THIRD EDITION

OUTCOMES

UPPER-INTERMEDIATE

Hugh Dellar

Andrew Walkley

**NATIONAL
GEOGRAPHIC**
LEARNING

Australia · Brazil · Canada · Mexico · Singapore · United Kingdom · United States

4

Contents 5

1 Entertainment

IN THIS UNIT, YOU:

- discuss how you spend your free time
- discuss different films and TV series
- talk about pictures and art

SPEAKING

1 **Work in pairs. Look at the photo and discuss the questions.**

   1 Why do you think the performance took place in this way? Do you think it's effective?

   2 Have you heard of any other unusual performances?

   3 Do you go to concerts much? What kind? What was the last one?

   4 What's the best concert, play, musical or other performance you've been to?

2 **Tell your partner about your other interests and how you spend your free time. Think about music, books, films, TV and hobbies. Find five things that you have in common.**

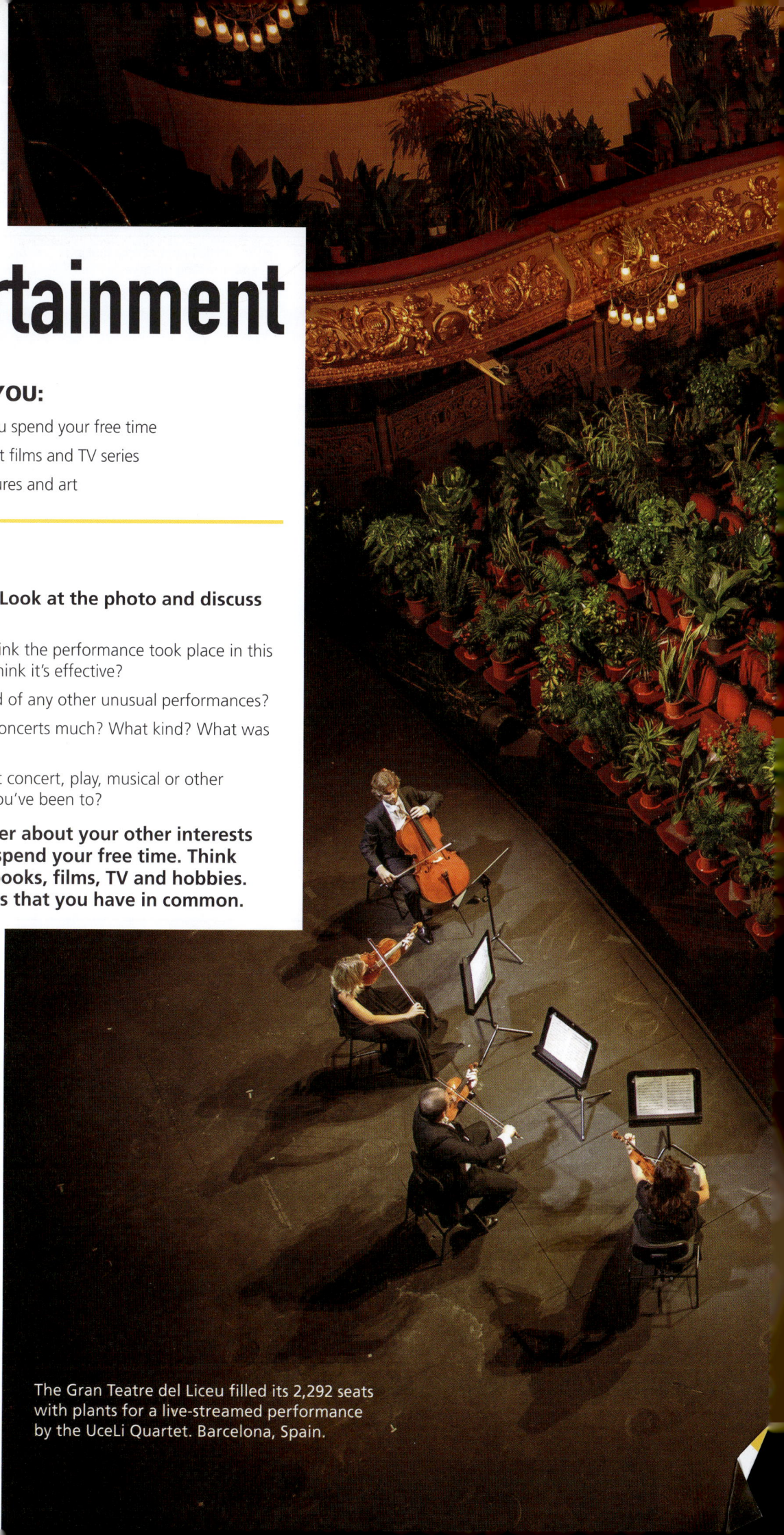

The Gran Teatre del Liceu filled its 2,292 seats with plants for a live-streamed performance by the UceLi Quartet. Barcelona, Spain.

What kind of things are you into?

IN THIS LESSON, YOU:
- discuss how you spend your free time
- describe films, books and music
- practise listening to people talk about films
- politely disagree with opinions

LISTENING

1 ▶ Eight people were asked questions using the structure *Do you … much?* Listen and write the question you think each person was asked.

GRAMMAR

Habits

To talk about habits, we use the present and past simple as well as structures such as *tend to* and *used to*. We also use words and phrases such as *rarely*, *not as much as I'd like to* and *all the time* to show how often.

a *My friends and I* **go out all the time**.

b *I sometimes* **played** *it* **for eight or nine hours a day**.

c *I* **don't tend to / I tend not to** *read much fiction*.

d **Did you (ever) use to** *watch 'Betty, la fea'?*

e *We'***d hang out all the time**, *but now we* **hardly ever do**.

f **Not as a rule**, *no, but I* **do listen** *to some jazz (every)* **now and then**.

2 Look at the examples in the Grammar box. Find:

1 three sentences about present habits.

2 a verb that describes a current habit – it means *(not) usually / generally*.

3 three different structures we use to talk about past habits.

4 phrases that mean *always*, *(not) normally*, *sometimes* and *almost never*.

3 Complete the sentences by adding one word in each gap.

1 I don't _____ to go to many concerts these days. I'm too busy working.

2 I mostly read stuff for work, but I do read novels every now and _____ .

3 He's basically on TikTok all the _____ . It's taken over his life.

4 We don't go to the cinema as much as we _____ to before we had kids.

5 I _____ ever read books, to be honest. I just read stuff online.

6 I used to go out a lot. I _____ often go clubbing four or five nights a week.

7 As a _____ , I tend not to listen to dance music. It's not my kind of thing.

8 _____ you ever use to go to the Teatro Colón when you lived in Buenos Aires?

4 Take notes on how your habits have changed. Think about these areas.

- work
- study
- holiday
- eating
- family

Share your ideas with a partner, using some of the structures from Exercise 2. Ask your partner questions to find out more.

G See Grammar reference 1A.

Sunday at the Cinema on the Champs-Élysées. Paris, France.

VOCABULARY
Describing films, music and books

V See Vocabulary reference 1A.

5 Complete the sentences with these words.

astonishing	catchy	commercial	disturbing	dreadful
gripping	hilarious	over-the-top	uplifting	weird

1 It's one of those tunes that's very easy to remember – very _____ .

2 It's _____ – just really, really funny.

3 It didn't do much for me. It's typical big-budget Hollywood – very _____ .

4 It's not an easy read. It's quite upsetting, quite _____ .

5 It's just too much for my liking – really _____ .

6 You can't stop reading it. It's so exciting, so _____ !

7 It's a really inspiring story, really _____ .

8 I can't explain it. It's really strange, really _____ .

9 It's just _____ – just a wonderful piece of music.

10 Don't go and see it! It's terrible, absolutely _____ .

6 P ▶ **Listen to words from Exercise 5 said on their own and then with other words. Practise saying them. Which words / phrases do you find hard to say? Practise saying them again.**

7 Write at least two words or phrases that are connected to each adjective in Exercise 5. Tell a partner the words you thought of. Your partner should guess the adjectives.

astonishing – *just incredible / amazed by it / made me think / watched it ten times*

LISTENING

8 FS ▶ **When said fast, three-word chunks often have linking between the words. Listen and write the words you hear.**

9 ▶ **Listen to two people talking about films. Which statement is true?**

1 They agree on everything.

2 They agree on most things.

3 They don't agree on very much.

4 They don't agree on anything.

10 ▶ **Listen again and answer the questions.**

1 Do the two speakers go to the cinema much?

2 What kind of films are they mainly into?

3 Have they seen any films recently?

4 What did they think of them?

DEVELOPING CONVERSATIONS
Disagreeing politely

You heard the speakers disagree with viewpoints like this:

Yeah, I guess, but **to be honest, I'm not that keen on** action movies.

It was all **a bit too** weird **for my liking**.

As I say, it's **not really my kind of thing**.

The Suicide Squad was OK / well made / not bad, **I suppose / guess, but** …

When disagreeing with someone's tastes, instead of saying directly *I don't like it* or *it's really weird*, we often soften our responses by using phrases such as *I'm not that keen on*, *I guess*, *I suppose*, *to be honest*, *for my liking*, etc. We also use *a bit* to soften negative adjectives.

11 M **Look at the Developing conversations box. Read three short conversations. Soften B's responses using some of the ideas from the box.**

1 A: I'm really into music from the 1990s. Nirvana, Pearl Jam, stuff like that.

   B: Yeah? I don't like it. It's the kind of stuff my dad listens to.

2 A: Do you like Tarantino? I love his films.

   B: He's all right, but I'm not keen on his stuff. It's very over-the-top.

3 A: Have you ever read anything by Daniel Alarcón? His books are fantastic.

   B: Yeah. I've read one. It was OK, but it didn't do much for me.

12 **Write a response to each of these sentences, disagreeing politely. Then work in pairs and have conversations using your ideas.**

1 I love crime novels like *The Girl With The Dragon Tattoo* and stuff like that.

2 I'm really into opera. It's fantastic.

3 I love pretty much any reality TV show.

CONVERSATION PRACTICE

13 **Work in pairs. Have conversations about your habits using this guide. Then swap roles.**

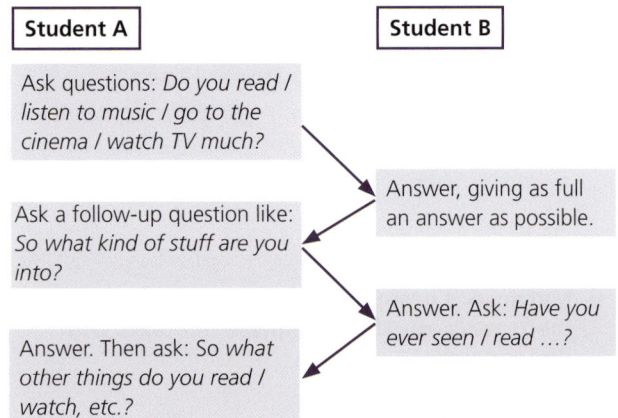

Student A	Student B

Ask questions: *Do you read / listen to music / go to the cinema / watch TV much?*

→ Answer, giving as full an answer as possible.

Ask a follow-up question like: *So what kind of stuff are you into?*

→ Answer. Ask: *Have you ever seen / read …?*

Answer. Then ask: So *what other things do you read / watch, etc.?*

1B

It's a big world out there

IN THIS LESSON, YOU:
- discuss different films and TV series
- read about the growth of non-English-language films
- summarize key ideas in a text
- explain the plot and the appeal of films you have seen

READING

1 Work in pairs. Discuss the questions.

1 Do you pay for any streaming services like Netflix? If so, which ones? Why?

2 Which country do most of your favourite shows and films come from?

3 Do you watch many shows or films from your country? Why? / Why not?

2 Read the article on page 11 about the boom in non-English-language programming. Answer the questions.

1 Why was the film *Parasite* significant?

2 What theory is suggested to explain the film's popularity?

3 What's behind the increase in non-English-language films?

4 How have technological developments helped?

5 What positive comment is made about American films?

6 What problems with them are also mentioned?

3 Work in pairs. You will each read about two films from different countries. Note down six words, phrases or facts that are most important for each film.

Student A: Read the text in File 1 on page 190.

Student B: Read the text in File 16 on page 197.

4 Work with a new partner who read the same file as you. Follow these steps.

- Compare the words, phrases and facts that you noted down. Explain your choices.

- Help each other with any words or phrases you aren't sure of.

- Discuss why you think the films have been so popular.

5 M Work with your partner from Exercise 3. Share what you learned about the different film industries and popular local films. Then discuss these questions.

1 Have you seen any of the films / shows mentioned in the article or in the texts at the back of the book? If so, which ones? What did you think of them?

2 Which of the four films you read about appeals the most / least to you? Why?

3 How would you explain the popularity of each film?

VOCABULARY Plots

6 Match each group of three words with one of the texts (a–d). Then complete the texts with these words.

tackles, twists, remake	flaw, adaptation, shot
sequel, smash, revolves	cast, touches, classic

a *Casablanca* is an all-time ¹_____ . I must've watched it more than twenty times and every time I notice something new in it. It's got an amazing

² _____ – including Humphrey Bogart and Ingrid Berman – and it ³_____ on the fears people experienced and the terrible things they lived through during the Second World War.

b *Old* is an ¹_____ of a graphic novel and it was ²_____ in the Dominican Republic. It's a very weird thriller about people on a beach who suddenly start getting old very quickly. If the film has a ³_____ , it's that it doesn't leave much to the imagination.

c *Captain America: The Winter Soldier* was a ¹_____ hit when it came out in 2014. It's the ²_____ to *The First Avenger*, which was released a few years earlier. The plot ³_____ around Steve Rogers – Captain America – who's in a race against time to stop a terrorist attack.

d *Hide and Seek* is an English-language ¹_____ of a South Korean film. It's a psychological thriller filled with shocking ²_____ and turns. Set in New York City, the film ³_____ issues around the wealth gap and the way certain areas are becoming ever-more expensive.

7 Work in pairs. Discuss the questions.

1 Can you think of five different **issues** a film might **tackle**?

2 Can you agree on five **all-time classics**?

3 Can you think of three films that are **adaptations of** books?

4 What's the opposite of a film that's filled with **twists and turns**?

5 Can you think of three films that are **sequels**?

6 Can you think of three common **flaws** many films have?

7 Can you agree on two films you both think have **an amazing cast**?

8 Can you think of any films that were **shot** in your town or region?

SPEAKING

8 Choose three of these topics and make notes on what you'd like to say about them.

1 the best film your country has ever produced

2 the best TV series you've seen recently

3 a film that all the family can enjoy

4 a film that made you cry

5 a film or TV series that makes you laugh out loud

6 the best film / TV series you've ever seen

7 a film or TV series from your country that you really hate

8 the film industry in your country

9 Work in groups. Share your ideas. Are there any recommendations you'd like to check out?

Bong Joon-ho's Oscar-winning film, *Parasite*.

A WORLD OF DIFFERENCE

21/3/2022   8 comments

Back in 2020, the South Korean film *Parasite* made history by becoming the first ever non-English-language film to win the prestigious Best Picture award at the Oscars. Directed by Bong Joon-ho and set in Seoul, the film is a sharp satire about two families from very different classes – one who live in poverty in a basement flat, and another very wealthy family who live in a huge house on top of a hill. Indeed, many feel that it was the focus on tensions around social divisions that made the film so popular with audiences around the world.

However, the success of *Parasite* is simply the tip of a much bigger iceberg. Over recent years, there's been an explosion of non-English-language films, driven largely by the desire of major streaming services like Netflix, Amazon Prime and HBO to expand their global reach. Local-language programming has helped attract new users as the platforms move into new markets, and shows from places like Germany, France, Spain and South Korea have all been popular both in their home countries and elsewhere. With more than 60% of Netflix viewers now outside the US, maybe it's not surprising

that series such as *Lupin*, *Squid Game* and *Money Heist* were so popular when they came out.

One of the main reasons for the success of many shows is the fact that dubbing technology has improved dramatically. This means it's now possible for people to watch films in their local languages – and the dubbing is no longer anything like as dreadful or as funny as it used to be.

In addition, the growth of interest in non-English-language content perhaps reflects a desire for different stories, and for more variety and creativity. Viewers also seem to enjoy finding common ground across different cultures. While American films are still big business at box offices everywhere, it is perhaps no real surprise that these changes are coming at a time when Hollywood is increasingly reliant on remakes of old classics, sequels to earlier successes and superhero movies. So as Hollywood becomes less ready to take creative risks, audiences are looking elsewhere for original entertainment.

In the picture

IN THIS LESSON, YOU:
- talk about pictures and art
- practise listening to a guide in a gallery telling visitors about two paintings
- present a description of a painting

SPEAKING

1 Work in pairs. Read the quotations about art. Discuss what you think each quotation means. How far do you agree with each one? Explain why.

Modern art = I could do that + Yeah, but you didn't.
—Craig Damrauer

Advertising is the greatest art form of the 20th century.
—Marshall McLuhan

Art is eternal, but life is short.
—Evelyn de Morgan

The more minimal the art, the more maximum the explanation.
—Hilton Kramer

VOCABULARY Talking about pictures

2 Work in pairs. Look at this painting. Discuss who the character might be and what you think is happening.

3 Read the definitions. With your partner, discuss which adjectives could describe the painting in Exercise 2.

1 **Bold** colours are very bright, strong and clear, whereas **subtle** colours are not strong or bright. They're softer and more delicate.

2 If a painting is **conventional**, it's traditional and not new or different in any way.

3 If a painting is **dramatic**, it contains a lot of exciting action.

4 If it's **atmospheric**, a painting creates a special mood – such as a feeling of romance or mystery.

5 **Abstract** paintings represent concepts, ideas or emotions, whereas **realistic** paintings show people, objects or events in a more photographic way.

6 If it's **ambiguous**, the meaning of the work isn't clear – it's **open to interpretation**.

7 If a painting shows a **domestic** scene, you see moments related to home and family.

4 Which of these sentences about the painting do you agree with?

1 The main character has his back to the viewer, which **creates** a feeling of mystery.

2 He **looks as if** he's lost in thought.

3 He's **obviously** a sad and lonely man.

4 He **seems to** be the most important thing in the painting.

5 He **appears to** be looking for something better than what he has.

6 He **looks** very proud. I **get the impression** he feels very pleased with himself.

7 He **looks like** a very wealthy man.

8 It **must** be somewhere in Europe. It **could well** be France.

5 Cover Exercise 4. Complete the sentences describing different paintings using words and phrases from Exercise 4.

1 I think it could _____ be Spain or Italy in this picture.

2 Everyone looks _____ they're having a really good time in this picture.

3 I get the _____ she's been crying. She _____ really upset.

4 They've _____ just moved in and are redecorating the whole flat, from the look of it.

5 They _____ all be students. That looks _____ a university canteen to me.

6 Everyone in this picture _____ to be queuing or waiting for something.

LISTENING

6 Work in pairs. Discuss these questions. Use language from Exercises 3 and 4.

1 What do you think the paintings on page 13 show?

2 Who do you think the people in the two paintings might be?

3 How do you think they're feeling – and why?

4 What might the connection between the two works be?

7 ▶ Listen to a guide in a gallery telling visitors about the two paintings on page 13. Which six adjectives from Exercise 3 does the guide use?

8 ▶ Listen again and answer the questions.

1 Where was the artist from?

2 Was he well known when he was alive?

3 In what way are the two paintings connected?

4 In what way might the viewer's first impression of the paintings be wrong?

5 Why did the painter include the globe and the Turkish rug?

6 Why did the painter include the landscape and seascape paintings within these paintings?

GRAMMAR

9 Look at these examples from the talk in Exercise 7. Then work in pairs to complete the rules.

> ### Adjectives and adverbs
>
> **Adjectives**
>
> *a symbol of the **difficult, stormy** nature of love*
>
> *She looks **calm** and **content**.*
>
> **Adverbs**
>
> *Look **carefully** and you'll notice that …*
>
> *These may look like **fairly** conventional, **fairly** realistic pieces.*
>
> ***Sadly**, though, he died at the age of 37.*

1 Adjectives are often used *before / after* nouns. Adjectives are also often used *before / after* the verbs *be, look, become, seem, get, taste*, etc. to describe the subject of the verb.

2 Most adverbs are formed by adding _____ to the adjective, but some have the same form as the adjective: *fast*, *hard* and *later*. Adverbs can be used to modify verbs, _____ , other adverbs and whole clauses or sentences.

10 Complete the sentences using the adjectives in brackets. Change the adjectives into adverbs where necessary.

1 _____ , Van Gogh did much of his best work while suffering from _____ depression. (severe / famous)

2 The painting was _____ damaged in a fire and, _____ , it couldn't be restored. (severe / unfortunate)

3 This _____ landscape is by the British artist, Kieron Williamson. _____ , he was only nine when he painted it. (amazing / lovely)

4 _____ , some people will just think it's _____ , but _____ some will like it and it may even change the way they think. (obvious / hopeful / weird)

5 _____ , Picasso's work was quite realistic, but it soon changed and _____ became more and more _____ . (experimental / gradual / initial)

6 There is a _____ debate about these _____ Chinese prints, because, well, _____ speaking, they were stolen before they were donated to the museum. (honest / serious / amazing)

G See Grammar reference 1C. »»

SPEAKING TASK

11 **M** Work in pairs.

Student A: Look at the painting in File 2 on page 191.

Student B: Look at the painting in File 17 on page 198.

Make notes on the following.

- what's happening in the painting
- the impression and feelings you have about it
- information about the painter and people in the picture (you can invent this if you want)
- additional comments you want to make about the painter and the painting. Start some comments with adverbs such as *Interestingly*, *Sadly*, *Actually*, etc.

12 Show the painting to your partner and present your comments and ideas.

■ MY OUTCOMES ■

> **Work in pairs. Discuss the questions.**
>
> 1 What conversations, listening texts or reading texts did you enjoy the most and why?
>
> 2 Can you talk about music, books and films more confidently? If so, why? How has this unit helped?
>
> 3 Which of the four skills (reading, writing, speaking, listening) do you find the most challenging? How has this unit helped with this skill?
>
> 4 What can you do outside the classroom to revise language or skills from this unit?

2
Sightseeing

IN THIS UNIT, YOU:

- practise showing people round a town or city
- discuss different festivals and carnivals
- share your feelings about future developments where you live

SPEAKING

1 **Work in pairs. Discuss the questions.**

1 Would you like to visit the tourist attraction in the photo? Why? / Why not?

2 What's the best / most disappointing place you have been to on holiday? Why?

3 Have you ever done any of these sightseeing activities? Tell your partner about your experience.

> go up a tower or a ferris wheel for the view
>
> go on a bike tour / a Segway tour / a bus tour
>
> visit an unusual museum / monument
>
> visit a temple / mosque / cathedral
>
> go to a theme park
>
> watch wildlife

2 **Work in pairs. Discuss the questions.**

1 Do you think your area is good for tourists? Why? / Why not?

2 Which sights or places would you show a friend who was visiting your area? Which activities would you do?

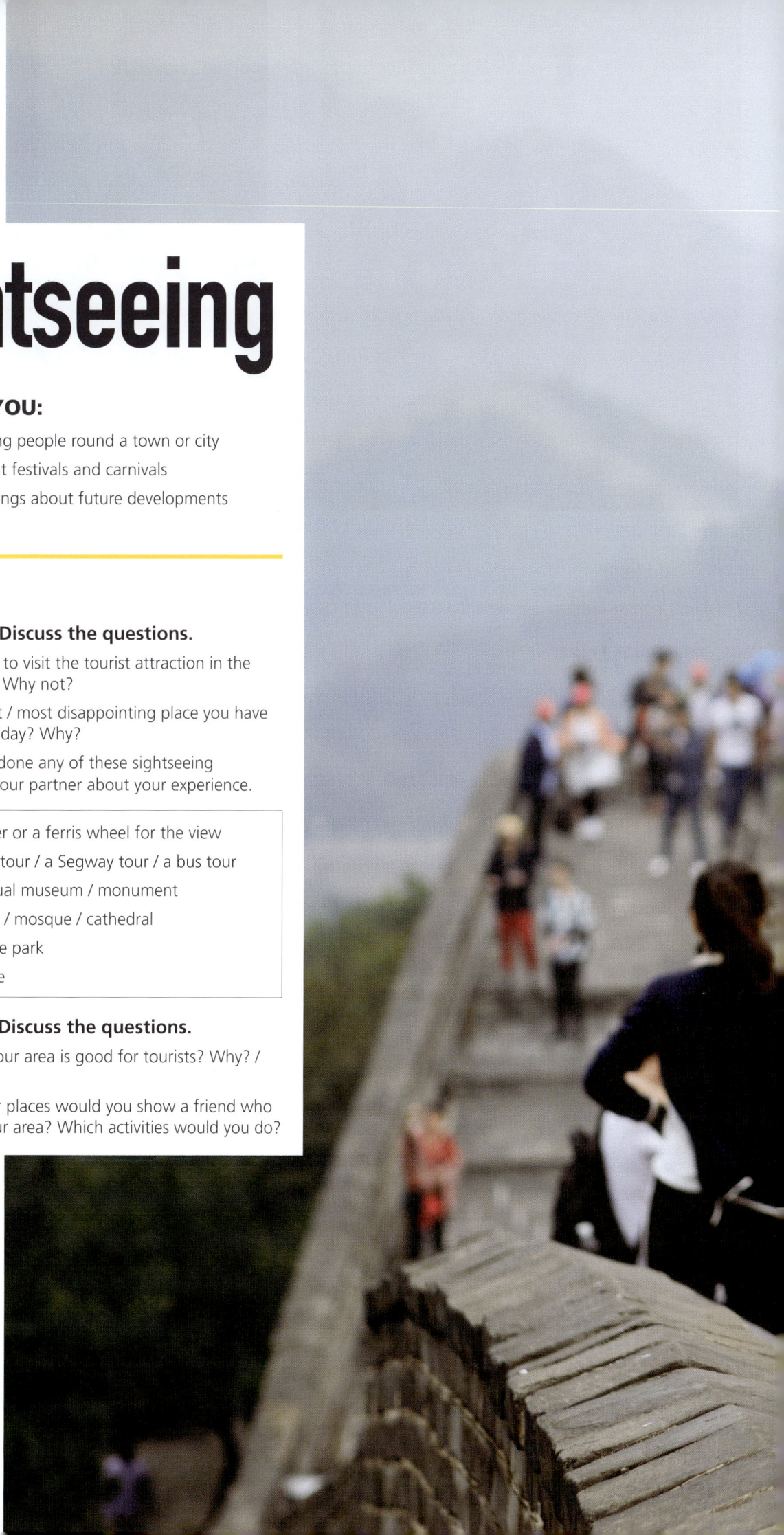

I'll show you round

IN THIS LESSON, YOU:
- practise showing people round a town or city
- describe buildings and areas
- practise listening to someone being shown round Belgrade
- use synonyms to agree

VOCABULARY Buildings and areas

1 Work in pairs. Discuss the questions. Use a dictionary if you need to.

1 What do you find in a **residential** area? Where are these areas usually?

2 What might you want to do to an incredibly **hideous** building or **monument**?

3 What might be good or bad about living in a **high-rise** building?

4 What kind of buildings and other things might you see in a **wealthy** area? What's the opposite of a wealthy area?

5 What might the government do to a **historic** area or building? Why?

6 What is bad about a **rough** area? What might be good about it?

7 What kinds of buildings might be described as **stunning**? And what do you call the opposite?

8 Why might an area become **trendy**? Why might it stop being the cool place to go?

2 Work in pairs. Which of the words in bold in Exercise 1 could you use to describe the area in the photo?

3 Complete the sentences with these words and phrases.

base	date back	do up
keep an eye on	knock down	open up

1 They're planning to _____ that building. I won't miss it. It's incredibly ugly.

2 It's a very wealthy part of town. Lots of embassies _____ their offices there.

3 Some of the buildings in the historic centre _____ over 600 years.

4 It's become quite trendy because of all the cool, arty cafés, but it is still a bit rough so _____ your bag.

5 A lot of high-rise buildings are going up here, so I expect a lot more shops and restaurants will _____ too.

6 They really ought to _____ that old building. I'm sure it'd look stunning if they did.

4 **P** ▶ Listen to words from Exercises 1 and 3 on their own and then in a phrase. Practise saying them. Which words or phrases do you find hard to say? Practise saying them again.

5 Work in groups. How many adjectives and verbs from Exercises 1 and 3 can your group use to describe buildings and areas where you live?

LISTENING

6 ▶ Listen to a Serbian woman and her friend as they drive through Belgrade. Number these things in the order they're mentioned.

a _____ a tomb

b _____ a famous landmark

c _____ little boats

d _____ embassies

e _____ a big entertainment venue

f _____ a museum

7 **FS** ▶ In fast speech, *it's* is often just said as /s/. This sound then joins together with the word that follows. Listen to four extracts from the conversation that start with *It's*. Write the words you hear.

world tour

world tour Nothing beats Belgrade in spring #Belgrade #Ilovemycity

8 **M** ▶ **Listen to the conversation in exercise 6 again. Take notes on what you hear about each landmark. Then work in pairs to compare your ideas.**

Landmark	Notes
New Belgrade	
the Arena	*Big concerts / sports events held there. One of the biggest entertainment venues in Europe.*
the Ada Bridge	
Manakova Kuca	
St Mark's Church	*Built late 1930s – on site of older church. Contains tomb of a great Serbian emperor.*
Kalemegdan Fortress	
the Victor Monument	
Dedinje	

GRAMMAR

Relative clauses

We use relative clauses to add information about nouns or previous clauses.

a *It contains the tomb of Stefan Dusan, <u>who was perhaps the greatest Serbian emperor ever</u>.*

b *Over to the right is the Arena, <u>where all the big concerts and sports events are held</u>.*

c *You might have seen it on TV. It's the place <u>they held the European basketball finals</u>.*

d *There's the Victor Monument up there as well, <u>which was put up after the First World War</u>.*

9 **Work in pairs. Look at the examples in the Grammar box and discuss these questions.**

1 Which sentences have a comma?

2 If you removed the underlined relative clauses, which sentences would still make sense?

3 Do we need a comma before adding a) essential or b) non-essential information?

4 Apart from *which* and *who*, do you know any other relative pronouns?

5 Do you always need a relative pronoun to add information after the noun?

10 **Rewrite each pair of sentences (1–7) as one sentence, using a relative clause.**

1 That statue is of our first president, Vaclav Havel. He was also a famous writer.

   That statue is of our first president, Vaclav Havel, who was also a famous writer.

2 We're coming up to Polanco. Polanco is one of the wealthier parts of the city.

3 Just behind us is the Grand Central Hotel. I was actually married in there.

4 And that building is the Courts of Justice. I got divorced there!

5 This shop on the left is run by my friend Zora. Her son plays professional football in Turkey now.

6 I started working over there in 2017. The area was already quite trendy then.

7 In that factory they make trainers. They export them to Europe.

G See Grammar reference 2A.

DEVELOPING CONVERSATIONS

Agreeing using synonyms

In the conversation in Exercise 6, you heard this:

A: *The houses are **lovely** round here.*

B: *Yeah, they're **amazing**.*

We often use some kind of synonym (a word with a similar meaning) to show we agree.

11 **Read the Developing conversations box. Work in pairs. Take turns to read out one of the opinions. Your partner should agree using synonyms.**

1 That's not a very nice-looking building.

2 All the houses round here are amazing, aren't they?

3 That castle is incredible!

4 The river looks wonderful, doesn't it?

5 Someone told me that area's not very safe.

6 This seems like quite a rich part of town.

CONVERSATION PRACTICE

12 **Imagine you are going to show a friend round your hometown, the area, town or city you are in now, or somewhere else you know well. Write the names of four or five places you will see. Think of:**

- details about the places.
- what you think of them.
- whether you'd recommend visiting them.

13 **Now roleplay the conversation. Follow this guide. Continue as long as you can. Then swap roles.**

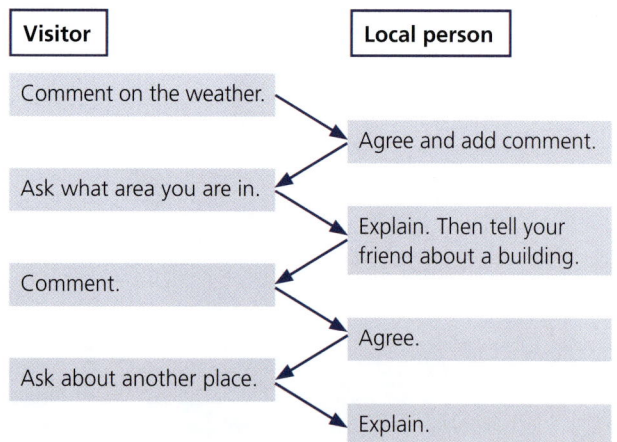

Visitor	Local person
Comment on the weather.	
	Agree and add comment.
Ask what area you are in.	
	Explain. Then tell your friend about a building.
Comment.	
	Agree.
Ask about another place.	
	Explain.

A carnival atmosphere

IN THIS LESSON, YOU:
- discuss different festivals and carnivals
- read articles about carnival in different countries
- decide if statements about a text are true or false
- practise guessing meaning from context

VOCABULARY Festivals and carnivals

1 **Work in groups. Look at the photos in the article on page 19 and discuss these questions.**

1 What do you know about the history of carnival? Where and when does it happen?

2 Why might local people like events like these?

3 Why might local people not like them?

2 **Which of these things can you see in the photos?**

bonfire	celebrations	costume	fireworks
float	mask	parade	sound system

3 **Match the nouns from Exercise 2 with the phrases (1–8).**

1 wear a ~ / hide behind a ~

2 take part in a ~ / a ~ through town

3 ride on a ~ / decorate a ~

4 set up a ~ / a really loud ~

5 make a ~ / hire a fancy dress ~

6 sit round a ~ / throw wood on a ~

7 adopt the ~ / take part in ~

8 set off ~ / watch a ~ display

4 **Work in pairs. For each of the nouns in Exercise 2, choose one of the collocations in Exercise 3. Think of an example from your own life. Tell your partner your example. Find out if your partner has had similar experiences.**

*A: I went to a fancy dress party last year and **wore** a scary monster **mask**.*

B: Really? I've never been to a fancy dress party.

Floats built by local artists parade in Viarreggio, Italy.

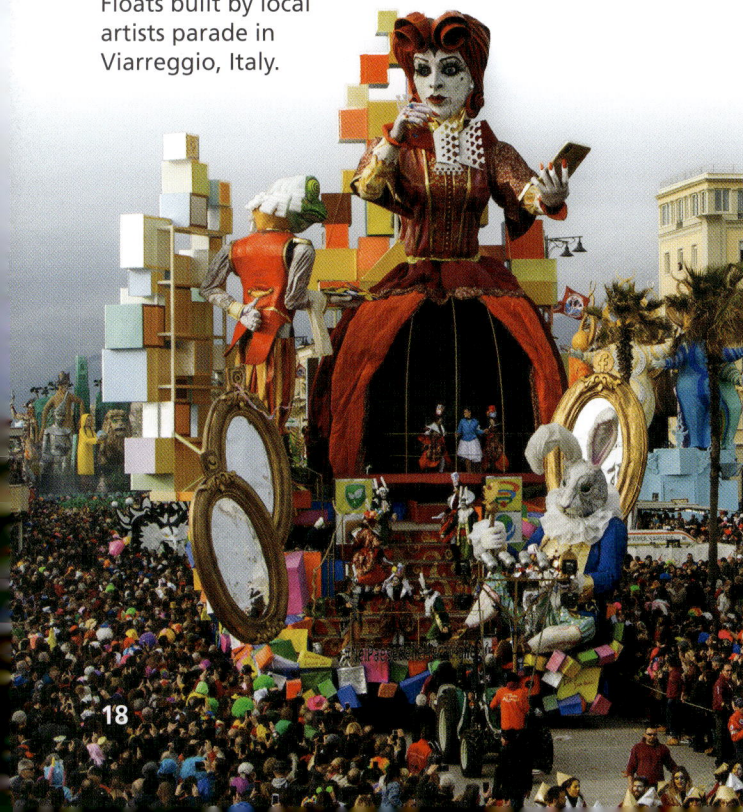

READING

5 **Read the introduction to the article about carnival on page 19 and choose the correct text type.**

a It's from an encyclopaedia entry about carnival.

b It's an article giving advice on holiday destinations.

c It's a blog about someone's experiences of carnivals.

6 **Read the texts quickly and decide which carnival destination appeals to you. Explain why to a partner.**

7 **According to the text, are the sentences true (T), false (F) or not given (NG)?**

1 The carnival in Port of Spain was originally a European festival.

2 Rich people in Trinidad don't take part in the carnival.

3 The carnival in Goa started to become really popular around 60 years ago.

4 Only local people can take part in celebrations in Goa.

5 There is a protest at every carnival in Dieburg.

6 A sweet food is commonly eaten at Dieburg Carnival.

7 Dieburg Carnival lasts the longest of the three carnivals.

8 The Goan Carnival is the oldest of the three events.

8 **Work in pairs. Read the words in bold in the text. Discuss what you think they mean.**

9 **Match the words in bold with their approximate meaning (1–8).**

1 reach the end

2 lines of rocks in the sea

3 people walking past a place

4 made fun of

5 not real / playful

6 starts

7 stand, sit or lie in a relaxed way

8 playing loudly

SPEAKING

10 **Work in pairs. Discuss the questions.**

1 Did you learn anything new about carnivals from the texts?

2 Think about your answer in Exercise 6. Would you still choose the same festival now you have read the texts again?

3 What carnivals or festivals are there near you? How similar are they to the ones you read about? Do you like to take part in them? Why? / Why not?

4 Have you ever been to any carnivals or festivals elsewhere? Where? When? What were they like?

Party round the world

For those with a party mindset, carnival offers the chance to travel the globe. While places like New Orleans and Rio de Janeiro will always grab the headlines, there are in fact carnivals in over 50 different countries. So, if you're looking for something different, we have some suggestions – as well as ideas for what's on offer once the singing and dancing is over.

PORT OF SPAIN, TRINIDAD

It's the largest of all Caribbean carnivals with 300,000 people on the streets in some of the most incredible costumes you're ever likely to see. Carnival here dates back to the 19th century when freed slaves adopted the European festival and made it their own through music and characters like 'Dame Lorraine', which **caricatured** posh people of that time. In the past, calypso musicians sang from the floats in the parade, but these days, you're more likely to hear soca music and the songs of Lord Shorty **blasting out** from the sound systems. Soca is a mix of African and East Indian beats which reflects the island's cultural mix; a mix that is also reflected in the popular carnival dish, *doubles*, a flatbread sandwich filled with vegetable curry.

When things have calmed down, Trinidad offers fantastic beaches and wildlife tours as well as cultural sites such as the Temple of the Sea. For the more adventurous, try scuba diving on the stunning **reefs**.

PANJIM GOA, INDIA

Goa hosts one of Asia's biggest carnivals. The idea of carnival was first introduced by the Portuguese 500 years ago, but it only really took off in the 1960s. Since then, it has grown to a four-day event and now includes many Goan and Hindu traditions. The festival **kicks off** with a ceremony led by a character called King Momo, who is played by a different local man each year. Among the celebrations that you can enjoy are huge bonfires, sports competitions, **mock** battles between people throwing eggs and dyed flour, and street theatre with the actors playing jokes on **passers-by**. Food favourites at the festival are spicy chicken Cafreal and chocolate pancakes with banana, and local people say they consume enough food and drink to feed a village during carnival.

After all the celebrations, you may want to just **lounge** on one of the many incredible beaches, but if you still have the energy, visit historic sites like Margao, with its stunning mix of classic Portuguese and Indian architecture.

DIEBURG, GERMANY

People in this tiny town have been celebrating what they call *Fünfte Jahreszeit* (the fifth season) since the 13th century. Events start in November but **culminate** in February with, among other things, Old Women's Day, which celebrates a women's protest in 1824 and now involves women cutting up the ties of male friends and family! There are fancy dress parades including traditional German bands, and some of the wildest partying of all the many carnival celebrations in Germany. One must-eat treat for partygoers are the *Krapfen*, delicious jam-filled doughnuts, which help them celebrate long into the night.

After it's all over and you've had all the jam doughnuts you can eat, take a few days exploring the nearby Black Forest with its stunning landscape and beautiful historic villages. For the more active there's also skiing. For the less active, there's more cake!

A welcome change

IN THIS LESSON, YOU:
- share your feelings about future developments where you live
- practise listening to people discussing issues around tourism
- discuss issues around tourism
- talk about plans and their impact on the future

SPEAKING

1 Work in pairs. Look at the photo. Discuss these questions.

1 What has your government or local council done to attract tourists or investment to your country or area?

2 Can you think of any new attractions for local people or tourists in your town or region? What do you think of them?

3 What is good about tourism generally? What might be bad about it?

LISTENING

2 ▶ Listen to five extracts where people comment on an aspect of tourism. Match the speakers (1–5) with the situations (a–f). There is one extra sentence.

a They're living in a popular tourist resort.

b They're at a protest against tourism.

c They're in a market.

d They're visiting a museum.

e They're in a meeting for investors.

f They're in a theme park.

3 ▶ Listen again. Match the speakers (1–5) with the correct sentences (a–f). There is one extra sentence.

a The speaker is looking forward to seeing something.

b The speaker is frustrated by a situation in their town.

c The speaker doesn't like souvenirs.

d The speaker regrets agreeing to something.

e The speaker broke something.

f The speaker plays a sport.

4 Work in pairs. Choose and discuss three sets of questions.

1 Do you like to buy souvenirs? Why? / Why not? What kinds of things have you bought?

2 How do you feel about theme parks? What's the nearest one to you? What are the best and worst rides you have been on?

3 Do you know any places with housing problems? What solutions do you think there are?

4 Would you like a new golf course in your area? Why? / Why not? What other sports facilities would be good to have?

5 Do you think a museum is a good place to go for a first date? Why? / Why not? What was the last museum you went to? What was it like?

People watch a famous clock strike in Prague's Old Town Square, Czech Republic.

GRAMMAR

Talking about the future

There is no future tense in English. Instead, there are different ways of talking about the future, such as *going to* + verb, *will* + verb, the present simple and the present continuous.

In many cases, more than one form can be used with little or no change in meaning. For instance, we often prefer the present continuous to talk about arrangements, but we can also use *going to* + verb.

I'm having *dinner with a client tonight.*

I'm going to have *dinner with a client tonight.*

5 **Work in pairs. Look at the Grammar box and discuss the questions.**

1 What can you remember about *going to, will*, the present simple and the present continuous?

2 Which forms do we use for:

a plans?

b decisions at the time of speaking and promises?

c future scheduled events?

6 **Read these sentences about the future. With your partner, discuss which option or options are incorrect in each set.**

1 a The move will improve things in the future.

b The move is improving things in the future.

c The move is going to improve things in the future.

2 a We're going to meet some friends later.

b We're meeting some friends later.

c We meet some friends later.

3 a It's going to cause problems at some point.

b It causes problems at some point.

c It'll cause problems at some point.

4 a What are you doing over the holidays? Any plans?

b What will you do over the holidays? Any plans?

c What are you going to do over the holidays? Any plans?

5 a I'll carry that for you. It looks heavy.

b I carry that for you. It looks heavy.

c I'm going to carry that for you. It looks heavy.

Due to, likely to, bound to

We often use adjectives to talk about the future.

a *The new hotel resort and spa are* **due to** *be approved next week.*

b *It's* **likely to** *attract tourists to the whole region.*

c *The same thing is* **bound to** *happen.*

7 **Match the examples in the Grammar box (a–c) with these explanations (1–3).**

1 This is almost certain to happen.

2 This is almost certain to happen; it's seen as highly probable by the speaker.

3 The action should happen at a particular time; it's expected to happen then.

G See Grammar reference 2C.

8 **Choose the correct option to complete the sentences.**

1 There are *due to / bound to* be problems when the new system is introduced.

2 I think we're *due to / bound to* arrive at something like twenty to ten.

3 If he keeps doing things like that, something bad is *due to / bound to* happen sooner or later.

4 The project is *due to / bound to* be completed in February, but we're well behind schedule.

5 Your mum's *due to / bound to* worry about you while you're away. It's only natural.

6 She can't travel at the moment as she's *due to / bound to* give birth any day now.

7 It is technically possible to get a visa to travel there, but it's *due to / bound to* be difficult.

9 **Think of two true examples for each of the following.**

- something which is due to happen in the next year
- something which is likely to happen in your country in the next year
- something which is bound to happen in the world at some point

SPEAKING TASK

10 **Work in pairs. Think about the place you live in. Discuss which of these areas need the most investment or improvement. Explain why.**

1 jobs for young people   4 affordable housing

2 attracting investment   5 leisure facilities

3 schools and education   6 protecting the environment

11 **M** **Read the instructions and do the tasks.**

1 Read the news item and decide if you support the plans or are against them.

2 Write ideas about the effect it will have on the areas in Exercise 10, using future forms where possible.

3 Work in groups to discuss your opinions. Try to reach an agreement about the plans, including any changes you would suggest. Report your ideas to the rest of the class.

> A local businessperson has been given planning permission to build one of the country's biggest hotels and leisure complexes near where you live. The complex will include a twenty-five storey hotel, three golf courses, a spa, a casino and a water park.

■ MY OUTCOMES ■

Work in pairs. Discuss the questions.

1 What interesting things did you learn about your classmates in this unit?

2 What useful language have you learned in this unit?

3 Which aspects of this unit do you feel the most and least confident with?

4 How could you practise using language from this unit outside of class?

Giving advice

IN THIS LESSON, YOU:
- write an email giving advice and making recommendations about a place
- use different ways of giving advice
- explain reasons for advice
- use more ways of describing places

SPEAKING

1 Work in groups. Discuss the questions.

1 How do you usually decide which places / towns and cities / countries to visit?

2 Have you ever left any online reviews? Where for? What did you say?

3 When did you last recommend a place in your area? Who to? Why?

USEFUL LANGUAGE

Advice and recommendations

There are lots of ways to give advice. Read the different ways of answering the question: *What would you recommend seeing there?*

I'd go to Itaewon (if I were you).

You should take a boat trip down the river.

You're best staying in an area called Gemmayazeh.

You could take a tour round the mountains (if you wanted).

You're better off taking the train. (= it's preferable)

We often use the structures above with an *if*-clause + present tense – or another expression that refers to a general topic.

If you want to relax, you should take a boat trip down the river.

In terms of accommodation, you're best staying in an area called La Candelaria.

2 Complete these sentences with advice for someone who is going to visit the area you are in now. Use your own ideas and a variety of structures.

1 If you've never been here before, _____ .

2 If you're into art or history, _____ .

3 If you like shopping, _____ .

4 If you want to go swimming, _____ .

5 If you want to escape the tourists, _____ .

6 As far as nightlife is concerned, _____ .

7 When it comes to getting round the city, _____ .

8 In terms of places to stay, _____ .

3 Work in pairs. Compare your sentences. Discuss whether you agree with each other's advice.

WRITING

4 A friend of a friend has written to Bash for advice about where to stay and what to do in Edinburgh. Read Bash's reply and decide which of the pieces of advice you would follow and which you'd ignore. Work in pairs and explain your decisions.

To: karim@hostzinga.fr
Subject Re: Edinburgh

Hi Karim,

Paul said you might write. I'll actually be away when you're here, so you could use my flat if you want. You'd be doing me a favour, as you could feed my cats. It IS in the suburbs, though – quite a long way from the city centre. As far as places to see are concerned, Edinburgh Castle is well worth visiting, although it's not super cheap. Almost all the museums are free, though. If you want to escape the crowds, I'd recommend Holyrood Park. It's really beautiful and if you go up to the top of Arthur's Seat, you get stunning views across the city on a clear day. You could even go wild swimming on Portobello beach if you're brave enough. While you're here, the Edinburgh Fringe Festival will be on. It's held in different places all over the city. There's comedy, theatre, live music, poetry, a firework display – all sorts of things. Check out the Ed Fringe website for more info. Apart from the festival, there's a huge choice of entertainment. When it comes to nightlife, I'd look online if I were you and see what you like the sound of. Otherwise, you'll miss out on all the city has to offer. Generally, I'd steer clear of most clubs in the Grassmarket as they can be a bit of a tourist trap. You're better off going to Leith – I think it's a bit trendier. In terms of eating out, Shezan and Dishoom are good for curry. If you want something more traditional, try Borough. It's a bit out of the way, but it's great. Other than that, lots of pubs do decent food. Anyway, if there's anything else you need, let me know.

Bash

5 Work in pairs. The email is written as one long paragraph and needs dividing up. Find expressions that show a new subject is being introduced and mark the beginning of a new paragraph with /.

VOCABULARY Describing places

6 Work in pairs. Discuss what good things or what problems there might be in the following.

- a tourist trap
- a rural area
- a posh area
- a lively area
- the suburbs
- a high-rise building
- a street market
- an up-and-coming area

Salisbury Crags, Holyrood Park with Edinburgh city and Castle in the background.

USEFUL LANGUAGE

Otherwise, other than, apart from

We use *otherwise* to show what the results will be if you don't do the thing you just mentioned.
I'd look online if I were you and see what you like the sound of. **Otherwise,** *you'll miss out on all the city has to offer.*

You can also use *otherwise* or *other than that / apart from that* to suggest alternatives.

It's great. **Other than that,** / **Apart from that,** / **Otherwise,** *lots of pubs do decent food.*

Note that you can use *apart from* and *other than* with a noun, but not *otherwise*.

Apart from / **Other than** / ~~**Otherwise**~~ *the festival, there's a huge choice of entertainment.*

7 **Look at the Useful language box. Decide if one or both options are correct in 1–7. Cross out the incorrect options.**

1 There's quite a lot of street crime, so don't leave anything valuable on café tables. *Otherwise, / Apart from that,* it might get stolen.

2 There's a small museum in the town, but *apart / other* from that, there's not much worth seeing.

3 *Otherwise / Other than* the main sights, I can't really suggest anything.

4 There are a few hotels in town which are pretty reasonable. *Otherwise / Apart from,* there's a nice campsite just outside town, if you have a tent.

5 *Apart from / Other than* walking, you're best taking taxis as they're not much more expensive than buses.

6 I'd put on plenty of sun cream even if you're not going to sunbathe. *Otherwise, / Other than that,* you'll get sunburned.

7 The Chinese restaurant in Havana Road is OK. *Otherwise, / Other than that,* there are a couple of decent pizzerias.

PRACTICE

8 **Work in pairs or groups. Together, choose a city or area in your country that you know well, or research a place you're interested in. Imagine a friend has written to you asking for this information. List the places and things you want to recommend.**

- where to stay
- what there is to see and do
- where to go at night / where to eat
- which areas to check out – or avoid

9 **Decide how many paragraphs you think you will write, and what will go into each one. Use the model in Exercise 4 to help you, if you need to.**

10 **Write an email of between 180 and 250 words giving advice to your friend about the city or area you chose in Exercise 8. Make sure you:**

- divide the email into paragraphs.
- use advice structures.
- use some of the expressions for introducing new subjects from Exercise 5.
- use *otherwise, other than* and *apart from* (*that*).

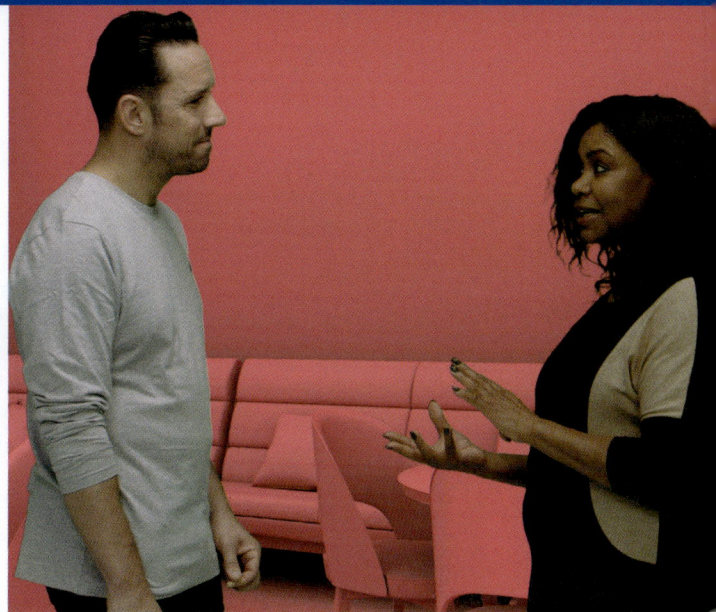

VIDEO Out and about

1 **Work in pairs. Discuss the questions.**

1 Do you have a carnival or big annual festival where you live?

2 What's it like? Do you enjoy it?

Understanding accents

Some accents replace an /ɜː/ sound with /ɔː/, so *work* /wɜːk/ may sound like *walk* /wɔːk/; *fur* /fɜː/ like *four* /fɔː/; and *bird* /bɜːd/ like *board* /bɔːd/.

2 📹 Watch the video. Which person has the closest experience to yours? What do they say?

3 📹 Match the statements with the speakers and explain your choices. Then watch again to check. There are three statements you do not need.

a It's one massive street party.

b It attracts tourists even in the run up to the main event.

c Motor racing isn't really my kind of thing.

d We give an offering to our ancestors.

e You can hear the practice sessions.

f Their version beats anything we do.

g People cheer on the dancers.

h There are firework displays all over the country.

i The traditions are slightly different to elsewhere.

4 **Tell your partner about one of the following you have seen or taken part in.**

a race	a firework display
a religious ceremony	trick or treating

VIDEO Developing conversations

5 📹 You are going to watch two people talking about the music they like. Watch and take notes on what they say.

6 📹 Work in pairs. Compare what you understood. Watch again if you need to.

7 **Discuss the questions with your partner.**

1 Which person is most like you? / Why?

2 Why might people (not) like opera or rock music?

3 What recommendations do you have for recent TV programmes, films, books or music?

8 FS 📹 Watch again. Complete the sentences with three to five words in each gap.

1 Lots of things really – _____ , bit of grunge …

2 Ah that's the best part! Crank up the drums, crank up the guitar, get _____ .

3 Maybe it's not _____ .

4 I _____ opera. Maybe I just didn't really understand it properly.

5 Let's say, if _____ check out opera – what would you recommend?

6 I think _____ *Carmen* would be nice.

7 Sounds good, but I think _____ drums, bass and guitar.

8 I mean _____ music is it's completely subjective.

CONVERSATION PRACTICE

9 **Work in pairs. You are going to practise a conversation.**

1 Choose a Conversation practice from either Lesson 1A or Lesson 2A.

2 Look at the language in that lesson.

3 Check the meaning of anything you've forgotten with your partner.

4 Have the conversation. Try to improve on the last time you did it.

Grammar and Vocabulary

GRAMMAR

1 Complete the text with one word in each gap.

I'm a big football fan. I've been going to watch my local club for nearly twenty years. I ¹ _____ to go with my grandad, ² _____ was a fan all his life. He ³ _____ usually pick me up early and take me for a burger before the game, so it was a real day out. My dad came with us every now and ⁴ _____ , but he isn't that keen on football, to be honest.⁵ _____ , my grandad died a couple of years ago, so now I ⁶ _____ to go on my own and meet friends ⁷ _____ I have made at the club.

The club has decided it's ⁸ _____ to move to a new stadium because it ⁹ _____ have a bigger capacity than the current one and they hope to host some matches in a big tournament ¹⁰ _____ will be held here next year. The old stadium is going ¹¹ _____ be knocked down and replaced with flats, ¹² _____ will be available at a cheaper price. I've applied to buy one and they have said that I'm highly ¹³ _____ to get one, ¹⁴ _____ is great.

2 Read the first sentence in each pair. Complete the second sentence so that it has a similar meaning. Use between three and five words, including the word in bold.

1 I think the next meeting is going to be in July.
  The next meeting _____ held in July. **DUE**

2 He said it's possible he'll be late, so start without him.
  He said to start without him as _____ late. **LIKELY**

3 There has been a gradual change in the city over the last ten years.
  The city _____ over the last ten years. **CHANGED**

4 They'll definitely change their minds about it.
  They _____ their minds about it. **BOUND**

5 I don't tend to go out much on a weekday.
  _____ at home during the week. **RULE**

3 Choose the correct option to complete the sentences.

1 Don't worry about it. I *sort / 'll sort* it out later.

2 *Apparent / Apparently*, it's quite a rough area.

3 As a rule, Monet *was painting / painted* outside.

4 This guy was looking at me *strange / strangely*. I felt really *uncomfortable / uncomfortably*.

5 The main character looks very *weird / weirdly* when he's in his disguise.

6 We spent the afternoon wandering round the old town, *which / where* was amazing!

7 Just to say, the traffic's pretty bad here, so *I'm probably arriving / I'll probably arrive* late.

8 This film, *who / whose* writer died shortly after it opened, has won a number of awards.

4 ▶ Listen and write the six sentences you hear.

VOCABULARY

5 Match the two parts of the sentences.

1	The film tackles	a	a teenage girl's experience of high school.
2	They're doing up	b	that hideous building – it's awful.
3	It dates back to	c	the celebrations.
4	The plot revolves around	d	the impression he's not happy where he is.
5	You can just hire	e	a lovely old house in the countryside.
6	The kids all took part in	f	the difficult topics of gender and identity.
7	The whole film was shot	g	the sixth century.
8	I always get	h	an eye on your stuff – just in case.
9	They should knock down	i	a car at the airport.
10	It's busy there, so keep	j	in black and white.

6 Decide if these adjectives describe a building, an area, a film or a song.

catchy	disturbing	gripping	high-rise
residential	rough	uplifting	wealthy

7 Complete the text with one word in each gap. The first letters are given.

You may know Notting Hill from the film of the same name, but perhaps you'd be surprised to know that it hasn't always been the ¹ we _____ area it is today. Forty years ago, it was quite a poor part of London, but people gradually bought houses there and then did them up. The changes since then have been ² as _____ and the area is now home to all kinds of ³ tr_____ bars and restaurants.

Notting Hill is also famous for its carnival, which is held every year in August. Each day, people take part in a ⁴ pa_____ through the streets, with many wearing masks or incredibly ornate ⁵ co_____ . There are also beautifully-decorated ⁶ fl_____ carrying musicians and dancers, and in the side streets, local people ⁷ s_____ up sound systems that ⁸ b_____ out lots of different music. It's amazing!

8 Complete the sentences using the correct form of the word in bold.

1 There's not much in the way of _____ in this town. **entertain**

2 I love the photo of the shadow of the pyramid. It's so _____ . **drama**

3 The meaning is open to _____ . **interpret**

4 It's quite an _____ scene in some ways. **upset**

5 It's a great piece of _____ film-making. **atmosphere**

6 The animals look very _____ in that painting. **real**

7 I'm not that keen on him, to be honest. I find his work dull and _____ . **convention**

8 I like their earlier music more. The new stuff is a bit too _____ for me. **commerce**

3
Things you need

IN THIS UNIT, YOU:

- discuss solutions to practical problems
- talk about tidiness and collecting things
- describe problems with things

SPEAKING

1 **Work in pairs. Look at the photo. Discuss the questions.**

1 Have you ever been in a vehicle that broke down? What happened?

2 Do you know any good mechanics or people who are good with machines?

3 Are you any good at fixing things? If not, do you know anyone who is?

4 Can you remember anything that needed fixing recently? Who did it?

5 What problems connected with these things do you know how to fix?

| bicycles | cars | computers | houses or flats |

6 What tools have you used? How well did you handle them?

7 Have you ever tried to fix something only for it to all go terribly wrong? When? What happened?

A mechanic repairs the wheel of a crash-landed Vimy aircraft in Indonesia.

Making do

IN THIS LESSON, YOU:
- discuss solutions to practical problems
- explain what useful things you may need or use
- explain what you need things for
- practise hearing chunks connected to asking for things

VOCABULARY Useful things

1 Work in pairs. Look at the pictures in File 3 on page 192 and discuss the questions.

1 Are there any things in the pictures that you've never used? Why? / Why not?

2 Which of the objects do you use: all the time / regularly / now and again / hardly ever?

3 Do you have any of these things on you now? Which of the things do you have at home?

4 Which of the things did you NOT know in English before?

2 **P** **▶** Listen to eight words from Exercise 1 and practise saying them on their own and in a phrase. Which phrases do you find hard to say? Practise saying them again.

3 Work in groups. How many useful things from Exercise 1 can you add to these categories?

clothes	DIY	first aid	kitchen	office / study

4 Work in pairs. Which thing(s):

1 are for putting up posters and notices?

2 are for making holes in the wall?

3 can be used to clear up some spilled coffee?

4 can be used to mend a tear in your clothes?

5 could be used to keep a packet of flour closed?

6 do you need to cut a tree down?

7 do you need in order to mend a leaking roof?

8 do you need if you have a small cut?

9 do you need if someone drops a glass and it smashes?

10 do you need to help you see what you're doing?

GRAMMAR

Explaining purpose

There are different ways we can define objects or explain what they are for and why we need them.

a *It's (used) for opening cans.*

b *You need it **if you** cut your finger.*

c *It **can / could be used** to hold a bunch of sticks together.*

d *Do you have a cloth **so I can** wipe this stuff off my shoe?*

e *I need a stepladder **(in order) to** get up on the roof.*

5 Look at the examples in the Grammar box. Answer the questions.

1 Which patterns explain the normal use of an object or a typical situation when you might use it?

2 Which pattern shows a possible use?

3 Which patterns show the specific reason you need something?

4 What verb forms are used after each pattern in bold?

6 Why would you use or need these things? Think of one common and one less common purpose for each.

a bandage	a bucket	a cloth	a needle	a peg

A cloth is for wiping away dirt.

If you can't open the top of a jar, you can put a cloth over the top so you can grip it better.

G See Grammar reference 3A. ⟩⟩

DEVELOPING CONVERSATIONS

7 ▶ Listen to two conversations. Which of the things in the picture are the people talking about?

Explaining and checking

Look at the ways the speakers explained things:

*That **stuff** – it's **a bit like** chewing gum **or something**.*

*They have **a sort of** clip **thing** that opens and shuts.*

You can check you understand by using these patterns:

*What? **You mean** Blu Tack®?*

*What? **You mean the thing you use to** connect yourself to the rope?*

8 Read the Developing conversations box. Think of two things in the office, home or garden that you don't know the name of in English. Then work in pairs. Take turns to explain your object and check understanding. Use words and phrases from the box. Does your partner know the English word?

LISTENING

9 ▶ Listen to a man asking for something. Answer the questions.
1 What does he want?
2 What does he need it for?
3 What does he use instead?

10 ▶ Work in pairs. Try to complete these extracts from the conversations with three words in each gap. Then listen again to check your ideas.
1 Ah, _____ , actually. I'm not sure I have,
2 I don't think there's one here. Can't you _____ ?
3 You need a _____ to push it down.
4 _____ do?
5 It wouldn't _____ .
6 What about a wooden spoon? You could _____ .
7 Don't worry about it. _____ .
8 You might want to _____ into that shirt or it'll leave a stain.

11 Work in groups. Discuss the questions.
1 Do you have a drawer or cupboard which is full of odd things? What's in it?
2 Can you think of a situation where you didn't have the things you needed and you had to improvise or make do?
3 Do you know any ways of removing different kinds of stains or dirty marks?

CONVERSATION PRACTICE

12 You are going to take turns to ask for different things and to solve different problems. Find your information and use the guide for each conversation.

Student A: Look at File 4 on page 193.
Student B: Look at File 18 on page 199.

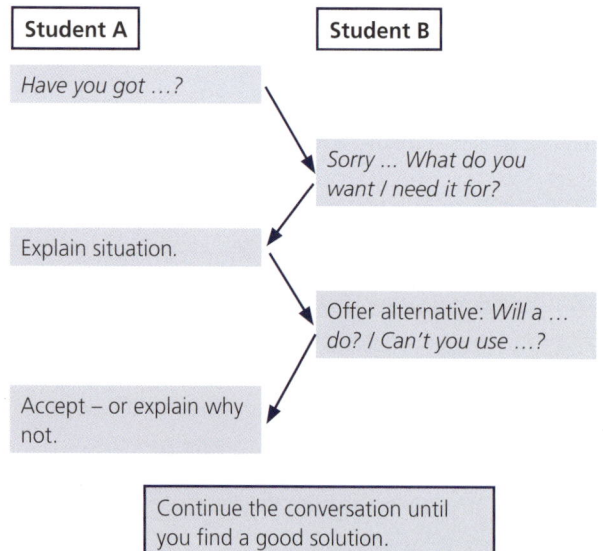

Student A	Student B
Have you got …?	
	Sorry … What do you want / need it for?
Explain situation.	
	Offer alternative: *Will a … do? / Can't you use …?*
Accept – or explain why not.	

Continue the conversation until you find a good solution.

Full house

IN THIS LESSON, YOU:
- talk about tidiness and collecting things
- read a blog post about collecting and hoarding

SPEAKING

1 Work in pairs. Do you know any people you might describe with these sentences? Explain why.

1 They're obsessed with keeping things clean and tidy.

2 They are really untidy. Their stuff is just dumped all over the place.

3 They keep stuff like plastic bags and concert tickets rather than throwing things away.

4 They have stuff they never use but refuse to get rid of it.

5 Their room / home has lots of lovely things they have acquired over time.

READING

2 In pairs, check you understand these words. Look at the title of the blog post and the photo. How do you think the writer might use the words?

acquire	attached	collect	psychology	store	value

3 In the blog post, you will also see other forms of the words in Exercise 2. What other forms of the words (e.g. noun, adjective) can you think of?

acquire, acquisition, acquisitive, acquisitively

V See Vocabulary reference 3B. »»

4 **M** Read the blog post. Work in pairs. Write four words or short phrases that summarize the four differences between collecting and hoarding.

5 Match the sentences (a–h) with the gaps in the blog post (1–7). There is one extra sentence that you do not need.

a It was basically an experiment to answer the question of how much one person might collect in a lifetime (22 grams over 32 years apparently).

b So how do we distinguish between them and when should we worry that someone has crossed that line and things are getting out of hand?

c As a result, they stop inviting people home, which reduces their social contact and can lead to social isolation.

d She recently had an exhibition displaying some of the 3,000 items in her collection in an IKEA store in London.

e The collector John Reznikoff set up his own auction house based on his interest in autographs, rare books and famous people's hair.

f As I mentioned last time, my friend has shelves of Star War figures, but he doesn't let anyone else touch them.

g In fact, the disorder can be triggered by the death of a loved one.

h But this is the point: collectors want to show off what they've acquired because they're proud of it.

6 Work in pairs. Choose and discuss two sets of questions.

1 Have you heard of any stories about hoarders? What happened? What kind of advice and help do you think they would need?

2 Do you subscribe to any video channels, podcasts, newsletters or forums? Which? Do you contribute in any way?

3 Do you go to museums much? Have you been to any odd ones? What's your favourite? What do you know about the collection?

4 What possession are you most attached to? Why is it so special? Have you ever been upset about losing / breaking something? What happened?

VOCABULARY Collecting things

7 Complete the sentences with these pairs of words.

curiosity / interest	got into / passion
impressive / storage	junk / bid
keen / trades	pride / show off
stickers / swap	will / donated

1 We all used to collect football _____ and if we had extras we would _____ them with each other.

2 My dad's a very _____ stamp collector. He also _____ them on online auction sites and sometimes makes quite a bit of money.

3 My brother has a very _____ collection of superhero figures and he's running out of _____ space.

4 I _____ collecting shells when I was on holiday one year and it's really grown into a _____ .

5 She takes a lot of _____ in her collection and often posts videos to _____ her favourite pieces.

6 I started it out of _____ , but then at some point I just lost _____ and decided to give them all away.

7 I pick up a lot of stuff in _____ shops and then I sometimes go to auctions and _____ for things.

8 He left his collection to his family in his _____ and they _____ it to the National Museum.

8 Work in pairs. Think of six questions you could ask the different collectors in the text and what you think they would answer. Use some of the language from Exercise 7.

SPEAKING

9 Work in groups. Talk about:

1 something you collect or used to collect.

2 a collector or collection you know or have heard about.

Should I worry about my friend's collecting habit?

📅 8/5/2022   💬 15 comments

Following my last post about a friend's Star Wars obsession, several readers expressed concern about the habits of people they know. Some sounded more like my friend, with a keen collecting habit, while others showed signs of the genuine psychological condition of *hoarding*. There's a fine line between the two and collecting can sometimes develop into hoarding. [1]_____ Well, research by psychologists has now helped to identify four main areas of difference.

The main focus for hoarders is with keeping stuff, whatever value it might appear to have. Often, it's literally junk from the street, but it may include more valuable things, such as piles of clothes which they've bought and then stored in a room with the price tag still attached. Collectors, on the other hand, typically have a clear motivation for collecting, even though their reasons may seem strange to others. For example, Graham Barker, who was listed in Guinness World Records for his collection of navel fluff (the tiny balls of cotton you find in your belly button), explained that he started it out of curiosity. [2]_____ Others, like Gladys Palmera, the world's biggest collector of Latin music, say it comes from a search for excellence. Rather than having a negative impact on their quality of life, it's about discovering forgotten artists and promoting the music she's loved since childhood, when her Panamanian father would bring back records from his business trips.

Both collectors and hoarders may need a lot of storage space and in Gladys Palmera's case that means hundreds of metres of shelving in her home near Madrid to display her 100,000 or so albums. [3]_____ Kelle Blythe, British collector of Pez® sweet dispensers, arranges national gatherings for collectors to come together and share their pride and joy. [4]_____ Collectors also tend to carefully arrange their things in alphabetical order or in clear categories, like Kelle Blyth's Pez collection in the photo, while hoarders' belongings are more likely to be untidy and chaotic. Their stuff is often piled all over the place, often taking over whole rooms that can no longer be used and, at worst, they turn their homes into a health hazard.

This untidiness can make hoarders feel ashamed. [5]_____ The opposite is often true of collectors, who frequently establish life-long friendships through sharing their passion. My Star Wars friend met his partner at a *Comic-Con* and he subscribes to various online forums and video channels where his friends comment, debate and share videos of favourite pieces or an unboxing of their latest acquisition.

Finally, hoarders typically refuse to get rid of anything and feel genuine distress if forced to, a feeling that psychologists say is connected to a fear of loss. [6]_____ Obviously, many collectors also feel strong attachments to certain items that they wouldn't sell at any price. However, most see swapping or trading pieces as part of the excitement of their hobby. Some even turn this into a profitable business. [7]_____

Collectors can even be quite willing to give up their whole collection. Gladys Palmera hopes to give hers away to someone who will allow the same access to it as she does. And as for Graham Barker? He eventually sold his navel fluff collection to the entertainment company, Ripley's.

Kelle Blyth displays her collection of Pez sweet dispensers.

3C

Finding fault

IN THIS LESSON, YOU:
- describe problems with things
- listen to part of a radio show about consumer rights and a problem a listener had
- use *should* and *should have* to give criticism, advice or suggestions
- talk about a time when you had a problem with something you bought

VOCABULARY How things go wrong

1 Match these items with the problems in bold in the sentences (1–10).

a desk	face cream	jeans	a kettle	a record
a scooter	shoes	a tablet	a top	a watch

1 When I took it out of the box, I found the screen **was cracked**.

2 When I tried to put it together, I realized it **had a piece missing**.

3 When I tried it on, I noticed there was **a mark** on the sleeve.

4 It was supposed to be for sensitive skin, but it **gave me spots**.

5 When I filled it the first time, I discovered it **had a leak**.

6 I only wore it for a week and the strap **came off**.

7 They **fell apart** after a month. The soles came off!

8 When I got home and tried them on, I realized the back pocket **was ripped**.

9 It turned out the brakes **were faulty,** which could have been really serious.

10 When I played it, I realized it **was scratched** and the needle kept jumping.

2 Take turns to think of two more items that can have one of the problems in Exercise 1. Tell your partner the items you are thinking of. Can your partner guess the problem they might have?

A: A boat and a pipe can have this problem.

B: OK. They can both have a leak.

LISTENING

3 ▶ Listen to part of a radio show about consumer rights and a problem a listener had. Answer the questions.

1 What problem did Fei have?

2 Which of these things happened when he complained about the problem?

a They didn't believe him.

b They said it was his fault.

c They gave him a refund.

d They gave him a replacement.

e He had to go back more than once.

f They offered a gift as compensation.

g They sorted it out eventually.

h He had to talk to several people.

4 Work in pairs. Discuss the questions.

1 Do you think Fei did the right thing? What about the company and its employees?

2 What advice would you give to the company if you were an expert on customer care? Why?

5 ▶ Listen to the customer care expert in the second part of the radio show. Do they agree with your ideas?

6 **FS** ▶ In speech, we often emphasize grammar words when we are making a contrast. The words around them can often be said very fast. Listen and try to repeat the words you hear.

1 Well, possibly, _____ can _____ deeper _____ .

2 _____ are _____ repeatedly.

3 However, _____ always _____ they do have _____ .

4 _____ do _____ doubts.

5 Absolutely. _____ doesn't _____ regular _____ .

6 Well, probably not, _____ some cultures do _____ different _____ .

7 ▶ Read the notes about the radio show. Think about what the missing information is. Listen to the second part again and complete the notes with one word or a short phrase.

1 John says a bad culture is where staff believe customers complain in order to be _____ .

2 As a result, shop assistants fail to _____ the customer.

3 John doesn't think the shop is always _____ when a customer complains.

4 Staff may have doubts, but it's important to think about _____ involved in sorting out the problem.

5 John suggests companies could save a lot in marketing costs by _____ customers.

6 For all types of business, _____ is the best way to advertise.

7 In Japan, when people complain they are interested in _____ .

8 It's important to remember that people who complain have _____ .

9 The final message is that companies should _____ in customer care.

8 Work in pairs. Discuss the questions.

1 What do you think of John Squire's advice? Is there anything else he could have said?

2 What's customer care like in your country? Does everyone get the same treatment? Why? / Why not?

3 Which companies have good or bad reputations for customer care? Why?

4 Do you ever have to deal with complaints? Who from? What about? How do you deal with them?

Returns and exchanges at IKEA®, Brooklyn, US.

GRAMMAR

Should and *should have*

We use *should* + verb to talk about the present and *should have* + past participle to talk about the past. The verb after *should* can be passive.

a He **should have checked** the shoes at the point of sale.

b Clearly, Fei **shouldn't have been treated** like that.

c You **should** always **start** from the view that they do have a valid claim.

d We say complaints **should be seen** in this way here too – as a gift.

9 Look at the examples in the Grammar box and answer the questions.

1 Which of the sentences give general advice or suggestions?

2 Which express a criticism or regret?

3 How are verbs made passive after *should*?

4 How are they made passive after *should have*?

10 Complete the sentences about the situation in the radio show. Use *should* and *should have* with the correct form of the verb.

1 If they don't want to continue to get a bad reputation, the shoe shop _____ (provide) more training for its staff.

2 Fei _____ (give) a free pair of shoes as compensation for what he went through.

3 The first shop assistant Fei spoke to _____ (fire) for treating him that way.

4 As they've treated him so badly, I think Fei _____ (spread) the word that it's a shop that _____ (avoid).

5 Fei _____ (leave) it so long before complaining. He _____ (learn) to be a bit more assertive.

11 Use *should* and *should have* to reply to these sentences with criticism, advice or suggestions.

1 It's my birthday today.
   You should have told me earlier. We should celebrate!

2 There's a bit missing.

3 There was a fault with the brakes.

4 I'm never going to get anyone to buy this car.

5 I never seem to have any money.

6 This whole holiday has been a complete disaster!

G See Grammar reference 3C. »»

SPEAKING TASK

12 Think about a time when you were in one of these situations. Tell your partner what happened and discuss if you handled the situation well.

• You had one of the problems in Exercise 1.

• You took something back to a shop.

• You complained about something.

13 **M** With your partner, decide what lessons you can learn from the experience and write a list of tips or advice you would give to other people in a similar situation.

■ MY OUTCOMES ■

Work in pairs. Discuss the questions.

1 To what extent did the topic and texts in this unit relate to your own interests and experience?

2 What are you better at now you have completed this unit?

3 Which of the four skills (reading, writing, speaking, listening) do you find the most challenging? How has this unit helped you with this skill?

4 What have you been doing outside the classroom to practise or revise language from the first three units?

4 Society

IN THIS UNIT, YOU:

- talk about the state of a country and the economy
- discuss global issues and solutions
- discuss news stories about social issues and think of solutions

SPEAKING

1 **Look at the photo. Work in pairs. Discuss the questions.**

1 What do you think causes situations like this?

2 What social issues do you think it shows?

3 Have you ever queued a long time for something? Where? Why? Do you think it could have been avoided? How?

People queuing up outside a bank in Jalpan, Mexico.

The state of the nation

IN THIS LESSON, YOU:
- talk about the state of a country and the economy
- practise identifying opinions on the state of the economy in a listening
- explain the causes and results of the state of the country
- practise providing new points of view in a discussion

VOCABULARY

The government, economics and society

1 Work in pairs. Read the sentences (1–12) and match the words and phrases in bold with the explanations (a–l).

1 Since she's **been in power,** the president's made a huge difference, especially for people on low incomes.

2 They need to cut **bureaucracy**. Businesses spend half their time filling in forms and dealing with officials!

3 The economy's in a total mess and we've gone into **a recession**. Unemployment has gone up massively.

4 The government is soft on crime. They should have more **punishments** to stop people who are caught dealing drugs or using violence.

5 They have set some tough targets to **tackle** the climate crisis. They want to ban all petrol cars by 2035.

6 The economy's **booming**. Lots of new businesses are starting up and plenty of new jobs are being created.

7 They've done a lot to tackle **corruption** and it means there's more money to spend on improving public services.

8 We've provided a lot of support for refugees, which has **boosted** our reputation in the world.

9 The **opposition** has agreed to work with the government to reduce hate speech on social media.

10 The cost of living is so high, people often have to do two jobs in order to **make ends meet**.

11 There's been a lack of **investment** in the health service, which is why we have a shortage of doctors and long waiting lists.

12 The government says they have too much **debt**, so they have cut spending and increased taxes to pay it back.

a money you borrowed and must pay back

b money you spend to improve things in the future

c a time when the economy becomes smaller

d had control of government and the right to make laws

e official rules and paperwork in an organization

f growing a lot or becoming very popular

g political parties not currently in government

h try to improve or solve a difficult problem

i helped to increase or improve

j fines or prison sentences, for example

k using your position in power to help yourself or your friends

l pay for all the basic things you need to live

Checking in voters. Bangalore, India.

2 **P ▶** Listen to the words from Exercise 1 in a phrase. Practise saying them. Which phrases do you find hard to say? Practise saying them again.

3 Work in groups. Decide if the sentences in Exercise 1 are positive or negative. Think of any examples of what the government might do in each case.

LISTENING

4 **▶** Listen to a woman and a man talking about their countries. Decide whose country is in a better situation and think of one reason why. Compare your ideas in pairs.

5 **▶** Work in pairs. Are the statements true (T), false (F) or not given (NG)? Listen again and check.

1 The president of the man's country has a bad reputation.
2 The president has done nothing to help the environment.
3 The man voted for the government, which is why he's disappointed.
4 There has been a recession in the man's country.
5 A lot of people borrow money because they don't earn enough.
6 Both speakers think voting is a waste of time.
7 The woman supports everything her government has done so far.
8 Her government has done a lot to boost tourism.
9 The man doesn't speak the language spoken in the woman's country.
10 There used to be more barriers to finding a job if you were from abroad.

6 Work in pairs. Discuss the questions.

1 Which country in the listening sounds more like yours? Why?
2 Use some of the ideas in Exercise 1 to say more about your country.

GRAMMAR

> ### So and such
>
> *So* and *such* are often used to link cause and result.
>
> *With **so** many people in debt, who knows what might happen?*
>
> *The economy is doing **so** well, the president's going to easily win the election.*
>
> *They've done **so** little to help the poor, that the number of people on the streets is rising.*
>
> *There's **such** a skills shortage that companies are paying really good money now.*

7 Look at the examples in the Grammar box and choose the correct options to complete the rules.

1 We use *so / such* before an adjective or adverb.
2 We use *so / such* before a noun or adjective + noun.
3 We use *so many / so much* before a plural noun and *so few / so little* before an uncountable noun.
4 We *have to / don't have to* start the result clause with *that* – especially in spoken English.

8 Complete the sentence starters with *so* or *such*.

1 Food prices have gone up _____ quickly …
2 We train _____ many doctors now …
3 Most people have to work _____ long hours …
4 The police made _____ a big mess of the investigation …
5 There's _____ little crime …
6 The government minister was involved in _____ a terrible public scandal …

9 Work in pairs. Write a possible ending for four of the sentences in Exercise 8. Work with another pair and compare your ideas

G See Grammar reference 4A.

DEVELOPING CONVERSATIONS

Showing understanding

To show we agree and understand when someone is talking about problems, we can use expressions such as:

I know! *Tell me about it!*

If we disagree or don't feel sympathy, we often soften our response:

I know what you mean, but … *Yeah, I guess. Mind you …*

10 **▶** Look at the Developing conversations box. Match the complaints (1–6) with the responses (a–f). Then listen and check your answers.

1 I don't know how people can make ends meet.
2 The job market is so competitive at the moment.
3 The pace of life is so fast here.
4 There's so much crime, you can't go out at night!
5 They haven't done anything to boost tourism.
6 This country is so bureaucratic!

a I know! It's exhausting. I feel like I spend my life just rushing around.
b Tell me about it! I only earn enough to cover the basics and I've got a good job.
c Tell me about it! I had to fill in four forms in three different places to be able to work here!
d I know what you mean, but if you're prepared to be flexible there's plenty of work.
e Yeah, maybe. Mind you, it's not like that everywhere. If you avoid certain areas, it's perfectly safe.
f Yeah, I know what you mean. Mind you, look what they've done to improve poor areas. That's great.

11 Now think of different responses to the complaints in Exercise 10. Practise your conversations in pairs.

CONVERSATION PRACTICE

12 **M** Work in pairs. Decide if you are Student A or B. Find your information. Spend five minutes preparing what you want to say. Then do the roleplay.

Student A: Look at File 5 on page 193 and follow the instructions.

Student B: Look at File 19 on page 199 and follow the instructions.

A better world

SPEAKING

1 Work in groups. List eight facts about the United Nations. Do some quick research if you need to.

VOCABULARY Development goals

2 Read the text about the United Nations sustainable development goals. Choose the correct options to complete the text.

In 2015, the 193 countries of the United Nations (UN) set themselves seventeen targets that they wanted to achieve by 2030. They are called 'The ¹*sustainable / sustainability* development goals' (SDGs). The first two targets are to end ²*poverty / the poor* (defined as living on less than $2/day) and to make ³*hunger / hungry* a thing of the past. Some of the goals focus on providing other basic things such as clean water, ⁴*improved / improvement* health, decent jobs and ⁵*afford / affordable* clean energy. Other goals focus on ⁶*economic / economist* issues and the environment. They aim to encourage ⁷*growth / growing* in the economy without involving ⁸*consumers / consumption* that damages the environment. Three goals are specifically about ⁹*preventative / preventing* measures against environmental disaster. Finally, the last set of goals is about creating a fair, ¹⁰*peace / peaceful* world where we have greater gender ¹¹*inequality / equality* and trying to stop ¹²*discriminated / discrimination* of any kind.

3 Work in pairs. Which SDGs are most relevant to your country, your area and you personally? Why?

READING

4 Read the article about SDG 10 – reducing inequality. Match the paragraph headings (a–f) with the paragraphs (1–6).
  a   Include everyone in the economy
  b   Prevention is better than cure
  c   Make tax and trade fairer
  d   Investment in schooling
  e   Get the wealthiest to contribute more
  f   Money for everyone

5 Work in pairs. Can you remember how these pairs of phrases were used in the six paragraphs of the article?
  1   investing in schools / more than halved
  2   preventative measures / death rates
  3   discriminated against / an annual award
  4   payment without conditions / succeed in education
  5   tackle inequality / a tax rate of 90%
  6   avoid paying tax / lose $14 billion

6 Work in pairs. Why do you think:
- Namibia spent a lot less on education before 1990?
- change for disabled people's rights is slow?
- a company prefers to pay tax in a particular country?

7 Tell your partner what you think of the article. Say:
- what you found surprising / interesting / obvious.
- what you agreed and disagreed with most.

GRAMMAR

Comparatives with *the ... , the ...*

We can show how changes in two or more things are related to each other by using two comparatives in the pattern *the* [comparative] .... , *the* [comparative] ...

The more equal a society is, **the happier** the people are.

The more people earn, **the fewer** problems they have.

The longer we wait, **the greater** the cost.

The **greater the equality** we have, **the less** hunger and poverty there will be.

8 Look at the examples in the Grammar box. Choose three of these sentence starters and complete them with your own ideas. Tell a partner.
  1   The more educated you are, ...
  2   The more tax the government collects, ...
  3   The less we spend on healthcare, ...
  4   The more coffee you drink, ...
  5   The more I work, ...

9 Work in pairs. Choose a sentence from Exercise 8. Make a chain of effects. Start each new sentence with the second half of the previous sentence.

  A: The more I work, the less free time I have.

  B: The less free time I have, the less exercise I do.

  A: The less exercise I do, ...

G   See Grammar Reference 4B.   »»

SPEAKING

10 Work in groups. Choose three other SDGs from the text in Exercise 2. Think of policies that could achieve each goal. Explain how they'd work.

Making the World More Equal

Research suggests that the more equal a society is, the happier the people are and the less poverty there is, so reducing inequality is key to meeting other sustainable development goals too. Here are six ways it could happen.

1 _____

Reducing income inequality may start from educating everyone to a similar level, which is why investing in schools is so important. For example, since Namibia gained independence from South Africa in 1990, it has spent a greater percentage of its budget on education than almost any other country in the world. The result is that poverty has more than halved (down from 53%).

2 _____

Governments may decide to build hospitals to improve health, but some countries have taken a different route. Back in the 1980s, Thailand chose to spend money on local medical services and preventative measures instead of new hospitals. More recently, Costa Rica established a similar programme of healthcare teams working in the community. In both cases death rates fell as access to healthcare rose dramatically. And both countries have seen their economies grow with Thailand also managing a 23% cut in inequality over the last 30 years.

3 _____

Of course, not all health issues can be prevented. Fifteen per cent of the world's population have a permanent disability, but unfortunately, they are often discriminated against and change is slow. The EU has an annual award for cities which make transport and public spaces more accessible to wheelchair users. Some countries, such as Germany, also give support to companies who employ people with disabilities. However, to make a bigger impact, we need more affordable support for people with disabilities and for their carers in their homes.

4 _____

Obviously, increasing minimum wages might reduce inequality, but others argue that an even better solution is a universal basic income (UBI) where every citizen receives a regular payment, without conditions, to spend as they wish. Countries such as Canada, Kenya and Spain have tried out UBI in certain communities, giving monthly payments of between $35 and $1,000. Despite opponents' fears, the results of these experiments show people tend to work the same amount and don't spend money on addictions. In fact, people receiving UBI usually see improvements to their physical and mental health and children in their communities are more likely to succeed in education.

5 _____

As well as raising incomes for members of society with the least resources, governments could also lower wealth at the very top. In theory, higher taxes on high earnings discourage the acquisition of excess wealth, and it may also have the benefit of reducing high-end consumption, like private jets. What's more, the greater the tax, the more governments can do to tackle inequality in health and education – *if* they can collect it. In the US, in the 1960s, there was a tax rate of 90% on a yearly income above $400,000 (around $4m today), but since then, as the rate's been cut, inequality has risen.

6 _____

But collecting tax can be difficult, especially where different countries have different tax rates. For example, many multinationals often avoid paying tax by a system called 'mispricing', whereby one part of the company in a low-tax country A, charges a very high price for the services it 'provides' to a different part of the company in a 'high-tax' country B. This means the company may actually make a loss in country B and pay no tax there at all. According to some research, African countries lose $14 billion a year in this way, in the mining industry alone.

Jakarta, Indonesia.

Stand up

IN THIS LESSON, YOU:
- discuss news stories about social issues and think of solutions
- talk about campaigns and campaigners
- practise hearing synonyms in news stories and taking notes
- give personal responses to news stories to develop a discussion

SPEAKING

1 Look at the photo and read the caption on page 41. Answer the questions.

1 Had you heard of the woman in the photo before or seen the film about her?

2 What other well-known campaigners have there been in your country or the world? What did they campaign for or against? Have they been commemorated in any way (e.g. films, books, buildings)?

3 Have you seen any films where someone was fighting for rights or had a legal battle? What happened? Do you like these kinds of films?

4 Have you heard any news stories recently about gender equality? Explain the story.

LISTENING

2 FS ▶ In news stories a key idea can be referred to in different ways. Listen and write down the three synonyms that are used for the key idea in each set of extracts.

3 ▶ Listen to five short news stories. Match the stories (1–5) with these topics (a–f). There is one extra topic.

a a campaign for change

b someone winning a prize

c an example of racism

d a project to solve a social problem

e an example of discrimination at work

f a discussion in parliament

4 Work in pairs. Make notes of what you remember about each story.

5 ▶ Listen again. Check your notes and add one more piece of information about each story.

6 Work in pairs. Match the verbs (1–6) with the words they went with in the news stories (a–f).

1 be awarded
2 be based
3 be debated
4 be damaged
5 be sued
6 reject

a in parliament
b for lies and abuse
c on evidence
d the argument
e compensation
f by human activity

@ellestreetart

7 Work in pairs. Discuss which of these phrases you might use to comment on aspects of each story. Explain why.

a It seems a bit over-the-top.

b It's quite shocking.

c It's unfair on other people.

d I just don't get the point of it. How will it help?

e That's good news for a change.

f They should do more to tackle the problem.

g It's just a ridiculous way to behave.

h At least they're doing something about it.

i It's sadly all too common.

VOCABULARY Campaigns

8 Complete the four news stories about campaigns using the correct form of the words in brackets. The words are not given in the correct order.

1 Crowds of protesters _____ outside the central court in _____ of campaigners who are _____ an oil company for $2 billion in compensation for destroying sea life, under a new law that protects nature. (**gather, sue, support**)

2 A new advertising campaign was _____ yesterday by women's groups trying to _____ the impact of poverty on young women and girls. They are also _____ the government to provide free sanitary products in all schools and colleges. (**call for, highlight, launch**)

Judge Ruth Bader Ginsburg was a leading campaigner for women's equality. Her first legal battles were made into the film *On the basis of sex*.

3 Protestors stopped traffic in the centre of town during a _____ against the government's _____ to provide adequate support for people with disabilities at home. _____ chained their wheelchairs together across the road. (**activist, demonstration, failure**)

4 An online _____ against the construction of a chemical factory near a residential area has received 10,000 signatures. Campaigners are also planning to _____ through the city centre to highlight the issue and _____ their right to clean air. (**defend, march, petition**)

9 Work in groups. Discuss the questions.

1 What do you think of each of the four stories? Would you support any of these campaigns? Which ones? Why?

2 Which way of campaigning or protesting is the most effective? Which aren't effective? Why?

10 Choose six of the words in Exercise 8. Underline other words that go with them.

Crowds of protesters **gathered** *outside the central court campaigners who are* **suing** *an oil company for $2 billion*

SPEAKING TASK

11 Think of a news story you have heard about or find a story online. It could be about the following.

- a campaign or demonstration
- an issue about the environment
- an issue about equality
- how the economy is doing
- social media

12 Spend five minutes preparing. Be ready to:

- explain what happened if your partner doesn't know already.
- comment on what you think about the story and if it shows a general problem in society.
- say what you think should happen next and how the problem could be solved.

13 M Work in pairs. Have conversations about your stories. Decide at least two things that should happen in response to the story.

14 As a class, decide which story is the most important and why.

■ MY OUTCOMES ■

Work in pairs. Discuss the questions.

1 Which reading or listening texts were the most interesting, and why?

2 After completing this unit, what sorts of conversations or discussions are you better at now? What phrases might you use?

3 Was this unit more or less difficult than earlier units? In what way?

4 What can you do at home to revise language from this unit?

Letters of complaint

SPEAKING

1 Work in groups. Discuss the questions.

1 What things have you bought over the internet?

2 Have you ever had any problems with online transactions? What happened? Did you sort it out?

3 Have you ever rung a customer helpline? What was the service like?

WRITING

2 Read the letter of complaint without filling in the gaps. Answer the questions from Exercise 1 for the writer of the letter.

Dear Sir / Madam,

¹_____ I am writing to complain about the digital camera I bought from your website on 18th July this year and the service I have received.

²_____ I was informed that delivery would take two weeks, but in fact it took over a month, arriving too late for me to take it on holiday. I sent a number of emails before I left, but they were never answered.

³_____ it was not exactly as advertised. According to your website, it was supposed to have 100GB of memory. However, it stated on the packaging that this was only with a memory card, sold separately. I rang to complain, but I was told that I should have looked more carefully and I was then directed to details on the website. However, the website simply has a link to a helpline.

⁴_____ when I called your helpline, it took me half an hour to get through and when I did, the three-minute conversation cost me five pounds and then I was told I would still have to write.

⁵_____ I feel that I should be sent the missing memory card free of charge.

Yours faithfully,

Jamila Benitez

3 Work in pairs. Match the sentence starters (a–f) with the paragraphs (1–5) in the letter. There is one extra sentence starter that you do not need. What is the purpose of each paragraph?

a To make matters worse,

b As compensation for the late delivery and the time and money wasted,

c When I finally received the camera,

d If I wanted to take the matter further,

e Following my telephone conversation today (15th September),

f When I ordered the camera,

4 Read the letter again and underline useful phrases that you could use in any letter of complaint.

5 Work in pairs. Discuss the questions.

1 Do you think the complaint is fair?

2 Do you think the company will agree to the compensation? Why? / Why not?

USEFUL LANGUAGE

According to

We use *according to* to say who gave us information or an opinion. In letters of complaint, especially, this introduces what **should** or **is supposed to** happen. We often contrast this with the actual situation using **however** or **but (in fact / in reality)**.

According to your website, it **is supposed to** have 100GB of memory. **However**, it stated on the packaging that this was only with a memory card, sold separately.

According to the advert, it **should** be delivered next day, **but in fact** I had to wait over a week.

6 Read the Useful language box. Complete the sentences with one word in each gap.

According ¹_____ your website, complaints should ²_____ dealt with within five working days. ³_____ , I am still waiting for an answer two weeks later.

When I received the parcel there were no batteries, ⁴_____ according to the advert they ⁵_____ supposed to be included.

According to the person I spoke to, legally I ⁶_____ have been ⁷_____ a full refund without any questions, but in ⁸_____ I was only offered a replacement – and then only after a long argument.

7 Complete the sentences with your own ideas.

1 According to your website, you provide a fast, efficient service. _____ .

2 According to your publicity, your staff are supposed to be highly professional, _____ .

3 According to the instructions, I should notice the difference within a week, _____ .

4 According to _____ .

Passive reporting verbs

In letters of complaint, we often use the passive forms of verbs to report speech, because it's more formal and we may not know the name of the person who spoke or wrote to us.

The woman I spoke to said you have to get in touch with the head office.

→ **I was told** *I should contact the head office.*

The guy I asked just said, 'Look at the small print, it's all there.'

→ **I was directed** *to the small print.*

8 Complete the sentences with a passive form of the reporting verb.

1 My husband _____ (tell) he should speak to the manager.

2 I _____ (offer) a full refund if I was not satisfied.

3 We _____ (inform) that the flight had been delayed by five hours only minutes before we were due to board.

4 I _____ (promise) a replacement. They wouldn't refund the money.

5 We _____ (ask) to arrive at the station 30 minutes before departure.

6 The holiday _____ (advertise) as all-inclusive.

9 Work in pairs. Rewrite the sentences to be more formal. Use a passive reporting verb and make any other changes you think are necessary.

1 The email you sent said it would take a couple of weeks to deliver.

2 The guy I phoned just said I should've looked more carefully. It's all there on the website.

3 He said if his reply wasn't good enough for me, I had to write to the company.

PRACTICE

10 Work in pairs. Look at the advert for a gift idea below. Make a list of things that could go wrong.

11 With your partner, decide which ideas you are going to use and plan a letter of complaint. Think about the following.

- what complaint(s) you are going to make
- how you will organize the letter into paragraphs
- what phrases from the model letter in Exercise 2 you could reuse
- what you want the company to do – offer compensation, apologize, etc.

12 Write your letter in 180–250 words. Then work with a new partner. Compare your letters. Discuss:

- whether you think the company would reply positively to the letter. Why? / Why not?
- one thing you like about the letter and one thing that would improve it.

Gifts Mapped Out

Looking for a gift which will provide memories and entertainment? Why not get a personalized jigsaw puzzle based on a special place? Use the location finder on our website and we'll create a puzzle of the map or photo of the area. Alternatively, you can send us a digital photo of whatever you like. Puzzles come in three sizes – 150, 250 or 500 pieces – and are packaged in a durable presentation tin.

We also have a range of gift cards, which you can add your own messages to. Orders normally take two weeks. Guaranteed delivery for Christmas on orders received before December 15th.

Visit us at giftsmappedout

VIDEO Out and about

1 Work in pairs. Discuss the questions.

1 How could we best reduce inequality?

2 How could we sort out the environment?

3 How could we best improve health care?

4 How could we best improve education?

Understanding accents

Some accents replace an /ɔː/ sound with /əʊ/, so *walk* /wɔːk/ may sound like *woke* /wəʊk/; *court* /kɔːt/ like *coat* /kəʊt/; and *more* /mɔː/ like *mow* /məʊ/.

2 ▣ Watch the video. Which person has the closest views to you? What do they say?

3 ▣ Work in pairs. Match the statements with the speakers and explain your choices. You may match statements with more than one speaker. Then watch again to check.

a People could be more understanding of other people's problems.

b Everyone can contribute to solving the issue in a small way.

c We need to be able to make informed choices in what we buy.

d We need to raise awareness of the problem and its consequences.

e The government should spend more money on it.

f There isn't enough diversity among trainers or materials.

g Young people could be stretched more by adopting different methods.

4 Discuss the questions with your partner.

1 What do you think is contributing most to ruining the environment?

2 Are there any lessons you wish they taught at school?

3 Why might it be important to diversify education / work?

4 How do you think you could increase people's empathy?

VIDEO Developing conversations

5 ▣ You are going to watch two people talking about two gadgets they have bought. Watch and take notes on what they say.

6 ▣ Work in pairs. Compare what you understood. Watch again if you need to.

7 Discuss the questions with your partner.

1 Which gadget would be most useful to you? Why?

2 What sounds do you find annoying?

3 What gadgets do you have in your office / kitchen? Are they any good?

8 FS ▣ Watch again. Complete the sentences with three to five words in each gap.

1 So _____ a hearing aid?

2 Kind of, but _____ instead of amplifying the frequencies, I can just mute them.

3 What's the battery life like? Do you _____ ?

4 What if you _____ alarm clock?

5 Exactly, and with this one _____ put it in and it does it for you.

6 The top just comes off – _____ the dishwasher.

7 … chilli and garlic … um _____ that stuff on your hands, especially garlic, it can smell …

8 After you wash your hands you can just rub your eye _____ so painful.

CONVERSATION PRACTICE

9 Work in pairs. You are going to practise a conversation.

1 Choose a Conversation practice from either Lesson 3A or Lesson 4A.

2 Look at the language in that lesson.

3 Check the meaning of anything you've forgotten with your partner.

4 Have the conversation. Try to improve on the last time you did it.

Grammar and Vocabulary

GRAMMAR

1 **Complete the text with one word in each gap.**

The Spirit Level by Richard Wilkinson and Kate Pickett argues that [1]_____ more equal a society is, the healthier it is and the [2]_____ social problems it has. Inequality in places such as the US has increased [3]_____ rapidly over the last decades that people have started to feel abandoned by the government, and there is more violence and addiction than in more equal societies. The authors suggest that governments should [4]_____ done more during the boom years [5]_____ reduce the wealth gap, because there is [6]_____ a lot of unemployment now that it is more difficult to tackle the situation. Nevertheless, the authors believe that change can happen. The government should [7]_____ more money on education and increase the minimum wage [8]_____ everyone feels valued for the job they do.

2 **Read the first sentence in each pair. Complete the second sentence so that it has a similar meaning. Use between three and five words, including the word in bold.**

1 Have you tried using a knife to open it?

Maybe _____ a knife to open it. **SHOULD**

2 What do you call that stuff you use if you've got a stain on your clothes?

What do you call the stuff you use _____ your clothes? **REMOVE**

3 The investigation was so poor, the chief of police had to resign.

The police _____ of the investigation that the chief of police had to resign. **MESS**

4 As the economy improves, we will see youth unemployment fall.

The better the economy performs, _____ will be for young people. **JOBS**

5 It was a mistake to invest so much in the Olympics.

I don't think the government _____ much in the Olympics. **SHOULD**

6 There's a positive correlation between practice and performance.

It's simple: the more you _____ performance will be. **BETTER**

3 **Complete the sentences with your own ideas.**

1 I need a cloth to _____ .

2 Have you got a screwdriver so _____ ?

3 There's such a shortage of housing, _____ .

4 When I was younger, I should _____ .

5 The more money I have, the _____ .

6 The more I study English, the _____ .

4 ▶ **Listen. Write the six sentences you hear.**

VOCABULARY

5 **Match the verbs (1–10) with the collocates (a–j).**

1 tackle — a for compensation / him for lying

2 boost — b more investment / government action

3 defend — c wealth / a huge collection

4 acquire — d consumption / his reputation

5 get into — e your rights / the city from attack

6 call for — f through town / against the war

7 march — g for things at auction / against someone

8 bid — h the climate crisis / a problem

9 sue — i collecting figures / politics

10 swap — j places / stickers with other collectors

6 **Complete the text with one word in each gap. The first letters are given.**

In times when the economy is in a [1] re_____ people often can't afford to buy new things or pay for repairs because they are struggling to make [2] e_____ meet. Many would like to turn to DIY or making things themselves. That's easy enough if you are [3] m_____ a strap which has come off a bag, or your shirt or trousers are [4] r_____ as most people have a [5] n_____ and thread. But what if it's a bigger repair, like your roof has a leak or a desk has [6] f_____ [7] a_____ ? Not everyone has the tools they need and they're expensive to buy. Well, one solution is visiting one of our network of tool libraries that have started up all around the country. You can borrow a [8] st_____ to climb up on the roof or a saw and [9] dr_____ to make a new desk and, just like a normal library, it's free. To find out more, visit our website. If you would like to [10] d_____ any tools, contact us on the number below. We will accept any that are slightly damaged – a little [11] sc_____ , for example – but we do ask that they have no parts [12] m_____ and are in working order. We'd also love to hear from you if you are interested in helping with our campaign to [13] hi_____ the services we provide, or maybe you'd even like to [14] l_____ a new library in your area.

7 **Complete the sentences using the correct form of the words in bold.**

1 It's important that kids learn to challenge _____ when they see it. **discriminate**

2 Health has improved in countries that have invested in _____ medicine. **prevent**

3 The economy is booming because of increased _____ from abroad. **invest**

4 Environmental _____ gathered in the central square in support of net-zero targets. **active**

5 The _____ have attacked the government's _____ to deal with price rises. **oppose / fail**

6 Child _____ in the country has _____ over the last 20 years. **poor / half**

7 _____ growth is not _____ unless we take care of the planet too. **economy / sustain**

8 There should be stricter _____ for people who are found guilty of _____ . **punish / corrupt**

5 Sports and interests

IN THIS UNIT, YOU:

- roleplay conversations about future arrangements
- talk about past mistakes and regrets
- discuss past and present interests

SPEAKING

1 Work in pairs. Discuss the questions.

1 Have you seen any films or videos about climbers? What happened in them?

2 What other extreme sports do you know? What do you think of them? What's the riskiest activity you've done?

2 Work in groups. Discuss which statements are true for you or people you know.

- I enjoy sports with a bit of a risk.
- I like outdoor pursuits – walking, camping, that kind of thing.
- I'm a member of a sports club.
- I belong to a music or drama group.
- I do volunteer work for a charity.
- I go to dance classes to keep fit.
- I like wandering round street markets and second-hand shops.
- I love doing puzzles – crosswords, Sudoku, stuff like that.
- I like sewing and knitting. I make my own clothes.
- I spend a lot of time on social media.
- At the weekend, I lie in bed till lunchtime and then just chill out at home.

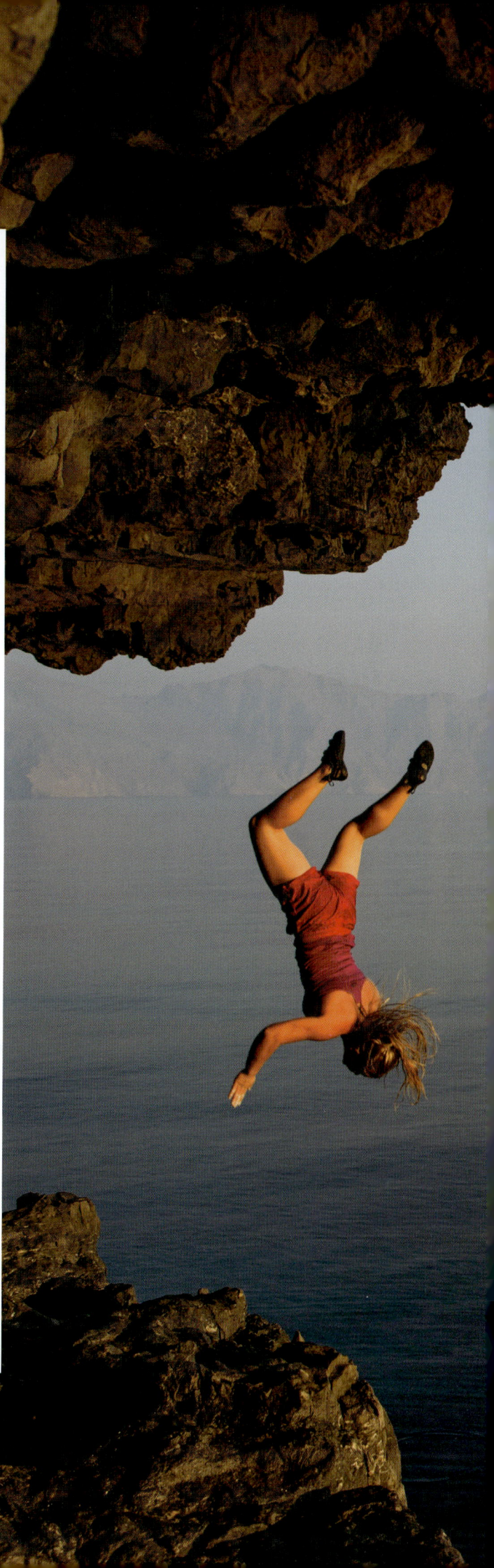

A woman who's free climbing without ropes falls into the sea in Oman.

Time out

IN THIS LESSON, YOU:
- roleplay conversations about future arrangements
- discuss health and fitness
- practise listening to three conversations about free-time activities
- practise checking what you heard

VOCABULARY Health and fitness

1 Complete the sentences with these words.

breath	chill out	junk	lie-in
shape	stamina	sweat	uncoordinated

1 I'm really unfit. I **work up a** _____ just running for the bus! It's awful!

2 I'm training for a marathon, so I run every day to **build up my** _____ .

3 I **get out of** _____ just walking up the stairs these days.

4 I'm so unfit. I really need to stop **eating** _____ **food**. The thing is, though, I know it's not good for me, but it's just so tasty!

5 I'm **totally** _____ – really clumsy. I'm always tripping over and bumping into things.

6 I'm **out of** _____ . I don't really do any exercise at all any more.

7 I usually work out on Saturday mornings and then just try **to** _____ and take it easy for the rest of the weekend.

8 I usually only manage to sleep five or six hours a night during the week, but on Saturdays I like to **have a long** _____ .

2 When one word ends in a consonant sound and the next begins with a vowel, we often link those sounds together.

Work in pairs. Look at the phrases in bold in Exercise 1 and decide which words you think will link. One phrase has no linking. Which one?

3 **P** ▶ Listen and check your ideas. Repeat what you hear. Which phrases do you find hard to say? Practise saying them again.

4 Work in pairs. Discuss these questions. Use vocabulary from Exercise 1 if you can.

1 How fit would you say you are? How much exercise do you do each week?

2 How often do you have a lie-in? How much sleep do you usually need?

3 What are the best ways to improve your coordination? Your stamina? Your general health? Have you tried any of these methods? How did you get on?

4 What sports and activities are you good and bad at? Why?

LISTENING

5 ▶ Listen to three conversations about free-time activities and answer the questions.

1 What is the second speaker in each conversation going to do?

2 How long have they been doing this activity?

6 **FS** ▶ Listen to nine extracts from the conversations. There is a word missing from the end of each extract. Try to work out the missing word and write it down.

7 ▶ Listen to the full extracts and check your ideas from Exercise 6.

8 ▶ Listen to the conversations from Exercise 5 again. Decide in which conversation (1–3) someone:

a is going to study with an expert.

b says that different parts of their body don't work well together.

c has successfully dealt with a problem.

d complains that they're out of shape.

e suggests their friend should be more open-minded.

9 Work in pairs. Discuss these questions.

1 Do you know anyone who has an unusual hobby – or have you ever discovered that someone had a hidden talent for doing something?

2 How long have they been doing it?

3 How did they first get interested in it?

DEVELOPING CONVERSATIONS

Checking what you heard

If we are surprised by what someone tells us and we want to check information, we often repeat part of the statement and add a question word with a rising intonation.

A: *I've got my knitting group tonight.*

B: **You've got what?**

10 Look at the Developing conversations box. Complete these conversations (1–5) with checking questions.

1 A: I usually run about ten kilometres most days.
  B: _____ ?
  A: Ten kilometres. I'm not that fast, though.

2 A: I do capoeira on Wednesday nights.
  B: _____ ?
  A: Capoeira. A Brazilian martial art dance.

3 A: I went to a comic fair at the weekend.
  B: _____ ?
  A: A comic fair. They had all these old Spiderman comics.

4 A: My mum's really into embroidery.
  B: _____ ?
  A: Embroidery. It's like sewing, but you use thread to make pictures or patterns on the cloth.

5 A: Well, I didn't get up till three on Saturday.
  B: _____ ?
  A: Three o'clock. I'd had a heavy week. I needed a lie-in!

11 Work in pairs. Practise reading the conversations in Exercise 10. Take turns to be B. Try to make the intonation in your checking questions go up.

CONVERSATION PRACTICE

12 Think about an unusual or surprising hobby and a future arrangement you have that is connected to it. Decide where you're doing it, who with, when, etc.

13 Write three questions people might ask you about your hobby, and the answers you would give.

14 Work in pairs and have similar conversations to those you heard in Exercise 5. Use this guide to help you. Then swap roles.

Student A	Student B
Ask about tonight or the weekend.	Explain your arrangement connected to hobby.
Check you understood.	Explain again (+ add info).
Ask and answer questions about hobby to continue.	

Practising capoeira at sunset, Brazil.

You should've been there

IN THIS LESSON, YOU:
- talk about past mistakes and regrets
- discuss different sports – and how you feel about them
- work out the purpose of a text
- provide evidence to support claims about a text

SPEAKING

1 **Work in groups. Discuss the questions.**

1 Do you know anyone who is a big sports fan? In what way? What team(s) do they support?

2 What are the most popular sports in your country? Why do you think they are so popular? Do you like them?

3 What do you think the most popular sports in the world are? Why?

VOCABULARY Sport

2 **Work in pairs. Read the sentences. Check any words in bold that you don't understand in a dictionary. Then discuss which sports the sentences might describe.**

1 She hit a great **shot** and made a hole in one.

2 He came off the **track**. He was trying to **overtake** on a corner and lost control of the car.

3 They almost scored – they hit the **bar** twice and a **post** once.

4 They called **a time-out** to discuss **tactics**.

5 They got promoted to the top **division** last season.

6 Oh no! That's my third double **fault** of the game.

7 I was **tackled** – just as I was about to **shoot**!

8 He ran from the halfway line to **score**.

9 I came on as a **substitute** after another player got injured.

10 He got a red card for a bad **tackle**.

11 She lost five first-round matches in a row so she **sacked** her coach.

12 I reckon the fight was **fixed**. I mean, the judges made some really weird decisions.

3 **Work in pairs. Which other sports can you use the words in bold from Exercise 2 to describe? Which words can you use to talk about other areas of life?**

Elections can also be **fixed** *– if the result is basically decided before people vote.*

4 **Work in pairs. Discuss the questions.**

1 Have you heard of anyone – or any team – who's been promoted recently?

2 Do you know any competitions that you think were fixed?

3 Can you think of any unpopular decisions that judges or referees have made?

4 Have you done or experienced any of the things in Exercise 2 when playing sport?

READING

5 **Write four possible benefits of doing or watching sport. Think about both individuals and society. Then compare your ideas with a partner.**

6 **Read the opinion piece on page 51. Does it mention your ideas?**

7 **Which of these statements do you think the writer of the article would agree with?**

1 If you did more exercise, you'd be more positive.

2 Forcing kids to compete undermines their confidence.

3 We shouldn't encourage people to read.

4 The most important thing is to win.

5 Sports clubs keep young people out of trouble.

6 It's OK for players to pretend to be injured.

7 Seeing great sports people in action is uplifting.

8 **Work in pairs. Which of the statements in Exercise 7 do you personally agree with? Find three more things in the article you strongly agree or disagree with.**

GRAMMAR

Past modals

should(n't) have, could(n't) have, would(n't) have

a *I* **shouldn't have overtaken**! *I* **wouldn't have crashed**.

b *I* **should have worked** *more. I* **could have bought** *a better car.*

9 **Work in pairs. Look at the examples in the Grammar box and complete these rules.**

To show we think something in the past was a good idea but didn't happen, we use [1] _____ + past participle. To show we think something that happened wasn't a good idea, we use [2] _____ + past participle. [3] _____ + past participle describes the likely consequence if a past situation had been different, and [4] _____ + past participle shows a possible consequence.

10 **Complete the sentences with the modal verbs in bold and the correct form of the verb in brackets. You may need to use negative forms.**

1 It was a close game. We _____ (try) any harder and there's no shame in losing to such a good team, but I still think we _____ (draw) with them. **could / should**

2 I don't know what I was thinking! I _____ never _____ (study) Art. Something like History _____ (be) much better for me. **should / would**

3 She _____ (think) before using social media like that. All the trouble she then got into _____ (be) avoided. **should / could**

G See Grammar reference 5B.

SPEAKING

11 **Work in pairs. Choose one of these topics and take turns to talk about it using past modals.**

- sporting event where something went wrong

- something you regret doing – or not doing

Quidditch match, Nantes, France.

SPORT – AND WHY I LOVE IT

Record numbers of people do no sport at all, while others don't even watch it. Let's look at the five main reasons they're missing out.

1 HEALTHY BODY, HEALTHY MIND

The first reason may be obvious, but it's still worth repeating: sport keeps you in shape. Moreover, people who are physically fit are, on average, happier. In fact, the British health service has recently experimented with giving people suffering from mild depression a course of exercise instead of medication.

2 PREPARATION FOR LIFE

A second reason is that sport makes you mentally stronger. Now, I'm not talking here about those odd non-competitive sports that some schools insist on: no winners, no losers and everyone gets a prize. Not only are such games dull and pointless for children, but life just isn't like that. Competitive sport teaches us to cope with losing and disappointments. Sure, we're not all naturally sporty, but then I'm rubbish at crosswords. You just have to find your own level and learn to enjoy your own performance. You can feel the same sense of achievement as Real Madrid winning a game by beating an opponent who is at a slightly higher (though still low!) level than you. Similarly, I'm happy completing a puzzle others would find easy.

3 IT'S SOCIAL AND FUN

What would we do without sport? Read? Play computer games? Hang around on the street? Obviously, these aren't necessarily all bad things – reading in particular brings many benefits – but the first two are hardly social, and the last not that interesting or purposeful. This brings me neatly to my third reason for playing sport: it helps to build relationships and teaches the importance of supporting each other, whether you win or lose. After bad games, players sometimes bond by comparing injuries they got. In the same way, sports fans often enjoy sharing the pain of their team losing almost as much as the joy of winning.

4 FAIRNESS AND HONESTY

Just to go back to hanging around on the streets, if you need proof that it's not that fun, why do so many of those kids end up in trouble? It's simply out of boredom – something which sport can often provide a solution to. So making sport more widely available is good for society. It also benefits society by showing children the importance of rules and moral choices. Of course people cheat and perhaps you've been denied the chance to win something as a result. You think 'I shouldn't have stuck to the rules! Then I would've won'. However, the rules are the sport and you know if everyone starts cheating, the game falls apart and stops being fun. That's how we learn about making the correct moral decisions in sport, but we also learn why, in life, cheats are looked down on or excluded.

5 SPORT IS LIFE

One final point I'd like to make here is that sport doesn't just involve learning about life. It IS life. I play tennis; I'm basically fairly hopeless, regularly serving double faults or weakly hitting the ball into the net. However, there are moments when somehow everything comes together and I hit a great shot down the line or serve a clean ace. I suddenly feel like a world-beater and it's a great feeling, even if the next ball flies miles out. Isn't life all about having those feelings? And sport – playing or watching – provides many of them. No one looks back at the end of their life and says, 'I should've worked more. I could've bought a better car' or 'I'll never forget that time my kids watched TV'. No, what we remember are things like Usain Bolt smashing the world 100-metre record in Beijing – beating everyone else so easily that he could actually slow down in order to start celebrating ten metres before he crossed the line. And we're more likely to think 'I should've played with my kids more' or 'I wish I'd done more sport'.

A bit extreme

IN THIS LESSON, YOU:

- discuss past and present interests
- practise listening to a conversation about an unusual character
- deduce the truth of statements about the conversation
- talk about accidents and injuries

LISTENING

1 Work in pairs. Look at these activities and discuss the questions. Use the sentence frames in the box below to explain your reasons.

ballroom dancing	handstands	hang-gliding
ice-skating	parachuting	shooting
tai chi	windsurfing	yoga

1 Have you ever done any of these activities? When?
2 Would you like to try any of them in the future? Why? / Why not?

I think it'd be fun / amazing / really hard.

I think I'd really enjoy it because I like other similar kinds of things.

I'm not flexible **enough**.

I'd be scared of break**ing** my leg.

I wouldn't be able to stand up.

2 ▶ Listen to three people – Chloe, Paola and Kyle – talking about Paola's uncle. Which of the activities in Exercise 1 has Paola's uncle done?

3 ▶ Work in pairs. Are the sentences about Paola's uncle true (T) or false (F)? Listen again and check.

1 He taught Paola and Kyle how to do handstands at his home.
2 He stopped ice-skating after an hour because Paola and Kyle were bored.
3 He used to go hang-gliding three or four times a month.
4 He gave up hang-gliding because he badly injured his neck.
5 He's only taken up windsurfing recently.
6 He lives by the sea now.
7 He drinks lemon juice every day because he thinks it's good for him.
8 Kyle admits Paola's uncle can be fun – but only for very short periods of time.

Yoga practitioner performs a handstand, Himalayas.

4 Discuss these questions with your partner.

1 Does Paola's uncle sound odd to you? Why? / Why not?

2 Do you know anyone who's unusual for their age? In what way?

3 Do you know anyone who's only OK in small doses? Why?

4 Do you know any other things (like lemons) that are supposed to be good for your skin, feet, hair, eyesight, etc.? Do you think it's true?

5 Do you know anyone who had a lucky escape? What happened?

VOCABULARY Injuries and accidents

5 Work in pairs. Discuss which problem (a–b) you think is worse in each case.

1 a He felt a bit dizzy.

b He passed out.

2 a I tore my knee ligaments.

b I strained a muscle in my neck.

3 a She knocked herself out.

b She had a hairline fracture of the skull.

4 a I had to wear a cast on my leg.

b I twisted my ankle.

5 a He grazed his knee.

b His knee is very swollen.

6 a The wound healed quite quickly.

b The wound got infected.

6 Work in pairs. Tell each other about an accident that had one of the results in Exercise 5. Do you think the accident or result could have been avoided? Why?

GRAMMAR

The present perfect simple and continuous

We use both the present perfect simple and continuous to talk about situations, changes and actions between some time in the past and now.

a I**'ve done** hardly any exercise since January.

b For the last few months he**'s been rubbing** lemon in his hair every day.

c I **haven't been feeling** very well the last few days.

d I **haven't been** to the doctor's about it yet, but I will if it gets worse.

e What **have** you **done** to your leg?

f How long **has** she **been doing** tai chi?

7 Look at the examples in the Grammar box. Then work in pairs. Answer these questions.

1 Which sentences use the present perfect continuous and which use the present perfect simple? How do you know?

2 Which structure do we use to describe things that have finished sometime before now? In the examples, how are these things connected to now?

3 Which structure do we use to show things started in the past and are still going on now?

8 Complete the conversations with the present perfect continuous or the present perfect simple form of the verbs.

1 A: _____ (you / manage) to buy the tickets for the game yet?

B: No. _____ (I / call) all morning, but I can't get through.

2 A: _____ (you / see) *The Lost City* yet?

B: No. _____ (I / mean) to for ages now, but _____ (I / just / not / have) the chance. Is it still on?

3 A: So why _____ (Wayne / decide) to leave? It's a bit sudden, isn't it?

B: Not really. _____ (he / think) about it for a while, but _____ (he / look for) the right job – and now he _____ (he / find) it.

4 A: I played tennis with her yesterday. She's really good, considering _____ (she / only / play) a few times.

B: I can imagine. _____ (she / always / be) good at sports. She's just got that natural fitness and coordination.

5 A: I'm really tired. _____ (I / not sleep) well recently.

B: That's not good. How long _____ (that / go on) ?

9 Work in pairs. Practise reading the conversations in Exercise 8. Add your own ideas to continue them for as long as you can.

G See Grammar reference 5C. ⟫

SPEAKING TASK

10 Think of three sports or interests that you (or people you know) have given up over recent years – and three things you (or people you know) have taken up.

11 **M** Work in groups. Share your ideas.

For the things people gave up, ask and talk about:

• why people stopped doing these things.

• how long they did them for.

• what was good or bad about them.

For the things people have taken up, ask and talk about:

• how people got into these things.

• how long they have been doing them for.

• what they like most about them.

12 In your group, decide on two different activities you'd all be happy to take up.

■ MY OUTCOMES ■

Work in pairs. Discuss the questions.

1 What interesting things did you learn in this unit?

2 Say how you would describe: a sports event you have been to; a leisure activity you regularly do; a sport or hobby you'd like to try.

3 What did you find the most difficult in this unit – the new language, the speaking activities, or the reading and listening texts? Why?

4 What can you do at home to revise language from this unit?

6 Accommodation

IN THIS UNIT, YOU:

- talk about places you have stayed in
- discuss culture shock and your experiences of it
- practise ways of resolving problems

SPEAKING

1 **Look at the photo. Work in pairs. Discuss the questions.**

1 Where do you think the place is?

2 Would you like to stay in a place like this?

2 **Discuss the advantages and disadvantages of staying in these places. Which have you stayed in? When? Where?**

1 a self-catering apartment

2 a posh hotel

3 a camper van

4 a tent

5 a youth hostel

6 a bed and breakfast

Getting a good night's sleep.

A great place to stay

IN THIS LESSON, YOU:
- talk about places you have stayed in
- express positive and negative views about places
- practise listening to two conversations about places people have stayed in
- practise using negative questions to express opinion and surprise

VOCABULARY Where you stayed

1 Read the sentences. Do they express positive (P) or negative (N) views about places, or could they be either (E)?

1 The whole place was really **muddy** and everything got **filthy**.

2 We had a **stunning** view from our room.

3 The service was really **efficient**.

4 The weather was just **unbearably hot**.

5 It **overlooked** a building site.

6 People were so welcoming, it was quite **overwhelming**.

7 The place was **a bit of a dump**, to be honest.

8 The **facilities** were absolutely incredible.

9 It was quite **isolated** – basically in the middle of nowhere.

10 The beach was **deserted** so we had the whole place to ourselves.

2 [P] [▶] **Listen to words and phrases from Exercise 1 and practise saying them. Which words or phrases do you find hard to say? Practise saying them again.**

3 Work in pairs. Think of ways to describe three places you have stayed in using the language from Exercise 1. Tell your partner about the places.

LISTENING

4 [▶] **Listen to two conversations where people talk about places they have stayed. Answer the questions.**

1 Where did the speakers stay?

2 In what ways did they have a good time?

3 What problems did they have?

5 [FS] [▶] **Listen to eight questions from the conversations. Write the first word in each question. Then listen again and try to write down the whole question.**

6 [▶] **Listen to the conversations again. Complete the phrases with three words in each gap. Contractions count as two words.**

1 It _____ this island in the middle of the Danube.

2 It _____ while we were there.

3 They _____ for a couple of nights.

4 We had a great time, _____ the weather.

5 In August? _____ a bit hot?

6 Look _____ . That's stunning!

7 It was a bit annoying, but _____ the place was, you couldn't complain.

8 It was a bit of a struggle climbing back up, but it was _____ .

7 Work in pairs. Discuss the questions.

1 Have you ever been to a music festival? If yes, which one? What was it like?

2 If not, would you like to go to one? Why? / Why not?

3 Has anyone ever put you up? When? Where?

4 What's the best sunset you've seen? Where? What were you doing?

GRAMMAR

Modifiers

Modifiers make adjectives, adverbs, verbs or nouns stronger or weaker.

Adjectives and adverbs can be made stronger with *very, really, absolutely, completely.*

Adjectives and adverbs can be made weaker with *a bit, quite, fairly, pretty.*

Nouns can be modified by *complete, real, a bit of, hardly any, almost no.*

Verbs can be modified by *really, absolutely, hardly (ever).*

8 Look at the Grammar box. Then work in pairs. Read these corrected sentences and discuss why the corrections are needed.

1 We got ~~very~~ **absolutely** soaked. (or **very / really wet**)

2 It was ~~absolutely~~ **really** hot. (or **absolutely boiling**)

3 Oh it was ~~too~~ **really** incredible. I loved it. (or **absolutely incredible**)

4 It was ~~quite~~ **a bit** too hot for my liking.

5 The food was ~~a bit~~ **quite** nice, but maybe a bit bland.

6 It was ~~completely a~~ **a complete** waste of time.

7 It was a bit /nightmare. **of a**

8 It was a bit dull. There were hardly /facilities. **any**

9 Match these modifiers with the groups of words (1–7). Which two groups of words can be used with more than one modifier?

a bit	a bit of a	absolutely	almost
fairly	hardly	really	very

1 pain / tourist trap / waste of money / dump / struggle

2 no one there / nothing to do / missed the bus / cried

3 cold / amazing / boiling / interesting / loved it

4 isolated / noisy / rough / too cold / overwhelming

5 posh / welcoming / efficient / dull / warm

6 filthy / amazing / gorgeous / deserted / enormous

7 anywhere to eat / anything to do / slept / noticed

10 Work in pairs. Use some of the language from Exercise 9 to talk about places in your town or city.

G See Grammar reference 6A.

DEVELOPING CONVERSATIONS

Negative questions

We often use negative questions to express our opinion or show that we find something surprising.

Couldn't you stay *somewhere else?*

Wasn't that a pain*, having to rely on the bus?*

Didn't they run *more often than that?*

11 Look at the Developing conversations box. Then complete the questions with negative forms.

1 A: _____ it a bit noisy?

B: Yeah, really noisy. The bar opposite had really loud music playing all night.

2 A: _____ you find it annoying, the way the sand always gets everywhere?

B: Yeah, a bit, but stony beaches are just really uncomfortable. They're no good for sunbathing.

3 A: _____ you ever heard of it? It's very well known.

B: Not in Asia it's not!

4 A: I don't really fancy diving myself. _____ you scared?

B: Not at all. I loved it. I'm thinking of taking it up.

5 A: _____ it really uncomfortable, camping?

B: It can be a bit, yeah, but we've got mattresses and chairs and stuff, so it won't be too bad.

12 Work in pairs. Respond to these comments with negative questions. Use the words in brackets. Then have conversations using your ideas.

1 'We stayed in a big five-star hotel in Cairo.' (expensive)

2 'Eight of us are going to share a room in a youth hostel.' (crowded)

3 'The area's quite rough, but the rent's really low.' (scary)

4 'I had to share a room with my boyfriend's mother.' (feel awkward)

CONVERSATION PRACTICE

13 Work with a new partner. Have a conversation about places you've been to. Begin by using this guide. Continue the conversation with comments, questions and responses. Then change roles and have another conversation.

Student A	Student B
Ask if B went away in the holidays.	Say where you went.
Ask about or comment on the place.	Respond.

A shock to the system

IN THIS LESSON, YOU:
- discuss culture shock and your experiences of it
- practise listening to an academic talk about what culture shock involves
- read a series of emails from a man living abroad for the first time
- identify tone and emotion in a series of messages

LISTENING

1 Work in pairs. Discuss the questions.

1 What do you understand by 'culture shock'?
2 When might you experience it?
3 What might it involve?

2 ▶ Listen to an extract from a radio programme about culture shock. How does the speaker answer the three questions in Exercise 1?

3 ▶ Listen again and answer the questions.

1 What two misconceptions about culture shock are mentioned?
2 What is *acculturation*?
3 What four stages do people go through?
4 What happens in each phase?
5 Why might it be a problem if you don't complete the cycle?

READING

4 Work in pairs. You are going to read some emails from a young man called Matt, who has moved abroad for the first time. Look at the photos of his hometown in England and the place he has moved to – Singapore. Discuss the questions.

1 What do you think Matt's life in England was like? Think about: social life, social circle, places to eat, nightlife, things to do in your free time, and so on.
2 How easy do you think he will find moving to Singapore? Why?
3 What things do you think Matt will have to get used to?
4 How would someone find moving the opposite way: from Singapore to a small English village?
5 Which place would you rather live in? Why?

5 Read email 1 from Matt to a friend back home. Answer the questions.

1 Which of your ideas from Exercise 4 does he mention?
2 Are you surprised by his reaction? Why? / Why not?

6 Work in pairs. Discuss what changes might have happened during Matt's first few weeks in Singapore. Then read Matt's second email and find out if you were correct.

7 Work in pairs. Discuss the questions.

1 Have you ever been homesick? When? Why?
2 What kind of things do you moan about in terms of school, work, family? Who do you moan to?
3 What kind of things do you think a foreigner might find difficult about your country?

8 Read Matt's third email and answer the questions.

1 What has Matt been doing since he last wrote to Jane?
2 How has his attitude to both Singapore and the UK changed?
3 What do you think has caused the change?

9 Before you read Matt's final email – written three years later – discuss the questions. Then read the email in File 6 on page 193 to see if you guessed correctly.

1 What do you think Matt's final email will say?
2 Why do you think there has been such a long gap between emails?
3 Where do you think he's living and how is he feeling?

10 Match the verbs (1–8) from the four emails with the words (a–h) they were used with.

1 pick up	a	my apartment
2 gaze	b	pride in what they do
3 get over	c	out of the window
4 slave away	d	very smoothly
5 sort out	e	at my desk
6 go	f	Matt at the airport
7 cope with	g	my jet lag
8 take	h	different variants of English

11 Read the four emails again. Underline examples of these features of acculturation. Compare your ideas with a partner.

1 wonder and joy
2 settling into a routine
3 swinging from one extreme to another
4 looking critically at your previous existence and its culture
5 insulting someone
6 refusing to mix with people
7 getting stuck in a phase

SPEAKING

12 Think of a time when you experienced culture shock and had to adapt to new ways of doing things (in another country, beginning a new job, etc.). Decide which language from this unit you want to use. Think about:

- what was strange for you.
- the different feelings you went through.
- how well you adapted.
- any things you just couldn't get used to.

13 Work in groups. Share your experiences.

1

To: Jacksonjane@shotmail.ml

Subject: Greetings from Singapore

Hi Jane,

Just a quick email to say I've arrived and am slowly finding my feet. It's been an absolutely mad few days. Got off the plane and was immediately hit by the heat – just unbearably hot and humid. I was picked up at the airport by David, who works for the company. He was taking the mickey out of me a bit in the taxi because he said I looked like a little boy who'd just arrived from the countryside. I suppose I probably did as I sat there gazing out of the window with my mouth hanging open. I mean, it's SO different. It's a bit overwhelming – but in a good way.

Anyway, after a couple of days getting over my jet lag and orientating myself a bit, I started at work. Mind you, I haven't exactly been slaving away at my desk. I seem to have spent most of my time being taken out for lunch, meeting people and partying! It's been pretty wild. I'd better start doing some proper work soon or the company will wonder what they're paying me for!

Anyway, they've already sorted out an amazing apartment for me – 15th floor, stunning view – so that's all gone very smoothly. I already know I'm going to love it here.

How are things with you?

Matt

Marina Bay, Singapore.

2

To: Jacksonjane@shotmail.ml

Subject: Too little time!

Hi Jane,

Sorry it's been a while. Things have settled down a bit since I last wrote. In fact, I've been working fairly long hours. People just don't seem to stop here. When I used to travel into London from the country, I thought the pace of life there was pretty fast, but here it's completely ridiculous! Then there's the heat – it's so hot and humid here I seem to be sweating all the time and I can only get to sleep with the air conditioning on full. I've also found the office culture a bit of a challenge: all the different variants of English are quite hard to cope with, and when I do understand people, I'm often shocked by how direct and to-the-point they are!

Luckily, though, I've made friends with this guy who joined around the same time as me and we go out and have a moan about things and just generally share our frustrations. David calls us The Moaning Twins, but who cares what he thinks? To be honest, I'm already thinking of leaving. I honestly can't bear it! I never thought I'd miss home so much! Call me sometime soon.

Matt

3

To: Jacksonjane@shotmail.ml

Subject: Why go back when you can go forwards?

Hey Jane,

I know I said I was going to be back in England over Easter, but then I thought why go back to the miserable weather, terrible food and dull conversation? In the end, I sold my plane tickets online and used the money to travel round south-east Asia a bit. There are some amazing places to visit and I've now seen quite a bit of Malaysia and Indonesia. The people are so much more in touch with their culture here. It's made me realize that back home, people just aren't interested any more. It's all reality TV and celebrities.

Have you ever thought of coming out here? There's a lot to be said for it. Life's a lot easier here. I have all my laundry done through a service in my block and someone comes in and cleans my flat every day. It's not like the poor service you get in England – it's far more efficient. People just take more pride in what they do here. And as for the food – honestly, I don't know how you lot eat the bland rubbish that gets served up there. Singapore is miles better. Anyway, I must dash – I've got my Mandarin lesson in ten minutes.

Matt

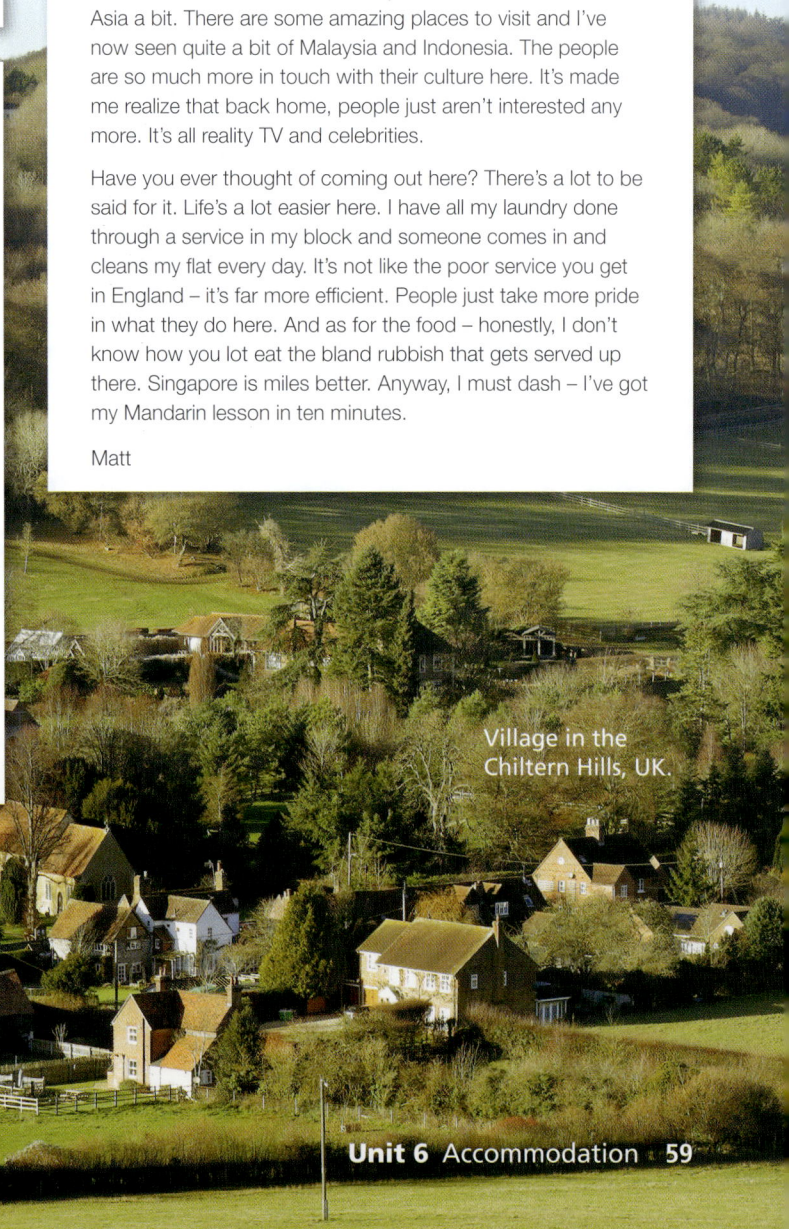

Village in the Chiltern Hills, UK.

Sorted!

IN THIS LESSON, YOU:
- practise ways of resolving problems
- discuss problems connected to different kinds of accommodation
- listen to four conversations about accommodation problems
- get a better understanding of idiomatic language

LISTENING

1 Work in pairs. Think of three common problems that people have in each of these situations. What's the worst problem in each case? Why?

1 staying in a hotel

2 renting a flat or house

3 sharing a flat or house

2 ▶ Listen to four conversations about accommodation. Decide what kind of place is discussed in each conversation and what the main problem is.

3 ▶ Listen again. Match two statements (a–h) with each conversation (1–4).

a Someone didn't know what was supposed to happen.

b Someone has ended up losing money because of a decision they made.

c There's no way to change the temperature in the room.

d Someone is sarcastic at the end of the conversation.

e Someone feels they're being cheated.

f Someone didn't do what they'd said they'd do.

g The person repeats their complaint in stronger language.

h Someone has paid to sort out a problem.

4 Work in pairs. Discuss what you would do in each situation in Exercise 2.

A: What would you do in the first situation?

B: I'd ask to see the manager.

A: How would that help?

GRAMMAR

Have / Get something done

You were right to **have it looked at** and to **get it repaired**.

I **had my bike stolen** from right outside the house.

5 Look at the examples in the Grammar box and choose the correct option to complete the rules (a–d).

a *get* or *have* + object + past participle is *an active / a passive* construction.

b We use this structure when we talk about someone doing something for us that we ask – or pay – them to do. It emphasizes *the action / the person who does it.*

c We *can also / can't* use this structure to talk about bad things that happen even though we didn't cause them.

d The structure *only focuses on the object of the verb / focuses on both the object of the verb and the person that the object belongs to.*

Lobby of Bellagio Hotel, Las Vegas, US.

6 Work in pairs. How many different ways can you complete these sentences using *have / get*?

1 You ought _____ your arm _____ .

You ought to get your arm seen by a doctor.
You ought to have your arm X-rayed.

2 You should _____ that picture _____ .

3 I should _____ this coat _____ .

4 She has _____ a tooth _____ .

5 I've just _____ my passport _____ .

6 I need _____ my computer _____ .

7 We _____ the house _____ last month.

8 I'm going _____ my hair _____ .

7 Use the ideas in Exercise 6 to talk about things:

- you've had / got done recently.
- you need to have / get done.
- you'd never have / get done.

G See Grammar reference 6C. »»

VOCABULARY Common idioms

V See Vocabulary reference 6C. »»

8 Match the idioms in bold in the sentences (1–8) with the definitions (a–h).

1 We shared a flat for a year and then one day she just left without paying her share of the bills, leaving me really badly **out of pocket**.

2 Our old place really wasn't that great! I think you're looking back at it **through rose-tinted glasses**.

3 Don't get me wrong. My roommate is great **in small doses**. It's just that after too much of him, I have an overwhelming desire to fall asleep!

4 I've told my landlord I'm not going to pay any more rent until he gets the heating fixed, so now **the ball is in his court**.

5 They pay a lot in rent, so they must be struggling to **keep their heads above water** now she's lost her job.

6 I don't know how they can afford a place like that, considering what they earn. It must have **cost an arm and a leg**.

7 They were all **taking the mickey out of** me because of my haircut. I didn't find it very funny though.

8 I only moved here a few months ago. It was really hard to begin with, but bit by bit I'm **finding my feet**.

a been very expensive

b for very short periods of time

c getting used to things

d have just enough money to pay for everything needed

e in an overly optimistic way

f it's his turn to react and do something

g making fun of

h short of money

9 Work in pairs. Choose three idioms from Exercise 8 and think of a situation for each. Discuss your ideas.

I paid someone to check that this apartment I wanted to buy was OK, but then the seller decided she didn't want to move after all and so I ended up out of pocket.

SPEAKING TASK

10 Read about four different situations. With a partner, choose two that you would like to roleplay.

- **Student A:** You rent a house. The bath has leaked and flooded the house.

  Student B: You are the landlord and you want Student A to pay for the damage.

- **Student A:** You share a flat with three other students. You're always tidying up after everyone else and it's annoying. You decide to talk to the messiest person.

  Student B: You are the flatmate. You think Student A has unrealistic expectations and needs to relax.

- **Student A:** You are in a hotel and need to get up early for a big meeting tomorrow. There's a huge party downstairs. You decide to go and ask them to be quiet.

  Student B: It's your wedding party and you're having a great time.

- **Student A:** You have been having big problems with your noisy neighbours. They have loud arguments, and they have a dog that barks at night. You've had enough.

  Student B: You are the neighbour. You don't like Student A's arrogant attitude.

11 Choose your roles. Prepare what you want to say.

12 **M** Roleplay the conversations with your partner. Try not to look at what you have written. Make sure you come to some kind of agreement.

■ MY OUTCOMES ■

Work in pairs. Discuss the questions.

1 What did you talk about in this unit? Do you feel more confident now about talking about these things? Why?

2 What useful language have you learned to talk about the topics in this unit?

3 What was the most challenging thing about the language you studied and used in this unit? Why?

4 What will you revise from this unit, and how?

A leaflet or poster

IN THIS LESSON, YOU:
- write a leaflet or poster for a club or organization
- discuss different clubs and organizations
- look at the function of different paragraphs
- explore when it's OK to leave out words

SPEAKING

1 Work in groups. Discuss the questions.

1 Have you ever belonged to any club or society?

2 What's good about being in a club? Are there any disadvantages?

3 What do you think people do when they meet in these organizations? Explain why you would – or wouldn't – join each one.

an athletics club	Boy Scouts / Girl Guides
a cycling club	a debating society
a drama club	a gastronomic club
a green activist group	a history society
a political party	a reading club

WRITING A leaflet or poster

2 Read the poster. Work in pairs. Would you join this team if it was near you? Why? / Why not?

3 Work in pairs. Discuss the questions.

1 What's the main group of people the club want to attract?

2 What's the wider group of people they are appealing to?

3 What's the purpose of each paragraph? Which ones give information and which ones aim to persuade you?

4 Can you find an example of these ways of persuading:

a a question posing a problem

b a call to action (e.g. Join us today!)

c positive adverbs (e.g. incredibly good)

d positive adjectives (e.g. easy to master)

WANTED! Touch Rugby Players

Feeling out of shape? Bored of working out in the gym? Looking for a sport with a great social vibe? Look no further: TOUCH RUGBY is the thing for you.

Touch rugby is rugby, but with all the tackling, kicking and rough stuff taken out. You have to pass the ball backwards to your teammates as you run and try to put the ball down behind the opposing team's goal line. The defenders stop you by lightly touching your body, at which point you stop and roll the ball to another player. After every six touches, the ball is given to the opposing team. It's a fantastically easy sport to pick up and remember, all it involves is a light touch, so there's no risk of injury. It's all about running, passing and having great fun!

And once you've learned how to play, it's something you can play whenever or wherever you like because it needs no special equipment other than a ball.

Most of our teams are mixed, so it's not just for men. Nor do you have to be especially athletic or coordinated, because there are teams for all levels. There are also lots of substitutions during the game, so if you're out of breath, you can always rest and chat to the others on the bench.

Our club runs training sessions with friendly games three nights a week (Mon, Wed and Fri) from 7 till 9 at the sports centre fields. We also have league matches on a Sunday. All sessions cost £5.

Come along! You'll find a warm welcome and enjoy a fantastic game.

4 Number the paragraphs from another poster in the correct order. What's the aim of the poster?

> **MEET THE WORLD!   A warm welcome wanted**
>
> a   Whichever way you take part, working with Home Host means you'll be helping people who would otherwise be unable to study here – and you'll make connections that will last a lifetime.
>
> b   Whether you can offer a room or a meal or a tour round town, Home Host will let you meet the world. Register today!
>
> c   Home Host matches you with visitors from abroad who need free accommodation. Through us, people from all over the world are able to attend training or conferences here, thanks to the generosity of people like you.
>
> d   Interested in meeting people from different cultures? Want to help people in need? Why not join us at Home Host?
>
> e   We need hosts all year round and ask people to commit to four hosting events a year. For more information and to register your interest, visit our website at homehost.org.
>
> f   And if you don't have space to accommodate someone, we're also looking for people to host a dinner or a night out with our guests.

5 Complete the useful expressions for persuading. Use one word from the posters in each gap.

1 _____ down and out of shape?

2 You'll receive a very _____ welcome.

3 You'll learn a skill that'll last a _____ .

4 You'll _____ _____ get fit, you'll also make friends.

5 You can join in _____ you like.

6 _____ you're a beginner or advanced, our school is the place for you.

7 _____ to the generosity of people like you.

6 Work in pairs. Tell your partner about:
- something you have experienced that will last a lifetime.
- a time you received a warm welcome.

USEFUL LANGUAGE

Whenever, wherever, however, etc.

We add -*ever* to question words to mean *It doesn't matter when / where / how*, etc.
*It's a sport you can play **whenever** or **wherever** you like.*

7 Complete the sentences by adding the correct words ending in -*ever*.

1 You can drop into our offices _____ you like.

2 _____ good you are, you'll find a group to suit you.

3 We'll get you into shape, _____ your fitness level.

4 _____ you live, you'll find a branch near you.

5 You can pay _____ you like, with the exception of cash.

6 _____ you are, and _____ your age, this is the sport for you.

Ellipsis

Ellipsis is when you leave out words – generally, grammar words such as subject pronouns or auxiliary verbs. You do this:
- for reasons of style or emphasis.
  Feeling out of shape?
- to avoid repetition.
  ... you can always rest and chat
- simply to be shorter or quicker, as in notes or emails.
  Gone to lunch. Back at 2. Andrew

When we leave out words, it should still be clear who or what the subject of the verb is and what tense it should be.

8 Read the information about ellipsis. What words have been left out in the examples in bold?

9 Cross out as many words as you can in these sentences without changing the meaning or making things unclear.

1 We are having a really great time. We wish you were here and we hope everything is fine with you. Karen.

2 Sara rang. She said she can't come this evening, but she will be at the meeting tomorrow.

3 I had to go out and I won't be back till 8. There's some dinner in the oven. I love you.

4 Are you planning to work abroad? This is your chance!

5 Do you worry about speaking in public? Do you get nervous in front of an audience or do you forget your words? Our course could help.

6 Have you never been to a gym before? We'll show you how the gym machines work and we'll give you support when you're training.

10 Work in pairs. Compare what you deleted. Is the subject and tense of each verb still clear?

PRACTICE

11 You are going to write a leaflet or poster. Work in pairs. Decide the following.
- the organization from Exercise 1 you want people to join
- the main group of people you want to attract – what problem might your club solve for them?
- the way a wider group could take part
- information you are going to give them
- any slogan or title you might use to attract attention
- how you will organize the leaflet / poster following the six-paragraph structure in the two models

12 Write the leaflet or poster. Add a design or illustration if you like.

13 Share your finished work in groups and discuss these questions for each leaflet / poster.

1 Would you join the club / organization? Why? / Why not?

2 Do you think any extra information should be included?

VIDEO Out and about

1 Work in pairs. Have you ever experienced culture shock? Where? And in what way?

Understanding accents

Some accents replace a /θ/ sound with /t/, *so three* /θrɪː/ may sound like *tree* /trɪː/; *thought* /θɔːt/ like *taught* /tɔːt/; and *both* /bəʊθ/ like *boat* /bəʊt/.

2 Watch the video. Which person has the closest experience to yours? What do they say?

3 Work in pairs. Match the statements with the speakers and explain your choices. You may match statements with more than one speaker. Then watch again to check.

a It took a while to get used to the mealtimes.

b I wasn't used to being in such a crowded place.

c It was pretty overwhelming at first, but I eventually got used to it.

d The street was noisier than I was used to.

e Travelling kind of made me see the weirdness of my own country.

f I was partially prepared for the experience, but it was still difficult.

g I'm still a bit wary of making some kind of social faux pas.

h People there helped me to settle in.

4 Discuss the questions with your partner.

1 How many different languages are spoken in your country? How fluent are you in them?

2 Has travel made you reassess anything in your country that is better, worse or just odd compared to other places?

3 What are the social norms where you are from around eating and mealtimes?

VIDEO Developing conversations

5 You are going to watch two people talking about activities they are going to do at the weekend. Watch and take notes on what they say.

6 Work in pairs. Compare what you understood. Watch again if you need to.

7 Discuss the questions with your partner.

1 Do you think you'd be any good at either activity in the video? Why? / Why not?

2 Are there any other reasons you would / wouldn't try them?

3 What relatively new activities for keeping fit or getting excitement have you heard of? What do they involve?

8 **FS** Watch again. Complete the sentences with three to five words in each gap.

1 So tell me, _____ getting up to this weekend?

2 It's not really. _____ three metres.

3 It sounds like a pretty extreme sport, though. Is it _____ exercise?

4 _____ daunting.

5 No, _____ you'll enjoy it so much.

6 So _____ a long, big foam surfboard.

7 _____ you must fall in the water a lot.

8 You can do an induction, you can, _____ the pointers.

CONVERSATION PRACTICE

9 Work in pairs. You are going to practise a conversation.

1 Choose a Conversation practice from either Lesson 5A or Lesson 6A.

2 Look at the language in that lesson.

3 Check the meaning of anything you've forgotten with your partner.

4 Have the conversation. Try to improve on the last time you did it.

Grammar and Vocabulary

GRAMMAR

1 Read the first sentence in each pair. Complete the second sentence so that it has a similar meaning. Use between three and five words, including the word in bold.

1 She took up golf around ten years ago.

She _____ about ten years now. **GOLF**

2 There was absolutely nothing worth seeing at the music festival.

Unfortunately, the music festival was _____ time. **COMPLETE**

3 He was incredibly lucky that he didn't kill himself.

Honestly, he _____ . He was lucky really. **DIED**

4 I knew the lock was broken and now we have been burgled.

I _____ fixed. We might not have been burgled. **SHOULD**

5 I wanted to go and see that game. Why didn't you tell me you were going?

You should've told me you were going. I _____ you. **WOULD**

6 The house is in chaos at the moment because it's being painted.

We _____ , so it's a bit chaotic at the moment. **REDECORATED**

7 It's not been a sudden decision to move to the country.

We _____ of moving to the country for a while. **HAVE**

8 He weighs eight kilos more than he did before he injured his leg.

He has _____ he got injured. **SINCE**

2 Choose all the correct options to complete the conversation.

A: How was your holiday?

B: ¹*Absolutely / Very / Really* fantastic.

A: Oh great. What did you do?

B: ²*Hardly / Almost / Nearly* anything to be honest. We just went to the beach most days.

A: Don't you find that ³*a bit / really / absolutely* boring?

B: No, not at all. I read and swim and play with the kids and being from the city, it's just a ⁴*really / real / bit of a* change. Do you know the east coast of Spain?

A: Not really – but ⁵*I've visited / I've been visiting* the big theme park near there a couple of times. Did you go?

B: No, we were told it's always ⁶*a bit / really / very* packed and you have to queue too long for the rides.

A: I know what you mean, but you ⁷*could've / should've / would've* gone. It's worth it even with the queues.

B: Well, ⁸*we've already talked / we've been talking* about going back there next year, so maybe we'll go then.

3 ▶ Listen. Write the six sentences you hear.

4 Write a sentence before and after the sentences from Exercise 3 to create a short conversation.

VOCABULARY

5 Match the verbs (1–10) with the collocates (a–j).

1 I get out of
2 We worked up
3 They hit
4 They sacked
5 We didn't discuss
6 I tore
7 The place overlooked
8 They got promoted
9 It left
10 She's always taken

a us quite out of pocket.
b tactics beforehand.
c the main square.
d great pride in her work.
e a bit of a sweat.
f the coach after six games.
g breath very quickly.
h the post twice.
i to the top division last year.
j a ligament in my ankle.

6 Decide if these words are connected to sport or places to stay – and in what way.

deserted	a dump	facilities	a landlord	overtake
self-catering	substitute	tackle	a time-out	a track

7 Complete the email with one word in each gap. The first letters are given.

Dear Juan,

Just a quick email to tell you how I'm getting on here in Tokyo. Sorry I haven't written sooner, but it took me a week to ¹get o_____ my jet lag and then, what with ²s_____ o_____ somewhere to live, I'm only just beginning to find my ³f_____ . I've finally found a flat – it's cost me an ⁴a_____ and a leg to rent, but it's very central and I have a ⁵st_____ view across the city. I sometimes just sit and ⁶g_____ out of the window for hours!

Anyway, people have been very ⁷we_____ and I think I'm going to love it here. Mind you, I've started reading that book you gave me about acculturation, so I'm trying not to look at everything through ⁸r_____-tinted glasses. That way, maybe then I won't be disappointed and swing to the other extreme.

Asher

8 Complete the sentence pairs by adding the same missing word in each gap.

1 a I need to start doing more exercise. I'm so _____ of shape.

b It was so hot my mum passed _____ on the bus yesterday.

2 a I guess he's OK _____ small doses, but I couldn't spend too long in his company.

b The car broke down _____ the middle of nowhere. It was awful.

3 a We carried on playing despite the rain – and _____ absolutely filthy.

b The wound somehow _____ infected so I had to go and get it looked at.

4 a I can pick you _____ from the station.

b It takes time to build _____ your stamina.

7
Nature

IN THIS UNIT, YOU:

- discuss different types of weather
- practise relating news stories about pets and wildlife
- discuss attitudes to nature through different quotes

SPEAKING

1   **Imagine you are the man in the photo. Prepare to describe what happened. Think about these questions.**

   1   Where do you live?

   2   When did the bad weather start?

   3   What effect did it have on your life?

   4   Did you sort out the problems? How?

2   **Work in pairs. Tell the story to a partner. Your partner should sympathize and ask extra questions. Then change roles.**

Flooding in Dordrecht, Holland.

Weather the storm

VOCABULARY Weather the storm

1 **M** **Work in pairs. Discuss what you think the words and phrases in bold mean in 1–10. Don't use a dictionary. Then complete the sentences using one weather word in each gap.**

1 There was a terrible _____ . I woke up in the middle of the night because the thunder was so loud and then there were these incredible **flashes** of lightning. It was quite scary.

2 The _____ was really **thick** and you could hardly see the car in front. We had to come off the motorway and wait for it to **lift**.

3 The _____ was **unbearable** and it was really humid and sticky. Then there was no air conditioning on the bus. Honestly, I thought I was going to faint!

4 It was just so _____ ! I lost all feeling in my fingers and my lips turned blue. I thought I was going to **freeze to death**!

5 It was incredibly _____ . Several trees were **blown down** near us and it even blew the roof off a warehouse near here.

6 When we left, it was fine, but then it suddenly **clouded over** and the rain started coming down. But then just as suddenly, the _____ came out and there was an amazing **rainbow**.

7 The ferry couldn't sail because the _____ was so strong, but it **eased off** after a couple of hours.

8 We were caught in that _____ on the way. It was pouring down and then it turned to **hail**. It was incredible. In the end, we had to pull over until it all eased off.

9 Honestly, _____ is very unusual for that time of year and we had to slow right down because it started to **settle**. We saw another car almost **slide** off the road.

10 It _____ **non-stop** for a week! The whole place was flooded. It was miserable.

2 **P** ▶ **Listen to words from Exercise 1 on their own and in a phrase. Which phrases do you find hard to say? Practise saying them again.**

3 **Work in pairs. Have you ever experienced anything like the situations in Exercise 1? Tell your partner.**

LISTENING

4 ▶ **Listen to two people sharing experiences of extreme weather. Answer the questions.**

1 Where were the people when they experienced the bad weather?

2 What kind of weather did each person experience?

3 How did they feel?

4 What did they do as a result of the weather?

Lightning storm strikes in San Francisco, US.

5 Work in pairs. Discuss the questions.

1 Which description did you like the best? Which bits did you like about it?

2 Do you know anyone who is good at telling stories or anecdotes? In what ways are they good at this?

3 Do you get weather events like this where you are? How often? What time of year?

GRAMMAR

Narrative forms

When we tell stories, we usually describe the main events in the order they happened and we use the past simple to do this. For example: in the story you heard, *'One moment we **were** in sunshine, the next we **saw** like a line on the road ahead and we **drove** through it and it **was** hail!'*.

Sometimes we have to use the past perfect and past continuous to show background information and explain the causes of events.

Read this summary of the story:

*When they **were driving** to Rome, it started to hail. They were terrified, as they'**d never seen hail that big**, so they pulled over and waited for it to stop.*

6 Look at the examples in the Grammar box. Work in pairs. Answer these questions.

1 Find an example of the past perfect simple and of the past continuous.

2 Which form shows an action was in progress at the same time as another, but was unfinished or interrupted?

3 Which form shows an action finished before a previously mentioned action or before the story began?

7 Complete this summary of the second story from Exercise 4 with the correct form of the verbs.

We were in Sardinia and we ¹ _____ (visit) this little village. It ² _____ (be) boiling all day and in the evening we ³ _____ (take) a walk along the beach when suddenly we ⁴ _____ (see) this incredible forked lightning. It ⁵ _____ (start) spitting and then just two seconds later, it started pouring down. As we ⁶ _____ (not bring) an umbrella, we just ⁷ _____ (run) to the nearest café we ⁸ _____ (can) find. It can't have been more than a minute, but we got absolutely soaked. I must have emptied a litre of water out of my shoes!

G See Grammar reference 7A.

8 Choose one of these sentences and use it in a story about weather. Imagine what happened before and afterwards. Use the past continuous and past perfect at least once.

1 We were absolutely soaked by the end of it.

2 The roads were really icy.

3 We couldn't see a thing.

4 The wind was so strong it nearly blew me over.

9 Tell your story to a partner.

DEVELOPING CONVERSATIONS

Making stories more dramatic

Read three patterns you heard in Exercise 4 that make the story more dramatic.

a *They were **as big as** golf balls.* (*as* + adjective + *as* to make comparisons)

b *Honestly, they were hitting the car **so hard**, they nearly broke the windscreen.* (*so* + adverb + result)

c *I must've poured **something like** a litre of water out of my shoes.* (*something like* + number)

10 Look at the Developing conversations box. Write four sentences about these things using patterns from the box. Share your ideas with a partner.

1 how hot / cold / wet / windy, etc. the weather is

2 how big / small / clean, etc. a place is

3 how posh / dangerous, etc. an area is

4 how good / bad, etc. a film or book is

CONVERSATION PRACTICE

11 Think of a time when you experienced extreme weather. Prepare to tell your story.

• Describe where you were, what you were doing and what happened.

• Think about when you could use the past continuous or past perfect and how to make the story dramatic.

12 Work in pairs. Take turns to tell your story. Show interest in your partner's story and ask questions. Use some of these phrases.

Do you know what happened to me [last night]?

I had this really [scary] experience when I was [on holiday] …

Really? What happened?

Actually, that reminds me of …

Animals making headlines

SPEAKING

1 Work in groups. Rank the animals from 1 to 8 for each category (a–d), where 1 is the least and 8 is the most (e.g. endangered).

bull	cat	dog	frog	rat	snake	tiger	whale

a most endangered   c most dangerous

b most useful   d best pet

READING

2 Work in pairs. Read the headlines and phrases from four news articles. Check any words you don't know. Discuss what you think the articles are about.

1 **Splendid Frog sounds alarm**

   a target for smugglers / be stopped, if not reversed

2 **Abandoned cat ensures business's success**

   at the point of going bankrupt / set up a shelter

3 **Victory in bullfighting fight**

   voted to lift a ban / subsidies are being reviewed

4 **Controversial research lab finally opens**

   investigate conditions / intimidate people

3 Work in two pairs within a group of four. Read your articles and check your ideas from Exercise 2.

Pair A: Read the articles on page 71.

Pair B: Read the articles in File 7 on page 194.

4 **M** Discuss what you understood with your partner. Decide what information from the articles you would NOT include if you had to explain them to someone else.

5 Change partners. Without looking at your articles, explain the stories to each other.

6 Now read the two articles you didn't read on page 71 or 194.

7 Work in pairs to complete the phrases from the articles. Each pair includes different forms in the same word family.

1 save it from *bankruptcy*   at the point of going *bankrupt*

2 be an ongoing _____   a _____ research lab

3 a sixth great _____   be declared _____

4 see it as under _____   send _____ letters

5 opponents highlight the _____   claim that vivisection is _____

6 _____'s own survival   the result of _____ activity

7 _____ are being reviewed   be _____ by local government

8 get an instant _____   _____ with demonstrations

9 their _____ is increasing   a _____ art form

GRAMMAR

Participle clauses

We can sometimes replace a relative pronoun + verb with an *-ing* or *-ed* participle of the verb.

a laboratory <u>which is funded</u> by Oxford University

*a laboratory **funded** by Oxford University*

carry out experiments <u>which investigate</u> conditions

*carry out experiments **investigating** conditions*

8 Look at the examples in the Grammar box. Then answer these questions.

1 Is the verb in bold in the sentences active or passive?

2 How would you say these sentences using a full relative clause in place of the participle clause in bold?

  a *Activists tried to intimidate people **involved in the project.***

  b *The numbers of people **attending bullfights** are in decline.*

9 Choose the correct option to complete the phrases.

1 the number of pets *abandoning / abandoned* by their owners

2 the number of species *dying out / died out*

3 the number of people *becoming / become* vegan

4 the number of people *curing / cured* of cancer

5 the amount of money *making / made* by supermarkets last year

6 the amount of forest *destroying / destroyed* each year

7 the amount of pet food *selling / sold* last year

8 the amount of support *giving / given* to oil companies

10 Work in pairs. Discuss the trends in Exercise 9 with reference to your country.

1 Do you think the numbers are going up or down?

2 What might be the cause or result of the change in each case?

3 Do you think the change is a good thing?

I think maybe the number of pets abandoned by their owners has gone up. You see more cats and dogs in the street. I think maybe it's because people bought a dog when they were spending more time at home. It's awful.

G See Grammar reference 7B.

SPEAKING

11 Work in groups. Tell the group about a story from the news or your own experience, on one of these topics.

- a pet or abandoned animal
- endangered or extinct animals
- animal rights campaigns
- activities involving animals

Cats roam over the model railway at the Diorama restaurant.

Abandoned cat ensures business's success

An abandoned cat has saved a restaurant from bankruptcy and ensured its ongoing success. The Diorama restaurant, in Osaka, was originally set up to show off the elaborate model railway built by the restaurant's owner, Naoki Teraoka. But Teraoka's business ran into trouble during the pandemic and he was at the point of going bankrupt when a tiny, ill kitten turned up.

Teraoka took pity on the abandoned animal and it was soon joined by the rest of its family. After giving shelter to the abandoned cats, he took photos of them walking around his models, like the great Godzilla monsters from the famous Japanese movies, and started posting the photos on Instagram. They got an instant response and he soon had visitors from all over coming to the café to see the cats for themselves. The business is now booming.

Cat cafés were already a big thing in Japan and their popularity has been increasing worldwide. People who are unable to keep pets, due to lack of living space or strict rules by landlords, can pay to come in the café and pet the animals. Other visitors come with a view to adopting a cat if they find a good match.

Mr Teraoka has now also set up a shelter, which has rescued over one hundred more abandoned cats.

SPLENDID FROG SOUNDS ALARM

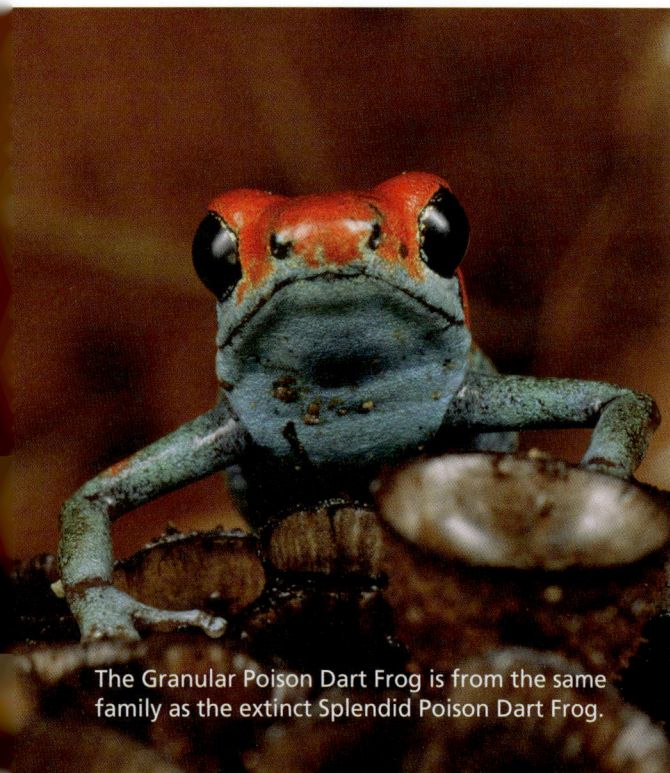

The Granular Poison Dart Frog is from the same family as the extinct Splendid Poison Dart Frog.

The Splendid Poison Frog of Panama was officially declared extinct last month, despite efforts to save it. Although the frog, a member of the poison dart frog family, had been hit by a disease, the extinction is considered mainly the result of human activity.

The frog's habitat in humid cloud forests had been severely reduced as trees were cut down for their timber and in order to create farmland. It had also been a target for smugglers, who would capture and sell the frog to collectors attracted by the species' brightly coloured skin.

The event has been offered as further evidence that the Earth may be entering a sixth great extinction, which could see hundreds of thousands of species die out and may eventually threaten humanity's own survival.

Unlike previous great extinctions, such as when the dinosaurs died out, the current crisis is largely man-made and could, according to experts, be stopped, if not reversed. New laws could protect vital habitats, while ongoing research could find cures for diseases affecting endangered species.

There are also more radical initiatives, such as a programme in Colombia where poison dart frogs are bred for collectors at a cheaper price than those smuggled from the wild.

Sadly, such initiatives are too late for the Splendid Poison Frog, but hopefully, not too late for other poison dart frog species.

Plant life

IN THIS LESSON, YOU:
- discuss attitudes to nature through different quotes
- practise listening for the main ideas in different conversations about plants
- share your knowledge of plants and nature
- practise recognizing new words or meanings you hear in context

SPEAKING

1 **Work in groups. Discuss the questions.**

1 Do you think it's important for people to spend time in the countryside? How much time do you spend there?

2 How much would you say you know about nature? Are you any good at recognizing and naming different trees, plants, birds, etc.? Do you know any names in English?

3 Do you have plants or flowers in your house? What state are they in? Do you have any problems with them? Who looks after them?

4 Have you ever done any gardening or helped in a garden or field? Did you enjoy it? Why? / Why not?

LISTENING

2 **FS** ▶ In conversations you may hear words you are unfamiliar with and want to ask about. Listen to five extracts and note down any words you are not sure of.

3 **Work in pairs. Ask your partner about your words from Exercise 2.**

A: What does … mean?

B: I'm not sure – let's look online.

4 ▶ **Listen to five conversations connected to plants and choose the best answers to the questions.**

1 The man is unhappy. Why?

a Some plants he bought had a disease.

b He's suffering from depression.

c He hasn't looked after some plants correctly.

2 The woman doesn't like the plants. Why?

a There are too many of them.

b They're not very pretty.

c They are damaging a building.

3 What was the problem with the flowers the woman gave?

a Big bunches of flowers aren't normally given as a gift.

b The flowers were a poisonous variety.

c The flowers are normally given when someone dies.

4 The two men talk about a hobby. What happens in the conversation?

a They compare their childhood experiences.

b One man refers to a bad experience he had.

c One man mentions a benefit of doing the hobby.

5 A man is talking to a woman. What's he doing?

a explaining the recipe for a new dish they're having

b describing a dish he liked when he was a child

c offering a cure for an illness

5 **Work in pairs. Compare your answers to Exercise 4. Explain your choices and why you think the other options are wrong.**

6 ▶ **Listen again. Note down any other words you are unsure of. Compare with a partner and see if they know what the words are.**

Fields of lavender in Brihuega, Spain.

7 Work in pairs. Choose two sets of questions to discuss.

1 Are there any invasive plants (or animals) in your country? What effect do they have? What's being done about it?

2 Are any flowers or plants connected to particular festivals or events in your country? Is there a national flower or tree? What do they symbolize?

3 Is there anything you swear by to solve different illnesses or problems?

4 Have you had any close encounters with animals? What happened?

VOCABULARY Plants and metaphor

V See Vocabulary reference 7C.

8 Work in pairs. Label the drawing of a plant with these words.

| blossom | branch | fruit | leaf / leaves | root | stem |

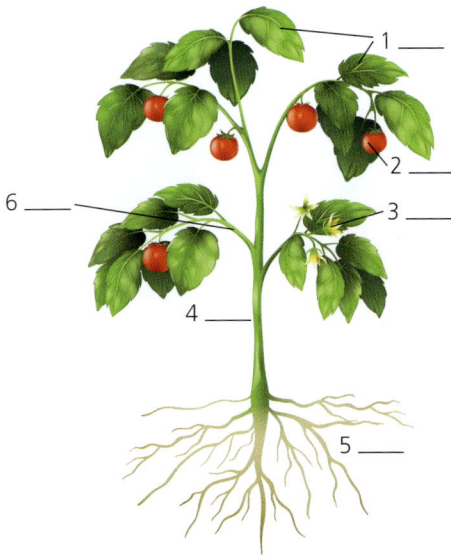

9 ▶ Listen to seven pairs of sentences. Decide if the words connected with plants in each sentence are used with the literal meaning from Exercise 8 (L) or a metaphorical meaning (M). Compare your ideas in pairs and discuss what the metaphorical meanings might be.

10 Work in pairs. Complete the sets of phrases with one word from Exercise 8. Decide which two phrases in each set are metaphorical. Do you have the same metaphor in your language?

1 buy some fresh _____
  the _____ of research
  the hard work is beginning to bear _____
  apples, bananas and other _____

2 take a _____ out of their book
  sweep up the _____
  the _____ look a bit dry
  _____ through a magazine

3 a fallen _____
  climb onto a _____
  _____ out into a new market
  a _____ of mathematics

4 it rots the _____s
  get to the _____ of the problem
  dig out the _____
  trace their _____s back to the 17th century

5 _____ yourself on the sofa
  _____ the idea in my head

water the _____s
sell pot _____s

6 cherry _____
  it's in _____
  have a _____ing career
  _____ into a major force

7 a strong _____
  break the _____ of a wine glass
  it _____s from the fact that
  _____ the flow of blood with a tissue

11 Work in pairs. For each word in Exercise 8, take turns to give an example sentence using the collocations in Exercise 10.

SPEAKING TASK

12 **M** Work in pairs. Read the quotes and follow the instructions.

There's no such thing as bad weather, only different kinds of good weather.

—John Ruskin

You drown not by falling into a river, but staying submerged in it.

—Paulo Coelho

The animals of the world exist for their own reasons. They were not made for humans any more than black people were made for white or women created for men.

—Alice Walker

The greatness of a nation and its moral progress can be judged by the way its animals are treated.

—Mahatma Gandhi

A tree has roots yet reaches for the sky. It tells us that in order to aspire we need to be grounded and that no matter how high we go, it is from our roots that we draw sustenance.

—Wangari Maathai

Friendship is a plant we must often water.

—German proverb

• Decide what the quotes mean or how you might translate them into your language.

• Think of an example from real life to illustrate each quote.

• Discuss how far you agree or disagree with each quote and why.

• Find one more quote online using a nature metaphor (or invent one!) to share with the class.

• As a class, decide on the best quote.

■ MY OUTCOMES ■

Work in pairs. Discuss the questions.

1 What conversations, discussions or roleplays did you find enjoyable?

2 How can you tell stories better to make them more interesting and dramatic?

3 What did you find challenging about the reading or listening texts?

4 What can you do at home to revise language from this unit?

8

Crime and punishment

IN THIS UNIT, YOU:

- have conversations about crimes
- relate and discuss recent trends including their causes and results
- debate different statements about crime and society

SPEAKING

1 Work in pairs. Look at the photo. Discuss the questions.

1 What places are they likely to be monitoring?

2 What kind of crimes do you think they might observe?

3 How effective do you think this kind of policing is? Do you know any instances it has been put to use?

4 What other ways can you think of to prevent or detect crime?

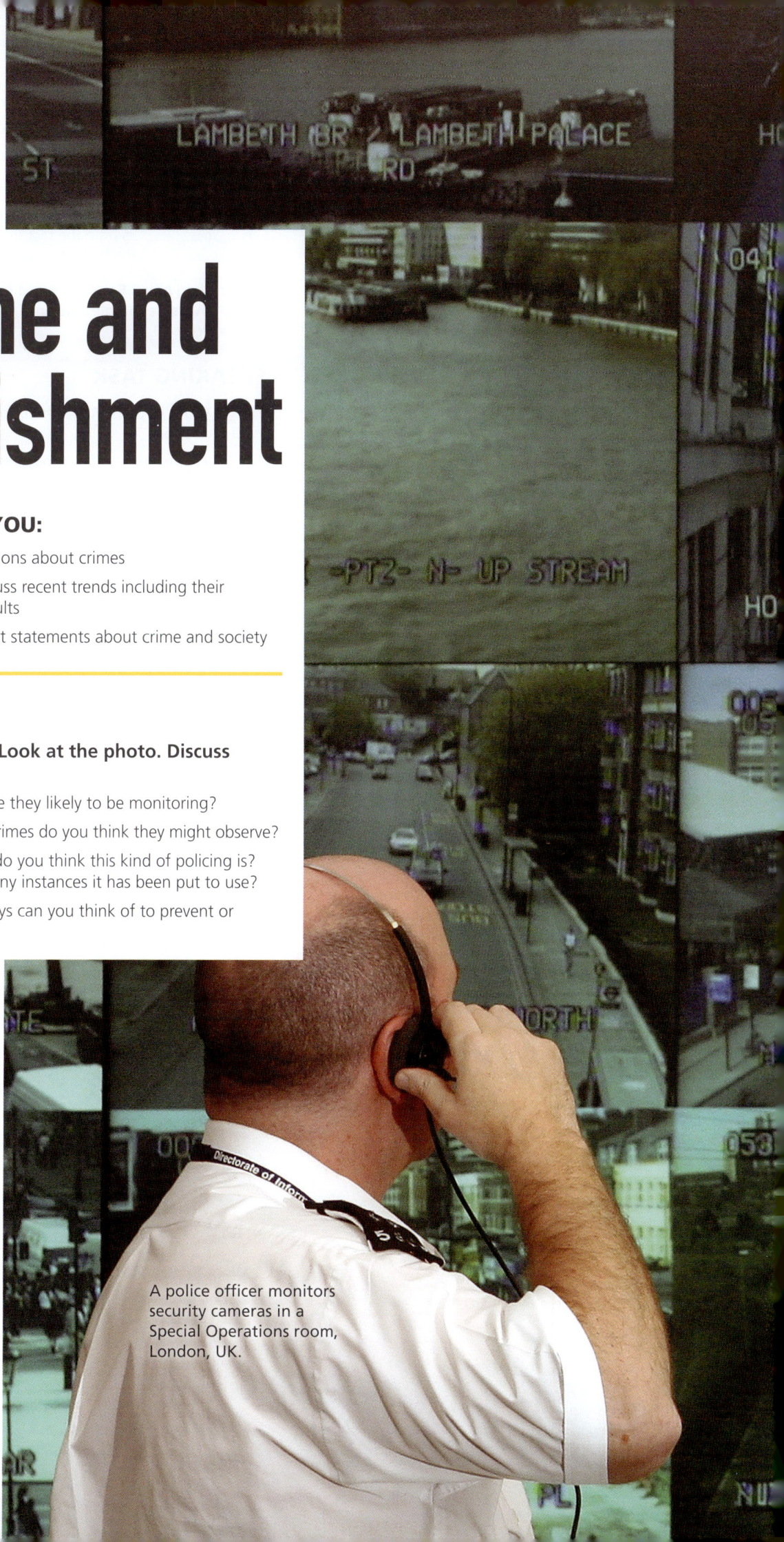

A police officer monitors security cameras in a Special Operations room, London, UK.

GUARDS AV / VICTORIA EMB.

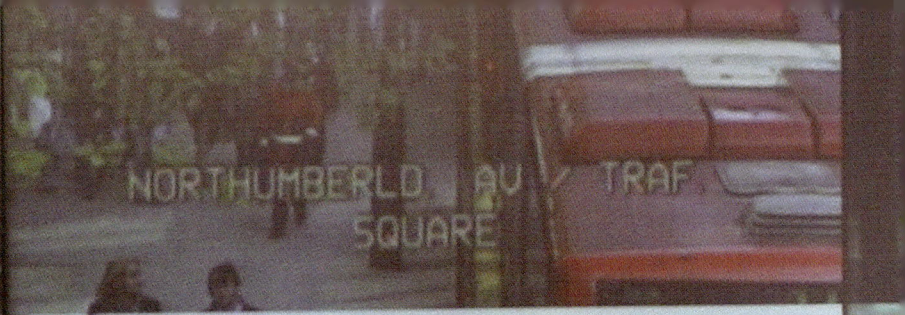

NORTHUMBERLD AV / TRAF. SQUARE

FERRY RD / MARSHAM ST

TWEEDY RD / SHERMAN RD

END RD / HARFORD ST

ROMFORD RD / VICARAGE LANE

YA124 Barking

CULAR RD / BARKING RD

Way North Circular

PAS Brent 5

Caught in the act

VOCABULARY Crimes

1 **Complete the sentences with the pairs of verbs. You may need to use the verbs in a different order.**

doing / caught	got hold of / gone	grabbed / came up to
killed / went off	raided / seized	set / smashed
stolen / broken into		vanished / came back

1 I got a phone call from the bank saying I'd _____ $1,000 into debt. Someone must've _____ my card details.

2 I was _____ on camera and had to pay a €100 fine. I was only _____ about 65!

3 She went out to the shops and never _____ . She just completely _____ .

4 They made such a mess. They _____ shop windows, threw rocks at police and _____ fire to cars.

5 When we got back, we found the house had been _____ . Fortunately, they hadn't _____ much.

6 I was standing outside the cathedral and this guy _____ me, _____ my bag and ran off.

7 Apparently, the police _____ this café near us and _____ five million dollars' worth of elephant ivory.

8 Luckily, it was very quiet when the device _____ so no one was _____ .

2 **Work in pairs. Match these crimes with the situations (1–8) in Exercise 1. There is one extra crime.**

a bombing	a burglary	a disappearance	fraud / identity theft
murder	a riot	smuggling	speeding
a street robbery			

3 **Work in groups. How many real examples can you think of for the crimes in Exercise 2? Explain what happened using some of the new vocabulary in Exercise 1. The crime might be:**

- something that's been in the news recently.
- a famous or historic crime.

LISTENING

4 ▶ **Listen to three conversations and answer the questions.**

1 What crimes from Exercise 2 do the speakers talk about?

2 How do the speakers know about the crime?

3 What happened?

Mounted police in London. UK.

5 ▶ **Work in pairs. Decide which conversation each group of words comes from and how each word was used. Then listen again and check.**

1 swipe / trainers / relief

2 stuffed / shock / drugged

3 directions / fortunately / spoil

6 Which of the three crimes from Exercise 4 is the most serious? Explain your reasons.

DEVELOPING CONVERSATIONS

Comments and questions

When listening to stories, we often make a comment and then follow it with a question.

Oh you're joking! What happened?

That's terrible! Did it have much in it?

7 ▶ **Look at the Developing conversations box. Write the words in the correct order to make comments and questions. Then listen and check your ideas.**

1 Was / dreadful / hurt / That's / anyone
   That's dreadful! Was anyone hurt?

2 been / must've / That / you / awful / Were / OK

3 anything / no / valuable / they / Oh / take / Did

4 parents / What / thinking / were / dreadful / That's / the

5 insured / a / What / shame / you / Were

6 police / Did / you / That's / terrible / report / to / the / it

7 did / joking / they / know / Do / who / it / You're

8 Work in pairs. Take turns to start a conversation using one of these sentences. Respond to your partner's statement with a comment and a question. Continue each conversation for as long as you can.

1 I had my camera stolen while I was on holiday.

2 We got caught in the middle of a riot.

3 We had our house broken into last night.

4 I had my bag snatched in the street.

5 Did you read about that guy who was murdered near here?

GRAMMAR

Showing degrees of certainty with modal verbs

We often use modal verbs (*must, can't, might* or *could*) to show degrees of certainty when we are giving opinions and speculating about what's true.

a *It **can't have been** very nice.*

b *Someone **must have got hold** of my card details.*

c *It **could have been** when I bought those new trainers on the internet, but then again it **might** equally **have been** in the local supermarket.*

d *That **must be** a relief.*

9 Look at the examples in the Grammar box. Then answer these questions.

1 Which two modals show the speaker is uncertain about what happened?

2 Which two modals show the speaker is almost certain about what happened?

3 How does the speaker show they're referring to a past event or feeling rather than the present?

10 Read about the situation and complete the sentences with one or two words.

> A 17-year-old boy has disappeared after having an argument with his parents. He's been gone for three days and they've just reported it to the police.

1 They must _____ a very serious argument for him to run away like that.

2 It can't _____ the first time it's happened or they would've reported him missing sooner.

3 His parents must _____ really worried, but they should've said something earlier.

4 He might _____ to a friend's house and he's too angry to get in touch.

5 Or he might _____ too embarrassed to phone because he thinks he's in trouble.

11 Work in pairs. Use *might, must, can't* or *should* to speculate about these situations.

1 Your neighbours have been buying a lot of expensive things recently. You've seen a man acting suspiciously outside their house.

2 You're walking past a shopping centre near where you live and you hear some shouting, then when you're nearer home you see several police cars speed past.

G See Grammar reference 8A. »»

CONVERSATION PRACTICE

12 Work in pairs. Follow the instructions.

• Choose a crime you discussed in Exercise 3 or another real one you know about.

• Think of some extra details and write down five key words on a piece of paper.

• Swap your paper with your partner and think of two comments and questions.

• Take turns to start the conversation.

Did you hear I got robbed / about that murder?

Rise and fall

IN THIS LESSON, YOU:
- relate and discuss recent trends including their causes and results
- discuss the crime rate where you are and ways of reducing it
- recognize arguments and supporting evidence in a report about falling crime
- describe statistics and trends

READING

1 Read the first two paragraphs of the article on page 79. Discuss these questions with your partner.

1 Does anything surprise you? Do you believe it? Why? / Why not?

2 How would you answer the question at the end of the second paragraph?

2 Discuss how falling crime might be connected to these topics. Read the rest of the article to check your ideas.

- education
- distraction
- population changes
- environment
- technology
- prison and policing

3 Match the missing sentences (a–h) with the gaps in the article (1–8).

a The more confidence the public has in the police, the more likely they are to help with enquiries.

b Increased levels in the blood and brain are known to be associated with violence.

c Remove the opportunity to start a life in crime and you reduce the number of criminals.

d Education, it is argued, makes us more civilized.

e This has resulted in less theft, which had previously been carried out to feed addictions.

f Once identified, police focused on these small areas to arrest criminals and discourage incidents.

g Essentially, when people are absorbed in a task, they are less likely to cause trouble.

h While Latvia fits the pattern, neighbouring Estonia reduced its prison population and still saw a similar fall in murders.

4 Work in pairs. Discuss the questions.

1 Which of the suggested causes for the fall in crime are seen in Riga and Latvia?

2 Do you agree with all the suggested causes? Why? / Why not? Which do you think plays the biggest role?

3 Which of these suggested causes have you seen in your country? Have they had the same results?

4 Are there any other factors that you think affect levels of crime?

VOCABULARY Trends and statistics

5 Replace the words in bold in the sentences with these words and phrases.

account for	coincided with	correlation	decline
declined	led to	peak	played a role
plunged	ranks	rise	soared
stems from			

1 During the 2000s, the number of cars that were stolen **fell sharply** by 70%.

2 The prison population hit a **high** of 450,000 in 2006 and has **slowly dropped** since then.

3 The fall in crime has **happened at the same time as** an increase in the numbers entering university.

4 There's a clear **link** between poor reading skills and crime.

5 As smartphone use has **increased sharply**, it has **resulted in** a similar rise in street crime.

6 It's argued that the **fall** in violent crime **is the result of** longer prison sentences.

7 The economic recession may have **been a factor** in the slight **increase** in the overall crime figures this year.

8 The fact that China **comes** second for billionaires may **be the reason for** the huge increase in sales of luxury cars there.

6 ▶ Listen to the phrases from Exercise 5 and practise saying them. Which phrases do you find hard to say? Practise saying them again.

7 Work in pairs. Discuss the statements in Exercise 5 and answer the questions.

1 Are these trends true for where you live?

2 Do the trends have any other causes or results?

SPEAKING

8 Work in groups to discuss recent trends.

- Individually, think of some recent trends or do a search of trends in the news using terms like *has soared, has plunged, a link between*, etc.

- Report your ideas to the other people in your group.

- Discuss what you think might be the causes of the trend and what it might lead to.

Riga, Latvia.

Riga-rous policing brings down crime

Jonas Grauza, a police officer from Riga in Latvia, gets out of his car to stretch his legs. While the nightlife in the old town is as lively as ever, for him it's been a quiet night. He's had to break up an argument and take a report of a stolen phone, but that's about it. He smiles when asked if it's a typical night. 'It's generally like this, yes, but I'm told 30 years ago it was very different. In the 90s, there were many more problems. Crime and policing has changed a lot.' And the statistics tell the tale. Although by EU standards, Latvia's crime rates are relatively high, they have been falling fairly steadily and violent crime has plunged, with the country seeing a 70% decrease in murders from their peak in 1993.

Similar trends have happened in many countries and it's led to a debate about the causes of falling violent crime and if it'll continue. Are people simply getting nicer?

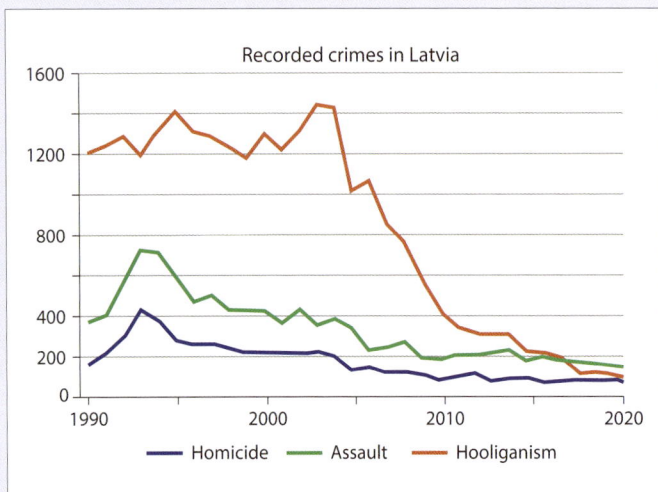

Recorded crimes in Latvia

EDUCATION

Some argue that through increasing awareness of issues, people are being turned off crime. Campaigns against drug and alcohol abuse have been successful in that young people are less likely to try illegal drugs than previous generations. [1] _____ Some have also pointed out that the fall in crime has coincided with an increase in the number of people going on to further education. [2] _____

DISTRACTION

However, it is not clear that education is the main cause. The vast majority of criminals are young and male. There is an argument that if young men are kept busy, they are less likely to commit crime. Involvement in education is one factor, the same argument may also explain recent findings that the popularity of video games may account for a percentage of the drop in crime. [3] _____

DEMOGRAPHICS AND ENVIRONMENT

The point that crime is fundamentally a young person's activity has also made researchers speculate that population changes have played a role. It is argued that crime peaked in the 1990s as a result of the children of the 1960s and 70s baby boom reaching their twenties. More controversially, it has been claimed that the banning of lead in petrol in the 70s is a factor, as previously the lead particles were released into the atmosphere and breathed in. [4] _____

TECHNOLOGY

While such environmental theories are not widely accepted, there is more agreement that technology and prevention have played an important role in the fall in certain crimes. For example, with more sophisticated locking systems installed in cars, it's far more difficult to steal them. Furthermore, in the past, car crime acted as a gateway crime – an easy first crime to commit, which might lead to further involvement in more serious things. [5] _____ Having said that, technology is also facilitating new types of crimes such as identity theft, though perhaps these attract a different kind of criminal.

PRISON AND POLICING

Other researchers argue that the fall in crime stems from jailing more people for longer, and from better policing. They point to the success of programmes in Los Angeles and New York, where police used statistical analysis to identify crime hotspots. [6] _____

THE RIGA EXPERIENCE

Proving causal links when assessing crime is always problematic, not least because correlations are rarely consistent. For example, in several countries, an increase in the prison population has coincided with the fall in crime, but this is not always the case. [7] _____

In the case of Riga, police targeted key establishments and drove out criminals. Their success allowed legitimate businesses to return as well as wealthier local people to move in. In addition, Latvia has experienced falling birth rates, while numbers of university students have almost tripled. More police and better training have also improved relations with the community and a multilingual section has been established to work with the increasing numbers of tourists. [8] _____.

More recently, as people have worked more at home, there's also been a reduction in property crime. Not that everything is perfect: pickpocketing and internet fraud have increased and the police themselves receive more complaints. However, Jonas Grauza is happy. 'If people complain, it shows the public trust us – and less violence means my wife worries about me less.'

Behind bars

VOCABULARY Crime and punishment

1 Complete the sentences with these words and phrases. You may need to change the verb form.

> appeal   be convicted   be given   be released   be treated
> cells   fine   offence   rehabilitation   served

1 Prisoners share / have tiny / are let out of their / are locked in their _____ .

2 He was jailed after _____ of fraud / murder / robbery / assault.

3 He _____ early / for good behaviour / after an appeal / for the day.

4 They need to place more emphasis on / undergo / try new approaches to _____ .

5 The prisoners _____ well / very harshly / with respect / like animals.

6 He _____ a small fine / a short sentence / life / the death penalty.

7 He only _____ half his sentence / eight years of a twelve-year sentence / a year in prison.

8 She's launched an / lost her / going to / won her _____ .

9 He committed a serious / his first / a minor / a repeat _____ .

10 She got a £50 / huge / small / €10,000 _____ .

2 Underline any other words that are new for you in Exercise 1. Where possible, notice the grammar they are used with.

3 Work in pairs. Discuss the questions.

1 What kind of crimes do you think should be punished with fines?

2 What do you think is more important – punishment or rehabilitation?

3 Do you know what the criminal justice system is like in your country? Is it effective?

LISTENING

4 **FS** ▶ Prepositions often merge with words around them in fast speech. Listen and write down the phrases you hear (1–8).

5 ▶ Listen to part of a radio programme. Take notes. Find out at least one piece of information about each of the following.

- Aniello Arena
- The Fortezza theatre company
- Crime and punishment in Norway
- Bastøy prison, Norway

6 Work in groups and compare your notes. How many different pieces of information do you have?

7 ▶ Work in pairs. Are the sentences true (T) or false (F) according to the programme? Listen again and check.

1 Aniello Arena is still in prison.

2 *Reality* is a crime film.

3 Arena admitted murdering three people.

4 Arena did acting before he was convicted.

5 The Fortezza theatre company provides prisoners with therapy through drama.

6 The public in many countries wouldn't support initiatives like Fortezza.

7 In Norway, reoffending after one year is around 50% less than in the UK.

8 Prisoners have often left school early because of problems with reading.

9 In Bastøy, inmates may learn a new profession.

10 In Norway, members of the public may talk or work with prisoners.

8 Work in pairs. Choose two sets of questions to discuss.

1 Do you think it's a good idea for prisoners to get involved in drama groups and acting? Should any prisoner be let out on day release to film and tour? Why? / Why not?

2 How do you feel about the Norwegian approach to crime and prisons? Would it work in your country? Why? / Why not? Can you think of any other ways to help rehabilitation?

3 Do you like any TV shows or films about crime? Which ones? Why? Why do you think crime shows and films are so popular around the world?

GRAMMAR

Nouns with prepositions

Nouns are often followed by a preposition and a noun, pronoun or noun phrase.

have **access to** <u>classes</u>

important **exceptions to** <u>this</u>

the **focus on** <u>what's</u> important

his **conviction of / for** <u>killing three people</u>

9 Look at the examples in the Grammar box. Work in pairs. Read this extract from the radio programme and answer the questions.

The Norwegian prison system has some **similarities** _____ *what the Fortezza theatre company does. Rather than placing an* **emphasis** _____ *punishing inmates, both give more* **attention** _____ *rehabilitation.*

1 What prepositions go after the nouns in bold?

2 What form of a verb follows a preposition?

3 What word means 'the thing(s) that' when it follows a preposition?

10 Complete the sentences using the correct form of the words in brackets and one or two other words.

1 In our country, we don't have a **problem** _____ (drugs).

2 The government has no **interest** _____ (improve) prisons.

3 There's a strong **focus** _____ (teach) citizenship at school.

4 I have great **respect** _____ (the police do).

5 There's never any **excuse** _____ (commit) crime.

6 There's no **point** _____ (try) rehabilitate some criminals.

7 We need a **return** _____ (the values / the past).

8 There's no **need** _____ (more investment / the police).

11 Work in pairs. Take turns to say a new sentence using the nouns in bold in Exercise 10. Does your partner agree with the new statement?

A: There's never any excuse for dropping litter.

B: I agree.

G See Grammar reference 8C. »

SPEAKING TASK

12 **M** Look again at the statements in Exercise 10 and follow the instructions.

- As a class, take a vote on each statement to find out who agrees / disagrees / is not sure.
- Choose the three statements where there is most disagreement.

- Individually, spend five minutes thinking about the reasons for your point of view for each statement – including why you are unsure.
- Work in groups with at least one person who has a different view of the first statement. Try to persuade your partners to change their view. Ask questions to encourage your partners to explain and justify their ideas.
- Change partners to discuss the second and third statements.
- Take a vote again to see what the class thinks after the discussions.

■ MY OUTCOMES ■

Work in pairs. Discuss the questions.

1 What interesting or surprising details about the topic of crime and punishment did you learn?

2 What sorts of conversations or discussions are you better at now? What phrases might you use?

3 Was this unit more or less difficult than earlier units? In what way?

4 What language do you need to revise from this unit?

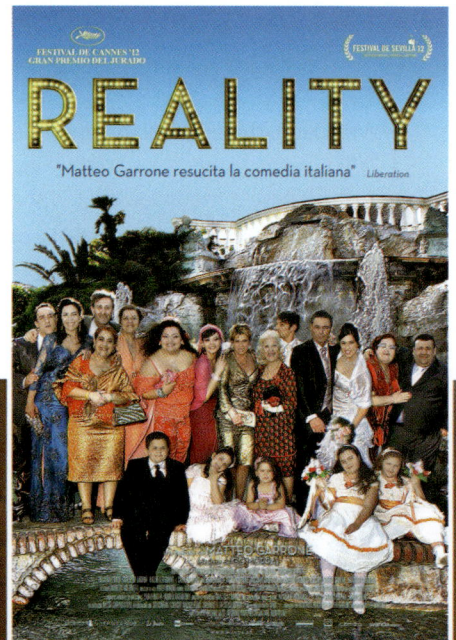

Aniello Arena on the set of *Reality*.

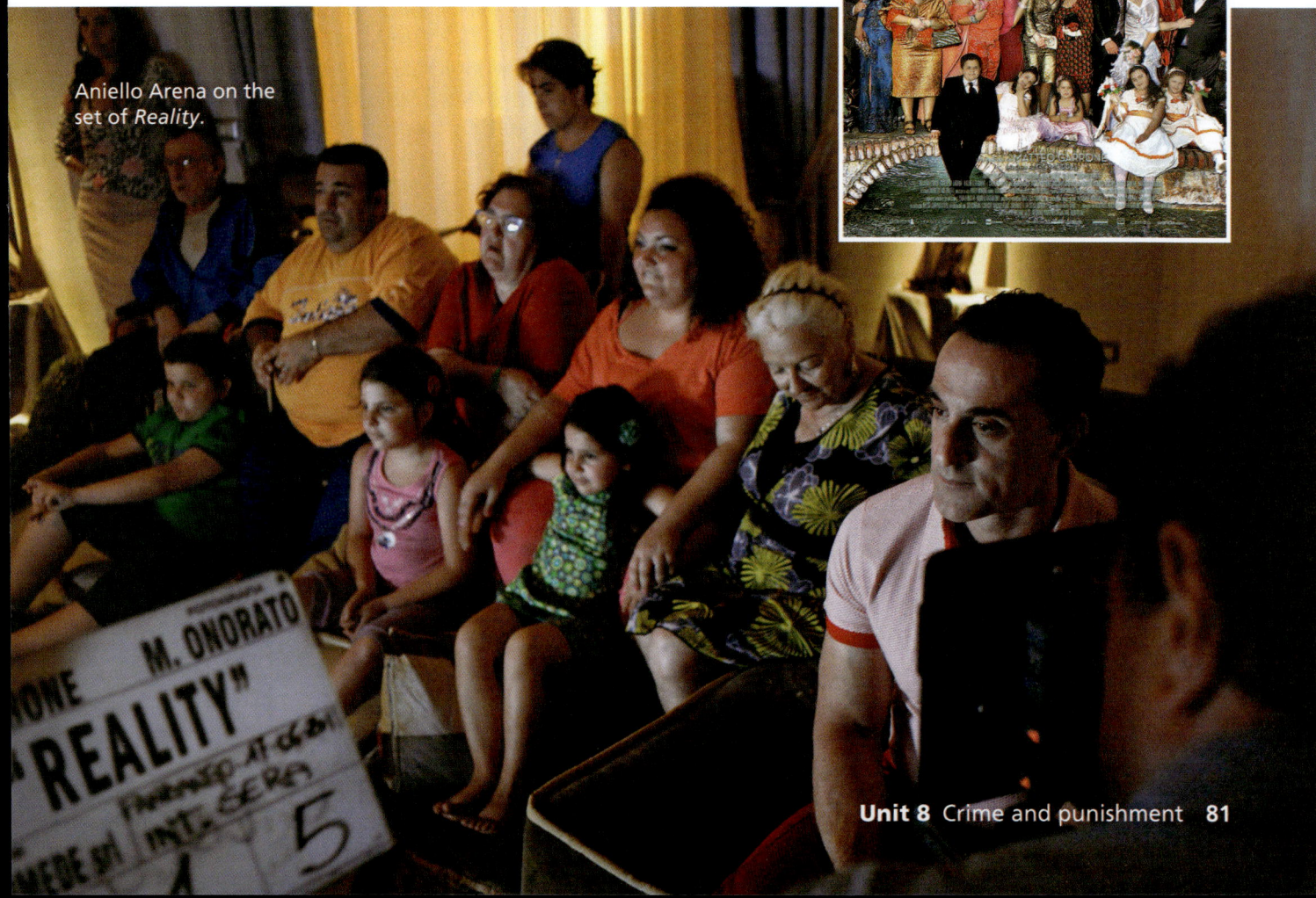

WRITING 4

Formal emails

IN THIS LESSON, YOU:
- write a formal email requesting information on an event
- talk about different types of formal writing
- recognize and practise using formal expressions
- decide on a good team-building event

SPEAKING

1 Work in groups. Discuss the questions.

1 In what kind of situations would you need to write in more formal language?

2 Have you received or sent any communications in more formal language? What were they about?

3 How much difference is there between formal writing in your language compared to speech? In what ways might it be different? How confident are you writing in that style?

4 Do you think communication with businesses, banks, customers, etc. is becoming less formal? Why? / Why not? Is that change a good thing?

WRITING

2 Read the email enquiring about a team-building event and answer the questions.

1 Why does Kathrin address the person she is writing to as *Ms*?

2 What kind of team-building event do they want to do? Why?

3 Do they have a fixed idea of how the event will be?

4 What information do they need to make their decision?

5 Why does she end with *Yours sincerely* instead of using a different closing phrase?

To: pennylee99@thehautecuisineschool.org

Subject: Corporate team-building event

Dear Ms Lee,

I am writing to **enquire** about the cookery demonstrations you **currently** offer at your school and whether they might be adapted to a team-building event.

We are a medium-sized design company and are planning an away day for 30 staff early next year. **Previously**, we have run a cake-baking competition in-house with some success, so we thought our staff would enjoy a cookery-related activity.

We **envisage** an all-day event where staff members can learn some new techniques and recipes and **have the opportunity to** practise them. However, we are very open to your suggestions.

I would be most grateful if you could send me details of what you would be able to offer, potential dates and an estimate of the cost. **In addition, I would appreciate it if you could** give me some information **with regard to** facilities for holding an informal reception or coffee breaks as part of the event.

Finally, **should there be** any issues **regarding** wheelchair access, please highlight these as one of those who will be attending is a wheelchair user.

I **look forward to hearing** from you soon.

Yours sincerely,
Kathrin Jacobson

---

3 Work in pairs. Discuss the questions.

1 What do you think of the suggested idea for the team-building day? Would you like to do it? Why? / Why not?

2 Can you think of any ways you could improve the event?

3 Have you ever had any away days with co-workers or classmates? What did you do? Did it help you all bond?

USEFUL LANGUAGE

Formal and informal language

The degree of formality that we use when writing depends on who we are writing to, how well we know them, and why we are writing. Generally speaking, more formal writing involves more multisyllable words of Latin origin, fewer phrasal verbs, fewer contractions (*I've*, *you're*, etc.) and fewer abbreviations. We also often join ideas in more complex sentences.

4 The email in Exercise 2 is quite formal. Match these informal expressions with the words or expressions in bold in the email.

about (x2)	are thinking of	ask	at the moment
before	can you (x2)	get to	hope to hear
if there are	on top of that		

5 Choose the more formal options to complete these sentences.

1 Thank you for *giving us a call* / *contacting* us and bringing this *matter* / *thing* to our attention.

2 *We are looking to* / *We want to* expand our team and currently have *lots of* / *a number of* vacancies available.

3 *We are sorry to tell you* / *We regret to inform you* that the item you *asked for* / *requested* is no longer in stock.

4 *If you need* / *Should you require* further *assistance* / *help*, please do not *hesitate* / *wait* to ask.

5 I *trust* / *hope* that this will not *be* / *prove* too much of *a pain* / *an inconvenience*.

6 *Is there any chance I can get* / *Would it be possible to obtain* a copy of your *newest* / *most recent* catalogue?

7 *In the event of* / *If there's going to be* a delay, we will contact you *ASAP* / *as soon as possible*.

8 If you *want to* / *wish to* create your own menu, I am sure we can *accommodate your needs* / *sort something out*.

9 *Do let me know* / *Tell me* if I can offer you any *more* / *further* information.

10 While I *appreciate* / *understand* the problems were partly due to external factors, I *feel* / *think* I should still expect to *receive* / *get* a full refund.

6 Complete Penny Lee's reply on page 83 using language from Exercise 2 and Exercise 5. Use one word in each gap. The first letter is given.

To: k.jacobson@topdesign.eul

Subject: Re: Corporate team-building event

Dear Ms Jacobson,

Thank you for ¹c _____ us, we very much ²a _____ it. Although we have never specifically run a corporate team-building event, we have ³p _____ organized demonstrations for closed groups and feel we could certainly ⁴a _____ your needs.

In ⁵a _____ to our cooking rooms, which each allow twenty people to share ten stoves, we have a special demonstration room which can seat up to 60 people. Furthermore, chairs can be removed to create a more open space.

I ⁶t _____ that you are planning to do the event on a weekday, in which case we have a ⁷n _____ of days available in January as well as good availability in February.

While we have disabled access to the building and demonstration area, I ⁸r _____ to say that the cooking rooms are not ⁹c _____ fully adapted. However, please ¹⁰d _____ let us know the specific needs and we may be able to make suitable adjustments.

With ¹¹r _____ to cost, the basic hire would be £4,000, but the final estimate will depend on the options you choose for the day. I suggest we discuss this in more detail by phone.

I am actually on annual leave from tomorrow till Monday. However, ¹²s _____ you ¹³w _____ to talk through the details before then, do not ¹⁴h _____ to contact me on the mobile number below.

I ¹⁵l _____ forward to discussing this ¹⁶f _____ . Thank you once again for considering us.

Yours ¹⁷s _____
Penny Lee

7 Work in pairs. Would you go ahead with this organization or not? Why?

PRACTICE

8 Work in groups. Discuss which activity would best encourage team-building skills among your group. Choose from the list or add your own idea. Then decide how you think the day would be organized.

- sword-fighting
- mountain climbing
- art classes
- ballroom dancing classes
- doing a quiz / treasure hunt
- sailing a large yacht

9 Individually, write a formal email to a company that might offer the activity you have chosen. Explain what you have in mind and ask for any relevant information such as:

- which day the activity is available on
- what time it starts / finishes
- how much it costs (and if there are any discounts)
- if you can have a brochure
- if there are any age limits
- how you can book
- disabled access

10 Share your emails in groups. Discuss:

- how well other students in the group presented the ideas you discussed.
- if they have asked for enough information.
- if they have used appropriately formal language.

VIDEO Out and about

1 **Work in pairs. Discuss the questions.**

1 Do you think it's good to spend time in nature?

2 How much time do you spend in nature? Where? Doing what?

Understanding accents

Some accents replace an /eɪ/ sound with /æ/, so lake /leɪk/ may sound like lack /læk/; rain /reɪn/ like ran /ræn/; and fate /feɪt/ more like fat /fæt/.

2 Watch the video. Which person has the closest views to you? What do they say?

3 Work in pairs. Match the statements with the speakers and explain your choices. You may match statements with more than one speaker. Then watch again to check.

a I don't get out to the countryside much.

b It's important to get away from social media.

c It gives you a moment to gather your thoughts and relax.

d The best way to keep fit is by hiking in the mountains.

e Not being out in nature can be bad for your mental health.

4 **Discuss the questions with your partner.**

1 Have you ever done anything challenging? How did it go?

2 What are other good ways to maintain your mental health?

3 How easy is it for people to access nature where you live?

VIDEO Developing conversations

5 You are going to watch two people talking about a trip to a city and two crimes. Watch and take notes on what they say.

6 Work in pairs. Compare what you understood with a partner. Watch again if you need to.

7 **Discuss the questions with your partner.**

1 Does the place sound like somewhere you'd like to go?

2 What do you know about the artwork?

3 Have you heard of any similar crimes? What happened?

8 **FS** Watch again. Complete the sentences with three to five words in each gap.

1 Northern Lights were there as well, _____ see the Northern Lights.

2 _____ comedy.

3 _____ he wrote 'thanks for the bad security'!

4 And then they _____ .

5 I think _____ in north Oslo.

6 They literally went into the gallery in broad daylight, while it was busy – _____ . They cut the painting out of the frame.

7 Apparently, it wasn't too damaged _____ salvage it and put it back up.

8 Yeah honestly, it's, um, _____ and there's so much in that gallery as well.

CONVERSATION PRACTICE

9 **Work in pairs. You are going to practise a conversation.**

1 Choose a Conversation practice from either Lesson 7A or Lesson 8A.

2 Look at the language in that lesson.

3 Check the meaning of anything you've forgotten with your partner.

4 Have the conversation. Try to improve on the last time you did it.

Grammar and Vocabulary

GRAMMAR

1 Read the first sentence in each pair. Complete the second sentence so that it has a similar meaning. Use between three and five words, including the word in bold.

1 I find politics totally boring.

   I have _____ politics at all.   **INTEREST**

2 I imagine she didn't hear you. She wouldn't ignore you.

   She _____ you. She wouldn't ignore you.   **HEARD**

3 It's possible that they're waiting for us outside.

   They _____ for us outside.   **MIGHT**

4 They should ban advertising which targets children.

   Advertising _____ should be banned.   **AIMED**

5 Destroying much of the forest led to increased flooding.

   There was increased flooding because they _____ many trees.   **DOWN**

6 I'm sure climate change is one cause of the increased number of storms.

   Climate change must be _____ the increased number of storms.   **ROLE**

2 Complete the text with the correct form of the verbs.

On Saturday 14th August at around 10 p.m., I ¹_____ (sit) in my living room watching TV with a couple of friends. It was unbearably hot, so we ²_____ (open) all the windows. Suddenly, we heard some loud bangs outside and I ³_____ (look) out of the window to see what was happening. A nearby car ⁴_____ (burn). I realized that someone must ⁵_____ (throw) some fireworks at it and it ⁶_____ (catch) fire. Just down the street I saw a group of youths acting suspiciously. I went out with a friend to see what they ⁷_____ (do), but they ran off. I ⁸_____ (chase) after them, but I couldn't keep up. Unfortunately, the number of teenagers ⁹_____ (cause) trouble like this has increased. It's coincided with a fall in the amount of support and activities ¹⁰_____ (provide) by the government.

3 Complete the sentences with the correct preposition.

1 There's no excuse _____ not being able to cook.

2 A return _____ old-fashioned values would be no bad thing.

3 We need to place more emphasis _____ staff development.

4 We haven't paid enough attention _____ the destruction of plant habitats.

5 Fraud accounted _____ 15% of all crimes in the UK last year.

6 Young people here generally have a lot of respect _____ their elders.

7 There are many similarities now _____ what happened in the seventies.

8 There needs to be a big decline _____ carbon emissions over the next few years.

4 ▶ **Listen. Write the six sentences you hear.**

VOCABULARY

5 Complete the pairs of phrases with one of these words.

bomb	commit	fog	lift	plunge
rank	sentence	snow	undergo	wind

1 the ~ didn't settle / the ~ has melted

2 there was thick ~ / the ~ eventually lifted

3 the ~'s easing off / the ~ blew away our parasol

4 the ~ was planted in a busy street / the ~ didn't go off

5 he's ~ing rehabilitation / the system's ~ing reform

6 they agreed to ~ the ban / they may ~ restrictions

7 the city ~s highly for safety / we ~ ahead of most places

8 prices have ~d / the country ~ed into a crisis

9 he ~ a minor offence / a major error

10 his ~ was reduced for good behaviour / he was given a life ~

6 Complete the sentences with the correct form of the words.

1 Violent crime such as armed _____ has fallen _____ in recent years.   **rob / sharp**

2 The prison has been accused of _____ because prisoners are treated so _____ .   **cruel / harsh**

3 The heat can be _____ in the summer if you don't have air conditioning, but then in the winter you might also freeze to _____ .   **bear / die**

4 The _____ of attending football matches shows no sign of declining even though _____ offences at grounds have increased.   **popular / crime**

5 It was a highly _____ decision to build the factory there because it _____ the habitat of several _____ species that are close to _____.
   controversy / threat / danger / extinct

7 Complete the text with one word in each gap. The first letters are given.

Pirates have ¹s _____ another ship off the east coast of Africa. Ten crew members are locked in a cabin on the ship and the pirates are demanding ten million dollars to ²r _____ the men and ³r _____ the ship to its owners.

A man is being questioned over the ⁴di _____ of a prize-winning dog. The dog ⁵v _____ without trace from the owner's garden and police believe it will have already been sold to another breeder. ⁶T _____ of pets is on the increase as the price of pedigree animals has ⁷s _____ over the last few years.

The government has agreed to give a ⁸su _____ to a company producing plant-based meat. It is hoped that it will help the company break out into new markets and keep prices low for consumers. Encouraging a vegetarian diet could ⁹l _____ _____ reductions in greenhouse gases that ¹⁰s _____ _____ the meat industry.

9
Careers and studying

IN THIS UNIT, YOU:

- roleplay conversations about how your job is going.
- talk about people and events that have had a big impact on you
- give a short presentation

SPEAKING

1 Work in pairs. Look at the photo. Discuss the questions.

1 What kind of qualifications do you think the people in the photo have?

2 What do you think this job might involve on a day-to-day basis?

3 What kind of qualities do you think you'd need to have to do this kind of work?

4 Could you do a job like this? Why? / Why not?

2 Change partners. Discuss the questions.

1 Are you working at the moment? Have you worked before?

2 If yes, what do you do and what jobs have you done in the past? What were they like?

3 If no, what would you like to do in the future? Why? What will you need to do to get the job you want?

People working on
the James Webb Space
Telescope at NASA.

The world of work

VOCABULARY Working life

1 Work in pairs. Read the sentences and discuss if the situations are usually positive or negative. What are the causes and results of each situation?

'I got promoted' is positive. It means you're doing well at work and get moved to a higher position. It usually happens because you're good at your job. One result is you usually get offered more money.

1 I got **promoted**.
2 I handed in my **notice** last week.
3 I got a **pay rise** last month.
4 I'm getting **on-the-job training**.
5 I actually got **made redundant** last month.
6 I'm slowly **getting the hang of** everything.
7 I'm **struggling to cope**, to be honest.
8 My boss never **delegates** responsibility to the rest of the team.
9 I'm finding it very **rewarding**.
10 It's really **stimulating**. I feel I'm really **stretching** myself.
11 The work's pretty **menial** most of the time.

2 **P ▶** Listen to the words and phrases from Exercise 1 and practise saying them on their own and in a longer phrase. Which words / phrases do you find hard to say? Practise saying them again.

3 Work in pairs. Which sentences in Exercise 1 have ever been true for you or for any of your friends or family? Say as much as you can about each situation.

My older sister actually got promoted quite recently. She works for this big international corporation and they just made her head of her branch. I'm really proud of her.

LISTENING

4 **▶** Listen to the first part of a conversation between two friends, Melissa and Richard. Answer the questions.

1 How is Richard feeling about his job? Why?
2 What does his job mostly seem to involve?
3 What are his plans for the future?
4 How does Melissa try to cheer Richard up?

5 **▶** Listen to the second part of the conversation. How do Richard and Melissa use these words?

1 training
2 college
3 clients
4 presentation
5 business trip
6 promotion
7 employee
8 firm

6 Work in pairs. Discuss the questions.

1 What advice would you give Richard? Why?
2 Do you know anyone whose job is going really well at the moment? In what way?
3 What do you see yourself doing in five years' time?
4 Think of two people you know well. What do you see them doing in five years' time?

GRAMMAR

Conditionals with present forms

We often use conditional sentences to talk about real or probable events now or in the future.

a **If I ask** about doing other stuff, **he** just **tells** me to be patient.
b **If it's** that bad, maybe **you should think about** handing in your notice.
c **It might get** better **if I** just **give** it a bit more time.
d **If you decide** to make a move, I'm sure **you'll be** fine.

7 Look at the examples in the Grammar box. Work in pairs. Discuss the questions.

1 What verb form is used in the *If* part of the sentences?
2 Which two sentences are talking about the future?
3 Which sentence is talking about now?
4 Which sentence is talking about something that's usually, generally true?
5 Which result clause is talking about a definite future result? How do you know?
6 Which sentence is giving advice? How do you know?
7 Which result clause is talking about a future possibility? How do you know?

8 Match the sentence beginnings (1–4) with two possible endings (a–h).

1 If you really want to get into the film industry,
2 If things really are that bad at work,
3 If I get made redundant,
4 If I get good enough grades,

a I might try and set up my own business.
b I'm going to do Law at uni.
c I'll put you in touch with a friend of my dad's who works as a sound engineer.
d you can always request a meeting with management to sort it all out.
e I don't need to sit the entrance exam.
f you have to start at the bottom and work your way up.
g maybe you should start looking for something else.
h at least I'll be able to live on the money I get for a while.

9 Write two conditional sentences you could say to someone in each of these situations. Try to use different patterns. Then compare your sentences in pairs. Do you agree with each other's ideas?

1 I had a big row with a colleague last week. It was awful.
2 I'm thinking of quitting my job and retraining in another field.
3 We want to try and launch our own website later this year.
4 We might send her overseas to study for her degree.

G See Grammar reference 9A. »»

DEVELOPING CONVERSATIONS

Feelings about the future

When we answer questions about the future, we use a range of different expressions to show how sure we are that something will happen.

*You**'re bound** to get lots of offers.* (= I'm 95% sure you will.)

*I **doubt I'll** pass the entrance exam.* (= I'm 90% sure I won't.)

10 ▶ Look at the Developing conversations box. Then look at five answers to the question *Do you think you'll get the job?* Choose the correct option. Then listen and check.

1 *I doubt it. / I'm bound to.* I'm not qualified enough.
2 *Definitely. / I might.* Stranger things have happened!
3 *Probably not / Hopefully not* – but it's worth a try.
4 *Hopefully. / Probably.* I really need the money!
5 *I'm bound to. / I doubt it.* They're desperate for new staff at the moment.

11 Write four questions about careers and studying using the pattern *Do you think you will (ever) …?* Work in groups. Take turns to ask questions and answer using the responses in Exercise 10.

Do you think you'll ever do a Master's?

CONVERSATION PRACTICE

12 Work in pairs. Choose a role.

Student A: Imagine you are working and your job is going really well. Think of at least three reasons why.

Student B: Imagine your job is going badly. Think of at least three reasons why.

13 Roleplay the conversation. Follow the guide. Continue as long as you can.

Student A	Student B
Greet Student B.	
	Greet Student A.
Ask, *So how're you finding your job? Is it going OK?*	
	Explain your problems.
Sympathize. Ask for more details.	
Give advice / make suggestions or offers.	
	Respond. Ask about A's job.
Explain what's good about your job.	

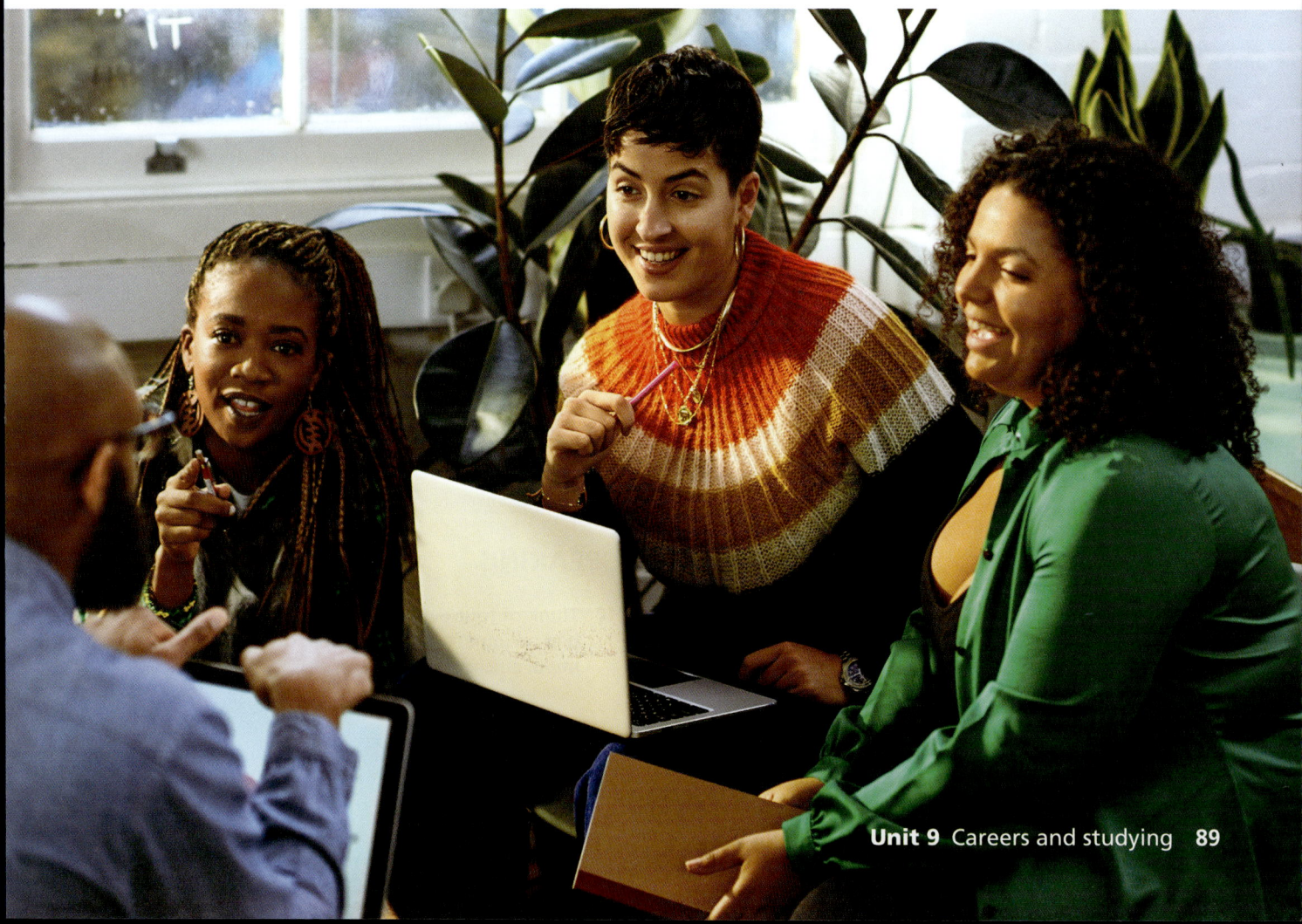

Starting out

IN THIS LESSON, YOU:
- talk about people and events that have had a big impact on you
- discuss work-related issues
- listen to a podcast about young people and the job market
- read about four first jobs

SPEAKING

1 Work in groups. Discuss the questions.

1 Do you know if there's a minimum age for a person to have a paid job in your country?

2 Are there any part-time jobs that young people in your country typically do when they are at school or at college or university? Would you do them? Why? / Why not?

3 What are the advantages and disadvantages of young people working while studying?

LISTENING

2 ▶ Listen to an extract from a podcast about young people and the job market. Take notes on any problems or solutions. Compare your notes in groups.

3 Work in pairs. Discuss the questions.

1 Do you think the advice given is good? Why? / Why not?

2 What other fields do you think are going to be growth areas in the coming years?

3 Do you know any other famous people who started out doing far more menial jobs?

READING

4 Read four texts about first jobs on page 91. Who do you think had the best first job?

5 Work in pairs. Decide which person:

1 was recommended for their job?

2 never got a break?

3 has a job that is sometimes misunderstood?

4 used to get a lift to work?

5 started to find their work a bit boring after a while?

6 received training?

7 now has doubts about 'facts' they hear about?

8 found their job didn't live up to expectations?

9 knew they were being exploited, but didn't mind?

10 had a manager that interfered a lot?

11 thinks certain people are better at a job?

12 feels more positive now about something?

6 Find the words that go with these nouns in the texts.

tables foot laugh labour word novelty benefits rank

7 Work in pairs. Discuss these statements.

1 I'd rather do manual work than office work.

2 People should never be forced to retire.

3 University students should also work, not just study.

4 The army is a good career choice.

5 Women are better at some jobs than men.

6 Getting a good job is often more about who you know than what you know.

GRAMMAR

Conditionals with past forms

We use conditional sentences with past forms to talk about imagined / hypothetical situations.

a *Even **if they doubled** my money, **I wouldn't want** to work near a beach again.*

b ***It would** probably **have been** a different story if **I'd been doing** it on my own!*

c *If **it hadn't been** for her, **I might never even have heard** about the job.*

d *If **I wasn't** in the army, **I would never have gone** somewhere like Haiti.*

8 Look at the examples in the Grammar box. Work in pairs. Discuss these questions.

1 Which sentence is a future hypothetical situation?

2 Which two sentences are past hypothetical situations?

3 Which sentence is talking about hypothetical situations now AND in the past? What's the reality of the situation?

4 Which sentence shows a possible hypothetical result – not a definite one? How do you know?

5 What forms are used in the *if* parts of each sentence? Which forms are used in the result clauses?

9 Complete the sentences with the correct form of the verbs in brackets.

1 To be honest, I _____ (not do) this job if I _____ (have) a choice, but I don't really. My parents aren't that well-off, so I basically have to.

2 I hated it, but the boss was a family friend. If my dad _____ (not get) me the job, I _____ (leave) sooner. In the end I stayed three years before quitting.

3 If it _____ (not be) for my old Geography teacher, I _____ (not become) a town planner.

4 If it _____ (not be) for my high school English teacher, I _____ (not give) this presentation to you today.

5 I love my job. Honestly, even if I suddenly _____ (win) loads of money, I _____ (not give up) work entirely.

G See Grammar reference 9B.

SPEAKING

10 Think of four events, situations or people that have had an impact on your life. In groups, explain their importance.

MY FIRST JOB

EDUARDO, BRAZIL

I got my first job this summer, working in a bar on a beach in Porto Seguro. It sounded ideal – chill out on the beach, get a suntan and earn some money before going back to university. Big mistake! I started work at two in the afternoon, cleaning the place, and then worked solidly through till five in the morning – restocking the bar, rushing from one table to the next, taking orders, carrying trays, clearing **tables** – it was non-stop! It didn't help that my boss was a complete control freak. By the time I got home, I was dead, and slept till one. I never actually set **foot** on the beach! Still, by the end of the summer, I'd saved enough to go on holiday with my girlfriend. It was great to have money I'd earned myself and to be able to spend it as I wanted, but to be honest, even if they doubled my money, I wouldn't want to work near a beach again. It's far too frustrating seeing what you're missing all the time!

JOCELYN, SCOTLAND

I grew up in a rural community where it was common for kids to help out on the nearby farms. When I was about fifteen or sixteen, I started working Saturdays picking potatoes. We'd be collected at seven in the morning and driven out to the fields, where we'd walk behind these huge machines and bag all the potatoes they'd dig up. It was exhausting, but I enjoyed being outside and we all had a **laugh** together. It would probably have been a different story if I'd been doing it on my own! Of course, as a teenager, I provided cheap **labour**, but that didn't really bother me – and I was very grateful for the money. It may sound funny now, but the £30 I earned each week – cash-in-hand, of course – felt like a fortune back then.

ELA, POLAND

I did Politics at university and I really wanted to go and see more of Europe, so I figured I needed a part-time job. A friend of mine did market research for this local company and she put in a good **word** for me. To be honest, if it hadn't been for her, I might never even have heard about the job. I mostly worked weekends, but once in a while they'd ask me to do the odd evening as well. I basically went door to door asking specific questions – what people drank, who they were planning to vote for, all sorts. It was fun to begin with, meeting so many new people, and the money was quite good too, but the **novelty** soon wore off. It got very repetitive. I don't regret it, though. I learned that a smile goes a long way – and as I know that some people were lazy and made up their data, I've learned to be sceptical about statistics too!

CARLA, CHILE

It sometimes surprises people when I tell them I'm an army logistics officer. I joined up after leaving school because I was quite restless and didn't really like 'academic' things or studying. Funnily enough, though, I've actually spent quite a lot of time in a classroom since I joined, as we get loads of on-the-job training. It's OK, though – you see the practical **benefits** more than at school, so I don't regret joining at all. In fact, I've done some amazing things. If I wasn't in the army, I would never have gone somewhere like Haiti. I went there as part of a UN humanitarian mission. For sure, people associate the army with war, but nowadays it's more about peacekeeping and helping people involved in conflicts. My area is all about solving problems and communication – and women are often better than men in these roles, so I'm certainly staying in the army and hopefully I'll achieve a high **rank**.

10 Socializing

IN THIS UNIT, YOU:

- plan a celebration with friends
- talk about embarrassing social mistakes
- discuss attitudes towards small talk

SPEAKING

1 **Look at the photo. Work in pairs. Discuss the questions.**

1 Where do you think these people are?

2 What do you think has been happening there? Why?

3 Have you ever heard of – or been to – any similar events?

2 **Work in pairs. Look at the list of occasions and answer the questions.**

birthday	Carnival	Christmas	Eid al-Fitr
Mother's Day	New Year	Valentine's Day	Workers' Day

1 Which of these occasions do you celebrate?

2 How do you usually celebrate them?

3 What is the biggest celebration of the year where you're from? What happens?

Two young people having fun in the Holi festivities.

Celebrate good times

IN THIS LESSON, YOU:
- plan a celebration with friends
- learn about different ways of celebrating things
- practise listening to people organizing a celebration
- suggest alternative times and places to meet

VOCABULARY Celebrating

1 Work in pairs. Read the sentences and check you understand the words in bold. Then discuss the questions.

a I had a small **get-together** at home with some friends.

b I **went clubbing** with a bunch of friends.

c I **treated myself** to a day in a spa.

d I had **a weekend break** in Prague.

e We hired **a venue** in town and got a kids' **entertainer** in.

f I wasn't really **up for** going out, so I just had a quiet night in.

g A bunch of us rented a **karaoke booth** for the night.

h My boyfriend took me out for a romantic dinner in this **posh** restaurant.

i I had a **big do** with about 150 people.

j A friend **threw a surprise party** for me.

1 Which of these things have you done to celebrate something?

2 When? What were you celebrating?

3 Which things would you not do to celebrate? Why not?

4 Can you think of three other ways of celebrating?

2 **P** ▶ Listen to the words and phrases from Exercise 1 and practise saying them on their own and in a longer phrase. Which words / phrases do you find hard to say? Practise saying them again.

LISTENING

3 ▶ Listen to three friends planning a celebration. Answer the questions.

1 Why are they going out to celebrate this Friday?

2 What do you hear about: Equinox? Rico's? Guanabara?

3 What time do they agree to meet?

4 ▶ Work in pairs. Complete the sentences from the conversation, using two words in each gap. Contractions (*it's*, *she's*, etc.) count as one word here. Listen again to check your answers.

1 So ＿＿＿＿＿＿ go out and celebrate on Friday, then?

2 I'd be ＿＿＿＿＿＿ that as well. Do you have anywhere ＿＿＿＿＿＿ ?

3 I thought that Equinox might ＿＿＿＿＿＿ .

4 I ＿＿＿＿＿＿ the music they play and besides, it's ＿＿＿＿＿＿ my kind of crowd there.

5 Well, personally, I'd ＿＿＿＿＿＿ to get something to eat at some point, if that's ＿＿＿＿＿＿ with you?

6 Rico's is always a ＿＿＿＿＿＿ .

7 Yeah, whatever. ＿＿＿＿＿＿ .

8 I'm working till six and it'd be nice if I could go home first, so could we ＿＿＿＿＿＿ eight?

GRAMMAR

The future perfect

We use the future perfect to show the point in the future by which something will (or won't) be complete.

*By four o'clock on Friday, we'**ll have finished** every single one.*

*Could we make it eight? I'**ll have had** time to get changed and freshen up a bit by then.*

*Don't call me before 12. I **won't have had** time to prepare otherwise.*

***Will** you **have finished** the meeting by two?*

5 Work in pairs. Look at the examples in the Grammar box and answer these questions.

1 How is the future perfect formed?

2 What references to time can you see?

3 Do the actions with the future perfect happen before those times or do they start at those times?

6 Complete the sentences with the future perfect form of these verbs. You may need to use a negative form.

| be | cook | eat | find | leave | lose | pass | process |

1 It's my grandparents' anniversary next Friday. They ＿＿＿＿＿＿ married for 50 years!

2 I'll order a takeaway for everyone. He said they were going to come straight from work, so they ＿＿＿＿＿＿ anything.

3 It's a shame you're not coming back till next Tuesday. I ＿＿＿＿＿＿ for Greece by then, so I'll miss you.

4 I sent my passport to be renewed ages ago, but apparently it ＿＿＿＿＿＿ in time for my end-of-year work trip. It's really annoying.

5 I'll have my results by the time you visit and hopefully I ＿＿＿＿＿＿ , so we'll be able to go out and celebrate.

6 Do you think he ＿＿＿＿＿＿ some lunch for us when we arrive tomorrow?

7 If you're already five kilos lighter, it means the diet's working. Imagine how much more you ＿＿＿＿＿＿ by the time summer comes around.

8 My dad's almost completely bald now – hopefully they ＿＿＿＿＿＿ a cure for that by the time I'm his age.

7 Spend three minutes thinking about how (a) your life and (b) the world will be different in 30 years' time. In pairs, share your ideas. Use the future perfect.

I imagine I'll have started losing my hair by then.

Hopefully, they'll have found a cure for cancer by then.

G See Grammar reference 10A.

DEVELOPING CONVERSATIONS

Arranging to meet

We often suggest alternative times or places to meet using *Can / Could we make it …?* We also explain why.

A: *So what time do you want to meet? Seven?*

B: *I'm working till six and it'd be nice if I could go home first, so could we make it eight?*

8 Look at the Developing conversations box. Complete B's responses in the conversations (1–5) with the explanations (a–e).

1 A: When do you want to meet? Would about nine tomorrow night be OK?

   B: Can we make it a bit earlier? _____

2 A: When would you like to meet? Would sometime this week suit you?

   B: Could we make it some other time? _____

3 A: What day works for you? Is Friday any good?

   B: Could we make it earlier in the week? _____

4 A: Where shall we meet? How about that new café on the other side of the river?

   B: Can we make it somewhere more central? _____

5 A: Why don't we meet at Janet's place?

   B: Can we make it somewhere nearer mine? _____

a It's quite awkward to get to, that place.

b I've got a lot on at work at the moment.

c She lives miles away from me.

d It's my girlfriend's birthday that day.

e I need to try and get an early night if I can.

9 Work in pairs. Have conversations. Take turns to ask these questions and to respond by suggesting alternatives and explaining why.

What time do you want to meet? Is … OK?

Where shall we meet? Would … suit you?

CONVERSATION PRACTICE

10 Work in groups of three. You're going to have a conversation like the one you heard in Exercise 3. Decide what you're going to celebrate. Then work individually and make notes on the following.

- two ideas for how to celebrate and why
- where exactly you would go

11 **M** Decide who is going to be Student A, Student B and Student C. Then have your conversation. Follow this guide.

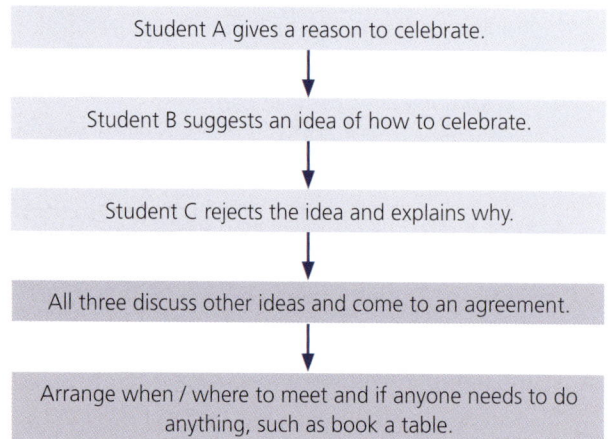

> Student A gives a reason to celebrate.
>
> ↓
>
> Student B suggests an idea of how to celebrate.
>
> ↓
>
> Student C rejects the idea and explains why.
>
> ↓
>
> All three discuss other ideas and come to an agreement.
>
> ↓
>
> Arrange when / where to meet and if anyone needs to do anything, such as book a table.

Putting your foot in it

IN THIS LESSON, YOU:
- talk about embarrassing social mistakes
- read about people who've committed a faux pas
- work out the function of different parts of an article
- discuss how serious different social mistakes are

READING

1 Read the dictionary definition of *faux pas*. Then discuss what faux pas might be made in each situation (1–4) and what the consequences might be.

> **faux pas** /ˌfəʊˈpɑː/ (n)
>
> If you *make* or *commit a faux pas*, you say or do something embarrassing by mistake. You can also say that you've *put your foot in it*.

1 An elderly parent sets up their first social media account.
2 A politician searches for an article on Twitter®.
3 An airline company wishes a national sports team well.
4 You ask someone how their partner is.

2 Read the article on page 99. Then work in pairs and discuss the questions.

1 What actually happened in each case?
2 Which situation do you think is the most embarrassing? Why?
3 Which situation is the funniest? Why?

3 Which paragraph in the article:

1 mentions a controversial social media post?
2 mentions something that made a bad situation even worse?
3 includes a conversation that ends in tears?
4 gives an example of something the writer found very hard to explain?
5 mentions a social media post that went viral?
6 shows the writer doing something they'd rather not have to do?
7 describes an unexpected benefit?

4 Complete these sentences (1–7) using the phrases in bold in the article. Use two or three words in each gap.

1 I nearly _____ in it with my brother last week. He's organizing a surprise party for my birthday and I forgot I wasn't supposed to know about it.

2 The mayor found himself in _____ after making some sexist comments at a dinner party. Unsurprisingly, the audience were not impressed.

3 I was his best man and before the wedding, I pretended I'd lost his ring. It was supposed to be a joke, but he didn't see the _____ and got really angry.

4 They announced this new car on Twitter without realizing the name they'd given it was actually a very rude word in German. In the end, they _____ and changed the name.

5 I was fed up with work, and my emotions _____ of me as I wrote an angry email to some colleagues. Unfortunately, I ended up accidentally sending it to my boss as well.

6 In the _____ the election, a politician posted and then deleted a terrible comment on social media. Someone managed to share a screenshot, though, and that went viral. The politician in question was clearly _____ by all the outrage and resigned.

7 The school sent out a message asking parents to help their kids get better at spelling, but people soon picked _____ the fact it was full of spelling mistakes! Epic fail!

5 Work in pairs. Discuss which of the seven mistakes in Exercise 4 you think are the most and the least serious. Explain why.

SPEAKING

6 Work in groups. Discuss the questions.

1 How careful are you about what you post online? What privacy settings do you use?
2 Can you think of any famous people who have made mistakes in public?
3 Have you ever put your foot in it – or done anything embarrassing in public? When? What happened?
4 Have any ads or comments caused outrage in the media in your country recently?

Put Your Foot In It?
WE'VE ALL BEEN THERE.

Jane Johnson can relate to everyone who's slipped up – both online and off!

"Johnson, did you just post #stupidmeetingssuck?"

A When my mum announced that she had created her very first social media account, I was slightly **taken aback**. She's really not the most tech-literate person I've ever met, but the modern world had clearly caught up with her, all her friends were now online and she felt like she was missing out. Fearing that she might embarrass me by uploading my old school photos or revealing personal information about me in her posts, I decided against sending her a friend request, but after a couple of weeks, curiosity **got the better of me** and I did have a peek at her page to see what she'd been up to. What I saw there was very confusing indeed. There were hundreds of posts, each of them just containing a single different name.

B Against my better judgement, I decided to call her and find out what was going on. After a bit of small talk about work and my love life, I casually asked how she was enjoying being on social media. 'It's all rather frustrating, I must say,' she replied. 'I've tried searching for hundreds of my friends, but none of them seem to be on there. Or maybe they're all just hiding from me. I don't know.' Once I'd managed to stop laughing, I did explain what she was doing wrong and thankfully, she **saw the funny side** of the situation.

C I reassured my mum that she was in good company. Take the former British politician Ed Balls, for example, who back in April 2011 decided to search Twitter for a recent article about himself, but then accidentally entered his intended search item term in the wrong box and sent a Tweet® simply reading 'Ed Balls'. People were quick to **pick up on** this little faux pas and the original Tweet has now been shared many thousands of times, with the incident now celebrated online every 28th April as 'Ed Balls Day'.

D Now, neither of these social media fails had any serious negative consequences for the people posting. In fact, in the case of Ed Balls, the slip allowed people to laugh at the mild misfortune of quite a serious politician who suddenly seemed to be like everyone's embarrassing dad. However, in the corporate world, committing a minor faux pas can have a major impact on your reputation and business.

E For example, **in the run-up to** a Six Nations rugby match between England and Wales, the airline company British Airways ended up **in hot water** for Tweeting their support for the England team. BA is the official airline partner of England Rugby, but is also supposed to represent all four countries that form the United Kingdom equally. The Tweet sparked an angry response from Welsh rugby fans, with a leading Welsh politician pointing out that this was a good way to annoy three million potential customers.

F In response to the outrage, the company **deleted the Tweet** and apologized, but the damage was already done. The moral for firms here seems to be: don't let keen sports fans decide your marketing messages. Oh, and in case you were wondering, England added insult to injury by travelling to Wales for the match and winning 24-13!

G It's clearly true that anyone can slip up, and I'm no exception. Indeed, after explaining to my mum what she'd been doing wrong, I called my son for a catch-up. At some point during the conversation, I asked how his girlfriend was, only for him to suddenly burst into tears! How was I supposed to know they'd split up the day before? So next time you **put your foot in it**, remember: it happens to the best of us.

Small talk

IN THIS LESSON, YOU:
- discuss attitudes towards small talk
- talk about different kinds of parties
- listen to five different people making small talk
- practise making small talk about different topics

VOCABULARY Parties

1 Work in pairs. Discuss when people might have these kinds of parties and what you'd usually expect to happen at each one.

1 a house-warming party	4 a fancy dress party
2 a farewell party	5 a hen party / a stag party
3 a dinner party	6 a street party

2 Match the words in bold in the sentences (1–6) with the meanings (a–l).

1 This guy kept trying to **chat me up**, and in the end I had to tell him to **get lost**. It was really awkward.

2 They set up a **marquee** in the garden and had a band playing in there. They must've spent a **fortune** on it.

3 Our neighbours' teenage son had a party while they were away and it **got a bit out of hand**. In the end, the police came and **broke** it **up**.

4 We threw a surprise party for my mum's 50th. She **didn't have a clue** we were going to do it and **burst into tears** when she saw everyone.

5 I felt a bit sorry for her, because hardly anyone **turned up** and she'd prepared loads of food, which all just **went to waste**.

6 I was invited to a wedding **reception**, but I hardly knew anyone there and no one really talked to me, so I felt a bit **left out**.

a go away and leave me alone
b a big tent used for events held outside
c ignored and not included
d large amount of money
e was left unused and was thrown away
f formal party
g became impossible to control
h had no idea
i stopped
j talk to me because he wanted a relationship with me
k came
l suddenly started crying

3 Work in groups. Discuss the questions.

1 Have you had any of the experiences in Exercise 2? When? Give more details.

2 What's your best and / or worst party experience ever?

3 Do you usually take a gift when you go to a party?

4 Do you usually arrive early, on time or late? Why?

5 What would your perfect party involve?

LISTENING

4 Work in groups. Discuss how you would feel in these situations, and what you would say or do.

1 A friend invites you to a party. When you get there, you don't know the host or anyone else apart from your friend, who spends the whole evening with someone else.

2 You decide to walk out of a lecture halfway through. You then meet someone else coming out of the lecture theatre.

3 You get talking to someone at a party. They seem OK to begin with, but it turns out that you don't really have much in common.

4 At a friend's house, you're offered a special dish – made from something you really don't like.

5 Someone you don't know interrupts a conversation you're having.

6 You're in a club or a café and there's a really long queue for the toilet.

5 ▶ Listen to five conversations. Match each conversation with a situation from Exercise 4. You can match one conversation with two situations.

6 FS ▶ When two vowel sounds meet, we often insert either a /j/ or a /w/ sound to make them easier to say together. Listen and say which sound you hear in each case.

7 ▶ Listen again. Choose from the list (a–h) what the speaker does in each conversation. There are three extra letters you do not need.

a embarrasses him / herself a bit
b upsets the host
c talks about a recent trip
d compliments someone
e makes their excuses and leaves
f shares a recipe
g invites themselves somewhere
h talks about the shop they run

8 Work in pairs. Discuss the questions.

1 In conversation 1, the speaker made an excuse and left. Would you have reacted in the same way?

2 Have you ever been to a party where you hardly knew anyone? What did you do?

3 Have you had any conversations recently with people you didn't know? What did you talk about? How did the conversations start and end?

GRAMMAR

Question tags

We often use question tags to ask for agreement or to ask for confirmation of an idea. Question tags are also used in polite requests.

a *They have music down there later on,* **don't they**?

b *You couldn't pass me the salt,* **could you**?

c *The speaker wasn't exactly helping either, though,* **was he**?

9 **Look at the examples in the Grammar box. Then answer these questions.**

1 How are the question tags formed?

2 Which sentence asks for agreement?

3 Which sentence asks for confirmation of an idea?

4 Which sentence is a polite request?

10 ▶ **Complete these conversations by adding question tags in the appropriate places. Listen and check your answers. Then work in pairs. Practise reading the conversations.**

1 A: Miserable weather.

   B: Yeah, awful. It's been like this for weeks now.

   A: I know. I can't remember when I last saw the sun.

2 A: You don't remember me.

   B: It's Li.

   A: No. It's Lian.

3 A: Excuse me. You haven't got a light.

   B: Yeah. Here you go.

   A: Thanks.

   B: You couldn't lend me a pound.

   A: No, sorry.

4 A: You missed the class on Monday.

   B: There wasn't one. The school was closed for the holiday.

   A: No. Mind you, you didn't miss much. It wasn't very interesting.

   B: Well, to be honest the whole course is a bit disappointing.

5 A: I love that jacket. It's from Zara.

   B: No, I got it from a vintage shop in town.

   A: Really? You wouldn't happen to have the address.

   B: No. Sorry. I honestly can't remember.

11 **Write four comments about the weather, the news, food or sport. Include question tags. Work with a new partner. Take turns to make a comment and think of a suitable reply.**

G See Grammar reference 10C.

SPEAKING TASK

12 **Work in groups. Look at the information and answer the questions.**

1 Does the information reflect your own experience? How do you feel about that?

2 Why do you think things are this way?

- Being able to make small talk with strangers can have a very positive effect on your mental and emotional health.

- Research in the US suggests men who make small talk before negotiations tend to get better deals than men who don't. However, whether or not female negotiators use small talk makes no difference to their success.

- Some research suggests that women in the US use more question tags, avoid swearing and use more precise grammar in small talk than men.

- In some cultures, small talk is generally seen as a waste of time and getting to the point is seen as being more important.

- In some cultures, family is a closed topic at work and in business, while in others, asking about family is seen as a way to show interest in the person you're talking to.

- Asking how much someone earns or about their finances is taboo in many cultures.

13 **M** **Work with a new partner. Think of advice for anyone wanting to make small talk with people from your country. Think about:**

- how topics and styles of small talk might change depending on age, gender, location, profession, class.

- things you'd advise them not to do – or talk about.

■ MY OUTCOMES ■

Work in pairs. Discuss the questions.

1 What did you find interesting about the reading and listening texts in this unit?

2 What useful language have you learned to talk about the topics in this unit?

3 Was this unit more or less difficult than earlier units? In what way?

4 When and how will you practise the language and situations from this unit in the future?

Personal statements

IN THIS LESSON, YOU:
- write a personal statement for a job / course of study
- discuss how best to structure personal statements
- look at different ways of describing your skills
- practise adding information using different linkers

SPEAKING

1 Work in pairs. Discuss the questions.

1 Have you ever written a personal statement? When? What for?

2 What kind of things did you put in it? Were you pleased with it?

3 How important is it to be honest when writing personal statements?

4 Do you think it's OK to be funny when writing personal statements? Why? / Why not?

WRITING

2 Niran is applying to do an MBA (a Master's Degree in Business Administration) at the University of Sydney in Australia. Look at the notes he made before writing his personal statement. Then discuss the questions in pairs.

Experience
Reasons for doing course
Personal qualities
Education and qualifications

1 What would you expect to read in each section?

2 What other areas do you think he could include?

3 What do you think is the best order to put all this information in?

University of Sydney campus in New South Wales, Australia.

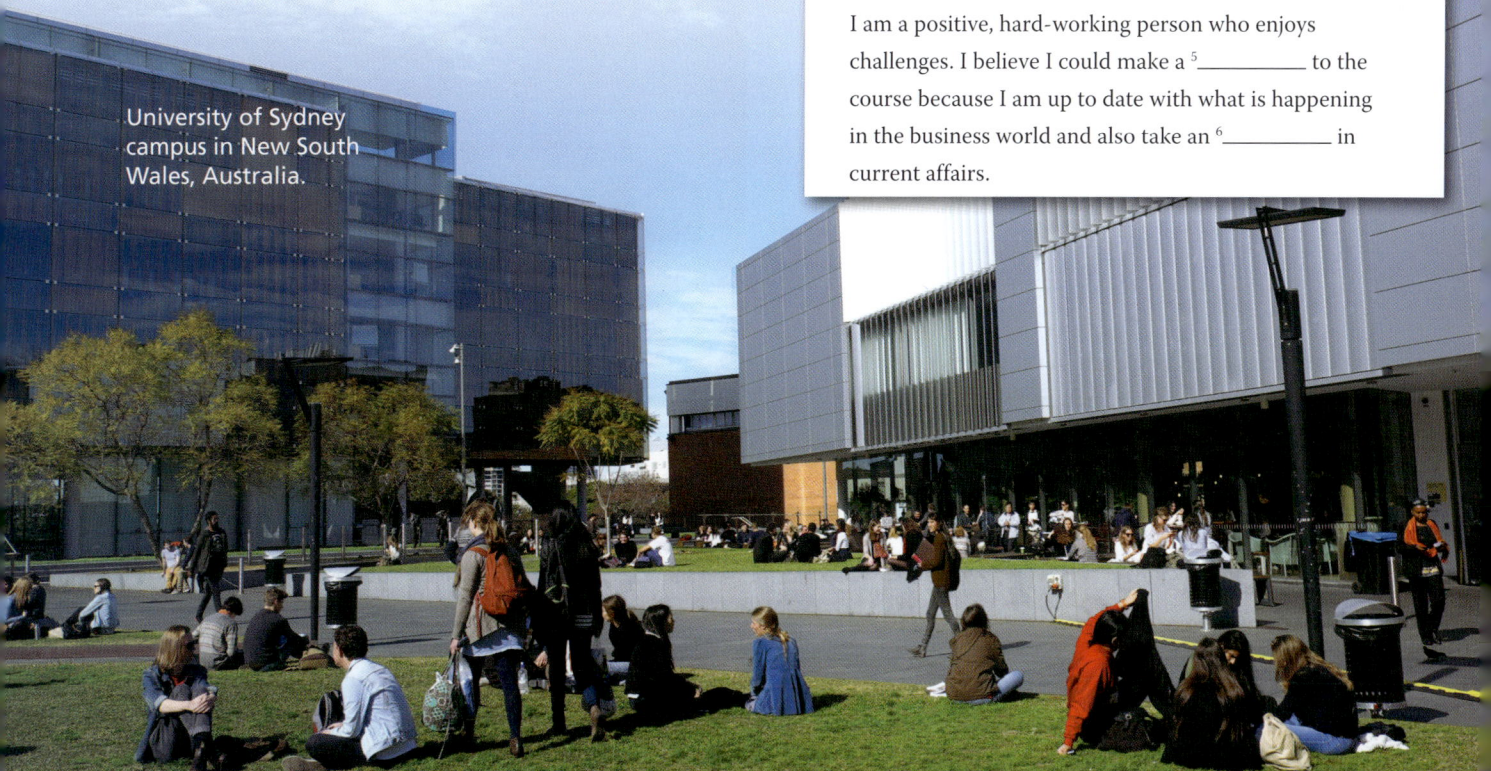

3 Complete Niran's personal statement with these collocations.

active interest	competitive advantage
extensive knowledge	invaluable insight
transferable skills	valuable contribution

I am applying for this course because I would like to broaden my understanding of the world of business and apply the theoretical and practical knowledge I have acquired to date. Furthermore, I feel an MBA will give me a [1]_____ in the job market.

As a teenager, I often accompanied my uncle to his office, where I gained an [2]_____ into how businesses are run. It was at this point that I decided to pursue a career in this area. My degree in Business Studies and Accountancy has given me [3]_____ of the field.

I am currently doing a part-time English course in order to improve my language skills. In addition to this, I have almost completed an online diploma in computing.

At present, I am on an internship at a media company. This experience has given me the opportunity to put into practice much of what I learned on my degree course.

Despite having been at the company for only a short period of time, I still believe I have acquired a set of [4]_____ that I can apply to any business environment.

I am a positive, hard-working person who enjoys challenges. I believe I could make a [5]_____ to the course because I am up to date with what is happening in the business world and also take an [6]_____ in current affairs.

SPEAKING

4 **Work in groups. Discuss the questions.**

1 What do you think is good about Niran's personal statement?

2 Is there anything you would change or add? Why?

3 Look at the list of transferable skills in the box. Which do you think you have? Give examples of when / how you have used them.

4 Are there any of these skills you'd like to develop further?

computer skills	language skills	leadership skills
negotiating skills	organizational skills	people skills
problem-solving skills	time-management skills	

USEFUL LANGUAGE

Describing yourself

In the personal statement, Niran gives a description of his character. Note that he doesn't just use an adjective. He also adds a comment to exemplify or clarify the description.

I am a positive, hard-working person who enjoys challenges.

5 **Match the descriptions (1–5) with the follow-up comments (a–e).**

1 I am a very ambitious person

2 I am very passionate about my studies

3 I am a highly sociable kind of person

4 I am very punctual

5 I can be very demanding

a and am determined to be a success in my field.

b and have a wide circle of friends.

c as I expect the best of people around me.

d and really love the subject.

e and have never missed a deadline.

6 **Now match these descriptions (6–10) with the follow-up comments (f–j).**

6 I am a very positive person

7 I am a very conscientious worker

8 I am quite a creative person

9 I am quite a well-rounded person

10 I can be quite a stubborn person

f who takes pride in doing things well.

g and am good at finding innovative solutions to problems.

h who finds it hard to see other people's points of view.

i and have a wide range of interests.

j who always tries to look on the bright side.

7 **Choose the five adjectives from Exercises 5 and 6 that you think best describe you. Explain your choices to a partner. Does your partner agree with your description of yourself?**

USEFUL LANGUAGE

Adding information

There are several different linking words you can use to add information. Some link two sentences together and are more commonly used after full stops; others are more often used to link clauses within a sentence.

8 **Look at the pairs of linking words in italics. For each pair, decide if both choices are possible or if only one is. Cross out any incorrect linking words.**

1 I believe I am well-qualified for the course. *In addition*, / *As well*, I have already gained considerable work experience in the field.

2 I speak fluent English and German. *Additionally*, / *In addition*, I speak very good French and basic Spanish.

3 I have read widely in the literature of the field and have relevant practical experience *too* / *as well*.

4 I am very keen on sport. I am a keen cyclist and play tennis regularly. *What's more*, / *In addition to*, I have been studying karate for the last six years.

5 *In addition to* / *As well as* being determined and ambitious, I am *also* / *furthermore* highly organized.

6 I spent a year studying Graphic Design in Canada. *Additionally*, / *In addition to this*, I have taught myself how to use specialist software such as InDesign and I *also* / *as well* have excellent web design skills.

9 **Compare your ideas with a partner.**

PRACTICE

10 **Decide on a course of study or job you would like to apply for. You are going to write your own personal statement of around 250 words. You will need to give information about the following.**

- your past and present education
- your work experience
- your skills and abilities

11 **Plan the content of each of your paragraphs. Use the model statement in Exercise 3 to help you.**

12 **Write the statement. Make sure you describe your skills and use linking words to add information.**

13 **Compare your statements with a partner. Say two things you like about your partner's statement and one thing (if anything) that would improve it.**

VIDEO Out and about

1 Work in pairs. Discuss the questions.

1 What was the last celebration you had? How did you celebrate?

2 Are you good at making small talk at parties?

Understanding accents

Some accents replace a /t/ sound with /d/, so *bet* /bet/ may sound like *bed* /bed/; *torn* /tɔːn/ like *dawn* /dɔːn/; and *matter* /mætə/ more like *madder* /mædə/.

2 🎥 Watch the video. Which person has the closest experience to yours? What do they say?

3 🎥 Work in pairs. Match the statements with the speakers and explain your choices. You may match statements with more than one speaker. Then watch again to check.

a I had a small leaving do.

b I had a little get together at my place with friends and family.

c I took a boat trip.

d My mother invited me over for a special meal.

e I went for a day out with a group of friends.

f We went to a new place which is part of a chain.

g I try and get people talking and help them feel at ease.

h I'd say I'm naturally pretty quiet and shy.

i I like socializing and meeting new people.

4 Discuss the questions with your partner.

1 Do you prefer a big or small affair for celebrations? Why?

2 Do you know anyone who is an introvert / extrovert? Give examples?

3 Do you have different personas in different situations? What might be good or bad about having different personas?

VIDEO Developing conversations

5 🎥 You are going to watch two people talking about their jobs. Watch and take notes on what they say.

6 🎥 Work in pairs. Compare what you understood. Watch again if you need to.

7 Discuss the questions with your partner.

1 What things did the two speakers in the video have in common?

2 What other kinds of problems might someone have with a boss or taking on a new role?

3 Do you know anyone who has taken on a new role recently? How is it going?

8 FS 🎥 Watch again. Complete the sentences with three to five words in each gap.

1 Well there's so much _____ up on.

2 Well, _____ exciting role, but it's just quite stressful.

3 _____ your manager?

4 The first few weeks are always the toughest, but, you know _____ get better.

5 Well _____ . So, how's your job going?

6 The hours are longer and there's _____ .

7 Hmm, well _____ new role it takes a bit of time to get used to it.

8 I guess you're right. _____ where I can make a difference.

CONVERSATION PRACTICE

9 Work in pairs. You are going to practise a conversation.

• Choose a Conversation practice from either Lesson 9A or Lesson 10A.

• Look at the language in that lesson.

• Check the meaning of anything you've forgotten with your partner.

• Have the conversation. Try to improve on the last time you did it.

Grammar and Vocabulary

GRAMMAR

1 Choose the correct option to complete the sentences.

1 If I get made redundant, I *set up / am going to set up* my own business.

2 I can't believe that in September I *have been working / will have worked* here for ten years already!

3 It was a fantastic party, *was / wasn't* it?

4 I'll call you when I *will have finished / have finished*.

5 Sorry I'm so late. I *would've called / would call* you if the battery on my phone hadn't died.

6 You wouldn't happen to know if they're taking on new staff, *would / do* you?

7 I would have told him to get lost too if he *spoke / had spoken* to me like that.

8 If the worst *comes / will come* to the worst, *I'll go back / I go back* and live with my parents.

2 Read the first sentence in each pair. Complete the second sentence so that it has a similar meaning. Use between three and five words, including the word in bold.

1 It was a shame there weren't more people at the party.
The party would have been better if more people _____ . **COME**

2 Would it be possible for you to give me a lift home?
You _____ home, could you? **DRIVE**

3 All staff are going to get training before we start using the new system with clients.
By the time the new system goes live, all staff _____ how to use it. **TRAINED**

4 The situation became quite chaotic because the police didn't intervene soon enough.
If the police had intervened sooner, the situation _____ out of hand. **GOT**

5 I want to do a Masters, but it depends on the cost.
I'm going to do a Masters if _____ too much. **COST**

6 It's pretty boring work, right?
The work _____ , is it? **INTERESTING**

3 Complete the email with one word in each gap.

Dear Simon,

I'm writing to say I don't think I ¹_____ make it to your leaving do. As you know, the new store's opening in two weeks and I'm finding things hard, to be honest. If my boss ²_____ actually taken on a couple more people as I asked him to, perhaps things wouldn't ³_____ so bad, but he just won't listen and, as he hardly sets foot in the office, he doesn't really know how much pressure we're under. If everything ⁴_____ to plan, I might ⁵_____ done everything I need to do before your party, but to be honest I ⁶_____ it. You know how it is – something unexpected is ⁷_____ to delay things.

So anyway, if I don't see you next week, let's get together soon, ⁸_____ we? We could even do some karaoke again, if you're up for it!

4 ▶ Listen. Write the six sentences you hear.

VOCABULARY

5 Match the verbs (1–10) with the collocates (a–j).

1	break up	a	into tears / out laughing
2	burst	b	in a good word for you / my foot in it
3	treat oneself to	c	the main reasons / the key points
4	go	d	clubbing / to this posh restaurant
5	have	e	the demonstration / the party
6	see	f	a quiet night in / a short break
7	achieve	g	a beauty treatment / a new outfit
8	put	h	a high rank / her main aim
9	hand in	i	the funny side / the practical benefits
10	summarize	j	her notice / her homework

6 Complete the introduction to a presentation with one word in each gap. The first letters are given.

Hello. Welcome and for those who don't know me, I'm Steffi. Today I'm going to ¹t_____ a look at a company called Global Xtra. Hands up how many of you have heard of it? Right. Well, it might surprise you to learn that it's currently the tenth largest company in the world with a market value of around $90 billion.

What I'm going to do today is tell you a bit more about this company and ²f_____ in more detail on where it currently stands. I'll begin by briefly ³ou_____ its main businesses and providing a short ⁴ov_____ of the company's history. I'll then ⁵m_____ on to ⁶re_____ its recent performance before ⁷hi_____ some of the current threats to growth and future opportunities. Finally, I'll ⁸t_____ a bit about how I see the company developing in the future.

7 Complete the sentences using the correct form of the words.

1 The company currently has 300 _____ (employ).

2 The report makes several _____ (recommend) on six key areas.

3 It's very _____ (reward) working with children.

4 Working in market research was fun to begin with, but the _____ (novel) soon wore off.

5 They spent a small fortune on their wedding _____ (receive).

6 I have to give a _____ (present) at the annual meeting. I'm so nervous!

7 It's ridiculous. She was made redundant only three months after they gave her a _____ (promote).

11

Travel and transport

IN THIS UNIT, YOU:

- roleplay a conversation to rent a car
- share and rate recommendations of travel media
- discuss your feelings about driving and transport

SPEAKING

1 **Work in pairs. Discuss the questions.**

1 Have you ever been on this type of transport? If yes, when and where? What was it like?

2 If not, would you like to? Why? / Why not?

2 **Work with a new partner. Discuss the questions.**

1 What's your favourite and / or least favourite way of travelling? Why?

2 What do you think would be good or bad about these kinds of travel?

- a guided coach tour
- mountain biking
- a sailing trip
- a trek by camel / horse
- hitchhiking
- a river cruise
- touring on a rail pass
- walking / backpacking

3 Which of the different types of travel have you – or people you know – tried? When? What were they like?

The Schwebahn floating tram in Wuppertal, Germany.

On the road

IN THIS LESSON, YOU:
- roleplay a conversation to rent a car
- talk about problems with renting vehicles
- practise listening to conversations with a rental firm
- express surprise and shock

VOCABULARY
Problems when renting

1 Complete the sentences with these nouns. Write one collocation for each noun.

brakes	chain	dent	deposit	engine
gears	insurance	small print	tank	tyre

1 They tried to sell us _____ to cover any damage to the windscreen or tyres.

2 The _____ cut out suddenly and we were drifting out to sea when they came to rescue us.

3 The _____ were very stiff and difficult to change. I kept putting it into third instead of fifth.

4 We started with a full _____ , but it obviously had a leak because we ran out of petrol quite quickly.

5 It took quite a few goes to get it started and the _____ were a bit dodgy. It's lucky we couldn't go that fast, especially with two of us on it.

6 I hit a rock going down the path and it bent the front wheel and put a _____ in the frame when I fell.

7 I got a flat _____ and they hadn't given us a kit to repair it, so we had to call the rental place to come and bring us back.

8 I hadn't read the _____ and I found out there was a $500 excess which wasn't covered by the insurance.

9 They weren't very well-maintained. The _____ was loose on mine and kept coming off.

10 They refused to return our _____ . They were pointing to a dent in the board and something to do with the sail, but I didn't really understand.

2 **P** ▶ Listen to the collocations from Exercise 1 and practise saying them. Which words / phrases do you find hard to say? Practise saying them again.

3 Work in pairs. Answer the questions.

1 What do you think was rented in each sentence in Exercise 1?

2 Use a dictionary to find one more collocation for each noun.

travel insurance / claim something on insurance / comprehensive insurance

3 Choose six collocations that you would be most likely to use and explain why.

4 Work in groups. Discuss the questions.

1 What things have you rented?

2 Have you ever had any of the problems in Exercise 1?

LISTENING

5 Work in small groups. Imagine you or your family wanted to rent a car. Discuss whether these features would be really important (***), quite important, but not essential (**) or not very important (*).

1 It's automatic.

2 It has a GPS / sat nav.

3 It's fuel-efficient.

4 It's diesel.

5 The insurance covers everything.

6 It has a great sound system.

7 You get unlimited mileage.

8 There's plenty of room in the boot.

6 ▶ Listen to a conversation in a car rental office. Which of the features in Exercise 5 apply to the car the man hires?

7 ▶ Work in pairs. Are the sentences true (T) or false (F)? Listen again and check.

1 The man is deciding whether to rent a car with this company or not.

2 He doesn't want an upgrade because of the cost.

3 He's supposed to return the car with an empty tank.

4 He can drive as far as he likes without extra charge.

5 There's some slight damage to the car.

8 ▶ Listen to a man calling a car rental office. Answer the questions.

1 What's the problem with the car the man has rented?

2 How does he feel about the proposed solution?

DEVELOPING CONVERSATIONS

Expressing surprise or shock

When we are surprised, shocked or annoyed by what we are told, we often repeat the information as a question and then add another question or comment.

A: *We guarantee they'll be with you within four hours.*

B: **Four hours?** *Is that really the quickest someone can get here?*

A: *I'll be able to come and look at your car next Wednesday.*

B: **Next Wednesday?** *That's almost a week away!*

9 Look at the Developing conversations box. Write responses to the statements. Repeat surprising information as a question and then add another question or comment.

1 A: The taxi fare to your hotel will be €100.

   B: _____

2 A: The cheapest ticket we have left is $875.

   B: _____

3 A: Our flight leaves at five in the morning.

   B: _____

4 A: It's a bit old, but it's a nice car! I could let you have it for £3,500.

   B: _____

5 A: If you just wait at the station, I should be able to get there within an hour or two.

   B: _____

6 A: I'm afraid the contract does state that there's a €50 penalty if you return the car more than an hour late.

   B: _____

10 ▶ **Listen and compare your answers. How similar are they?**

11 Work in pairs. Practise reading the conversations in Exercise 9 using your own extra questions and comments. Continue each conversation for as long as you can.

CONVERSATION PRACTICE

12 Work in pairs. You are going to roleplay a conversation in a car rental office. Find your information and plan some of the things you will say. Then have the conversation.

Student A: Look at File 8 on page 195.

Student B: Look at File 20 on page 199.

13 Roleplay a second telephone conversation. Use some of the language from the box and these details.

Student A: Phone Right Car Rentals and report a problem. Decide if you are happy with B's response.

Student B: Listen to Student A. Deal with the problem however you want to.

> *I wonder if you can help me.*
>
> *I'm calling because we have a problem with the car we're renting from you.*
>
> *I'm so sorry to hear that.*
>
> *I'm not sure we'll be able to help you, I'm afraid.*
>
> *I'm sorry, but I don't think that's acceptable.*
>
> *That's the best we can do, I'm afraid.*

Travelling life

IN THIS LESSON, YOU:
- share and rate recommendations of travel media
- discuss attitudes to travel and travel experiences
- practise understanding collocations / phrases in context
- practise describing length, age, cost, etc. of journeys and places

SPEAKING

1 Read the introduction to a blog post. Work in pairs. Discuss if you or anyone you know:

- have the travel bug.
- love comic books like *Tintin*.
- like geography and maps.
- enjoy watching, reading or hearing travel stories.

READING

2 Work in two pairs within a group of four. Read the recommendations made by the writer of the blog and decide if you'd like to watch / listen to / read each one.

Pair A: Read the recommendations on page 111.

Pair B: Read the recommendations in File 9 on page 195.

3 With your partner, check you understand the collocations in bold. Discuss which recommendation sounded most interesting and why.

4 **M** Change partners and work with a student from the other pair.

- Summarize the recommendations you read and agree on which three recommendations you think are best.
- Tell each other if you know any other good films, books or podcasts about travel.

5 Work with the same partner. Complete the collocations in bold from the recommendations. Use one word in each gap.

1 What's better, having a **clear** _____ or wandering where you fancy?

2 What might be good about travelling on **a** _____ **budget**?

3 Do you know anyone who's **dropped everything** to _____ on a new life?

4 Have you ever found yourself in **a tight** _____ ? How did you get out of it?

5 Have you ever been _____ **for a prize or won an award**?

6 Where would you go to see **stunning** _____ in your country?

7 Have you ever had an experience that **opened your** _____ or **made you** _____ **what's important**?

8 Have you ever _____ **great hospitality** on a trip?

9 What **difficulties** have you had to _____ – while travelling or in life?

6 Work in groups. Choose five questions from Exercise 5 to discuss with your partner.

GRAMMAR

Compound adjectives

We sometimes turn phrases into adjectives which can be used in longer, more complex sentences.

The path goes along the coast for a long distance.
a long-distance *coastal path*

The Appian Way was built 2,300 years ago.
the **2,300-year-old** *Appian Way*

He is a travel writer who has won an award.
an award-winning *travel writer*

7 Look at the examples in the Grammar box. Then correct the mistakes in these sentences.

1 I bought a third class train ticket.

2 It was a 3,000-kilometres round trip.

3 It's a Spanish-spoken country.

8 Rewrite these sentences using two adjectives. At least one should be a compound adjective.

1 Angkor Wat is a temple in Cambodia built 900 years ago.
Angkor Wat is a _____ temple.

2 We went on a trip round the world for six months.
We went on a _____ trip.

3 We were stuck in traffic which was moving slowly in a line that didn't seem to end.
We were stuck in a _____ line of _____ traffic.

4 The Burj Al Arab Jumeirah hotel has five stars and is a luxury hotel.
The Burj Al Arab Jumeirah is a _____ hotel.

5 We rented a flat with three bedrooms in the city centre.
We rented a _____ flat.

9 Make a list of different journeys you make / have made using compound adjectives.

a five-minute walk   *a five-hour flight*
a half-hour bus ride   *a seven-week trip*

10 Work in pairs. Compare your lists and ask questions about the different journeys to find out more.

G See Grammar reference 11B.

SPEAKING

11 Work in pairs. Say what you think of these quotes. Explain your opinions.

'Travelling – it leaves you speechless and then turns you into a storyteller.' attributed to Ibn Battuta

'Take only memories, leave only footprints.' attributed to Chief Seattle

'Wherever you go becomes a part of you somehow.' Anita Desai

TRAVELLING
from your sofa

I think I caught the travel bug before I even had the capability of catching a bus on my own, let alone hitching a ride. At the age of seven, I first came across other worlds through an old copy of *The Adventures of Tintin*. I would look up the places from the stories in an old atlas my parents had, and this then developed into a fascination — some would say obsession — with maps of all sorts. I'd spend hours planning different routes crossing continents and wondering if there was some kid like me in these distant cities, doing the same as me … with their mother also telling them to get their head out of a book and go outside and get some exercise. Now I am older, I have been lucky enough to fulfil some of those early dreams, but between trips I am constantly creating new dreams and finding inspiration from a host of films, books, blogs and podcasts. Here are some of my latest recommendations.

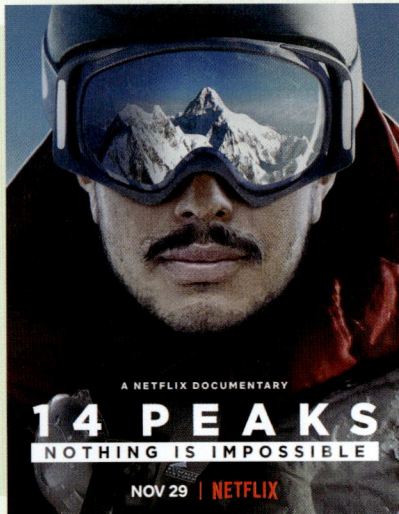

14 Peaks

I have to admit I love mountaineering films. Apart from the **stunning scenery** and the daring people they feature, I think it's maybe because I'm just a bit too scared to do what they do. *14 Peaks* is about a team of Sherpas, led by the inspirational Nirmal Purja, who **embark on the seemingly impossible challenge** of reaching the summit of all fourteen of the world's 8,000-metre mountains in just seven months. Just as a comparison, the record at the time they started the attempt was just under eight *years*. Apart from the excitement of the climbing and the race to complete the record, the film offers some **interesting insights** into the relationship between Sherpa people and the wealthy western climbing teams that they usually work for.

The Salt Path

Raynor Winn's is an uplifting book about how travel can provide a purpose and restore hope. The book starts with her life crashing down as she and her husband, Moth, find themselves bankrupt and homeless, just as they discover that Moth has been diagnosed with a terminal disease. In the face of these difficulties, they choose to embark on a 630-mile **hike along a coastal path** in south-west Britain, camping wild and living off a meagre 48-pound-a-week unemployment benefit. Through the twists and turns of their long-distance walk, the couple connect with nature and **re-evaluate what's important** in their lives. The book **was shortlisted for a major prize** in the UK.

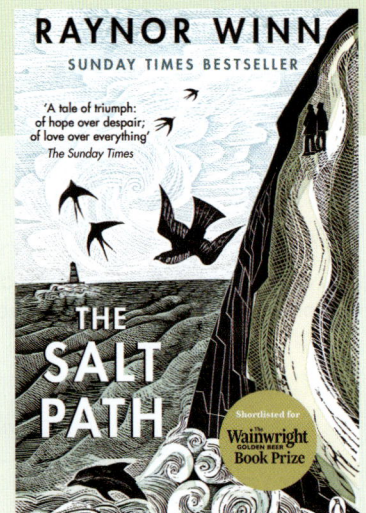

Overheard

The weekly podcast from National Geographic is **an eclectic mix** of science, the arts, exploration, the environment and of course travel. Recent episodes looked at restoring a man's arm and sense of touch; an interview with Jessica Nabongo, the first black woman to visit every country on Earth; efforts to turn the industrial city of Pittsburgh green and a walk down the 2,300-year-old Appian Way in Italy. From time to time it also includes some odd stories, such as an episode from 2020 about a travelling circus from Guatemala which **gets stranded** in Honduras because of the pandemic restrictions. The podcast tells the story of how they managed to **get out of the tight corner** they were in and make it back home.

What drives me mad

VOCABULARY Driving

1 Match the verbs (1–10) with the groups of words (a–j).

1	drive	a	a red light
2	flash	b	by a car coming off the motorway
3	overtake	c	really close behind you
4	get cut up	d	your lights
5	go through	e	the car in front
6	run over	f	20 mph over the speed limit
7	swear	g	a guy crossing the road
8	lose	h	to avoid hitting the dog
9	do	i	your licence
10	swerve	j	at the other driver

2 Work in pairs. Discuss what might be the reasons for and / or results of the ten actions in Exercise 1.

LISTENING

3 FS ▶ Listen and read the phrases. Do you hear the word *that* added at any point? Where?

1 the flat we were staying in
2 What annoyed me was the only
3 They said I could appeal
4 The thing I find most difficult is
5 but to be fair I think even that was
6 What annoys me is the fact I have
7 Riders seem to think rules

4 ▶ Listen to five speakers. Choose from the list (a–f) what had recently happened to each speaker. There is one statement you do not need.

a passed a driving test
b nearly got hit by someone
c had a mechanical breakdown
d broke the law while driving
e got a penalty for parking
f had an accident

5 ▶ Listen again. Choose from the list (a–f) what each speaker complains about. There is one topic you do not need.

a the poor quality of roads
b attitudes of other drivers
c worrying too much about something
d the amount of roadworks
e other road users causing danger
f signs not being clear enough

GRAMMAR

Emphatic structures

In English, we sometimes change the order of words in a sentence to emphasize how we feel.

a *The only sign warning that there was a market was 60 metres away, which was really annoying.*

b ***What*** *annoyed me* ***was (the fact) that*** *the only sign warning there was a market was 60 metres away.*

c ***The thing*** *I found annoying* ***was that*** *the only sign warning there was a market was 60 metres away.*

6 Look at the examples in the Grammar box. Work in pairs. Discuss the questions.

1 Which two sentences emphasize how you feel?
2 In your language, can these sentences be constructed in the same way?

7 Complete the sentences with these pairs of words.

annoys / the number	concerns / the amount	
drives / the whole	find / sitting	hate / the fact
gets on / parking	scares / the way	's / how

1 What _____ my nerves is people _____ on the pavement so you can't walk past.
2 The thing that _____ me is _____ some people swerve in and out of the lanes.
3 What I _____ the most boring is _____ in traffic jams all morning.
4 The thing that _____ me the most is _____ of pollution there is in the city centre.
5 What _____ incredible is _____ some men can still believe that women aren't good drivers.
6 What _____ me is _____ of speed cameras there are.
7 What _____ me mad is _____ one-way system and the lack of signposting.
8 What I really _____ is _____ that so much money is spent on cars.

G See Grammar reference 11C.

8 Write responses to the complaints in Exercise 7. Use these patterns. Then work in pairs. Take turns to say the complaints and reply.

I know. It's really …

I know. They should …

Really? That doesn't bother me. What (annoys me more) is …

Really? I don't mind that. I think …

A QUESTION OF TRANSPORT

1 **What stops people using public transport the most?**

   a the cost

   b the fact that it doesn't run frequently enough

   c the amount of crime you get on buses and trains

   d the fact that it's filthy and run-down

   e the fact that it's so crowded

2 **Which of these do you think is a real problem with transport?**

   a the shortage of parking spaces in the city centre

   b the lack of investment in cycle lanes and facilities

   c the fact that public transport is badly coordinated

   d the speed limits that are imposed on drivers

   e the sheer number of cars on the roads

3 **Which single thing would most improve your town or city?**

   a introducing a charge for vehicles to enter the centre of town

   b the introduction of stricter speed limits

   c reducing the number of bus stops

   d creating a new underground line

   e getting rid of all parking restrictions

4 **Which of these is the scariest?**

   a being in a car when the driver texts while they're driving

   b being in a car when the driver overtakes on a corner

   c being on a very bumpy flight

   d cycling in the city on a busy main road

   e being stuck in a tunnel on a train

5 **What bad driving habit do you find the most annoying?**

   a people sticking to the middle lane on the motorway

   b people driving too slowly

   c people not indicating before they pull out or turn

   d drivers not giving enough space to cyclists

   e drivers not stopping to let pedestrians cross the road when they're waiting at a crossing

6 **What do you like the best about train travel?**

   a the fact that you can work during the journey

   b the fact that you can relax and sleep

   c the amount of space you have

   d the fact that you get to meet new people

   e the fact that I hardly ever have to do it

7 **Which behaviour do you find the most strange?**

   a standing in the queue to board a plane an hour before it starts boarding

   b leaping up to get off the plane as soon as it lands

   c people wearing masks when cycling or walking to work

   d parents taking their kids to school by car

   e people taking cabs when there's perfectly good public transport available

8 **What concerns you the most?**

   a the amount of pollution caused by traffic

   b the number of accidents on the roads

   c the high rate of bicycle thefts

   d oil running out sometime in the not-too-distant future

   e the ever-increasing number of aeroplanes in the skies

SPEAKING TASK

9 Read the transport questionnaire and choose one answer for each question. Think of your reasons.

10 Work in groups of three. Find out more about your partners by discussing your choices.

11 Write one more possible answer to each of the questions in the questionnaire. Then share your ideas.

▮ MY OUTCOMES ▮

Work in pairs. Discuss the questions.

1 Which reading or listening texts were the most interesting, and why?

2 What useful phrases have you learned to talk about travel and transport?

3 What did you find new and hard to learn or use in this unit?

4 What do you most need to revise from this unit? How will you do that?

12
Health and medicine

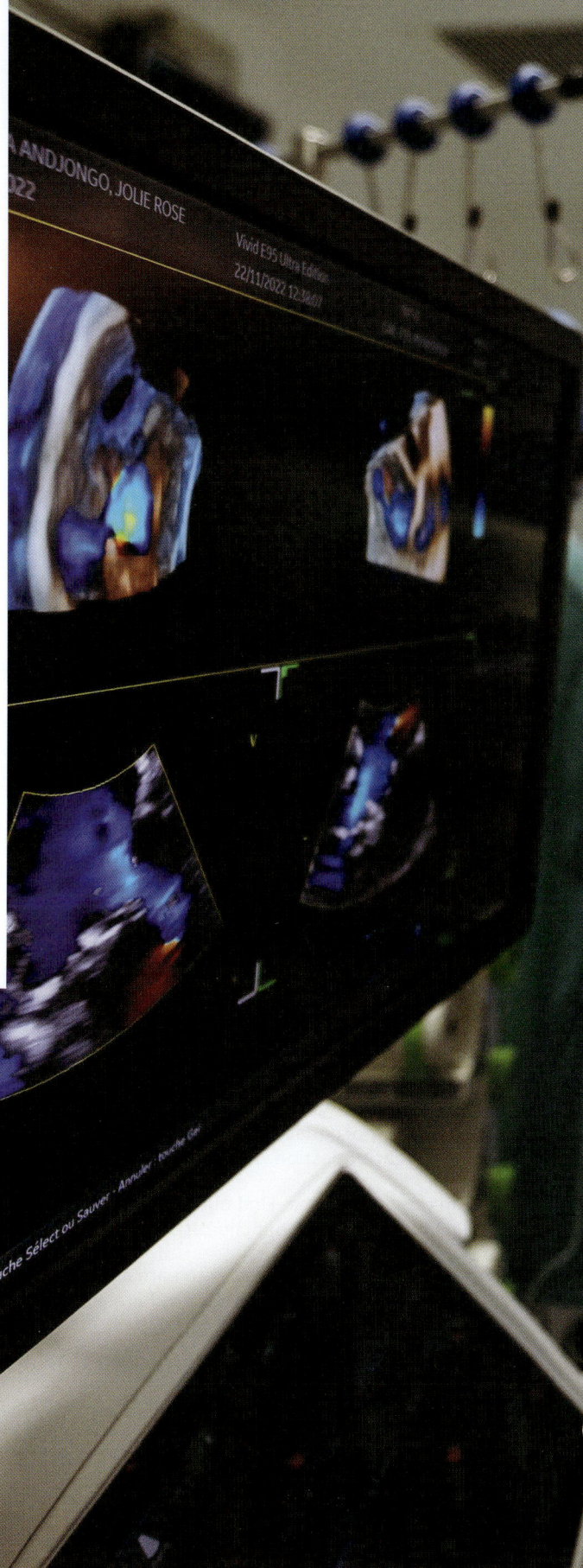

IN THIS UNIT, YOU:

- explain a health problem and sympathize
- discuss the connections between humour and health
- share opinions on medical tourism

SPEAKING

1 Work in pairs. Discuss the questions.

1 What kind of skills and character do you need to be a heart surgeon?

2 What do you know about the process of becoming a surgeon? How difficult is it?

3 Do you know anyone who works in medicine? What exactly do they do? Do they enjoy it? Why? / Why not?

2 Change partners. Discuss the questions.

1 When was the last time you were ill?

2 What symptoms did you have?

3 What did you do to get better?

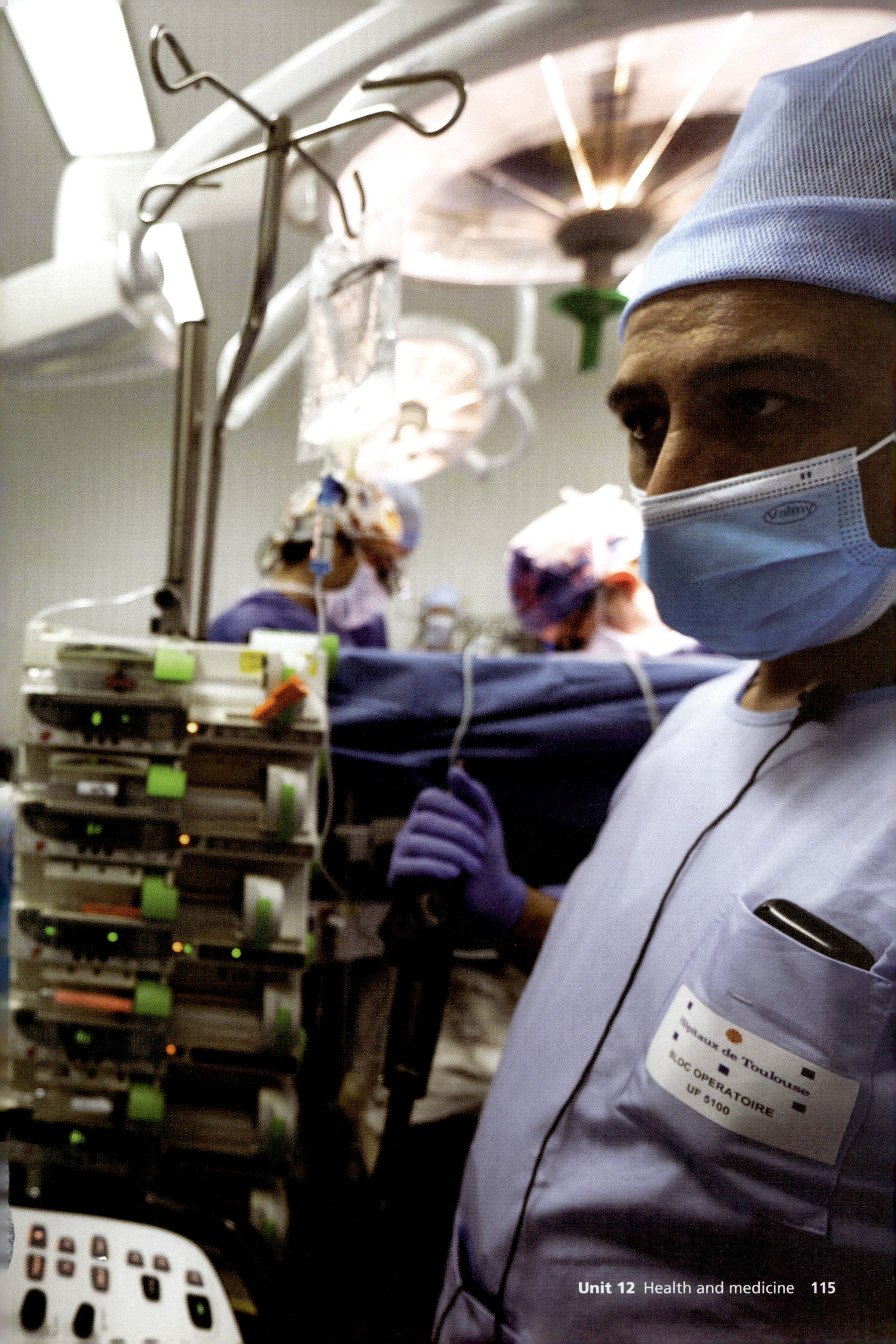
Valmy
Hôpitaux de Toulouse
BLOC OPERATOIRE
UF 5100

I feel awful

IN THIS LESSON, YOU:
- explain a health problem and sympathize
- practise listening to people explaining why they can't make a meeting
- practise passing on sympathetic messages
- practise explaining changed plans

VOCABULARY Health problems

1 Complete the descriptions of health problems with these words.

burned out	chronic	an inhaler	panic
physiotherapy	poisoning	rough	runny
therapist	tight	toss	violent

1 I'm pretty sure it was food _____ . When I got home I felt a bit _____ and then I suddenly threw up and was up the rest of the night, which wasn't very pleasant.

2 He has a lot of allergies. Sometimes it just causes a _____ nose or a nasty rash, but he's also had some more _____ reactions where his face swelled up, which was very scary.

3 She suffers from _____ back pain. She has regular _____ , but she still has to take quite strong painkillers to manage the pain.

4 He suffers from anxiety and sometimes gets _____ attacks. It's partly because of stress but he's also seeing a _____ to talk through some other issues.

5 I have so many things I'm trying to deal with in my life. I can't switch off when I go to bed and then I _____ and turn all night. I feel completely _____ .

6 I suffer from asthma. Using _____ manages it most of the time, but I had an attack recently when my chest felt so _____ I was struggling to breathe, which was quite frightening.

2 **P** ▶ Listen to the phrases from Exercise 1 and practise saying them. Which phrases do you find hard to say? Practise saying them again.

3 Work in pairs. Choose and discuss three sets of questions.

1 Do you know anyone who has an allergy? What to? What reaction do they have?

2 Do you know anyone with a chronic condition like asthma or back pain? How bad is it? How do they manage it?

3 Do you know anyone who has had stress-related health problems? Why? What happened?

4 Do you know anyone who's had any kind of therapy? What for? Was it helpful?

5 Do you know anyone who's had food poisoning? When? What happened?

LISTENING

4 ▶ Listen to two telephone conversations. Answer the questions.

1 Why are the people phoning?

2 What health problems have the speakers' partners had?

5 ▶ Listen again. Are the sentences true (T) or false (F)?

Conversation 1

1 Yusuf's girlfriend, Katie, passed out earlier.

2 She's not been sleeping well.

3 Katie is seeing a therapist.

4 Michelle gives Yusuf some advice.

Conversation 2

5 It was an allergy they knew about before.

6 They had to call an ambulance.

7 Lachlan will stay in hospital until tomorrow.

8 Nina is annoyed they'll miss the concert.

6 Work in pairs. Discuss the questions.

1 Which problem sounds worse to you – Katie's or Lachlan's? Why?

2 What advice would you give each of them?

3 Have you ever missed something important or nice because of illness or an accident? What happened?

GRAMMAR

Positive expectations and changed plans

We often use *be meant to / be supposed to* and *should(n't) / ought to* + verb to talk about plans and expectations.

a We**'re meant to be going** away for a few days next week.

b I**'m supposed to be coming** to the concert tonight.

c It **shouldn't be** too late.

d We **ought to get** to yours by lunchtime.

7 Look at the examples in the Grammar box. Then work in pairs. Discuss these questions.

1 Which two sentences talk about something that has already been organized, but which the speakers may not be able to do?

2 Which two sentences contain the meaning *I (don't) expect + will*? Are they being positive about the future or negative?

G See Grammar reference 12A.

8 Complete the sentences (1–6) with a verb or phrase from the Grammar box and the verb in brackets.

1 The medicine the doctor gave me is working really well, so I _____ (be) back at work soon.

2 I _____ (meet) a friend later, but I think I'm just going to go home to bed. I feel really rough.

3 It might feel a bit sore for a while, but it _____ (hurt) too much.

4 He _____ (have) the operation next week, but they're not sure if the hospital will have a bed for him, in which case they'll need to delay it.

5 Apparently, it's not a bad break so it _____ (take) long to heal. Hopefully, she'll only be on crutches for a few weeks.

6 I _____ (go) to a concert tonight, but I'm feeling a bit burned out. You don't want to buy my ticket, do you? It _____ (be) really good! They're a great band.

9 Change partners. Tell each other about:

- something you're supposed to be doing sometime soon, but might cancel.
- something that's supposed to be happening sometime soon, but might not.
- something happening soon that you think should be good.
- something you're doing soon that shouldn't be too hard / shouldn't take too long.

DEVELOPING CONVERSATIONS

Passing on messages

In the first conversation, Michelle showed sympathy for Yusuf's girlfriend, Katie, like this:

Tell her there's no need to apologize and I understand.

Send her my love and **tell her** I'm thinking of her.

We use imperatives to ask people to pass on messages like this to be more polite.

10 Look at the Developing conversations box. Write the words (1–8) in the correct order to make messages.

1 best / them / regards / give / my

2 me / her / a / hug / give / from

3 coming / them / not / apologies / give / for / my

4 thinking / tell / say / I'm / hi / and / of / them / them

5 tell / not / love / her / send / worry / my / and / to / her

6 to / tell / soon / him / better / it / take / and / get / easy

7 himself / need / there's / tell / him / apologize / to / look / and / after / no / to

8 give / tell / the / baby / my / them / wait / and / them / can't / congratulations / I / to / see

11 Are there any messages in Exercise 10 that you don't like or would feel uncomfortable saying? Why?

CONVERSATION PRACTICE

12 Roleplay the conversation. Follow this guide. Continue as long as you can. Then swap roles.

Student A	Student B
Explain that a friend / family member is ill, so you can't … (*I'm just ringing to let you know we're not going to make it to … because …*)	
	Show concern. Ask more about the problem. (*Oh dear! What's up? / that's terrible! Is she all right now?*)
Give some more details.	
	Comment / ask further questions. (*That sounds awful. How did it happen? / Poor thing! When did it begin?*)
Respond	
	Pass on message and end conversation. (*Well, give him a hug from me and tell him to get better soon.*)

A dose of humour

IN THIS LESSON, YOU:
- discuss the connections between humour and health
- identify evidence for statements in an article about humour and health
- explain other research you have read or heard about
- practise telling jokes connected to medicine

READING

1 Work in pairs. Look at the photo and discuss the questions.

1 What is happening? Why?
2 Have you heard of or seen anything similar?
3 What effects might laughter or a sense of humour have on health? Why?

2 Read the article as quickly as you can. Is the author writing the article to criticize or support clowns in hospitals?

3 Read the article again. Which of the following does research show, according to the article?

1 Children don't want to be visited by clowns in hospital.
2 People who hadn't watched a comedy movie needed more painkillers after their operation.
3 People with a sense of humour had a longer life expectancy.
4 People don't get a positive effect from humour if they don't actually laugh.
5 Doctors tell jokes to each other in stressful situations.
6 Doctors don't talk to their patients enough.
7 You can inherit a sense of humour.
8 Doctors make patients laugh more after they have done a course.

4 Work in pairs. Choose four sets of questions to discuss.

1 Why do you think people have a fear of clowns? Do you have any fears?
2 Why do you think it's important that patients choose their comedy movie for it to help with pain relief? What would you choose?
3 Why might the kind of jokes doctors may tell each other not be appropriate for their patients? Do you speak differently to different groups of people? How?
4 Why might it be important for doctors and nurses to use humour? What health professionals have you talked to? What were they like?
5 Do you think all humour is healthy? Why? / Why not?
6 How do you think you can learn to be funnier? Do you make people laugh much? How?

5 Work in pairs. Check you understand the words in bold in the article and use some of them to complete the sentences. Use one or two words in each gap.

1 Over 25% of those who were _____ stated they had suffered stress-related conditions.
2 The study showed that financial literacy is essential if the financial system is to be run effectively, which in _____ would have a positive effect on the economy as a whole.
3 The study provided _____ that laughing has a positive _____ on productivity at work.
4 The study _____ how nurses interacted with patients on hospital wards.
5 The research _____ that much back pain was, in fact, the result of an infection in the spine.
6 The survey was _____ over the phone with people from 26 countries.
7 The study appears to _____ what researchers had long suspected: ape and human laughter share a common origin.
8 The study stresses _____ of green space for feelings of well-being.

6 Work in pairs. Tell a partner about any research you have heard reported in the news recently.

SPEAKING

7 Read this joke to yourself. Follow the stresses and pauses that are marked. Guess how the joke might end.

A man goes to a **doctor** // and **says**, // 'Doc. // I think there's something **wrong** with me. // Every time I **poke** myself // it **hurts**. // **Look**!' // And he starts **poking** himself. // He pokes himself in the **leg**. // '**Ouch**!' // He pokes himself in the **ribs**. // '**Aagh**!' // He pokes himself in the **head** // and he literally **screams** in agony. // '**Aaaaagh**! // You **see** what I mean, Doc? // You see how **bad** it is? // What's **happening** to me?'// And the doctor **replies**, // 'Yes …

8 Tell a partner the joke with your ending.

9 ▶ Listen. Find out the actual ending.

10 Work in groups of three. Find your information, read the jokes and choose your favourite.

Student A: Look at File 10 on page 195.
Student B: Look at File 21 on page 199.
Student C: Look at File 15 on page 197.

11 Prepare your favourite joke. Mark the words that are grouped together and those that are stressed. Practise saying the joke quietly to yourself.

12 Take turns to tell your jokes. Use actions if you think they will help.

JUST CLOWNING AROUND

A clown working with children in a hospital.

Gene Clark discovers hospital entertainers still have a role to play.

Hospitals can naturally be difficult places to be, filled as they are by stress, illness and alarms ringing. In an attempt to provide a more positive environment, many children's hospitals have painted pictures of clowns and cartoon figures on the walls. However, a survey **conducted among** 250 children revealed that they would all prefer not to see the wards decorated with clowns' faces. While the children liked the bright colours, even some of the teenagers **who were questioned** found the faces 'scary'. Fear of clowns is, in fact, quite a common phenomenon and can provoke sweating, shortness of breath and panic attacks – hardly the reaction the hospitals were after!

These findings might also lead us to **question the value of** real-life clowns working in hospitals, which has been an increasingly common practice all over the world. However, Pau Pujol, a hospital clown from Barcelona, explains that 'most clowns in hospitals don't use the traditional heavy make-up because we're aware it can scare kids. We're only about magic and joy and contributing to the recovery of patients.'

There is certainly **some evidence that** humour can **have a positive impact on** health. One study has found that patients with a good sense of humour had better outcomes in cases of kidney failure. Another found that patients who had watched a comedy film of their choice following an operation required substantially less pain medication afterwards than a **control group**.

Exactly why that is is not entirely clear. The act of laughter is known to release chemicals in the brain, which reduce stress as well as exercise the lungs and muscles. However, a Norwegian study, which showed how a sense of humour reduces mortality up to retirement age, **stresses that** laughter is not always necessary for humour to work. The **lead researcher**, Sven Svebak, says 'Commonly, people with the same sense of humour tend to enjoy themselves together and can communicate humour without huge gestures. A twinkle in the eye can be more than enough.' He argues that humour builds stronger communities (and vice versa), **which in turn** leads to less insecurity and stress. And that seems to be backed up by **research which found** that humour is often used by doctors and nurses to reinforce their working relationships. It also enables them to cope with the stress of being surrounded by illness and death.

However, it seems that this use of humour doesn't extend to interactions with patients, where doctors apparently prefer to present a colder, more professional front. Some argue that this way of communicating **contributes to** a wider problem in modern health services. With new technology and drugs, the focus can be too much on technical solutions, and the importance of individual attention and warm, human contact in the healing process is sometimes lost. While clowns and comedy can obviously help to fill that gap, it is argued that the nurses and doctors themselves should use more humour in their daily interactions with patients.

But what if they are not 'naturally' funny? Is it something they can learn or are they born that way? A study that **looked at how** twins reacted to Gary Larson cartoons **showed that** a sense of humour wasn't genetic, but **was due to** environmental factors such as family and friends. Svebak's research seems to **confirm** this and he believes humour is learnable.

In fact, there are now a number of courses available for health professionals to improve their humour skills. Courses look at how to tell jokes and funny stories better, as well as how to notice opportunities for humour in everyday conversation or when it is best avoided. As Pau Pujol says, 'Clowning is a skill which you have to work on and scaring people is really a sign of inadequate training rather than a problem with the idea of clowns in hospitals.'

Foreign bodies

IN THIS LESSON, YOU:
- share opinions on medical tourism
- talk about different medical procedures
- practise listening to a discussion on medical tourism and identifying opinions
- practise emphasizing important facts in a discussion

VOCABULARY
Parts of the body and operations

1 Label the picture with these words.

brain	chest	elbow	hip	kidney	knee
liver	lung	rib	spine	toenail	wrist

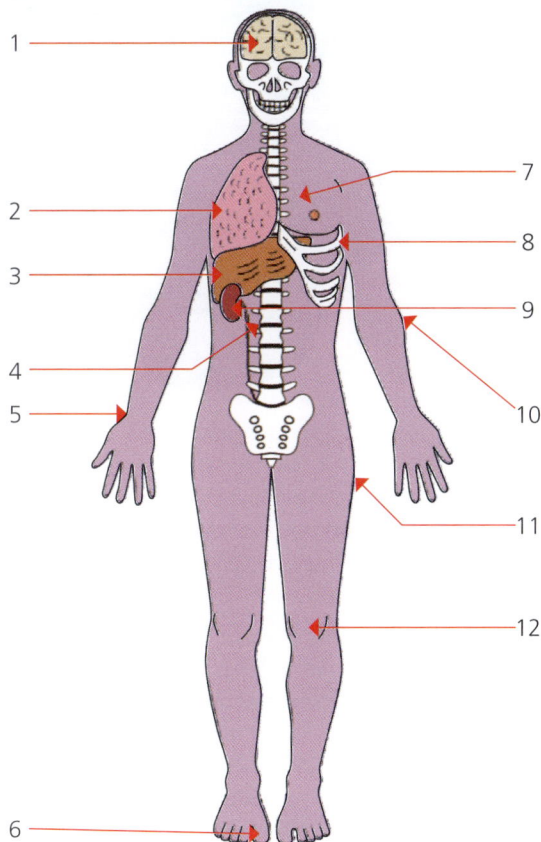

2 Work in pairs. Which parts of the body from Exercise 1 could these sentences be about?

1 It was badly broken and she had to have an operation to **put a pin in it**.

2 In the end the only option was to **have a transplant**.

3 It was causing him a lot of pain, so he had an operation to **replace it**.

4 She had major surgery to **remove the tumour**.

5 He **tore a ligament** and he had to have an operation to sort it out.

6 It was **a minor operation**. She was only in hospital for the day.

3 Do you know anyone who has had an operation on any of the parts of the body in Exercise 1? Tell your partner.

LISTENING

4 Read the Fact File about medical tourism. Do you find each fact interesting, surprising, shocking or unsurprising? Explain why.

FACT FILE

Canada is the top medical tourism destination, according to the Medical Tourism Index.

Singapore receives 500,000 medical tourists a year – half of whom come from Indonesia.

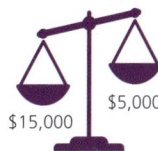

Some cosmetic procedures that cost $15,000 in the US only cost $5,000 in Spain.

$15,000 $5,000

India's government has introduced special visas to make it easier for people to visit for medical treatment.

VISA

Budapest, Hungary, claims to be the dental capital of Europe, attracting large numbers of German and Austrian clients.

5 ▶ Listen to the introduction to a radio programme about medical tourism. Complete the notes using between one and three words in each gap.

1 Following the 2020 pandemic, medical tourism is expected _____ .

2 People have to wait a lot longer for _____ like hip replacements.

3 Unsurprisingly, people are choosing _____ .

4 Destinations for medical tourism combine affordable _____ with great _____ .

5 Medical tourism may include _____ treatment or having _____ .

6 FS ► Adverbs like *personally* often get reduced in fast speech. Listen to eleven extracts and write the adverb you hear.

7 ► Work in groups. Discuss the questions. Then listen and find out what the speakers say.

1 What problems do you think might be connected to medical tourism?

2 What do you think the different benefits might be?

3 Do you have any other questions you'd like answered?

8 ► Do these sentences reflect the opinions of Karl (K), Ila (I) or Pepa (P)? Some may apply to more than one person. Listen again and check.

1 You should stick to providers with a good reputation.

2 Medical tourists can catch unexpected illnesses.

3 Most medical tourists don't travel very far away.

4 It can be difficult to get complaints resolved.

5 Medical tourism won't improve healthcare for everyone.

6 Countries like India are losing qualified medical staff to wealthier nations.

7 If people don't have money, they can get help.

9 Work in groups. Discuss two sets of questions.

1 Do you know if there's much medical tourism in your country? What do you think about it?

2 Would you ever go abroad for treatment? Why? / Why not? Do you know anyone who has been? How did it go?

3 Have you heard any stories about operations going wrong? What happened? How easy is it to complain about medical services or sue hospitals?

GRAMMAR

Not only / Not just …

We often use *not only* / *not just* to show that two facts about a situation are important.

a *Many decide to go private – **not only** within their home countries, **but also** abroad.*

b *Medical tourism **isn't just** about minor operations, **it's also** about treating serious illness.*

We sometimes start the clause with *not only*.

c ***Not only do private hospitals take** doctors from the public sector, they also attract staff to big cities.*

d ***Not only was it** expensive, but the service was absolutely terrible.*

10 Look at the examples in the Grammar box and answer the questions.

1 In each sentence, which of the facts do you think is more expected / well known?

2 What linking words often appear in the second part of the sentence?

3 What happens to the word order when you start the clause / sentence with *Not only*?

11 Read the first sentence in each pair. Complete the second sentence so that it has a similar meaning.

1 There can be problems during any operation and during the recovery period.

There can be problems not just _____ .

2 Apart from the treatment, the hospital organizes all travel to and from your home.

The hospital not only _____ to and from your home.

3 The capital city has fantastic hospitals as well as the great tourist facilities we are familiar with.

The capital city not only _____ .

4 Having dental work done abroad was cheaper and I had a holiday as well.

Not only _____ had a holiday.

5 I had never had an operation before and on top of that it was my first time abroad.

Not only _____ .

G See Grammar reference 12C. ⟫

SPEAKING TASK

12 Work in pairs. Discuss whether you agree or disagree with each statement. Think about the situation in your country and the wider world.

1 It's inevitable that care will vary a lot between hospitals.

2 Doctors shouldn't be allowed to work in private hospitals if they didn't pay for their training.

3 Healthcare should be free to all users and paid for through taxes.

4 All medical staff should be paid more.

5 There are too many people suing hospitals and doctors.

6 Patients should always have a choice about how or where they are treated.

7 Medical tourism overall is a bad thing.

13 M Work in groups. Find three statements from Exercise 12 that you can all agree with and two that you all disagree with. Then explain what you chose to the class.

■ MY OUTCOMES ■

Work in pairs. Discuss the questions.

1 What speaking or writing activities did you find enjoyable?

2 In what new ways can you now talk about your health and health problems?

3 What vocabulary problems did you have with the reading or listening texts?

4 What will you do outside the classroom to revise language from this unit?

Reports

SPEAKING

1 Discuss the questions in groups.

1 How might a report differ from an essay, a brochure or a leaflet?

2 Have you ever taken part in a survey? What for? Do you know what the results were?

3 Have you heard of any government / company reports being published recently? What were their findings / conclusions?

4 Do you ever read or write reports for study / work? What on?

WRITING

2 Read the introduction to a report about public transport and car use and the list of its main findings. Discuss the questions in pairs.

1 What do you think the statistics would be if the report was about your city or area?

2 Considering the aim of the council, which of the statistics do you think is good news and which is bad? Why?

3 What action would you recommend to the council?

INTRODUCTION

The survey that led to this report was conducted with people in the Northsea area. It aimed to find out how people travelled and the reasons for their choices, with a view to the council developing policies to discourage car use.

Main findings:

- 75% use the car as their main form of transport.
- In the previous month, four out of five people had used some alternative – train, bus, bike, motorbike or (electric) taxi.
- 90% said they would be willing to use alternative transport to the car.
- 83% of journeys by public transport were by bus.
- Only one tenth of those surveyed felt public transport provision was good or very good.
- The main reasons cited for not using public transport were cost and inconvenience.

3 Read the summary of the findings and complete the text with these words.

examples	factor	favourably	interviewed
long	majority	mentioned	minority
rated	respondents	vast	widely

SUMMARY OF FINDINGS

While the findings of the survey showed that cars remain the main form of transport, there was some hope in the fact that there were high numbers of people willing to change. Only a small ¹_____ felt they would continue to use their car, no matter what.

Most ²_____ had used buses, and the ³_____ said they would use them more often if they were cheaper and more convenient. ⁴_____ of inconvenience that were ⁵_____ on numerous occasions were the lack of timetable information and buses running infrequently and failing to connect with other routes.

Even though bus travel actually compares ⁶_____ to car travel, cost-wise, the perception of the ⁷_____ majority of people ⁸_____ was that it was more expensive. Interestingly, those using the train ⁹_____ it highly, **despite** it being more expensive than the bus. This suggests comfort is also a ¹⁰_____ .

RECOMMENDATIONS

If the council is to encourage less car use, it clearly needs to develop bus services. It should improve timetabling and make information more ¹¹_____ available, for example through a website. In the short term, a campaign to raise awareness of the relative costs of buses and cars – as well as increasing parking fees in the centre – could help. **However**, to make a real difference, the council needs to invest in new buses in the ¹²_____ term to increase frequency and comfort.

Bus driving past the Tarell Valley, Wales, UK.

4 Work in pairs. Discuss the questions.

1 What extra information is included in the report outside the main findings of the survey?

2 Do you think the report gives a fair summary of the main findings? Why? / Why not?

3 Do you agree with the recommendations?

USEFUL LANGUAGE

While, despite, however, even though

Despite this can be used instead of *however*, and *despite the fact that* can be followed by a clause.

Despite the fact that *I told him not to, he took the car.*

However can come in the middle of a sentence as well as at the beginning.

Cars are expensive to run. There are, **however***, ways to save.*

5 Look at the words in bold in the report on page 122. Then discuss these questions in pairs.

1 Which word contrasts an idea with an idea in the previous sentence?

2 Which three words help to link two parts of a sentence?

3 Which word is followed by a noun / *-ing* form?

4 Where are the commas in the sentences with words in bold?

6 Choose all the correct options to complete the sentences. Cross out any incorrect options.

1 *While / Despite / Even though* student numbers fell this year, the school is confident it can grow in the future.

2 Most students were satisfied with their classes, *even though / despite / however* there was a lot of noise from ongoing repair work.

3 The school doesn't have enough resources. *However / While / Despite this*, the teachers do an excellent job.

4 Profits were down last year, *despite / however / even though* having more students.

7 Rewrite the sentences using the words in bold. The meaning should stay the same.

1 Despite the government investing in buses, most people still prefer to travel by car. **EVEN THOUGH**

2 While the cost of air travel to passengers has been falling, the cost to the environment has increased. **HOWEVER**

3 Most people rated the service as poor. However, the majority also praised the quality of the food. **WHILE**

4 Things have improved, but we're still struggling. **DESPITE**

Be to

In the report, you read:

If the council **is to encourage** *less car use, it clearly needs to develop bus services.*

be to + verb is often used in an *if*-clause to show a desired future result. Negatives are formed as *is not to* or *isn't to*. The main clause shows what must be done first, using *need / must / have to*, etc.

We **must do** *something now if the situation* **is not to** **deteriorate** *further.*

8 Look at the examples with *be to* and write sentences using these ideas.

1 the government / invest in green technology / meet their carbon targets

The government needs to invest in green technology if they are to meet their carbon targets.

2 the government / win the next election / change their policies now

3 we / improve our marketing / boost sales

4 we / reduce crime / increase the number of police

5 the company / reduce its debts / not go bankrupt

6 the council / build more cycle lanes / encourage more people to cycle to work

7 discourage waste / the government / introduce a tax on the amount of rubbish people throw away

PRACTICE

9 You are going to write a report on improving public health services in your area. First, complete the findings in the box with what you imagine the statistics are for your area.

> **MAIN FINDINGS**
>
> _____% of people use private instead of public health services.
>
> _____% visited their local hospital or clinic in the past year.
>
> _____% of those who saw a doctor required no treatment.
>
> _____% of medical conditions are due to lifestyle choices.
>
> _____% of respondents felt public health was good or very good.
>
> _____tenth(s) of people could get an appointment with their doctor within 48 hours.
>
> The main reasons for using private healthcare were _____ , _____ and _____ .

10 Work in pairs. Compare your statistics and discuss:

- which the worst statistics / trends are and which are good.

- what the cause of these statistics / trends might be and possible consequences if they get worse.

- how these aspects of the health service might be improved.

11 Write a report of 200–300 words (excluding the main findings above). Include:

- an introduction to the report to explain the survey and its purpose.

- a summary and analysis based on the statistics you wrote.

- a conclusion about how things could be improved.

12 When you have finished, give yourself a mark between 1 and 5 in the following categories.

- How easily can you follow the content of the report?

- Is it well organized?

- Does it summarize the statistics well?

- Does it have good recommendations?

- Does it use good language for a report?

13 Swap your work with another student and give their report a mark. Discuss the marks you gave each other. Do you agree?

VIDEO Out and about

1 **Work in pairs. Discuss the questions.**

1 When was the last time you were ill?

2 What symptoms did you have?

3 What did you do to get better?

Understanding accents

Some accents replace an /aɪ/ sound with /ɔɪ/, so *bye* /baɪ/ may sound like *boy* /bɔɪ/; *tie* /taɪ/ like *toy* /tɔɪ/; and *ply* /plaɪ/ more like *ploy* /plɔɪ/.

2 ▶ **Watch the video. Number the speakers' experiences from 6 (worst) to 1 (least bad). What do the people say?**

3 ▶ **Work in pairs. Match the statements with the speakers and explain your choices. You may match statements with more than one speaker. Then watch again to check.**

a It took me quite a while to recover.

b It was incredibly painful.

c I had to make new arrangements.

d I can't really remember the last time.

e I injured myself when I was out.

f I make a special drink which always helps.

g It didn't take long to get over it.

h I took a day off and lay down in the dark.

4 **Discuss these questions with your partner.**

1 Do you know anyone who is hardly ever ill? What's their secret?

2 Have you ever twisted your ankle / strained a muscle / done your back in?

3 Do you know anyone who suffers from migraines or another condition? Explain.

4 When was the last time you had to rearrange something? Why?

VIDEO Developing conversations

5 ▶ **You are going to hear two people talking about a problem on a journey. Watch and take notes on what they say.**

6 ▶ **Work in pairs. Compare what you understood. Watch again if you need to.**

7 **Discuss the questions with your partner.**

1 What other questions would you have asked the storyteller?

2 What would you have done in the situations the storyteller describes?

3 Have any of the situations in the story happened to you or someone you know? What happened?

8 FS ▶ **Watch again. Complete the sentences with three to five words in each gap.**

1 Hey _____ ?

2 I tried to call a garage but _____ .

3 How long _____ ?

4 It took me five hours to go back home. _____ ?

5 I had to call my landlord _____ a spare key.

6 Yeah _____ late already.

7 Oh no! _____ ! What did you do after?

8 Well, I hope _____ and the car.

CONVERSATION PRACTICE

9 **Work in pairs. You are going to practise a conversation.**

1 Choose a Conversation practice from either Lesson 11A or Lesson 12A.

2 Look at the language in that lesson.

3 Check the meaning of anything you've forgotten with your partner.

4 Have the conversation. Try to improve on the last time you did it.

Grammar and Vocabulary

GRAMMAR

1 Read the first sentence in each pair. Complete the second sentence so that it has a similar meaning. Use between three and five words, including the word in bold.

1 I can't believe how much some sports stars are paid.

What _____ that some sports stars are paid such unbelievable amounts of money! **ANNOY**

2 It really scares me, the way people still trust him and are happy to vote for him.

The thing that I _____ people will still vote for him, after everything he's done. **SCARY**

3 I've arranged to meet a friend later, but I could cancel.

I'm _____ a friend later, but I could always cancel. **SUPPOSED**

4 I expect everything will be fine.

There _____ problems. **SHOULD**

5 It's an expensive treatment and it doesn't really work.

As a treatment it's _____ it doesn't actually work very well. **ONLY**

6 They provide five-star accommodation and on top of that organize all transport.

_____ five-star accommodation, they also organize all transport. **NOT**

2 Choose the correct option to complete the sentences.

1 We stayed in a *three-stars* / *three-star* hotel.

2 Not only *it was* / *was it* cheap, but it was also very central.

3 *It* / *What* really annoys me that you can't leave negative feedback on their website.

4 There are plenty of *well-paid* / *well-paying* jobs in tourism, but few are all year round.

5 I ordered it yesterday, but the postal service is so slow! I bet *it'll* / *it should* take ages to arrive.

6 Shall we try and get there about six? *I shouldn't be* / *I'm not supposed to be* too busy then.

7 I can give you some *fast-acted* / *fast-acting* tablets to deal with the vomiting.

8 We stayed in a *400-year-old* / *400 years old* castle.

3 ▶ Listen. Write the six sentences you hear.

VOCABULARY

4 Match the verbs (1–10) that go with both collocates (a–j).

1	embark on	a	the tumour / a stain
2	get out of	b	the pain / asthma
3	manage	c	on a budget / light
4	remove	d	and turn / a coin
5	toss	e	a new life / a long journey
6	put	f	a therapist / a specialist
7	see	g	a tight corner / trouble
8	drop	h	a survey / a trial
9	conduct	i	it into gear / a dent in it
10	travel	j	everything / the subject

5 Decide if these words are connected to transport and travel or to health and medicine – and in what way.

the brakes	the chain	a chest	a condition
a hip	an itinerary	a kidney	physiotherapy
a reaction	scenery	a spine	a tank

6 Write at least one adjective or noun from the units that goes with each noun in Exercise 5.

a full tank, a kidney transplant

7 Complete the sentences with the correct prepositions.

1 He suffers _____ severe back pain.

2 I've been talking _____ some issues with a therapist.

3 There's evidence that exercise has a positive impact _____ mental health.

4 The research looked _____ how poor diet might contribute _____ burn out.

5 The swelling was due _____ an allergic reaction, which _____ turn led to difficulties in breathing.

6 They were driving _____ the speed limit and went _____ a red light.

8 Complete the story with one word in each gap. The first letters are given.

A few years ago I drove to a town at least ten hours from my home. It's quite dangerous, because the main road is quite narrow, but people often [1]d_____ at 120 kmh or more and are always trying to [2]o_____ – even if they're on a bend or there's a long line of cars in front of you. They will drive up really close [3]b_____ you and [4]f_____ their lights as if you are in their way. Sometimes you can even see them in the mirror [5]sw_____ at you. Then when they come past they suddenly [6]c_____ you up because they have to [7]s_____ to avoid a car coming in the opposite direction! I hate it, so on this occasion, I tried a different route. I was in the middle of nowhere and hit a big hole, getting a [8]f_____ tyre and some other damage. My phone had no coverage and I was completely [9]st_____ . It's the first time I'd ever [10]en_____ such a situation and I got a [11]p_____ a_____ . Luckily, a woman driver saw me and stopped. She calmed me down and phoned the emergency breakdown. Unfortunately, my insurance didn't [12]c_____ this kind of incident, but at least I survived!

13
Life-changing events

IN THIS UNIT, YOU:
- share news about people
- share good and bad advice
- discuss values and ideas that are important to you

SPEAKING

1 **Work in pairs. Discuss the questions.**

1 What do you think the cones are for? What do you think might happen at the ceremony?

2 How are kids introduced to school where you live? Are there any special processes or acts? What's good about how it's done?

3 What do you remember about your first days at school, work or university?

2 **Change partners. Make a list of eight other life-changing events. Discuss which you have already experienced and what you remember about them. Which changed you the most? Why?**

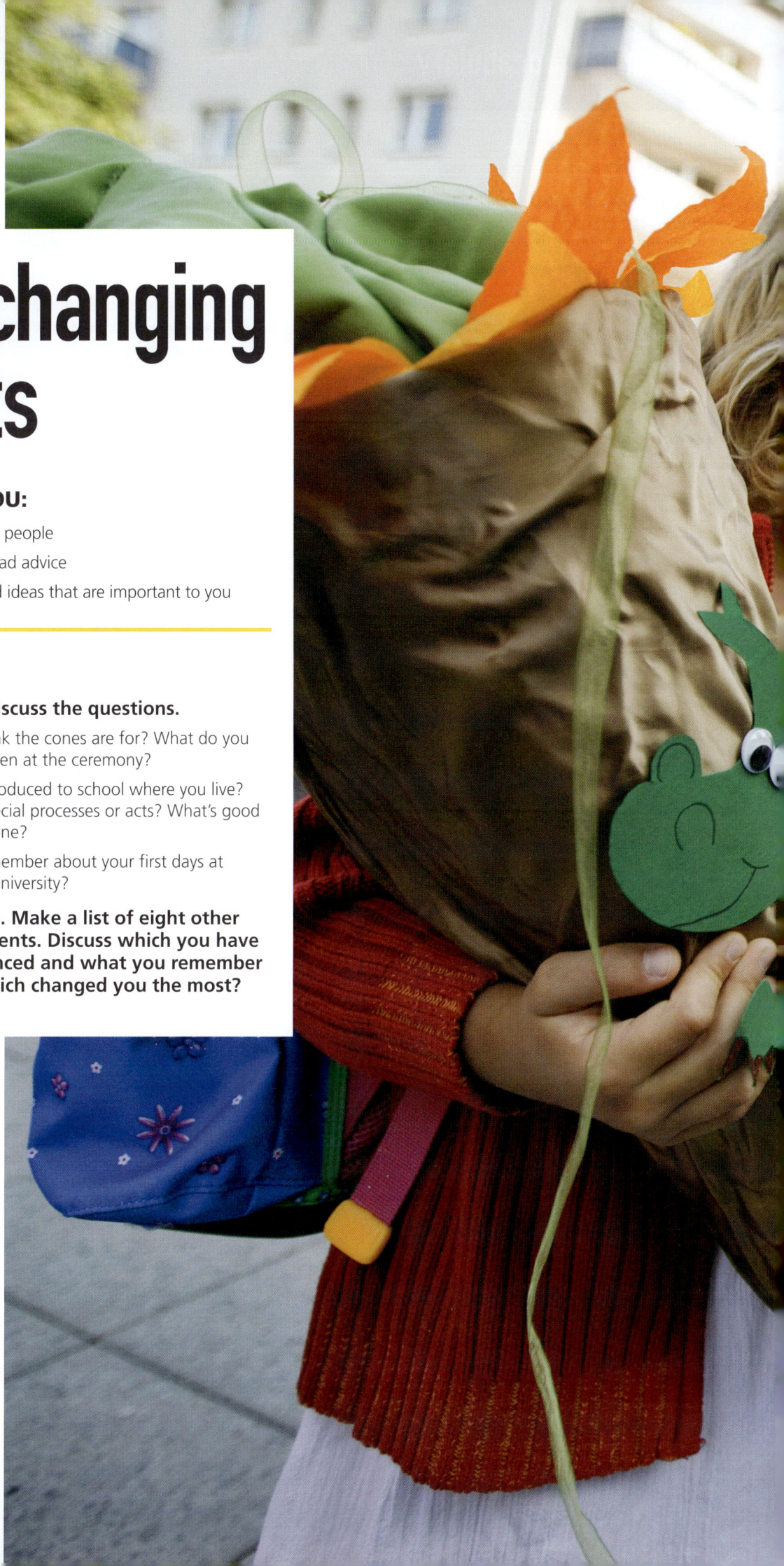

First graders hold their 'school cone' (Schultüte) as they wait for the enrolment ceremony for their first day at Merian school in Frankfurt am Main, Germany.

Life's a journey

IN THIS LESSON, YOU:
- share news about people
- describe major life events in some detail
- practise listening to conversations about big change in people's lives
- report information you're not 100% sure of

VOCABULARY Major life events

1 Complete the sentences with these pairs of words.

cheating on / straw	mortgage / interest
respects / funeral	graduation / dropped out
pregnancy / labour	vows / anniversary
groom / bride	

1 It had been quite an easy _____ but then I ended up being in _____ for almost 30 hours.

2 They decided to renew their _____ to mark their 20th _____ , which was very sweet.

3 He was buried last week. I went to pay my _____ before the _____ .

4 It's her _____ ceremony next month. It's amazing, really, because she almost _____ at the end of her first year.

5 We saved up for a deposit and then managed to find a good _____ that had a fixed _____ rate for the first five years.

6 He had to give a speech at the reception because the _____ was one of his oldest friends and he'd known the _____ for ages too.

7 She found out he was _____ her and I think that was the final _____ for her.

2 **P** ▶ Listen to the words from Exercise 1 in phrases and practise saying them. Which phrases do you find hard to say? Practise saying them again.

3 Work in pairs. Which major life events do you think are described in Exercise 1? Choose three of these events each and think of examples you have heard about. Take turns to say as much as you can about each one.

LISTENING

4 ▶ Listen to two conversations. Answer these questions for each conversation.

1 What major life events do they mention?

2 What caused each event?

5 ▶ Listen again. Decide which of these points are made.

1 It wouldn't have been that long until Kerry's graduation ceremony.

2 Kerry had talked about splitting up with her partner before.

3 They'd been together for quite some time.

4 Ollie and Leila had been seeing each other a couple of times a month.

5 Leila has quite a long commute into work.

6 Ollie might change careers if he can't get the kind of job he's looking for.

6 Work in groups. Discuss the questions.

1 What other reasons for dropping out of uni can you think of? Do you know anyone who has done this?

2 Why else might couples split up?

3 Do you know anyone who has been in a long-distance relationship? How did it work?

4 Would you ever consider moving to a different country for love? If not, why not?

5 Do you know anyone who's changed careers? From what to what? Why?

GRAMMAR

The past perfect simple and continuous

Past perfect forms emphasize that something happened before another past event which has already been mentioned.

A: *I was told he was doing well there.*

B: *He was, but he'd actually **been thinking** about leaving for a while.*

A: *So what brought that on?*

B: *As I understand it, she'd recently **split up** with her partner.*

7 Look at the examples in the Grammar box. Then work in pairs. Answer the questions.

1 Which of the structures in bold is the past perfect simple? Which is the past perfect continuous?

2 What is the form of each structure?

3 Which structure describes something that happened just once? And which describes something that happened over a period of time?

4 Which time expression shows the period of time?

8 ▶ Complete the sentences using the past perfect simple or continuous form of the verbs. Then listen and check your answers.

1 When I found out I _____ (win), I was speechless. I just couldn't believe it.

2 Apparently, they discovered she _____ (steal) money from them for months.

3 I suddenly realized I _____ (leave) the fire on, and by the time I got back to the house, the whole place was in flames.

4 She _____ (suffer) from the illness for some time, but she _____ (not tell) anyone about it.

5 He _____ (struggle) with the course for a while and in the end, he just decided he _____ (have) enough and dropped out.

G See Grammar reference 13A. »»»

9 Think of a response to each of these sentences using the past perfect simple or continuous. Then work in pairs. Take turns to ask the questions and give responses.

1 So why did your father decide to take up running?
2 But how come she didn't have any money?
3 What made them decide to move to Brazil?
4 How come he gave up playing basketball?
5 So how come you sold your flat?

DEVELOPING CONVERSATIONS

Showing uncertainty

We use lots of different expressions to show we are reporting information that we're not sure is true.

As I understand it, she'd recently split up with her partner.

Apparently, she's got a really good job there.

10 Look at the Developing conversations box. Complete the conversation using one word in each gap. The first letter is given for you.

A: Hey, did you hear about Gavin getting married?

B: Yeah. It was a bit sudden, wasn't it?

A: Exactly! As ¹f _____ as I know, they'd only been going out for five weeks!

B: Really? ²A _____ I understand it, they'd actually been at school together.

A: Right. Well, ³f _____ what I've heard, she's a really nice woman and, ⁴a _____ , very rich.

B: Really? I was ⁵t _____ they didn't invite many people to the wedding because they couldn't afford it.

A: Well, ⁶a _____ to my friend Justin, she fell out with her father because he didn't really approve.

11 You are going to have a conversation like the one in Exercise 10, about an imaginary man called Bill. Invent 'facts' about his life. In pairs, have the conversation using your ideas and expressions from Exercise 10.

A: *Did you hear about Bill moving?*

B: *Yeah. From what I've heard, he's gone to Greece.*

CONVERSATION PRACTICE

12 Think of some news you've heard recently about someone you know or someone famous. Then work in pairs and have similar conversations to the ones you heard in Exercise 4. Use this guide to help you get started. Then swap roles.

Student A	Student B
Ask if your partner knew / has heard about …	
	Say no. Ask for more details.
Give more details about the news. Include some information you're not sure is true.	
	Ask more questions and / or add comments.
Answer any questions. Continue to give more details and extra information.	

A brand new you

IN THIS LESSON, YOU:
- share good and bad advice
- discuss self-care
- read an article on how best to deal with changes
- practise identifying the main topic in parts of a text

READING

1 You are going to read an article about self-care. Work in groups. Discuss the questions.

1 What do you understand by the idea of 'self-care'?

2 Do you practise self-care at all? If so, in what way?

3 When is it most important to do self-care? Why?

2 Work in pairs. Look at these words and phrases from the article. Use a dictionary if you need to check their meaning. How do you think they might be connected to the idea of self-care?

fly the nest	uncharted waters
forge new bonds	friends you can count on
trigger people	put on a brave face
take its toll	keep a track of how you're feeling
beat yourself up	step outside yourself

3 Read the article on page 131. Match the headings (a–i) with the paragraphs (1–8). There is one extra heading you don't need. In pairs, check your answers and explain your choices.

a   Broaden your social circle

b   Try and see the bigger picture

c   Change takes as long as it takes

d   Healthy body, healthy mind

e   Don't let stress get the better of you

f   Understand who your real friends are

g   Don't draw comparisons

h   Stop worrying about what others think

i   It's fine to not be fine

4 Work in pairs. Explain how the phrases in Exercise 2 were used. Read again to check.

5 **M** Work in groups. Discuss these questions.

1 Do you agree with all the suggestions made in the article?

2 What do you think the best piece of advice is? Why?

3 Has anyone you know ever been in any of the situations mentioned in the text, or a similar situation?

4 What advice from the text could you use to help them? What other advice could you give them?

GRAMMAR

Be always / constantly -ing, wish and would

We can use the present continuous and *I wish + would / wouldn't* to show our feelings about habits.

a   He**'s constantly screaming and shouting** at us.

b   She**'s always texting** to see how I'm doing.

c   I **wish you'd** call a bit more often.

d   I **wish people wouldn't** criticize me like that.

6 Look at the examples in the Grammar box. Then work in pairs. Answer the questions 1–3.

1 Which structure emphasizes habits that could be positive or negative?

2 Which two adverbs are used with the present continuous?

3 Which structure shows you'd like someone to behave differently (but don't expect them to)?

7 Add a second sentence to these comments using the ideas in brackets with the present continuous + *always / constantly,* or *wish + would.*

1 He's very romantic. (buy me roses and say he loves me)
   He's always buying me roses and saying he loves me.

2 She's not a very good listener. (shut up and let others speak sometimes)

3 She's the best friend I've got. (text me and check how I'm doing)

4 He's not good at talking about his feelings. (tell me what's wrong)

5 She's so serious about everything. (relax a bit and have a bit more of a laugh)

6 He's always beating himself up about things. (learn to be a bit kinder to himself)

7 He's just not a very nice person. (make fun of everyone in the office)

8 Work in pairs. Talk about the following.

- Two people you know with the characteristics in Exercise 7. Use the structures:
  She's / He's always / constantly -ing … and *She / He never …*

- Three people you know who should change their habits. Use the structure:
  I (sometimes) wish … would(n't) …

G See Grammar reference 13B.

SPEAKING

9 Choose three of these topics and make notes on each one.

- the best piece of advice you've ever been given

- advice you'd give your younger self

- advice that you've given a friend who was going through changes

- advice you wish your parents had been given

- good relationship advice

- some terrible advice you were given or you gave

10 Work in groups. Share your ideas. Then decide what the best piece of advice is.

SELF-CARE
In Times Of Change

Tired of thinking 'I wish you'd be a bit more supportive', you finally walk out on your long-term partner. Fed up with a boss who's constantly screaming and shouting at everyone, you decide to hand in your notice at work. On leaving school, your children fly the nest and you find yourself home alone.

Life-changing events come in many different shapes and sizes, but one thing's for sure: they can often leave you feeling insecure and worried about what happens next. Let's explore some ways in which you can navigate your way through uncharted waters.

1 When your life changes, you'll need to change the way you live it. Leaving a job or a partner can often mean losing your social circle and you may need to find a new one. It can be hard to put yourself out there and forge new bonds, but there are few things better than hitting it off with someone and realizing they get what you're going through. Get out and join a book club or do volunteer work, find a local sports club or get involved in local community groups.

2 Life change can be a way of sorting out which friends you can count on and which you can't. It's good to spend time with old friends who want to help, but it's also good to let go of those who no longer give you what you need. Focus on those who are there for you and accept that we all lose people on our journey through life.

3 Of course, not everyone will agree with decisions you make and how you might choose to live your life. Some might react badly and may openly criticize you. Rather than wishing people wouldn't bad-mouth you, recognize that this may be because they're jealous or even scared of what you've decided to do. You've dared to do something they haven't, and this is going to trigger some people. That's just the way it is.

4 Focusing on your own wellbeing is vital during times of stress and the more you do things that make you feel positive, the better. It can be easy to let yourself go when the going gets tough, so watch what you eat and drink, stay in shape and exercise. Maybe join a gym as that can help you meet new people too.

5 Big changes can be emotionally draining. Many of us simply put on a brave face and pretend that everything is fine, even when life is really taking its toll on us. It's important to remember that during times of change, it's normal to feel a mix of emotions – anger, fear, anxiety, sadness, exhaustion … often all at once! Keeping a diary can be a great way to keep track of how you're feeling – and getting feelings down in words can help to reduce their power.

6 There's little point in worrying about why other people who've experienced similar things to you don't feel the same as you do. The answer is simple: it's because they're not you. We all respond to things in our own unique way and life's stressful enough already without measuring yourself against others.

7 Don't beat yourself up if you find yourself still missing your kids and wishing they'd call more a year after they've left home, or if you still think a lot about a loved one who died two years ago. Things don't always happen when we want them to and we often need to allow ourselves more time to adjust to new stages in life.

8 There's an old saying that when you're wrapped up in yourself, you make a very small parcel. It's important to try and step outside yourself sometimes and take a longer view. Ask yourself what the teenage you would say about where you're currently at in life. Would the seventy-year-old you worry as much as you do – or would they think you're doing just fine?

It's good to seek advice when you reach a fork in the road.

From the cradle to the grave

IN THIS LESSON, YOU:
- discuss values and ideas that are important to you
- talk about birth, marriage and death
- listen to four people describing different ceremonies
- use parts of a spoken text to show why statements are true or false

SPEAKING

1 Work in pairs. Discuss the questions.

1 Do you know anyone who's had a baby recently?

2 Do you know any rites or ceremonies around pregnancy and birth?

3 When do people come of age in your country? What might people do to mark the event? Are there any other special ages that people celebrate?

4 Have you been to any weddings? What were they like?

5 Do people usually celebrate wedding anniversaries in your country? How? Are there any special anniversaries?

6 Are funerals big events in your country?

LISTENING

2 Work in pairs. Look at the groups of words (a–d) and, without using a dictionary, discuss the questions (1–2).

1 Which words do you already know the meaning of?

2 What kind of ceremony or rite do you think links the words in each group? How?

  a reception / a toast / groom / vows

  b turn twenty / traditional outfits / mayor / gather

  c preserve / coffin / respects / grave

  d lips / a blessing / labour / an astrological chart

3 ▶ Listen to four people talking about different ceremonies and rites. Answer the questions.

1 What ceremony or rite does each person talk about?

2 How are the words in Exercise 2 used?

A Hindu wedding ceremony, India.

4 **FS** ▶ Listen to three groups of three phrases. In each group, one word appears in all three phrases. Write the word you hear repeated.

5 ▶ Work in pairs. Are these statements about the ceremonies in Exercise 3 true (T) or false (F)? How do you know? Listen again and check your ideas.

Speaker 1

1 The speaker is a good singer.

2 The person who says 'I do' loudest will be the decision maker in the relationship.

Speaker 2

3 The girls spend thousands of pounds on their outfits.

4 They receive a present at the ceremony.

Speaker 3

5 The body is always displayed in a coffin before the funeral.

6 Taking photos of the dead is a sign of respect.

Speaker 4

7 The speaker is very positive about the Hindu rites carried out at birth.

8 The rites connected with new babies happen ten days after birth.

6 Work in groups. Discuss the questions.

1 What aspects of the four experiences you heard about are different in your culture? What happens in your culture?

2 Do you like the sound of any of the traditions the speakers talk about? Which ones? Why?

3 Are there any traditions around birth, coming of age, weddings and funerals that are changing? Why? Is it a good thing?

4 Are there any traditions you'd like to change? Why? / Why not?

VOCABULARY Values and concepts

V See Vocabulary reference 13C. ⟩⟩

7 Complete the quotes with these nouns.

ambition	compromise	courage	happiness
honesty	integrity	justice	responsibility

1 'Money can't buy you _____ , but it does mean you can be miserable in comfort!'

2 'Children should be given _____ from an early age or they will never become adults.'

3 '_____ is always the best policy in life. Lies will always get you into trouble.'

4 'You need _____ and greed to get ahead in life.'

5 'The key to a successful marriage is friendship and _____ . Love fades and you can never have everything you want.'

6 'Freedom and _____ for all is something worth dying for.'

7 'It's better to have _____ and experience failure, than to lose your principles and have success.'

8 '_____ is not only what it takes to stand up and speak, it's also what it takes to sit down and listen.' (attributed to Winston Churchill)

8 Work in pairs. Discuss the questions.

1 How far do you agree with each of the quotes in Exercise 7? Explain why.

2 What might people do to demonstrate the values in Exercise 7?

3 What core values do you think guide you?

4 What do you think are the core values that might guide the following?
   – a doctor
   – a soldier
   – a school
   – a business

SPEAKING TASK

9 Choose three of these ideas / concepts. Add an extra one that's important to you.

Curiosity   Dignity   Success   Friendship   Loyalty   Faith   Liberty   Hatred

- Write your own 'quotes' for each one – or find good quotes about them online.
- Find images that capture what each one means to you.
- Decide why you value the ideas / concepts you've chosen the most highly.

10 **M** Work in groups. Share your quotes and discuss how you far you agree with each one. Explain why you chose your images. Then try to agree on which of your ideas / concepts is the most important and why.

■ MY OUTCOMES ■

Work in pairs. Discuss the questions.

1 What interesting information did you learn about the topic of the lesson ?

2 What collocations have you learned?

3 Was this unit more or less difficult than earlier units? In what way?

4 What language from this unit do you need to revise and practise?

14 Banks and money

IN THIS UNIT, YOU:

- roleplay conversations about money problems
- talk about wishes and regrets
- take part in a debate about money

SPEAKING

1 Work in pairs. Discuss the questions.

1 What do you think is happening in the photo? Why?

2 Have you ever given or received money as a present? If so, when?

3 Do you like the idea of giving money as a present? Why? / Why not?

4 In which situations do you think it's OK to give people money?

2 Change partners. Discuss the questions.

1 How good with money are you? In what way?

2 Do you know anyone who has ever won any money? How?

3 Are you earning money at the moment? Are you happy with what you make?

4 Do you know anyone who has invested money in anything? What?

5 How do you feel about getting into debt? Why?

Elderly people in the Temple of Tay Kak Sie in Semarang City, Indonesia.

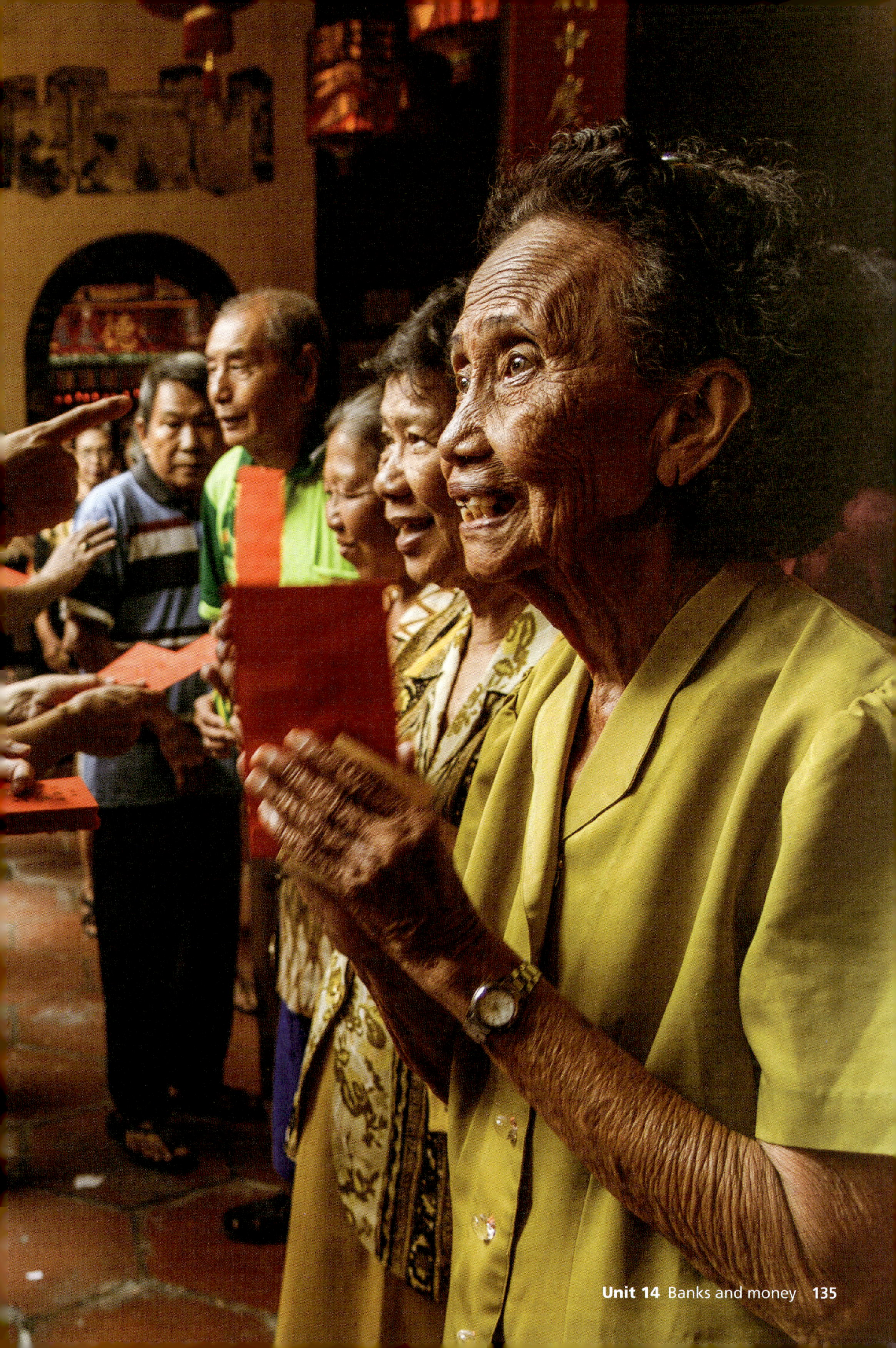

Money troubles

IN THIS LESSON, YOU:
- roleplay conversations about money problems
- discuss different kinds of money problems that people have
- practise listening and deciding if statements are true or false
- practise apologizing and offering explanations

VOCABULARY Money problems

1 Complete the sentences with these pairs of words.

balance / overdrawn	cashpoint / withdraw	inflation / pace
budget / debt	commission / rip-off	savings / pension

1 I wanted to change some money, but they charged 10% _____ , which is a total _____ .

2 _____ was around 10% and wages weren't keeping _____ , which led to lots of strikes.

3 The _____ outside the supermarket ate my card while I was trying to _____ some money.

4 Her grandparents lost all their _____ , so now they just have to live on the state _____ , which is tiny!

5 He's never learned how to manage a _____ so he's always getting himself into _____ .

6 It was pretty depressing. I checked my _____ online and found I was _____ .

2 **P** ▶ **Listen to the words from Exercise 1 said on their own and in a phrase. Practise saying them. Which words / phrases do you find hard to say? Practise saying them again.**

3 **Work in pairs. Discuss the questions.**

1 Have any of the problems in Exercise 1 ever happened to people / economies / countries you know? When? What happened?

2 What other money problems often affect (a) individuals? (b) banks or private companies? (c) national economies?

3 What are the worst problems that can affect a–c in question 2? Why?

LISTENING

4 ▶ **Listen to two conversations involving problems with banks and money. Answer the questions for each conversation.**

1 What does the customer want?

2 What problems does the customer encounter?

3 What happens in the end?

5 **FS** ▶ **In fast speech, often you hardly hear *will*. Listen to eight extracts and decide which don't include *will*.**

6 ▶ **Listen again to the conversations. Decide if the sentences are true (T) or false (F).**

Conversation 1

1 The customer can prove where he's currently living.

2 He pays a regular monthly sum of money towards the bills.

3 He wants to pay some cheques into an account.

4 No fees need to be paid during the trial period for a current account.

Conversation 2

5 The customer wants around £500 worth of foreign currency.

6 The bank usually holds some Venezuelan currency, but doesn't have any left.

7 The customer is pleasantly surprised by the exchange rate.

8 They charge 3% commission when they change money.

7 **Work in pairs. Discuss the questions.**

1 Have you ever opened a bank account? What kind? Who with? Was it easy to do?

2 Are banks generally seen in a positive light in your country? Why?

3 Who do you think are the best or worst banks to be with? Why?

4 Have you ever had any problems changing money or using cashpoints abroad? If yes, what happened?

GRAMMAR

Passives

a *The £30* **will be refunded***.*

b *I'm not sure what it***'s called***.*

c *They***'re** often **accepted** *instead of the local currency.*

d *I***'ve been caught out** *before thinking that.*

8 **Look at the examples in the Grammar box. Then answer the questions.**

1 Why is the passive used in each sentence?

2 How is the passive formed in each case?

3 Do you know how to use the passive in any other tense?

9 **Complete the sentences with the correct active or passive form of the verbs.**

1 I only realized that my card details ¹_____ (copy) last Saturday when I was doing my shopping in my local supermarket and the machine wouldn't ²_____ (process) the transaction. I ³_____ (call) my bank and they said my card ⁴_____ (stop) because of suspicious activity over the previous few days.

2 His business had serious cash flow problems last year and he ¹_____ (run up) huge debts trying to keep things going. In the end, he ²_____ (go) bankrupt. All his employees ³_____ (make) redundant, the bank ⁴_____ (take) his house and he ⁵_____ (leave) without a penny to his name.

A woman walks past a pawn broker and gold seller in Dover, UK.

3   A well-known politician ¹_____ (accuse) of fraud. Councillors believe that last year Michael Hurley, 46, ²_____ (involve) in a plan to steal local government money, and that he ³_____ (transfer) over £1.3 million from a local council account to a secret account in Belize. He ⁴_____ (arrest) last week after a lengthy police investigation. If he ⁵_____ (find) guilty, he could face up to ten years in jail. Mr Hurley ⁶_____ (claim) he has done nothing wrong.

G See Grammar reference 14A.

DEVELOPING CONVERSATIONS

Apologizing and offering explanations

In formal settings, we can use these expressions to apologize:

I'm really / terribly / awfully sorry.

I do apologize.

When dealing with problems in business situations, it is common for people to apologize and then offer a polite explanation or solution.

I'm awfully sorry, Madam, **but I'm afraid** you're out of luck.

I'm terribly sorry this is taking so long, madam. The computers aren't usually this slow!

10 ▶ Look at the Developing conversations box. Write the words in the correct order to make explanations that follow apologies. Then listen and check your answers.

1   the / look / at / once / I'll / into / matter
2   are / the / very / being / today / computers / slow
3   have / some / of / there / been / kind / must / mix-up
4   down / at / the / I'm / our / moment / is / afraid / system
5   can / we / absolutely / afraid / nothing / there's / I'm / do
6   afraid / to / make / decision / I'm / not / authorized / I'm / a
7   word / can / see / manager / do / and / I'll / a / with / my / what / I / have

11 Work in pairs. Take turns to say and respond to these sentences. When responding, apologize and offer an explanation or solution.

1   Why is it taking so long?
2   Why don't you have any record of my deposit?
3   My driving licence should be enough identification, shouldn't it?
4   The cashpoint outside has eaten my card.
5   I keep forgetting my PIN number. Can I change it?
6   I've just had my bank statement. Why am I being charged every time I withdraw money from my local cashpoint?

CONVERSATION PRACTICE

12 Work in pairs. Find your information. Spend a few minutes preparing what to say. Decide which language from this lesson you want to use.

Student A: Look at File 11 on page 195.

Student B: Look at File 22 on page 200.

13 **M** Roleplay the conversations. Take turns to be the customer and the bank clerk. Sort out the problems that arise.

14C

The luck of the draw

IN THIS LESSON, YOU:
- take part in a debate about money
- discuss how you feel – and what you know – about lotteries
- explore metaphors connected to money
- practise listening to people presenting arguments in a debate

SPEAKING

1 **Work in pairs. Discuss the questions.**

1 Are there lotteries in your country?

2 What do you know about them?

3 Which of the facts about lotteries below do you find interesting, surprising or unsurprising? Explain why.

- The first lottery occurred in China about 200BC. The Great Wall of China may have been partly funded by it.
- Winners of Dutch lotteries in the 17th century sometimes received paintings.
- 85% of people who win the lottery in the UK choose not to have their name made public.
- Lotteries were banned in the United States between 1890 and the mid-1960s.
- The hardest lottery to win is the Italian SuperEnalotto – with odds for the top prize of over 622 million to one.
- The biggest ever jackpot win for a single person is currently $2.04 billion.
- At least 28% of the money spent on the lottery in the UK goes to 'good causes'. These include charities, preserving British heritage, funding Olympic athletes and subsidizing theatre and the arts.

VOCABULARY
Metaphors connected to money

V See Vocabulary reference 14C. »»

2 **Complete the sentence pairs (1–8) with one of these words. You may need to change the form.**

bet	earn	gamble	jackpot
lottery	odds	stake	waste

1 a He doesn't _____ much. He's still a junior in the firm.

 b After all that hard work, I think we've _____ a break.

2 a I wish we hadn't bought it. It was a _____ of money!

 b I wouldn't _____ your breath. You'll never persuade him to change his mind.

3 a He _____ £50 on a horse to win, but it came second.

 b I _____ it was nice to have a break after all that work.

4 a I don't _____ at all. I don't even do the lottery. I'm just not lucky.

 b A recent report has warned that people are _____ with their lives by buying cheap medication online.

5 a He's the clear favourite to win at _____ of 2 to 1.

 b She recovered from the illness against all _____ .

6 a I won £10 on the _____ . I got three numbers out of six.

 b Finding a decent restaurant there is a bit of a _____ .

7 a There's a rollover on the lottery because no one won last week. The _____ is something like $30 million now.

 b He hit the _____ when he got that job. It's great.

8 a I do sometimes bet on the football results with friends, but only for a very small _____ each – ten cents a time!

 b It's important voters understand the issues because there's a lot at _____ – people's jobs and their future security!

3 **Work in pairs. Choose one of the questions to talk about.**

1 What aspects of life do you think are **a lottery** in your country? Explain why.

2 What do you think is **at stake** in the next election in your country? Explain why.

3 Can you think of someone you know or have heard about who survived – or achieved something amazing – **against great odds**? Explain what happened.

4 Do you know anyone who's ever **hit the jackpot**? How? What happened?

LISTENING

4 **Work in groups. List reasons someone might give for banning a lottery.**

5 ▶ **Listen to the first speaker (Zak) in a debate about banning lotteries. Note what reasons he gives for banning them.**

6 Explain the points Zak was making when he mentioned the following.

1 promising to give people $2.6 million in the next quarter of a million years
2 the focus of the marketing of lotteries
3 subsidizing opera and Olympic sportsmen
4 only having to choose six numbers to get rich
5 dreaming of a mansion and a Ferrari
6 the story of John from Sydney

7 ▶ Listen again and check your ideas. Then discuss the questions.

1 What mark out of ten would you give Zak's speech?
2 Do you agree with his points? Why? / Why not?
3 What counter-arguments could someone make?

8 ▶ Listen to the opposing speaker, Stacy, in the debate. Take notes on Stacy's reply to Zak.

9 Compare your notes in pairs and then in groups.

10 Work in groups. Discuss the questions.

1 What mark would you give Stacy?
2 Who do you think won the debate? Why?
3 Do you think any of the points they made were irrelevant, clever, stupid or confusing?

SPEAKING TASK

11 Work in groups of four or five and prepare a debate similar to the one you heard between Zak and Stacy. Decide which of the topics (1–5) you want to debate – or suggest your own topic.

1 The love of money is the root of all evil.
2 The best things in life are free.
3 The world would be a better place without banks.
4 Everyone should have to vote.
5 Debating should be part of everyone's schooling.

12 Divide your group into two teams. One team should argue for the topic you have chosen; the other team should argue against it. Prepare your arguments.

13 Nominate a speaker for each team. Then have your debate in front of another group. The other group will give each team marks out of ten and decide the winner. Your group will then do the same for them.

■ MY OUTCOMES ■

Work in pairs. Discuss the questions.

1 What topics and texts in this unit were the most useful?
2 What phrases have you learned to talk about money?
3 What listening or reading texts were difficult, and why?
4 What can you do to extend language from this unit?

Arguing your case

IN THIS LESSON, YOU:
- write an essay that argues a particular point of view
- discuss your thoughts about – and experiences of – zoos
- look at how to structure a short, written argument
- indicate and dismiss weak arguments

SPEAKING

1 Work in groups. Discuss the questions.

1 Can you remember the last time you went to a zoo? Who did you go with? What did you see?

2 Can you think of three reasons why keeping animals in captivity is a good thing?

3 What are the alternatives to zoos?

WRITING

2 Look at the title and four paragraphs of a student's essay. Put the paragraphs in the correct order.

> ## 'ZOOS ARE NOT SOMETHING WE NEED IN THE 21ST CENTURY.' DISCUSS.

a Nevertheless, the positive work done by zoos has become increasingly important and is surely sufficient reason for their continued existence. For instance, zoos do a lot to protect endangered species. Many zoos have breeding programmes, which are essential if we want these animals to survive. A good example here is the orangutan. The natural environment of these animals is rapidly being destroyed and, as a result, they are now almost extinct. Given this, zoos represent the final chance of survival for orangutans. Anyone that attacks zoos is, in fact, helping to bring about the end of these beautiful animals.

b If you add to this the excellent work many zoos do in raising awareness of the problems facing animals in the wild, then you surely have sufficient reasons for supporting the continued existence of this endangered public institution.

c Over the last twenty years or so, there has been a fierce debate about the place of zoos in society. People often claim that zoos are an old-fashioned form of entertainment and should be closed down. However, over recent years, there has been growing appreciation of the work zoos do both in terms of protecting endangered animals and in terms of public education.

d One common argument against zoos is that they are cruel. They are seen as a kind of prison for animals that should, supposedly, be left in the wild to wander freely. Some people also believe that zoos normalize the idea that it is acceptable to capture animals and to keep them in captivity, and this then encourages all manner of cruelty towards animals in society in general.

3 Compare your ideas with a partner and explain how you made your decisions.

4 Decide which paragraph:

1 gives opposing arguments

2 gives a closing statement supporting one side of the argument.

3 gives an overview of the main argument on each side.

4 gives details of one side of the argument.

5 Work in groups. Discuss the following.

1 Does the writer agree or disagree with the idea of zoos? How do you know?

2 Do you agree with this point of view?

3 What is the function of each of the three sentences in the opening paragraph?

4 Underline the words / phrases that the writer uses to introduce ideas they do not agree with.

USEFUL LANGUAGE

Indicating weak arguments

A common way of structuring an argument is to first present arguments that other people hold and that we feel are weak, before then dismissing them. We use specific words and phrases to indicate that we are doing this. They show the reader we are distancing ourselves from these views.

*Zoos **are seen as** a kind of prison for animals.*

***People often claim (that)** zoos are an old-fashioned form of entertainment and should be closed down.*

***One argument against** zoos is that they are cruel.*

6 Find three more words or phrases that the essay writer uses to indicate what they see as weak arguments.

7 Complete the sentences with these words.

argument	believe	claims	common	seen	supposedly

1 Some research _____ that animals in zoos live much longer lives.

2 Zoos are _____ enjoyable places to visit.

3 Many people _____ that nature programmes and documentaries will gradually make zoos redundant.

4 One _____ in favour of zoos is that they perform valuable work by breeding endangered species and then returning them to the wild.

5 Animals are often _____ as having no individuality or personality.

6 One _____ reason for attacking zoos is the idea that we don't have the right to deprive animals of their freedom.

Orangutan baby Duran plays in his enclosure next to his mother Djudi in the zoo of Dresden, Germany.

8 Underline the words and phrases in Exercise 7 that you can reuse in your own writing.

Dismissing weak arguments

When we have presented a weak argument, we often start the next sentence with *However* or a similar word to show the contrast with our own (stronger) ideas. We present our ideas as facts, using the present simple. For example:

One argument against zoos is that *they are cruel.* **However, it is also necessary to consider** *the cruelty of the wild. Many animals actually live longer, healthier lives in captivity than they would in the wild.*

9 Work in pairs. Think of why each of the arguments in Exercise 7 might be seen as weak. Write a contrasting sentence starting with *However*.

10 Compare the sentences you've written with another pair. Do you agree with them? Why? / Why not?

PRACTICE

11 Work in pairs. Choose one of these essay titles. Think of reasons why people might agree or disagree with the statement, and then discuss your own opinions.

- 'It is morally wrong to test drugs on animals.' Discuss.
- 'Long prison sentences stop people from committing crimes.' Discuss.
- 'Professional sport causes more pain than pleasure.' Discuss.
- 'Staying at home for your holiday is better than travelling somewhere.' Discuss.

12 Plan your essay. Organize your ideas into four paragraphs, following the structure discussed in Exercise 4.

13 Write your essay. Use as much language from this lesson as you can.

VIDEO Out and about

1 Work in pairs. Discuss how far you agree with the following statements.

1 'Money is the root of all evil.'
2 'The best things in life are free.'
3 'The world would be a better place without banks.'
4 'Everyone should have to vote.'

Understanding accents

Some accents replace a /r/ sound with /w/, so *red* /red/ may sound like *wed* /wed/; *rot* /rɒt/ like *what* /wɒt/; and *treat* /triːt/ more like *tweet* /twiːt/.

2 ▶ Watch the video and answer the questions.

1 Which statement do the speakers discuss?
2 Which person has the closest views to you? What do they say?

3 ▶ Work in pairs. Match the statements with the speakers and explain your choices. You may match statements with more than one speaker. Then watch again to check.

a Ultimately, even things that are free require an investment of time and energy.
b There's something in the statement, I suppose, but I don't really think its true.
c I fully agree with this statement.
d There are things I love which I obviously have to pay for.
e It doesn't cost you anything to give someone a hug.
f Just being with children and enjoying the sunshine is free.

4 What things have you invested time and energy in? Did it pay off? Discuss with your partner.

VIDEO Developing conversations

5 ▶ You are going to watch two people talking about some news. Watch and take notes on what they say.

6 ▶ Work in pairs. Compare what you understood. Watch again if you need to.

7 Discuss the questions with your partner.

1 Do you think Jacob has made the right decision? Why? / Why not?
2 What other problems can people encounter at university?
3 How easy / difficult is it to get ahead in life with a fine art degree or without a university education?

8 **FS** ▶ Watch again. Complete the sentences with three to five words in each gap.

1 Apparently, he's split up with that girl _____ .
2 Yeah, he's taken some time out, you know, I think _____ quite hard.
3 And he's gone home. _____ a job.
4 Probably like a year. _____ travelling.
5 _____ do the same course again?
6 I think he's _____ fine arts.
7 _____ have a catch up with him.
8 We should. See _____ .

CONVERSATION PRACTICE

9 Work in pairs. You are going to practise a conversation.

1 Choose a Conversation practice from either Lesson 13A or Lesson 14A.
2 Look at the language in that lesson.
3 Check the meaning of anything you've forgotten with your partner.
4 Have the conversation. Try to improve on the last time you did it.

Grammar and Vocabulary

GRAMMAR

1 Complete the text with one word in each gap. Contractions (*it's, you're, wasn't,* etc.) count as one word.

After we had [1]_____ married for a few years, my husband and I decided to close our separate bank accounts and put all our money into one joint account. He [2]_____ been telling me what a good idea it was for ages and in the end, I just gave in. Looking back on it, though, I wish I [3]_____ agreed to it. The problems started a few weeks ago. My joint card [4]_____ rejected a couple of times and when I phoned the bank about it, they said our overdraft [5]_____ been used far too much over the preceding weeks. At first I thought perhaps our account had [6]_____ hacked into, but when I spoke to my husband about it, he admitted he'd been spending too much. We're so badly in debt now that we're going to have to sell our car. I wish we [7]_____ have to, but what can we do? Still, at least everything should [8]_____ paid back by the end of this year!

2 Read the first sentence in each pair. Complete the second sentence so that it has a similar meaning. Use between three and five words, including the word in bold.

1 She never really helps me with the housework.
   I _____ me with the housework.   **WISH**

2 I wish he wouldn't take my things without asking me first.
   He _____ things without asking me.   **ALWAYS**

3 He's always talking over the top of everyone else.
   He _____ anything anyone else says!   **NEVER**

4 I hate being so short.
   I really _____ taller.   **WISH**

5 Unfortunately, my car is with the mechanic.
   Unfortunately, my car _____ at the moment.   **FIXED**

6 I can't accept this cheque. There's no signature on it.
   I can't accept this cheque. It _____ .   **SIGNED**

3 Choose the correct option to complete the sentences.

1 When I came out of my house this morning, I saw that our car *was / had been* broken into.

2 I'd *been looking / looked* forward to it for so long, but in the end it was a bit disappointing, really.

3 Have you seen the news? Something terrible *has been / has* happened in the city centre.

4 Of course they all denied *been / being* involved in the scandal.

5 I wish *I'd / I wouldn't have* never met you.

6 I wish I *didn't have / hadn't had* to do military service. They were the worst two years of my life.

7 I wish he *hadn't been / wasn't* so selfish. He only ever thinks of himself.

8 I feel so useless. I wish there *was / is* something I could do to help.

4 ▶ Listen. Write the six sentences you hear.

VOCABULARY

5 Match the verbs (1–8) with the collocates (a–h).

1 drop out   a 10% commission / a small fortune
2 charge   b your vows / your passport
3 live on   c a diary / track of your money
4 waste   d of university / of society
5 renew   e your 25th anniversary / the event
6 keep   f your breath / money
7 manage   g ten pounds a day / the state pension
8 mark   h the situation / a budget

6 Complete the sentences using the correct form of the words.

1 I'm in charge of 35 people, so the job carries quite a lot of _____ (responsible).

2 We've known each other since we were kids. It's maybe the most important _____ (friend) of my life.

3 It was a difficult _____ (pregnant). There were quite a few complications.

4 The national bank collapsed, and that totally wiped out all our _____ (save).

5 This is a whole new experience for us. Basically, we're into _____ (chart) waters now.

6 It's my daughter's _____ (graduate) ceremony next week.

7 Decide if these words are connected to life-changing events, banks or gambling – and in what way.

my balance	the final straw	in labour	the jackpot
a lottery	odds	an overdraft	pay my respects
stake	vows		

8 Complete the story using one word in each gap. The first letters are given.

Basically, he just [1]v_____ . One day he was there, the next day he was gone. From what I've [2]h_____ , the board basically decided to let him go quite a while ago. [3]Ap_____ , he didn't get on with some of the other directors. Someone told me he accused them of lacking [4]h _____ – or of being liars if you prefer! Then when the company started suffering during the crisis, he got the blame. He was accused of getting the firm into serious [5]d _____ so, as I understand it, despite the official statement saying how he's always acted with absolute [6]in _____ and everything, he really got fired! I'm not that surprised, to be honest. He was never someone who liked to [7]co _____ . It was always his way or not at all! He was [8]e _____ good money, though, so I'm guessing they had to pay him compensation when he left.

15 Food

IN THIS UNIT, YOU:

- have conversations about how to make dishes
- discuss food, meals and cookery
- explain and discuss food-related news stories

SPEAKING

1 Work in pairs. Discuss the questions.

1 What do you think the relationship between the people in the photo is?

2 What do you think they're cooking? Why?

3 How do you think they might cook the food they're preparing?

4 Have you ever done any cooking like this?

2 Change partners. Discuss the questions.

1 Can you cook? If so, what's your best dish? If not, what's your favourite dish to eat?

2 How did you learn to cook or would you like to learn?

3 Is there any food you typically prepare together with your family or friends? When?

4 Do the men or women in your family do most of the cooking? Or does it depend?

Tzutujil Mayan women preparing traditional food together in San Pedro la Laguna, Guatemala.

What's cooking?

IN THIS LESSON, YOU:
- have conversations about how to make dishes
- practise listening to someone explaining a dish
- practise hearing and using vague language in descriptions
- improve your explanations by using linking words

VOCABULARY Food and cooking

1 Look at the pictures in File 12 on page 196. In pairs, discuss the questions.

1 Are there any foods here that you've never tried?
2 Are there any you didn't know in English?
3 Are any of them difficult to buy where you live?
4 Which five of these foods do you like the most?
5 Are there any you can't stand? Why not?
6 Are there any foods you love that aren't pictured?

2 Complete the sentences with these verbs.

bake	beat	blend	chop	crush	dip
melt	peel	simmer	soak	sprinkle	squeeze

1 _____ the avocados and remove the stones.
2 _____ the whole trout in the oven for twenty minutes until it's cooked through – the flesh will be soft and should come away from the bones easily.
3 Put the chickpeas in some water and _____ them overnight.
4 _____ the chocolate in a bowl over some boiling water and mix in the raisins.
5 Cut a grapefruit in half and _____ some juice over the salad.
6 _____ an egg and mix with some flour and iced water. Then take slices of courgette, _____ them in the mixture and deep-fry them till they are golden brown.
7 _____ the almonds and _____ on top of the cake.
8 Finely _____ some parsley and sprinkle it onto the soup.
9 Add the coconut milk and wait till it starts to boil. Then turn down the heat and _____ for twenty minutes, stirring occasionally.
10 When the vegetables are soft, _____ everything in a food processor until it's smooth.

3 Work in pairs. Look again at the verbs in Exercise 2. Which of these things have you done in the past month? Think of two more foods you could use with each verb.

You can peel bananas and potatoes.

LISTENING

4 **FS** ▶ Listen to eight extracts from a recipe. How many times do you hear the word *of* in each extract?

5 ▶ Listen to two people talking about a dish one of them is cooking. Note down the ingredients.

6 **M** ▶ In pairs, discuss what you remember about how the dish was made. Then listen again and take notes. Finally, compare your notes in groups.

7 Work in pairs. Discuss the questions.

1 Do you like the sound of the recipe? Why? / Why not?
2 Do you know anyone who has a special diet or who avoids certain things like salt? What do they have to eat or avoid? Why?
3 Who's the best cook you know? What are their best dishes?

DEVELOPING CONVERSATIONS

Vague language

We can show something is not exact by adding *-ish* to adjectives or *-y* to nouns. We can also add *kind of* or *sort of* before adjectives and verbs.

*It's a grey**ish** white stick. It gives a **kind of** citrusy flavour.*

*It looks **sort of** like a spring onion.*

With quantities, we use words such as *roughly / about / or so.*

*Use **roughly** a cupful.*

*Leave it to boil for fifteen minutes **or so**.*

8 Look at the Developing conversations box. Make the sentences less exact by adding the words and suffixes in brackets in the correct place. There may be more than one answer.

1 You bake it in the oven for twenty minutes. (roughly)
2 I generally sprinkle some herbs on top and two teaspoons of crushed pistachios. (about)
3 If you add a squeeze of orange, it gives it a sweet finish, which is really nice. (kind of)
4 The colour put me off at first. It was green blue, but it tasted great. (kind of / -ish)
5 It has an odd oil texture and a weird egg smell. (-y / -y)
6 You need a large pan, because you add two litres of fish stock. (-ish / or so)
7 If it's a small chicken and isn't stuffed, then it should only take 40 minutes to roast. (-ish / or so)
8 It's like a potato, but it's rounder and it's got purple skin and the flesh is orange. (-ish / kind of)

9 Work in pairs. Using vague language, describe different foods for your partner to guess.

A: It's biggish with a yellowish skin, very juicy flesh and a kind of lemony flavour. It's quite bitter.

B: Is it a grapefruit?

GRAMMAR

Linking words

You have learned a number of words in this book that make the relationship between two ideas within a sentence or between two sentences clear. For example, you may want to show:

order and time (*and, when, after, once, then, afterwards, while, during,* etc.)

reason and purpose (*as, so, to*)

contrast (*although, even though, however*)

a condition (*if, in case, provided*).

10 **Look at the examples in the Grammar box. Then choose the correct options to complete the recipe.**

First you chop some onions ¹*and / after* put them in some oil. Fry them for a few minutes. Actually, you should heat the oil a bit beforehand and ²*when / then* you put the onion in, it should sizzle. ³*Then / After* you need to turn the heat down, ⁴*as / so* you want the onion to cook slowly ⁵*then / so* it becomes nice and sweet. I also like to add some garlic, ⁶*although / however* I know most people don't. Anyway, ⁷*while / during* the onion is cooking, peel about four big potatoes and cut them into little pieces – quite small, ⁸*otherwise / unless* they'll take ages to cook.

⁹*Once / Afterwards* the onion has started to turn brown, add the potatoes and continue to cook everything ¹⁰*until / when* the potato is soft. The onion won't burn ¹¹*provided / unless* you mix it in with the potato and stir the mixture now and then.

Break about eight eggs into a bowl and beat them with a touch of milk. Spoon the cooked mixture into the beaten eggs – without any of the oil ¹²*if / in* case you can avoid it – and mix it all together.

You then pour away the oil in the pan – apart from about a spoonful – and heat up the pan again so it's very hot. ¹³*When / Then* pour the egg and potato into the pan and after about a minute, turn it down low and let it cook ¹⁴*for / during* about ten minutes. You then need to get a big plate or flat lid which you place on top of the omelette ¹⁵*for / to* turn it over and cook the other side.

G See Grammar reference 15A. 〉〉

CONVERSATION PRACTICE

11 **Work in pairs. Discuss how many of these different kinds of dishes you could cook. For each dish, decide what ingredients you'd need and how you'd cook the dish.**

- a stir-fry
- a pasta dish
- a stew
- a vegetarian dish
- a tart or a cake
- a rice-based dish
- a curry
- a salad

12 **Choose one of the dishes from Exercise 11 that you think you could cook best. Change partners. Have conversations similar to the one in Exercise 5. Follow this guide. Then swap roles.**

Student A	Student B
Start by saying: *Mmm! This is delicious! What's in it?*	
Ask questions about the taste and about how to make the dish.	Explain what's in the dish.
Check details when you're not sure about ingredients or what to do.	Answer the questions as best you can.

15B

This takes me back

SPEAKING

1 Work in pairs. Discuss the statements. How far do you agree with them?

1 Complicated recipes aren't really necessary.

2 If you want good food, you have to pay more for it.

3 People eat too much junk food.

4 How good we think something tastes can be influenced by descriptions and price.

5 TV cookery competitions are a bad idea.

6 You shouldn't throw away food.

7 There's no good or bad when it comes to food – just different tastes.

8 The people you eat with are more important than the food.

READING

2 Read the blog post on page 151 quickly. What does the writer think of these films and programmes?

1 *Sour Grapes*   2 *MasterChef*   3 *Ratatouille*

3 Work in pairs. Which opinions in Exercise 1 do you think the writer holds? Which do you think the writer would disagree with? Underline the evidence in the blog post.

4 Work in pairs. Can you remember why the writer mentions the following?

- art
- auctions
- flattery
- food banks
- leftovers
- a spoiler
- taking the mickey

5 Work in pairs. Discuss these questions.

1 How far did you agree with the author of the blog? Did they change your mind in any way? Would you recommend the blog to anyone?

2 What cookery programmes or films about food do you know? Do you like them?

3 If you could follow any of the hyperlinks in blue, what do you think they might lead to? Which would you click on? Why?

VOCABULARY Prefixes

V See Vocabulary reference 15B.

6 Read about the meanings of different prefixes. Complete the examples (1–12) with these prefixes.

| dis | ex | mis | multi | non | out |
| over | pre | pro | re | semi | super |

1 many – as in a _____ *cultural* society or _____ *lingual child*

2 no longer – as in an _____ *-soldier* or an _____ *-president*

3 wrongly – as in _____ *manage a situation* or _____ *inform the public*

4 better or more than – as in _____ *perform competitors* or be _____ *played*

5 too much – as in _____ *cook the fish* or _____ *do it in the gym*

6 not – as in a _____ *-stick frying pan* or *my social life is* _____ *-existent*

7 the opposite of – as in _____ *obey an order* or _____ *qualify a contestant*

8 before – as in a _____ *-war leader* or _____ *heat the oven*

9 again – as in _____ *play a game* or _____ *read a book*

10 partly – as in a _____ *-professional player* or *being left* _____ *-conscious*

11 in favour of – as *in* _____ *-GM food* or a _____ *-democracy campaigner*

12 higher than normal – as in a _____ *power* or *the* _____ *-rich*

7 **P** ▶ Listen to twelve phrases from Exercise 6. Practise saying them. Which words / phrases do you find hard to say? Practise saying them again.

8 Work in pairs. Challenge each other to think of a new word for each prefix and use it in a collocation or sentence.

A: *pre-*

B: *pre-cooked*

A: *I buy a lot of pre-cooked meals.*

SPEAKING

9 **M** Work in pairs. Choose two of these ideas and write a comment for the blog.

- a food or smell that reminds you of someone or some time
- a special meal you remember having
- a smell / food you can't stand because of a past experience
- an opinion you agree with in the post with an example from your own experience
- an opinion you disagree with in the post – explain why
- what's good about *MasterChef* or similar programmes
- a film connected to food
- research connected to food

10 Share your comments with other students in the class.

A little less description, a lot more conversation

As you know, this blog is about celebrating food and eating. In terms of the recipes we feature, we like to keep things simple with a few ingredients mixed with some common herbs or spices: a one-pot stew; some lamb chops or sardines on the grill; a tasty salad sitting in the middle of the table for everyone to dig in. And we're not snobbish about food. Of course, fresh is usually best, but tinned can be good, and those sad-looking leftovers in your fridge can be made into something delicious. We like chips, we like hot dogs and we love sharing a bag of sweets on a long journey. But if you want a better idea of what our philosophy is … and what it's not – take my TV viewing this week.

First up on Monday evening was *Sour Grapes*, the award-winning documentary about the auction market in rare and fine wines. Not being a wine drinker or a fine diner myself, I've often wondered if spending even $50 on something to drink can really be worth it, but in *Sour Grapes* we see over-priced taken to a whole other level. We follow one seller who persuades wealthy people to buy bottles that cost literally thousands through the description of the wine's 'complex' flavours, which only the highly 'sophisticated' taste of the consumer might appreciate. It turns out that rather than sophisticated tastes, those consumers have more money than sense, because they're actually being sold some blended supermarket brands with a forged label and a lot of flattery.

It's this focus on appearances and 'sophistication' which has made me fall out of love with *MasterChef*, which I saw on Wednesday. I still like some of the early rounds, where you see quite a variety of styles and people, but as the competition goes on, it seems to become about ever-more fancy dishes, which take five minutes to describe and are arranged into some kind of piece of art. In Wednesday's episode, the contestants were put through their paces in a real, high-end restaurant. At one point, the chef shouted at them, not because the dish was overcooked or under-seasoned (or as we prefer to say, 'not enough salt'), but because the tiny dots of sauce round the edge of the plate were unevenly spaced! He actually chucked the whole plate in the bin and told them to start again! Apart from the criminal waste at a time of increasing numbers of food banks, I'm thinking, dude, just lighten up. Cooking and eating really shouldn't be stressful, and if it is, you're doing it wrong.

Which brings me to Saturday, when I watched the Pixar film *Ratatouille* with my dad. Since I was about ten, we have established a tradition to spend an evening together once a year and watch *Ratatouille*. We start off by making pizzas together. My dad used to make the bases, but I've taken over that job as I'm basically better at it. We select our own toppings – anchovy and olives for me, while my dad (despite me taking the mickey) still insists on ham and pineapple. We then settle down to the film.

If, for some inexplicable reason, you haven't seen the film, *Ratatouille* tells the story of a rat who wants to become a chef, and a miserable restaurant reviewer who is only interested in finding fault and destroying reputations. When faced with trying to impress this critic, the rat, rather than taking the *MasterChef* approach, prepares a simple vegetable stew called ratatouille. It can't possibly work, can it? But [spoiler alert] with the first mouthful, the critic remembers his childhood and the same dish his mother prepared when he was upset and needed love and comfort. The critic smiles, and so do we – well I do. My dad usually cries!

This is what cooking and eating should be about. It's about the people you're with, the joy it gives, and the conversation and memories it creates.

PREVIOUS POSTS
granny's apple pie; first picnic of the year; simple stews; how wine experts never say the same thing twice

Those dots of sauce are not spaced correctly!

Come on! He could be a top chef!

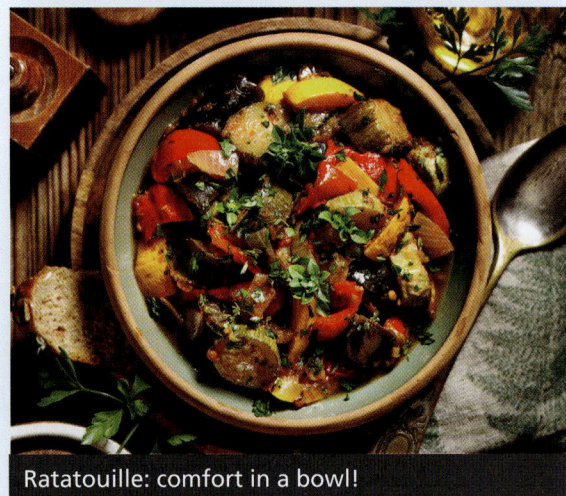
Ratatouille: comfort in a bowl!

Food for thought

IN THIS LESSON, YOU:
- explain and discuss food-related news stories
- read news headlines and discuss possible content
- listen to news items about food and practise taking notes
- practise summarizing and reporting what people said

LISTENING

1 Work in pairs. Look at the news headlines and discuss the questions.

1 What do you think of each headline?

2 Which stories would you want to read? Why?

3 Which would you include on a front page? Why? Try to agree.

a Fast-food chain's ice cream creates a stir on social media

b Research suggests gut bacteria offers key to obesity crisis

c Burger business and football club win climate action awards

d Report shows meat industry donates millions to political parties

e SUPERMARKET PULLS AD PROMOTING VEGANISM

f Campaigners Demand Action After Report Into Food Waste

g 'SCALLOP DISCO' LIGHTS THE WAY FORWARD

h OVERFISHING COULD WIPE OUT FISH STOCKS BY 2048

2 ▶ Listen to four news stories about food. Match each story (1–4) with one of the headlines from Exercise 1 (a–h).

3 Work in pairs. Discuss which phrases go with which story and why the speakers used these words. What else do you remember about the stories?

suffering from severe hunger	a crime against humanity
possess a particular gene	scrape the seabed
pioneered plant-based burgers	offset the carbon from
with small fish as bait	promote good habits

4 ▶ Listen again and take notes about other key information in each story.

5 Work in pairs. Using your notes, how many of these questions can you answer?

1 How much food is wasted worldwide?

2 Which countries have anti-waste laws, according to the news report?

3 What is special about the football team?

4 How much food is wasted at Max's?

5 What was accidental about the fishing discovery?

6 How many eyes do scallops have?

7 What flavour sauce was added to the ice cream?

8 How long is the ice cream on sale for?

6 Work in pairs. Discuss the questions (1–5).

1 Which story would you be most likely to tell someone else about? Who? Why?

2 Are there any anti-food waste laws in your country? Are they strict enough?

Members of Ocean Rebellion in Lisbon, Portugal, protest against overfishing.

3 Are there any foods that you don't eat, or that you eat less of, for environmental reasons?

4 Have you heard of any interesting marketing that has caused a debate on social media?

5 What food companies do you like / not like? Why?

GRAMMAR

Patterns after reporting verbs

When we report what people said, we sometimes use a verb to more or less report the direct speech (*say, state, claim, announce*) and sometimes we use a verb to summarize the main idea (*promise, accuse, recommend,* etc.). These verbs are followed by different patterns.

It **promises** to make 50% of all sales plant-based.

The report also **urges** governments and businesses to do more.

Campaigners **accused** the government here of failing.

Some **claimed** the dessert was a fantastic blend.

Climate experts **recommend** moving to a vegetarian diet.

7 Read the examples in the Grammar box. Match the verbs in bold with these patterns (1–6). Do any of the verbs fit more than one pattern?

1 verb + *to* + verb

2 verb + person + *to* + verb

3 verb + *-ing*

4 verb + preposition + *-ing*

5 verb + person + preposition + *-ing*

6 verb + (*that*) clause

8 Work in pairs. Match these verbs with one or more of the patterns in Exercise 7.

advise	agree	apologize	confess	consider	deny
encourage	imagine	insist	intend	refuse	remind
suggest	threaten	warn	worry		

9 Read the first sentence in each pair. Complete the second sentence so it has a similar meaning. Use between two and five words, including the word in bold.

1 We strongly recommend that the company rethinks its policy.

We would _____ its policy on this matter.   **URGE**

2 The government have accepted an offer for the farmland from a private company.

The government _____ the farmland to a private company.   **AGREED**

3 My son is three now and he never wants to eat anything healthy.

My son just totally _____ anything healthy at all.   **REFUSES**

4 My grandmother always makes her special apple pie every time we go and visit her.

My grandmother always _____ her special apple pie every time we go and visit her.   **INSISTS**

5 A friend of mine said we should try this new Vietnamese place near here.

A friend of mine _____ this new Vietnamese place near here.   **SUGGESTED**

6 Given the cod shortages, fish and chip restaurants are suggesting that customers try alternatives.

Given the cod shortages, fish and chip restaurants are _____ alternatives.   **ENCOURAGING**

7 The company has expressed regret after it was caught selling contaminated meat.

The company _____ contaminated meat.   **APOLOGIZED**

8 The firm rejected all accusations of involvement in the scandal.

The firm categorically _____ involved in the scandal.   **DENIED**

G See Grammar reference 15C.

10 Work in groups. Tell a partner some examples of things that:

- people are currently being urged to do – or not do.
- someone famous has been accused of doing recently.
- you've promised to do recently.
- you've had to apologize for doing recently.
- someone famous has been criticized for recently.
- you have refused to do.

SPEAKING TASK

11 On your own, spend ten minutes preparing a discussion for a 'podcast'.

- Think of a food story you've heard about where you are from (e.g. food shortages, health issues, farming, etc.) and check details if you need to, or look for a story on the internet. (You can find a story in your own language and explain it in English if you like.)
- Decide why the story might be of interest to other people.
- Think about how you will explain it to others.
- Think of at least two questions related to the story to ask other people in your group. They could be about their own experience or opinions.

  What do you think they should do about …? Have you ever …?

12 **M** Work in groups. Choose one person to be the host and manage the discussion. They should invite different people to explain their stories and ask their questions. Make sure everyone takes part and ask further questions to keep the conversation going.

■ MY OUTCOMES ■

Work in pairs. Discuss the questions.

1 What conversations did you practise, and which did you enjoy the most?

2 How has this unit helped you listen or read more confidently?

3 What did you find challenging in the unit? Why?

4 How can you now practise language from this unit outside the classroom?

16 Business

- call about a business issue and arrange a meeting
- discuss the qualities of successful people
- present and discuss ideas for a business investment

SPEAKING

1 Work in pairs. Discuss the questions.

1 When and where do you think this photo was taken?

2 Who do you think the trader is talking to on the phone? What about?

3 Why do you think there are no women in the photo?

2 Work with a new partner. Discuss the questions.

1 Would you like to work in business? Why? / Why not?

2 Do you think discrimination exists in business in your country? Why? / Why not?

3 What was the last call you made to each of the following? What about? How did it go?

a a client or employee

b your bank or other service provider

c your workplace or school

d a family member

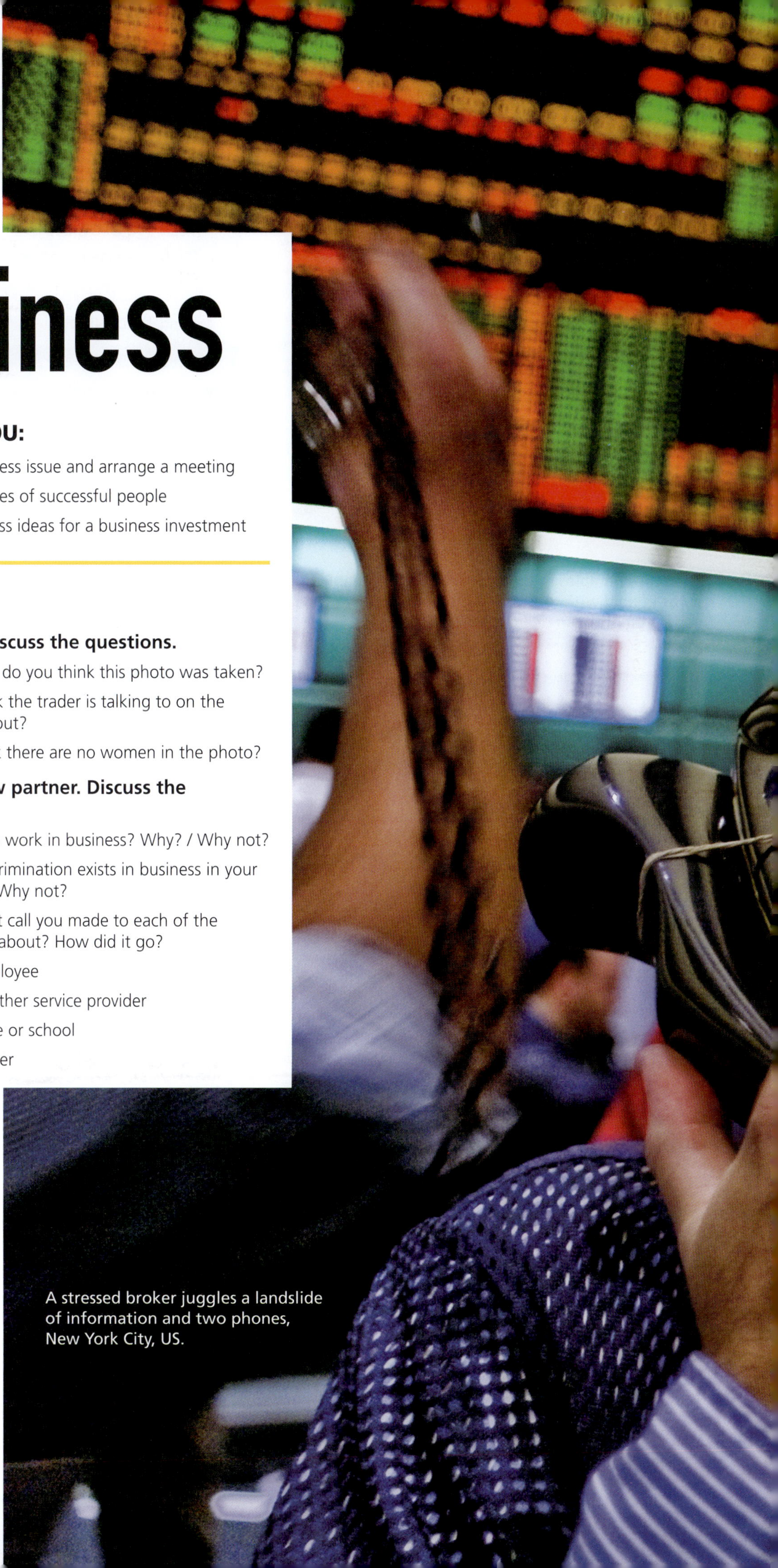

A stressed broker juggles a landslide of information and two phones, New York City, US.

16A

I'll chase it up

IN THIS LESSON, YOU:
- call about a business issue and arrange a meeting
- practise listening to phone calls and taking notes
- practise making communication more formal
- explain how plans can fit with previous arrangements

VOCABULARY
Business meetings and communication

1 Complete the sentences with these verb phrases. Decide what the 'it' refers to in each case.

came up with it	chase it up	implement it	note it down
pencil it in	placed it	put it forward	take it on

1 We sent you an **invoice** a couple of months ago and I'm just phoning to _____ as the payment is now **overdue**.

2 We're having a meeting to talk through the new marketing **strategy** and how we are going to _____ as we go forward.

3 If Friday afternoon suits you for the meeting, can you _____ ? I'll send you **confirmation** once I've spoken to everyone.

4 I just wanted to say we loved your **proposal** and we're going to _____ at our next management meeting.

5 I just wanted to announce that the name we've gone for is *Lime Explosion*. Well done to Tara who _____ and thanks to everyone for your **input**.

6 I'm really sorry. I **processed** your order when you _____ , but I can see now it hasn't been sent out. I'll call the warehouse now.

7 It's so **hectic** now, I can't do the extra admin on top of everything else. Can't we ask the new guy to _____ ?

8 We have a webpage for applications. Do you want to _____ ? The url is jimjams dot a u **forward slash** new, then a **dash**, and then jobs. You can also email me your CV to jane **underscore** brent at jimjams dot a u.

2 **P** ▶ Listen to the verbs from Exercise 1 said with *it* and then with the noun collocate. Practise saying them. Which words / phrases do you find hard to say? Practise saying them again.

3 Work in pairs. Discuss the questions.

1 Can you write out the email address and url in Exercise 1?

2 What kinds of things might you need to chase up?

3 What kinds of things might someone come up with?

4 Why might you take on someone else's work? Why might a company take on staff?

5 What's good about asking for everyone's input on a proposal or plan? What might be bad?

6 Do you have any meetings or events pencilled in? Why might the dates change?

7 What do you think someone would do to process an order or a passport application?

8 What might a marketing strategy involve? When else might people need a strategy?

LISTENING

4 ▶ Listen to a conversation between two colleagues. Answer the questions.

1 Why is Ivan calling Claudine?

2 What does he suggest?

3 How does Claudine respond?

4 What arrangements do they end up making?

5 ▶ Now listen to a second conversation between a client and a customer services operator. Complete the notes as you listen.

Order no.: _____
Date placed: _____
Client's name: _____
Email address: _____
Action: _____

DEVELOPING CONVERSATIONS

Using *would* to show formality

One way we can make sentences sound more polite and less direct is to use *would*. It is often used in more formal contexts. We also use other more formal words with *would*.

*I **was wondering if** you**'d** like to join us?* (formal)

Do you want to come with us? (informal)

6 **M** Look at the Developing conversations box. Rewrite the sentences using *would* and the words in brackets so that they sound softer and more polite.

1 Is Friday good for you? (at all)

2 Can you make the 29th? (able / at all)

3 Do you have the address there? (happen)

4 Can you just spell the street name? (mind)

5 Do you want to come with us? (wondering / like)

6 Can you email me over the details? (possible)

7 Any day next week is good for me. (suit)

8 If it's OK with you, I don't want to. (mind / rather)

7 Work in small groups. Arrange a time and place for a meeting. Each student should reject at least two suggestions. Use polite expressions including *would*.

GRAMMAR

The future continuous

We occasionally use a future continuous form to show a future event will be in progress when another one happens. We therefore often use it to explain how a new plan fits with something we've already arranged.

a I'**ll be visiting** Barcelona for a trade fair the week after next, so I'**ll be able to** fit in a day with you then.

b Some orders **will be going out** from the warehouse later today, so I'**ll add yours** to the delivery and it should be with you tomorrow morning.

8 Look at the examples in the Grammar box. Then work in pairs to answer these questions.

1 Which of the forms in bold is the future continuous?

2 Which form shows a previous arrangement?

3 Which form shows the new plan we are making?

9 Complete the sentences (1–5) using *will / won't* and a simple or continuous form of the verbs in brackets.

1 _____ (visit) the head office when you're in Japan? We could have a meeting then.

2 I'm sorry we've got nothing available now, but it's worth contacting us again in the run-up to Christmas as we _____ (take on) new staff then.

3 I _____ (go) to the Cairo office later on today, so I _____ (try) and chase up the projected sales figures.

4 We _____ (open) a new flagship store in Tokyo soon, so that _____ (boost) our profile quite a bit.

5 Thanks for the offer, but I _____ (arrive) late tonight, so I _____ (not be) able to make the dinner.

G See Grammar reference 16A.

CONVERSATION PRACTICE

10 Work in pairs. You are going to roleplay a business-related conversation and arrange a meeting. Read the roleplay cards and spend five minutes preparing what to say.

Student A: Look at the roleplay card in File 13 on page 197.

Student B: Look at the roleplay card in File 23 on page 200.

11 Take turns to call your partner. Explain why you are calling, have a brief discussion and then arrange your meeting.

16B

A major success

IN THIS LESSON, YOU:
- discuss the qualities of successful people
- practise reading a profile of a successful entrepreneur
- notice collocations around business and success and put them to use
- share different stories of successful people from your country

SPEAKING

1 Work in pairs. Read about the characteristics of successful people. For each characteristic, discuss what mark you'd give yourself from 1 (definitely not me) to 5 (definitely me) and explain why.

DO YOU HAVE WHAT IT TAKES TO BE SUCCESSFUL?

Some people may be born with the qualities to be successful, but you can develop them too. Here at *Knowyourbusiness* we have put together a top-ten list. How many of these qualities do you have?

1 Successful people set high standards and put in the hours needed to meet them.

2 They were high achievers at school and are always keen to learn more through reading widely.

3 They're social animals. They have a wide circle of friends and acquaintances and are always networking.

4 They're perfectionists and always focused on improving their company's performance.

5 They display a healthy degree of impatience and tend not to perform well in bureaucracies.

6 They're creative and they're innovative.

7 They don't waste time moaning or looking for people to blame. They accept responsibility for their actions, learn and move on.

8 They're keen observers and often take notes, so they tend to notice changes and opportunities quicker than others.

9 They maintain their cool and their sense of humour under pressure.

10 They have what's called a 'tolerance of ambiguity'. They don't have to have complete knowledge or certainty before making a decision or seizing an opportunity.

2 Add up your score and compare it with a new partner. Discuss the questions.

1 Do you agree with the ideas in the text? Why? / Why not?

2 What do you think the website means by 'successful'? How else could you define success? Would those definitions require different characteristics?

READING

3 Quickly read the profile of Tunde Onakoya on page 159. Find out what his business is and what makes him remarkable.

4 Complete the profile with these sentences. There is one extra sentence that you do not need.

a Even so, while the business was ultimately unsustainable, Tunde had discovered a passion for teaching and seen further proof that chess can boost kids' self-esteem and academic abilities.

b Since embarking on the new venture, Onakoya has proved himself an adept fundraiser and skillful organizer.

c The players ignored Tunde's pleas to teach him how to play, but he still picked up the rules by closely observing the games over time.

d As well as bringing awards for Onakoya, the project has attracted attention from the media in Africa and beyond.

e Not only did he become a chess master, achieving a rank of thirteen in Nigeria, he also gained academic success.

f It proved to be an instant success, attracting first five, then twenty, and eventually almost 100 kids, all keen to have a go.

g However, in his case, the two years he had out of school may have proved to be a blessing in disguise.

5 Work in pairs. Which of the ten characteristics of successful people do you see evidence of in Tunde's story?

6 Discuss these questions with your partner.

1 Did the profile change your view about what a successful business and businessperson can be? Why? / Why not?

2 What challenges do you think Onakoya might face as he tries to expand? How might he overcome those issues?

3 Would you contribute in some way to Chess in Slums Africa? How? / Why not?

7 Work in pairs. Look back at the profile and missing sentences in Exercise 4. Find the verb and adjective collocations that go with these nouns.

potential	hardship	scholarship	challenges	doubts	cut
effort	market	experience	plans	venture	success

8 For each collocation, write one sentence which says something true about yourself or a person or business you know.

SPEAKING

9 **M** Choose one of these topics. Spend a few minutes researching some details and thinking about what to say. You can look up information in your own language.

- How a famous entrepreneur in your country achieved success.
- How a businessperson used their wealth positively.
- How a famous person overcame hardships.
- How a well-known person achieved success but not riches.

10 Work in groups. Tell each other what you know and decide which story you all like the best.

New African Entrepreneurs

This week we profile Tunde Onakoya, the 28-year-old social entrepreneur and winner of the Future Africa award for community action.

Tunde Onakoya is the remarkable founder of Chess in Slums Africa, which teaches chess to deprived children to help them fulfil their true potential. Through CISA's innovative chess programme, the kids learn language, literacy and critical thinking skills that help with their schooling. CISA also provides financial support to particularly vulnerable individuals, who otherwise may be forced to drop out of school. And as a child of the slums himself, Onakoya knows how easy it can be to miss out on education.

When he was young, Tunde Onakoya's family experienced financial hardship and he sacrificed his place at secondary school so his younger brother could complete his primary education. Tunde eventually got a place at an English-speaking private school when his mother took on work as a cleaner in exchange for his fees. [1]_____ It was during that time that he first came across the game of chess, which was to change his life forever.

Onakoya started going to a local barber's, initially to play on a Playstation® 1 they had there. However, once there, he was drawn to chess games that were also going on in the shop and was immediately fascinated by the pieces. [2]_____ So although his limited English initially made life in his new school difficult, he was ready to excel in the chess classes the school provided.

And he certainly did excel. [3]_____ He won a partial scholarship to study at university and graduated in 2015. However, graduation brought fresh challenges as the Nigerian economy was slowing and there was rising unemployment.

Onakoya's first venture was a scheme to set up chess clubs in private schools. He managed to overcome various doubts school leaders expressed about the project and established a number of clubs around the city. The kids' parents paid a termly fee, but the schools typically took a very large cut, which squeezed his profits and left him frustrated by how little he was earning for the huge effort he was putting in. [4]_____ Perhaps he just hadn't found the right target market or business model for chess classes. And that was about to change.

On a visit to Majidun, another very deprived area in his city, Onakoya saw the kids running in the streets instead of being in school and, reflecting on his own experience, he decided to bring some friends and chess boards to teach them how to play. [5]_____

Among the crowd was a smiling five-year-old girl who was especially eager to take part, and when Onakoya spoke to her on a return visit, she told him she wanted to become a nurse. He was so impressed by her ambition, despite her young age and lack of education, that he told her story via social media. The post went viral and among the comments was an offer to pay for the girl's education. It was the real turning point and Chess in Slums Africa was born.

[6]_____ In the first four years of the project, he raised over $400,000, providing ongoing school scholarships for over 200 slum kids. His team of voluntary teachers also delivered courses to over a thousand kids in five slum communities, with positive impacts on school attendance. He now has ambitious plans to expand the programme in and beyond Nigeria.

In chess, the weakest piece (the pawn) can become the strongest (the queen), by reaching the final row of the board. For some, children in slum communities can be seen as dispensable pawns in the economy, but for Tunde Onakoya, with the right person and the right push any child has the potential to become a queen or king.

The mother of invention

IN THIS LESSON, YOU:
- present and discuss ideas for a business investment
- explain how businesses are doing
- practise listening to a discussion about a business show
- talk about changing obligations and abilities

VOCABULARY How's the business doing?

1 Work in pairs. Don't use a dictionary. Discuss what you think the phrases in bold mean or decide how to translate them into your first language.

1 We decided to sell **a** 60% **stake in the company**.

2 We've **poured our own money into the business** and remortgaged the house.

3 We'd like to **expand our business into new territories** and we're looking for **potential partners** to help us.

4 We have **doubled our turnover**, but we're still making a small loss.

5 We're looking to **branch out and diversify** away from our core business.

6 The company's been going for six years, but we've decided to **cease trading**.

7 We invested a lot in new technology, and we're beginning to **see a big return on that investment**.

8 We've developed a new device to detect cancer early and **we have a patent**.

9 Things had been a bit slow, but recently we've been **flooded with orders**.

10 The company made a loss in the first three years, but it **broke even** this year.

11 **My company was taken over** and I resigned as **CEO**.

2 Work with a new partner. Discuss how well you think each business mentioned in Exercise 1 is doing and why.

LISTENING

3 ▶ Listen to the introduction to a radio discussion about a reality TV programme. Complete the notes.

Shark Tank started in ¹_____ and has been broadcast in over ²_____ . Four or five budding entrepreneurs present their proposals to several ³_____ . The sharks are very ⁴_____ .

The rules of the show mean the sharks can only negotiate a higher ⁵_____ in the company.

The companies that have won investment include BuggyBeds, Piñata2Go and ⁶_____ .

4 Work in pairs. Discuss the questions.

1 Have you heard of the programme before? Is there a version in your country?

2 Is it popular where you are? Why? / Why not?

3 What questions do you think the Sharks ask the entrepreneurs?

5 ▶ Listen to the next part of the discussion. Answer one of the questions.

1 If you know the show, do you think the discussion is fair to the programme. Why? / Why not?

2 If you don't know the show, does the discussion make you more or less likely to watch it? Why?

6 FS ▶ Listen to five extracts. Decide what word you hear in all of them.

7 Which of these arguments are made during the discussion?

1 People like the programme because it helps people get rich.

2 People like the programme because it shows how businesses can grow.

3 People like the programme because they like to see failures as well as successes.

4 The sharks provide a lot of good advice throughout the show.

5 Some businesses on the show are just never going to work.

6 The Tangle Teezer shows how even a bad pitch can lead to an investment.

7 Just being on the show can help a business take off.

8 The sharks aren't always as clever as they think they are.

8 Work in groups. Choose three questions to discuss.

1 Do you think reality TV shows / talent shows like this are positive? Why? / Why not?

2 Why do you think businesses fail?

3 Why do you think some businesses succeed?

4 Have you got any ideas for a business? How likely is it that you will do it?

5 Do you know anyone who has a business? How successful is it?

GRAMMAR

Expressing obligation and ability

We use ***must*** to show a present obligation / necessity but a form of ***have to*** when we need a present perfect / past form, etc. or the sentence requires an *-ing* form or infinitive. Where we want to be clear something creates an obligation for someone, we use ***force someone + to + verb*** or ***make someone* + verb**.

*By not **having to repeat** the process, customers save time and money.*

*So maybe they need some vicious criticism **to make them stop**.*

*No one**'s forcing anyone to accept** an offer.*

We use ***can*** to show a present ability / possibility but a form of ***be able to*** where we need a present perfect / future form, etc. or the sentence requires an *-ing* form or infinitive. Where we want to be clear something creates a possibility for someone, we use ***allow / enable someone + to + verb*** or ***let someone* + verb**.

*We **haven't been able to** raise sufficient money to go ahead with the project.*

*The programme **allows** hard-working people to succeed.*

*The investment might **enable** people to become millionaires.*

*It's a brush for long hair that **lets** you get rid of knots painlessly.*

9 Look at the examples in the Grammar box. Then look at the mistakes crossed out in these sentences. In pairs discuss how each sentence should be corrected.

1 This deal means I'll finally ~~can~~ give up my day job.

2 If the loan is approved, it will ~~able~~ us buy more stock and take advantage of the interest we've generated.

3 The feedback ~~made~~ us to look at the design again.

4 The device allows you to share files without you ~~must~~ rely on a computer.

5 Over the last few years, we ~~can~~ keep ahead of our competitors by developing new products.

6 We were forced to cut costs ~~for to able us~~ compete.

7 Thanks to all the effort everyone put in, in the end we ~~can~~ fulfil all our orders before Christmas. Well done!

8 If we'd done more market research before launching the first model, we would not have ~~must~~ redesign it so soon. It would've ~~forced~~ us think about our product a bit more.

9 It's a risk more investors are going to ~~must~~ take.

10 We'll soon ~~can~~ generate all our own electricity, which will ~~can~~ us cut costs massively.

10 Work in pairs. Tell each other about six of these things.

• something you haven't been able to do recently

• something you're glad you won't have to do in the future

• something you used to be able to do, but can't any more

• something everyone should have to do

• something you'd like to not have to do

• something you'd love to be able to do

• something a little more money would enable you to do

• something a lot more money would allow you to do

• something getting a particular qualification would enable you to do

• something which you have to force yourself to do

G See Grammar reference 16C. ⟫

SPEAKING TASK

11 Work in pairs. You are going to try to pitch products to others in the class. As a class, organize yourselves into A pairs and B pairs. Then, with your partner, choose one of the products on your card and prepare what you are going to say.

Pair A: Look at the list of products and businesses for investment in File 14 on page 197.

Pair B: Look at the list of products and businesses for investment in File 24 on page 200.

12 Join with a different pair. Take turns to pitch one of your products to the other pair. If you like the product, offer to invest in their company. Negotiate what percentage of the company you want in return – and specify any other conditions.

■ MY OUTCOMES ■

Work in pairs. Discuss the questions.

1 How useful and / or interesting was the topic of business for you?

2 Having completed this unit, what sort of conversations can you do better?

3 What did you find challenging about language in this unit?

4 What have you been doing outside the classroom to practise or revise language from the coursebook?

Two sisters present their business idea to possible investors in *Shark Tank*.

Stories

IN THIS LESSON, YOU:
- write a story with a given first line
- use descriptive language
- use different verbs to add interest
- include a summary sentence

SPEAKING

1 Discuss the questions.

1 When you were at school, how often did you write stories? Did you like it? Why? / Why not?

2 Why might it be good to write short stories in your own language? What about in English?

WRITING

2 Read the task from an exam. Individually, think of answers to the questions.

> Write a story for our magazine. The story must begin with this sentence.
>
> *Juana heard a knock, but when she opened the door of her flat there was no one there.*
>
> The story must include:
> - a package
> - an apology

1 What kind of person could Juana be? What could she do next?

2 What could be in the package? What purpose could there be for it?

3 Why might Juana need to apologize? Why might someone need to apologize to Juana?

3 Compare your ideas in groups and think of one more possibility to answer each question.

4 Read the story. Were any of your ideas similar? Do you like this idea or do you prefer your own?

Juana heard a knock, but when she opened the door of her flat there was no one there. She heard someone going down the stairs. She went to the stairs, but there was no one there. When she came back, she saw a small package by the door. She opened the box. Inside was a watch, some money and a note.

The note said: When I was a young girl, I used to come into your shop and buy things for my parents, but I also stole from you. I had a lot of problems. I knew it was wrong, but I still did it. You were always very kind to me. Now I'm older, I want to say sorry.

Juana thought about all the young people who came into her shop and smiled.

Creative writing can help develop language and other skills.

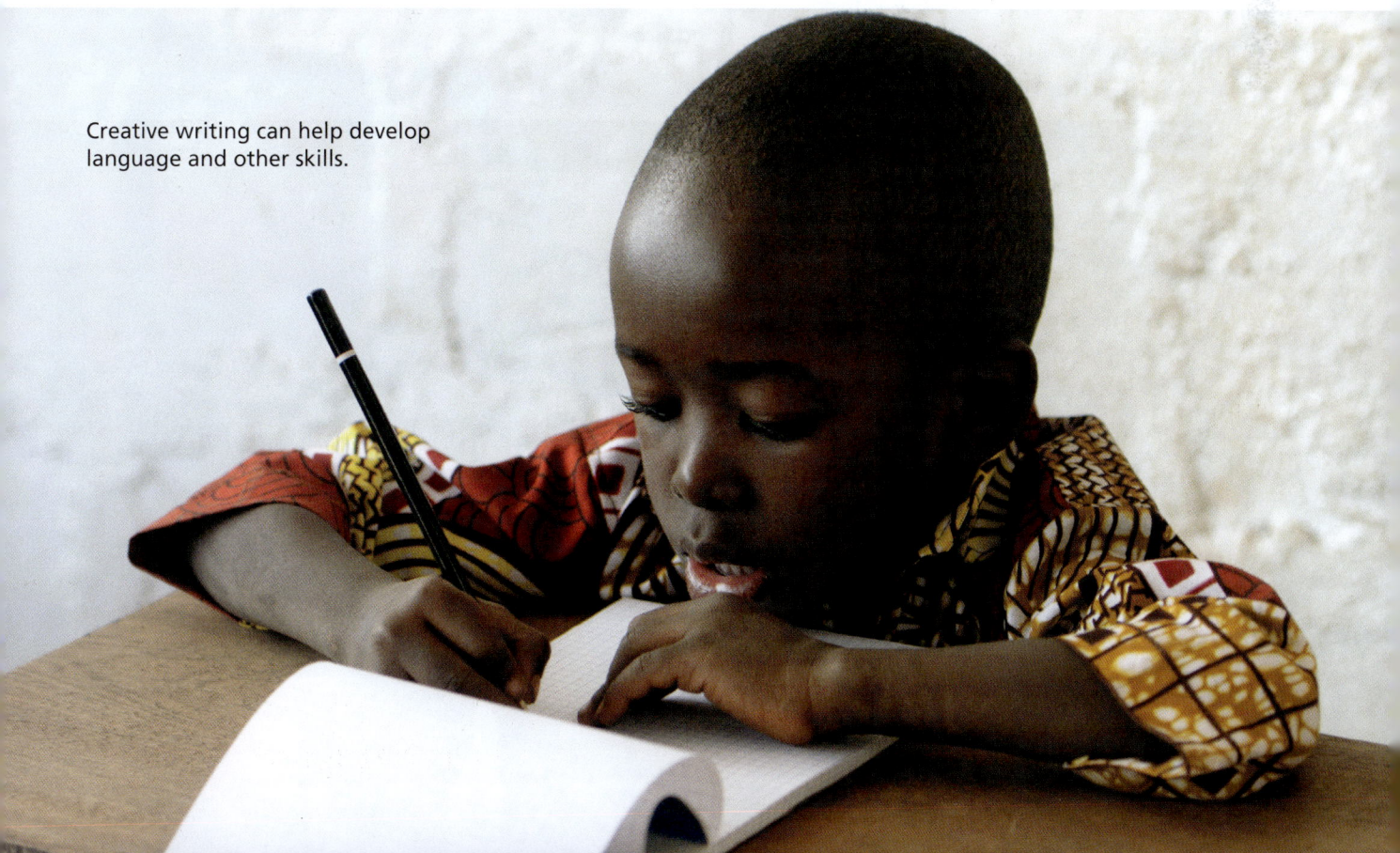

5 **M** Work in pairs. Look back at the story and decide where it could be improved:

- using descriptive adjectives (e.g. tiny, huge)
- using descriptive adverbs (e.g. run quickly, walk slowly)
- using descriptive verbs that show how you did something (e.g. rush, bend down, grab, whisper)
- varying verb forms (e.g. was -ing, had done, should have)
- avoiding repetition
- adding a twist or 'lesson' learned at the end of the story.

6 Read a second version of the story. Find examples of the six ways to improve a story in Exercise 5.

Juana heard a knock, but when she opened the door of her flat there was no one there. She heard someone running off down the stairs. In her younger days, she might have raced after them. Juana was about to close the door, when she noticed the small neatly wrapped box someone had left on the floor outside. She struggled to bend down and picked it up. Back inside her flat, she carefully unwrapped the package and stared at what was inside. A beautiful gold watch, a roll of money and a handwritten note.

The note said: Dear Juana, when I was a young girl, I used to come into your shop and buy stuff for my parents. You were always kind to me and would sometimes give me a sweet, saying what a good girl I was, but actually I was stealing from you. I'd often grab things and slip them into my bag. I had a lot of problems then. I knew I shouldn't be doing it, and I sometimes wish you'd caught me, but you never did. Anyway, now I'm older and wiser, I just want to say sorry.

Juana thought about all the young people who had come into her shop. She smiled and whispered to herself, 'Thank you'. As she'd always said to her husband, 'There's good in everyone – even those who do bad.'

7 Discuss these questions about the story.

1 What else do you learn about Juana? What kind of person is she?
2 Why didn't the girl talk to Juana, do you think?
3 What do you think of the final message?

USEFUL LANGUAGE Interesting verbs

8 Read the pairs of opposites in these sentences. Choose the option that suggests doing something quietly or slowly.

1 He *glanced / stared* at his phone.
2 He *crept / raced* down the corridor.
3 She *whispered / screamed*, 'Watch out!'
4 The door *banged / clicked* shut behind him.
5 She *struggled / leaped up* from her seat.

9 Work in pairs. Try to think of reasons for each of the actions in Exercise 8.

He glanced at his phone to check the time.

He stared at his phone in disbelief. The message said he'd won a million dollars.

Story endings

We often finish a short story with a kind of summary sentence explaining what message we should take from it, or what happened afterwards.

As she'd always said to her husband, 'There's good in everyone – even those who do bad.'

And they all lived happily ever after.

In an exam, thinking of common endings may help you frame your story and include different verb forms.

10 Complete these story endings with the correct form of a verb.

1 I had been incredibly lucky. It _____ have been so much worse.
2 If she hadn't done that, I wouldn't _____ here today.
3 It was the last time he _____ ever see her again.
4 And that _____ how my mother met my father.
5 I just wanted the ground to open up and I _____ never been so embarrassed since that day.
6 It _____ been the best day of her life and one she was never _____ to forget.
7 It just goes to show that you _____ never judge a book by its cover.
8 It just goes to show that if at first you don't succeed, _____ trying and one day you _____ .

11 Work in pairs. Decide how many of the story endings in Exercise 10 you could use for these story tasks. You can change words like pronouns if you need to. Explain how the ending would relate to the rest of the story.

1 Begin your story: *David looked out of the tent and couldn't believe his eyes.* (include a storm / a lake)
2 Begin your story: *We were tired after a morning's sightseeing, so we stopped for a rest.* (include a phone / help)

PRACTICE

12 Work in pairs. Choose one of the tasks in Exercise 11. Follow these instructions.

- Individually, brainstorm ideas about possible people, the place, the actions in the story, and the ending.
- With your partner, compare your ideas and choose the ones you like or think of something new.
- Individually, write an initial draft describing the basic events. (100–150 words)
- With your partner, compare your texts and discuss how you might improve them with different vocabulary or verb forms, etc.
- Rewrite the text in 140–200 words.

VIDEO Out and about

1 Work in pairs. Answer the questions.

1 What does success mean to you?

2 What does a person need to be successful?

Understanding accents

Some accents replace a /w/ sound with /v/, so *wet* /wet/ may sound like *vet* /vet/; *went* /went/ like *vent* /vent/; and *wary* /weərɪ/ more like *vary* /veərɪ/.

2 📹 Watch the video. Which person has the closest views to you? What do they say?

3 📹 Work in pairs. Match the statements with the speakers and explain your choices. You may match statements with more than one speaker. Then watch again to check.

a It's about finding happiness rather than wealth.

b For me it's not about getting to the top in your career.

c Sometimes society can impose its own idea of how you should be.

d You can't give up easily. You have to keep going.

e You need to have clear goals and get on with them.

f People recognizing that you're doing a good job.

g Successful people aren't shy and insecure.

h You have to create your own opportunities.

i For me, success is any time I meet a deadline.

4 Discuss the questions with your partner.

1 Who do you know who is determined, pro-active and/or self-confident. Give examples.

2 What recognition have you received for work you have done?

3 Have you ever missed a deadline or come close to it? When? What happened?

VIDEO Developing conversations

5 📹 You are going to watch two people talking about a recipe. Watch and take notes on what they say.

6 📹 Work in pairs. Compare what you understood. Watch again if you need to.

7 Discuss the questions with your partner.

1 Would you make this dish? Why? / Why not?

2 What else might you want to know about the recipe?

3 Do you think cooking should be taught at school? If so, what aspects should kids learn?

8 FS 📹 Watch again. Complete the sentences with three to five words in each gap.

1 What was that _____ yesterday?

2 Then it's a layer of _____ stewing for thirty minutes.

3 . . . bit of cheese and then you _____ with the pasta sheets.

4 How many cherry tomatoes _____ in that recipe.

5 Yeah, yeah, yeah and then _____ vegetables when you're making it.

6 . . . _____ vegetable stock in there as well.

7 I put a bechamel sauce in, _____ .

8 OK, _____ creamy, right?

CONVERSATION PRACTICE

9 Work in pairs. You are going to practise a conversation.

1 Choose a Conversation practice from either Lesson 15A or Lesson 16A.

2 Look at the language in that lesson.

3 Check the meaning of anything you've forgotten with your partner.

4 Have the conversation. Try to improve on the last time you did it.

Grammar and Vocabulary

GRAMMAR

1 Complete the text with one word in each gap.

This show has sometimes been accused ¹_____ showing off and suggesting dishes that take too long to prepare, and if that's ever been the case, then it's obviously something we'd be keen to apologize ²_____ . ³_____ , the recipe we ⁴_____ be showing you today is one of the easiest things you'll ever cook. It's a stir-fry and, to be honest, the most important thing is the equipment. Make sure you have a good wok – a Chinese frying pan. Personally, I can't imagine ever ⁵_____ anything but a Fissler. They're not cheap, but they're the kind of thing that can ⁶_____ even a beginner look good. They ⁷_____ you to cook a huge range of Chinese food and are super-easy to clean and store – ⁸_____ , as I said, they can be rather expensive.

2 Read the first sentence in each pair. Complete the second sentence so that it has a similar meaning. Use between three and five words, including the word in bold.

1 To ensure the beans are soft, soak them overnight.

Soak the beans overnight, _____ too hard.
OTHERWISE

2 There was widespread opposition, but they still went ahead and built the factory.

The factory was built _____ . **DESPITE**

3 To avoid further strikes, we would urge the management to increase its offer.

_____ its offer, there will be further strikes. **IF**

4 The company is accused of putting profit above people.

The company is _____ putting people first.
CRITICIZED

5 Don't call between nine and ten, OK? My favourite TV show is on then.

Don't call between nine and ten as _____ my favourite TV show then. **BE**

6 They made me do it even though I didn't want to.

I _____ it even though I didn't want to. **FORCED**

7 The terrible weather has prevented us from visiting you.

We _____ visit you because of the awful weather.
ABLE

3 Choose the correct option to complete the sentences.

1 I'm happy to lend it to you, *in case / provided / once* you can pay me back this week.

2 Leave to cook slowly *during / once / for* it has come to the boil.

3 *I'll be teaching / I'll teach / I teach* when you get here so I'll ask reception to show you to the room.

4 We'll soon *can / be able to / let* attract further investment.

5 He strongly denies *doing / to do / about doing* anything wrong.

6 In the end, he confessed *to steal / stealing / to stealing* the money.

4 ▶ Listen. Write the six sentences you hear.

VOCABULARY

5 Match the verbs (1–10) with the collocates (a–j).

1	pencil in	a	a late payment / the matter
2	chase up	b	the onions / some wood
3	implement	c	trading / to exist
4	overcome	d	an order / an ad in the paper
5	place	e	the garlic / the opposition
6	bake	f	a meeting / the date
7	cease	g	the strategy / the new policy
8	soak	h	doubts / various obstacles
9	chop	i	a loaf / in the oven
10	crush	j	overnight / in hot water

6 Decide if these words are connected to cooking, business or both – and in what way.

dip	fulfil	leftovers	melt	place	process
put forward	sprinkle	squeeze	stake	take over	target

7 Complete the sentences using the correct form of the words.

1 He was _____ (qualify) for cheating.

2 The situation got worse because it was _____ (manage).

3 She overcame great financial _____ (hard) to achieve her success.

4 We have very _____ (ambition) plans for expansion.

5 We have _____ (perform) all our competitors in four of the last five years.

6 The UK is now an incredibly _____ (culture) society. People from all over the world live there.

7 I _____ (do) it at the gym so I was stiff this morning.

8 I got food poisoning from some _____ (cook) chicken.

8 Complete the story with one word in each gap. The first letters are given.

Ten years ago, my brother invented an energy-saving device for the home. He took out a ¹p _____ to protect his invention and we set up a business to sell the device. We ²p _____ a lot of our money into the business and we didn't ³b _____ e _____ for the first four years, although our ⁴t _____ grew steadily. Then one year, energy prices soared and we were suddenly ⁵f _____ with orders. The business ⁶e _____ rapidly as we built a new factory and ⁷t _____ o _____ over 100 new staff. We also decided to ⁸d _____ by investing heavily in research and development to come up with new products. We were beginning to see some ⁹r _____ on this investment when a big tech company offered to buy the business. After the takeover, I could have stayed on, but I decided to resign as ¹⁰C _____ and take time off, as I was burned out. My brother also left the company, but he's immediately started a new ¹¹v _____ and is looking for ¹²p _____ partners to join him.

Grammar reference

1 ENTERTAINMENT

1A HABITS

Present

To talk about present habits we generally use the present simple. We can also use *tend to* + verb.

*I **listen** to music all the time.*

*I **tend to watch** films on demand these days.*

Note that there are two possible negative forms for *tend to*.

*I **don't tend to** go to the cinema that much.*

*I **tend not to** go out during the week.*

DID YOU KNOW?

We can use *do / does* + verb in an affirmative sentence when we want to emphasize a contrast to a habit.

*I'm mainly vegetarian, but I **do** occasionally eat meat.*

*She works at home, but she **does** occasionally go into the office.*

Past

To talk about past habits, we can use the past simple, *used to* + verb, or *would* + verb. *Used to* and *would* (usually contracted to 'd) have a similar meaning when talking about past habits. However, using *would* in negatives and questions is less common.

*I **listened** to music all the time when I was younger.*

*I **used to play** computer games all the time.*

***Did** you **use to watch** that cartoon when you were a kid?*

*I **didn't use to go** out much.*

*I **never used to do** much sport.*

*I**'d watch** a lot of reality TV when I was in my teens.*

Note that for *used to,* there is technically no final *-d* in negatives and questions. However, you may sometimes see it written with a final *-d*. The pronunciation is the same with or without the *-d*. When forming the negative with *never,* we keep the final *-d*.

Note also that we only use *used to,* and not *would,* to talk about past states (e.g. *I **used to have** long hair*. NOT *I ~~would have~~ long hair*.)

We often use adverbs and adverbial phrases to express the frequency of the habit. Some common and useful examples include:

always / constantly / all the time

often / normally / usually / generally / as a rule

sometimes / occasionally / (every) now and again / (every) now and then / from time to time / hardly ever / rarely / once in a blue moon

phrases of specific time: *once a week / two or three times a month / a couple of times a year,* etc.

*We **usually** eat out a couple of times a month.*

*I **mostly** eat vegetarian food **as a rule**. I guess I eat meat maybe **once every couple of weeks**.*

*I **hardly ever** watch football these days. I used to watch it **all the time**.*

*He's **often** late for work. The traffic is **sometimes** unpredictable.*

*We see each other **every now and again**. **Once a month**, maybe.*

We also use phrases with *don't … as much as I'd like to / I want to / I used to / we did before.*

*I don't go out **as much as I used to**.*

*We don't see each other **as much as we'd like to**.*

Exercise 1

Read the first sentence in each pair. Complete the second sentence so that it has a similar meaning. Use between three and five words, including the word in bold.

1 I only go to the cinema once a year at most. **HARDLY**
   I _____ cinema.
2 We used to fight constantly when we were kids. **TIME**
   We used _____ when we were kids.
3 As a rule, people don't read on public transport here. **TEND**
   People here _____ public transport.
4 We'd never get homework at my old school. **USED**
   We _____ at my old school.
5 He was fitter before because he cycled 50 km every day. **WOULD**
   He used to be _____ cycle 50 km every day.
6 I did it all the time when I was younger, but I don't do it so often now. **AS**
   I don't do it _____ to.

Exercise 2

Complete the sentences so they are true for you, using at least one frequency word or phrase.

1 I go to the cinema …
   I go to the cinema from time to time, maybe once a month.
2 I eat vegetarian food …
3 At school, we used to get homework …
4 As a child, I'd get into trouble …
5 I go out during the week …

Common mistakes

- *I ~~was going~~ **went** / **used to go** swimming a lot when I was younger.*
  Don't use the past continuous to talk about past habits.
- *I ~~would have~~ **used to have** long hair when I was younger.*
  Don't use *would* to talk about past states.
- *I don't go **as much** ~~how~~ **as** I'd like to.*
  Don't use *how* instead of *as* in comparatives.

Exercise 3

Find the mistake in each sentence and rewrite the sentence correctly.

1 I was reading lots of sci-fi books in my teens. I must've read hundreds of them.
2 My parents never used to go out late at night because we would live in quite a rough area.
3 We're both so busy these days, so we don't see each other as much how we used to.
4 As a rule, I don't use to watch TV much these days. There are too many annoying ads.

DID YOU KNOW?

Would is actually more common than *used to* to talk about past habits. We generally use *used to* to express facts and *would* to express tendencies. So while we often introduce a topic with *used to*, we tend to give the details with *would*.

*'**Did** you **use to watch** that children's news show that was on TV when we were kids?' 'Yeah, I**'d watch** it from time to time. My parents **would** usually watch it with us.'*

1C ADJECTIVES AND ADVERBS

Adjectives

Adjectives can generally go in two positions:

- directly before the noun

  The film had a really **uplifting** ending.

  It's a pretty **catchy** soundtrack.

  It looks like a very **old** painting.

- after noun + linking verb, such as *be, become, get, go, feel, grow, look, remain, seem, smell, stay, sound, taste* and *turn*.

  The ending was really **uplifting**.

  The soundtrack is pretty **catchy**.

  The painting looks very **old**.

Note that most adjectives can occur in both positions. However, some adjectives can only go in one position.

That's the main reason. NOT ~~That reason is main.~~

Some people were asleep. NOT ~~There were some asleep people.~~

Adverbs

Many adverbs are formed by adding -ly to the adjective, but some adverbs have the same form as the adjective: *fast, hard, early, late, right, daily, yearly.*

We arrived **late** for the meeting.

Did I do it **right**?

Adverbs can go in a number of positions:

- before or after verbs (and after the object if there is one)

  They **slowly** wandered from room to room.

  He always paints **quickly**.

  She studied the manuscript **carefully**.

- before adjectives

  His writing is **absolutely** impossible to read.

  It was a **strangely** moving film.

- before other adverbs

  The traffic was moving **really** slowly.

  She speaks **incredibly** quickly.

- at the start of sentences or clauses. This is to comment on, or to show an opinion about, the whole sentence or clause.

  Fortunately, no one was injured in the accident.

  I meant to be here earlier, but, **stupidly**, I got halfway here before I realized I'd left your address at home.

Exercise 1

Choose the correct option to complete these sentences about the paintings on page 13.

1 The two pieces were painted *short / shortly* before the artist's death.

2 Gabriel Metsu was both *wide / widely* admired and *reasonable / reasonably* successful during his lifetime.

3 *Unfortunate / Unfortunately*, he died at the height of his fame.

4 *Initial / Initially*, they may strike you as fairly *traditional / traditionally* portraits.

5 The young man sitting in the chair looks *calm / calmly* and is *obvious / obviously* thinking *hard / hardly* about what to write.

6 Dogs in paintings were a *frequent / frequently* symbol of loyalty and trust.

Exercise 2

Complete the sentences with these adjectives, changing them into adverbs if necessary.

beautiful	disturbing	famous	hard
interesting	regular	recent	

1 You can buy a season ticket for the museum if you're going to be a _____ visitor. It works out a lot cheaper.

2 I've been working really _____ to improve my English and I feel I'm making progress at last.

3 The artist Vincent van Gogh _____ cut off part of his left ear.

4 A _____ report has found that children are being exposed to _____ high levels of violence in video games.

5 _____ , this is one of only two portraits he ever painted, but as you can see it's _____ done – a real masterpiece.

Exercise 3

Write the sentences with the adverb in brackets in the correct place.

1 I've seen him all day. (hardly)

2 He reacted badly to the news. (fairly)

3 I think that new graffiti is awesome. (really)

4 She really worked and got a grade A. (hard)

5 The car was completely destroyed, but he escaped without a scratch. (amazingly)

6 The special effects are amazing – realistic. (incredibly)

7 He escaped with no injuries. (unbelievably)

8 They got married in 2005, but he died after. (sadly, shortly)

2 SIGHTSEEING

2A RELATIVE CLAUSES

Sometimes we use a relative clause to give information about someone or something. The relative clause comes immediately after this person or thing.

Defining relative clauses

A relative clause can give essential information about someone or something. This is sometimes called a defining relative clause, and the sentence would not make sense without the relative clause. We do not need a comma before a defining relative clause.

He's the man **that / who led our country during the war**.

Highgate is the place **where Marx is buried**.

Bristol is the place **where I met my wife**.

We can miss out the relative pronoun in a defining relative clause if it is the object of the clause.

He's the man **(that) I spoke to earlier.** (I spoke to the man; the man = the object)

Non-defining relative clauses

A non-defining relative clause gives extra, non-essential information about someone or something. The sentence would be clear and complete without the relative clause. This kind of relative clause always has a relative pronoun and we always separate the relative clause from the main clause with a comma.

I met my wife in Yonhi-Dong**, which is a suburb of Seoul.**

Vaclav Havel**, who was also a famous writer,** was the first Czech president.

Smith**, whose books have been translated into over 30 languages,** was born in 1966.

Chosica**, where Emmanuel grew up,** is a town near Lima.

Pronouns

In both kinds of relative clause, we can use the relative pronouns *who* or *whom* for people, *which* for things and *whose* for possession. We can also use the relative adverb *where*. In a defining relative clause, we can use *that* instead of *which* or *who*.

Exercise 1

Underline the relative pronouns and add a comma where it is necessary.

1 That was the home of Abram and Beatty Zimmerman, <u>whose</u> son is the famous singer, Bob Dylan.
2 We're meeting Jaime later. You know, the guy whose brother got us the tickets for the match.
3 Apparently, the hotel where we're staying in Vienna overlooks the river.
4 The 19th of July celebrates the day that we gained independence.
5 The first place we will stop at is the Cavern Club which is famous for its connection with the Beatles.

Exercise 2

Rewrite each pair of sentences as one sentence, using a relative clause.

1 The house was designed by Lutyens. He is considered one of the UK's greatest architects.
   The house was designed by Lutyens, who is considered one of the UK's greatest architects.
2 After lunch, we went to check out the castle. It was very grand.
3 We spent two days in Bergen and then drove down to Stavanger. My girlfriend has family there.
4 Chen's grandfather still lives at home with the rest of the family. His grandfather is 97.
5 She was born in Valencia. Valencia is Spain's third biggest city.
6 In the small village where he was born, there is a statue of Arnold Schwarzenegger. He has been described as 'Austria's most famous living son'.
7 The palace dates back to the early 1700s. It has been home to the monarch for over a hundred years.
8 Claremont is a small town near Los Angeles. Smith grew up there.

Commenting on a clause

We also use a non-defining relative clause with *which* to comment on, or to give our opinion of, the whole of the previous clause. This is common in spoken English.
*We spent a week hiking in the jungle, **which was an incredible experience.***
*We got lost, **which meant we missed the start of the performance.***

Common mistakes

- *We went on a guided tour round the old town, ~~that~~ **which** was nice.*
  Do not use *that* in a non-defining relative clause.
- *He was born in Mendoza, **which** ~~it~~ is near the foothills of the Andes.*
  Do not use another pronoun as well as the relative pronoun. The relative pronoun replaces the other pronoun.
- *She studied at Bologna University, which is the oldest university in the world.*
  Remember to use a comma before the relative pronoun.

Exercise 3

Complete the sentences with a non-defining relative clause, using the information from these sentences.

It was very cheap.	It was a huge relief.	It's in north Italy.
They were all amazing.	It was very kind of her.	It meant we had to get a taxi.

1 We saw the Pyramid of Tenochtitlán, Coyoacán and the Frida Kahlo Museum, <u>which were all amazing</u> .
2 I finally found my passport, _____ .
3 We missed the last bus, _____ .
4 The meal only cost €20, _____ .
5 My parents live in Bergamo _____ .
6 A passer-by offered to help, _____ .

Exercise 4

Complete the sentences with your own ideas.

1 I was born in <u>Gdansk</u> , which <u>is a city in the north of Poland</u> .
2 I was born in _____ , which _____ .
3 I live in _____ , which _____ .
4 I recently visited _____ , which _____ .
5 One day, I'd love to visit _____ , which _____ .
6 My favourite place in the world is _____ , which _____ .

2C TALKING ABOUT THE FUTURE

There is no future tense in English. We use different forms depending on what we want to express.

It's important to note that the distinction between the uses of future forms is often not clear or not important and we can sometimes use the forms interchangeably. For example:
I'm staying in this evening. OR *I'm going to stay in this evening.* (for a plan / intention / arrangement)
You'll love Prague. OR *You're going to love Prague.* (for a prediction)

The rules and explanations below are guidelines about how we talk about the future.

Present simple

We use the present simple to talk about something that is fixed as part of a timetable, itinerary or programme.
*My train **leaves** at nine.*
*When **does** the exhibition **start**?*

Present continuous

We use the present continuous to talk about arrangements, or something that is agreed or finalized in some way.
*I'm **meeting** a friend later.*
*We're **returning** to the UK next year.*
*I'm **staying** in this evening.*

Be going to

We use *be going to* to talk about future plans and intentions that were made before the time of speaking.
*I'm **going to do** some exam revision tonight.*
*We're not **going to say** anything to him.*

Will

We use *will* to talk about decisions made at the time of speaking. This includes promises, offers and requests.
*I'll **call** her now and see what she says.*
*I'll **help** you with that.*
*Thanks. I'll **pay** you back tomorrow.*

Predictions

- For predictions based on direct present evidence (e.g. what we can see or hear or other information available), we usually prefer *be going to*.
  Look at the traffic. We**'re not going to get** there before six.
  It**'s going to be** a nice day.
- For predictions based more on personal feeling or opinion, we usually prefer *will*. We often begin with *I think* and sometimes add *probably* between *will* and the verb.
  I think you**'ll love** Prague. It's a great city.
  I**'ll** probably **regret** this tomorrow!

Exercise 1

What are the phrases in bold expressing in the conversations? Match the phrases in bold (1–8) with the uses (a–d).

a something fixed, such as part of a schedule.
b an arrangement
c an intention or plan
d a decision made at the time of speaking

1 A: Have you emailed Simona about the trip yet?
  B: Ah, no, I haven't. Thanks for reminding me. ¹**I'll do it in a minute**.
2 A: Do you want to go for a bite to eat this evening?
  B: Sorry, I can't. ²**Jackie and Mark are coming round** for dinner.
3 A: Why are you wearing those old clothes?
  B: ³**I'm going to clean the windows**.
    A: Oh, right. Well, ⁴**I'll give you a hand** if you like.
4 A: I think Chris Briscoe needs to see you – something about the Munich conference.
  B: Yes, I know. ⁵**I'm going to arrange a meeting** with him as soon as I have a moment. Do you know when ⁶**the conference is**, exactly?
  A: Yes, the last weekend in November.
  B: Ah, OK. And ⁷**are you going?**
  A: I can't, sadly. ⁸**My brother's getting married** that weekend.

Exercise 2

Choose the best options to complete the conversations.

1 A: What time *is the train / will the train be* this afternoon?
  B: 3.30, I think.
  A: OK. So, *I'll meet / I'm meeting* you at the station around quarter past, then.
2 A: *I'll see / I'm seeing* Mary later. Do you want to join us? *We're going to try / We try* that new pizza place.
  B: Thanks, but I've got my final exam tomorrow. *I stay / I'm going to stay* in tonight and do some last-minute revision. But *I won't do / I'm not doing* anything tomorrow night, if you fancy doing something?
  A: Sure. Let's do something then. *It'll be / It's going to be* good to help you celebrate the end of the exams.
3 A: I'm so excited about Paris next weekend! I can't wait!
  B: Lucky you! *It'll be / It's being* amazing. *When's your flight / When will your flight be*?
  A: Thursday afternoon. That reminds me, actually. I need to book a cab to the airport before I forget.
  B: *I'll give / I'm going to give* you a lift, if you want. It's not a problem.
4 A: Look at this traffic. *It's being / It's going to be* a long journey.
  B: Yeah. What time do you think *we'll get / we're getting* there?
  A: Well, *it's / it's going to be* six at the earliest, I'd say.
  B: OK, *I phone / I'll phone* Sandy and tell her *we're being / we're going to be* a bit late.

Be due to

We use *be due to* to talk about when things are scheduled to happen. This is often for formal or officially arranged events or situations.
The bus **is due to arrive** in five minutes.
Entry requirements **are due to change** next year.

Be likely to and be bound to

- We use *be likely to* to talk about things that are probable – we think they will happen. We use *be unlikely to* to talk about things that are improbable – we don't think they will happen. We can use *highly* and *quite* to show the degree of likelihood.
  We**'re unlikely to** arrive before midnight.
  It**'s highly likely** the exhibition will be extended.
- We use *be bound to* to talk about things we see as (almost) certain to happen.
  There**'s bound to be** a delay. There always is.
  It**'s bound to be** sunny in July.

Exercise 3

Read the first sentence in each pair. Complete the second sentence so that it has a similar meaning. Use between three and five words, including the word in bold.

1 I'm almost sure they'll be late. **BOUND**
  They _____ late.
2 It's very possible that the traffic will be bad at that time of day. **LIKELY**
  The traffic _____ at that time of day.
3 I'm pretty certain the concert will sell out. **HIGHLY**
  It _____ that the concert will sell out.
4 According to the itinerary, we get back to the hotel at six. **DUE**
  According to the itinerary, we _____ to the hotel at six.
5 I don't think the restaurant will be full. **UNLIKELY**
  The restaurant _____ full.

3 THINGS YOU NEED

3A EXPLAINING PURPOSE

We can use the phrases in bold to explain the purpose or function of something:
It's used for clean*ing* bottles.
It's used to clean bottles.
You use it for measur*ing* angles.
You use it to measure angles.
It's for peel*ing* vegetables.
It's to peel vegetables.

Note the use of *for* + *-ing* and *to* + verb.

We use the following phrases with *can* and *could* to explain a possible use of something:
You can use it to open a jar.
It could be used to unblock a sink.

Exercise 1

Complete the responses using the correct form of these verbs.

clean	count	cycle	massage
measure	remove	run	

1 A: What's a pedometer?
  B: It's like a watch. You use it to _____ how many steps you take each day.
2 A: What's an anemometer?
  B: It's a device used for _____ wind speed and direction.
3 A: What's this?
  B: You use it to _____ your back and your neck. Perfect after a stressful day!
4 A: What's this for?
  B: It's for _____ ice from the car windscreen. You can use it for _____ the mud off your shoes too!
5 A: Is it possible to walk along the river?
  B: Well, there's a pathway, but it's mainly used for _____ and _____ .

to / in order to, so and if

We can use *to / in order to, so* and *if* to explain the reason or purpose for using something.

to / in order to

We use *to* + verb or *in order to* + verb. While *to* and *in order to* can be interchangeable, *in order to* is generally more common in formal contexts.
*I need a hammer **to** hang up this picture.*
*I could do with some scissors **to** open the packet.*
*A cable is required **in order to** connect the device to the computer.*

So

We can use *so* or *so that* with the same meaning. We use *so (that)* + clause.
*Have you got a bin bag **so** I can clear the table?*
*Use a cloth **so that** you don't mark the table.*

DID YOU KNOW?

So (that) is often followed by *can*.
*Do you want to borrow a torch **so you can see** where you're going outside?*
*Pass me a cloth **so that I can grip** the lid of this jar better.*

If

We can use an *if*-clause to talk about possible situations in which something might be necessary.
*This is useful stuff to have **if you need** to remove stains.*
***If you can't find** anything else, hang it up with a nail.*

Exercise 2

Complete the sentences using *so, if* or *to*.

1 Have you got a dustpan and brush _____ I can clean up this mess I've made?
2 I must buy some wire _____ hang this new photo up with.
3 _____ you want to put those shelves up properly, you'll need a drill.
4 You'll need an adaptor _____ you're going to use your laptop in the States.
5 Put some cream on _____ protect yourself from the sun.
6 Can I borrow your stepladder _____ I can change the light bulb in the hall?

Exercise 3

Complete the sentences using *so, if, to* or *in order to* and the ideas in brackets. You may need to add some extra words.

1 We need some matches _____ the stove. (light)
2 Maybe you should wrap some tape round where there's a crack _____ . (it / not / get) any worse.
3 You'll need wire cutters _____ that – not scissors. (you / want / cut)
4 Have you got something I can stand on _____ this light bulb? (I / can / change)
5 Have you got a clip _____ these papers together? (keep)
6 A microscope is needed _____ the organization of cells. (examine)

3C SHOULD and SHOULD HAVE

Use

We use *should* to say what we think is the correct or best thing to do. We often use *should* to give general advice, suggestions or criticism.

Form

- We use *should (not / never)* + verb to talk about the present.
  *You **should see** complaints as an opportunity to improve.*
  *You **shouldn't lose** your temper when making a complaint.*
  *We **should never give** terrorists what they want.*
  *Stop distracting me. We **should be working** not chatting.*
- We use *should (not / never)* + *have* + past participle to talk about the past. We often use the form *should've*, especially in more informal contexts such as speaking.
  *He **should've checked** the shoes at the point of sale.*
  *They **shouldn't have parked** here. They've blocked me in.*

Note that we can use the continuous form with *should*.
*You don't know what to do? Well, you **should've been paying** attention.*

Exercise 1

Complete the three conversations with the correct form of *should* and the verbs in brackets.

1 A: You [1]_____ (come) bowling with us. We had a great time.
  B: Well, you [2]_____ (not tell) me so late. It was too late to rearrange things.
  A: I know. Sorry. But maybe we [3]_____ (go) next week sometime if you fancy that.
2 A: Did you hear that Sally's been sacked? Someone saw her in a shopping mall the other day when she [4]_____ (work). Apparently, she'd phoned in to say she was ill and she said that the doctor had told her that she [5]_____ (stay) in bed for a few days. I think this wasn't the first time that had happened.
  B: Well, fair enough, to be honest. She really [6]_____ (know) better. She's only got herself to blame.
3 A: The neighbours kept me awake last night again.
  B: Really? Maybe you [7]_____ (report) them next time.
  A: I have already, but the police don't seem to want to do anything.
  B: They [8]_____ (come and warn) them at least.
  A: Well, maybe, but I guess they had more important things to do.
  B: Did you tell them how often it's happening?
  A: Not really. Maybe I [9]_____ (not be) so calm when I spoke to them. Perhaps I [10]_____ (sound) a bit more desperate!
  B: Yeah, maybe.
  A: I don't know. Maybe we [11]_____ (just move).
  B: Yeah, but you [12]_____ (have to). That's just wrong!

DID YOU KNOW?

We often use the passive with *should*.

- For the present, we use *should + be +* past participle.
  *The shop assistant **should be sacked**.*
- For the past, we use *should + have been +* past participle.
  *The shop assistant **should have been sacked.***

Exercise 2

Complete the sentences with *should* and the correct passive form of these verbs.

not allow	check	close down	never post

1 The website _____ before it went live. The contact details are not correct.
2 The restaurant is filthy. It really _____ . I won't be going there again, that's for sure.
3 Fake news like this _____ . It _____ in the first place. Social media platforms need better policing.

Common mistakes

- *We should ~~to~~ go. We're already late.*
- *I should ~~working~~ be working in the office today, but there's a public transport strike.*
- *He should ~~took~~ have taken it back to the shop sooner.*
  You may also sometimes see or hear people use *of* instead of *have*. This is a common mistake.
- *They should ~~of~~ have had it fixed by a professional.*

Exercise 3

Find the mistake in each sentence and rewrite the sentence correctly.

1 I should rang you earlier, but I forgot. Sorry.
2 It's terrible I have to work tonight. I should celebrating my birthday with my friends!
3 When you take it back, you should to ask for some kind of compensation.
4 I sometimes think I should never gone to university because I didn't enjoy it much and I have a huge debt now.
5 They should of tried to sort it out instead of blaming me.

4 SOCIETY

4A *SO* AND *SUCH*

Use

We use *so* and *such* to emphasize the degree of something.
*It was **so** interesting.*
*It's **such** a great idea.*

We also use *so* and *such* to link cause and result. The *so / such* clause expresses the cause and this is followed by a clause that expresses the result.
*I'm **so** tired, I can hardly stay awake.*
*It was **such** a boring film that many people left before the end.*

Form

- Use *so* + an adjective or an adverb.
  *I'm **so disappointed**.*
  *Things change **so slowly**.*

We also use *so + few / many +* countable noun and *so + little / much +* uncountable noun.
***So few** people voted for him.*
*There are **so many** homeless people these days.*

- Use *such* + noun and *such* + adjective + noun.
  *It's **such** a **shame**.*
  *It was **such** a **great day**.*

We also use *such a lot of* + noun.
*There's **such a lot of rubbish** on the streets.*

Cause and result

When we use *so* and *such* to express cause and result, using *that* to link the result clause is optional.
*There's **so** much traffic, it's usually quicker to walk.*
***So** few people had bought tickets **that** they decided to cancel the event.*
*They did **so** badly in the elections **that** their leader resigned.*
*It was **such** a surprise, I didn't know what to say!*

Exercise 1

Choose the correct option to complete the clauses expressing a cause (1–8). Then match them with the clauses expressing the result (a–h).

1 Our situation sometimes looks *so / such* bleak,
2 He was involved in *so / such* a terrible public scandal,
3 The government have lied *so / such* many times,
4 Food prices have gone up *so / such* quickly,
5 The earthquake caused *so / such* a lot of damage,
6 *So / Such* few women are having babies these days,
7 They've got *so / such* poor hospitals,
8 There's *so / such* little crime now,

a there have been riots in the street markets.
b that most kids can't even get basic health care.
c they're actually making police officers redundant!
d I've just lost faith in them.
e the government's introduced tax breaks for big families to boost the birth rate.
f that it's hard not to feel pessimistic about the future.
g that tens of thousands are feared dead.
h that in the end he was forced to resign.

Exercise 2

Complete the sentences with *many*, *much*, *few* or *little*.

1 There's so _____ poverty in the world that surely tackling that has to be our main goal.
2 So _____ people bothered to vote that the election results are almost meaningless!
3 So _____ people turned up to vote in the election, there were the longest queues ever at the polling stations.
4 So _____ new jobs have been created that there are actually a lot of posts which are unfilled.
5 So _____ research has been done into the problem that it's hard to say what's causing it.

Exercise 3

Read the first sentence in each pair. Complete the second sentence so that it has a similar meaning. Use between three and five words, including the word in bold.

1 The meeting was so boring, I almost fell asleep. **SUCH**
  It _____ , I almost fell asleep.
2 There is such a lot of fake news these days, you just don't know what to believe. **SO**
  There _____ these days, you just don't know what to believe.
3 It's been such terrible weather recently, I've hardly been outside. **SO**
  The weather _____ recently, I've hardly been outside.
4 The news has been so depressing recently that I've stopped watching it. **SUCH**
  It's been _____ recently that I've stopped watching it.

4B COMPARATIVES WITH *THE ... , THE ...*

We can show connections using the following basic patterns:

- *the* + comparative + noun + verb, *the* + comparative + noun + verb.

   The more affluent the area is, **the nicer** the cars are.

   The bigger you are, **the more difficult** it is to find nice clothes.

   The older people get, **the more forgetful** they become.

   Note that we can sometimes omit the verb *be*.

   The more affluent the area, the nicer the cars.

- *the more / less* + noun + verb, *the more / less* + noun + verb

   The more I earn, **the more** I buy.

   The less you want, **the more** you have.

- *the more / less / fewer* + noun, *the more / less / fewer* + noun

   The more traffic, **the more** pollution.

- It is possible to combine the patterns.

   The more money people have, **the greedier** they get.

   The hungrier you are, **the more** you want to eat.

   The more you practise, **the easier** it will become.

   The less I know, **the better**.

Exercise 1

Complete the sentences with one word in each gap.

1 _____ richer the country, _____ lower the birth rate.
2 The better educated people _____ , the _____ money they are likely to earn.
3 The stronger _____ economy, the _____ unemployment there is.
4 The hungrier people are, the _____ desperate they tend to be and the more conflicts _____ will be.
5 The happier people are, the _____ illnesses they _____ .

Exercise 2

Complete the sentences with the pattern *the ... , the ...* and the correct form of the word in brackets.

1 _____ (money) a person borrows, _____ (great) the risk is for the bank.
2 _____ (long) you wait, _____ (pleasurable) the reward.
3 _____ (colourful) the flower, _____ (powerful) the smell needs to be.
4 _____ (a liquid) heats up, _____ (unstable) it becomes.

DID YOU KNOW?

There are some useful fixed phrases with *the ... , the ...*

The bigger, the better.	*The fewer, the better.*
The sooner, the better.	*The more, the better.*
The simpler, the better.	*The more, the merrier.*
The faster, the better.	*The older, the wiser.*

Exercise 3

Write a short reply to each question using *the ... , the better*.

1 What size boxes do you want?
2 What kind of camera are you thinking of buying?
3 When do you want this done by?
4 How do you want your coffee?
5 How many people should we invite?

5 SPORTS AND INTERESTS

5B PAST MODALS

Use

Should(n't) have

We use *should have* + past participle to show we think something in the past which didn't happen was a good idea or the correct or best thing to do.

We **should've set off** earlier to miss the traffic.

I **should have phoned** you. I forgot, sorry.

We use *shouldn't have* or *should never have* + past participle to show you think something that happened wasn't a good idea or wasn't the correct thing to do.

You **shouldn't have hit** him. It was wrong of you.

I **should never have spoken** to him. I regret it now.

Would(n't) have

We often add a comment using *would have / wouldn't have / would never have* + past participle to show the likely consequence if a past situation had been different.

I should've paid more attention. I **wouldn't have made** that mistake.

It's your birthday? You should've said. I**'d have bought** you a present.

We should've got here earlier. We**'d've got** a better seat.

Could(n't) have

We can add a comment with *could have* + past participle to show a possible consequence if a past situation had been different.

They should've acted sooner. They **could have saved** his life.

They shouldn't have substituted the striker. They **could've** won.

We use *couldn't have / could never have* + past participle to show that something was not possible.

I should've asked for help. It was obvious I **couldn't have done** it on my own.

Form

The past form of most modal verbs is modal + *have* + past participle. *Have* is often contracted to *'ve*, especially in more informal contexts, such as speaking. *Would* is often contracted to *'d*.

I **should've** known.

We **could've** got it cheaper.

They'd have changed their mind.

Exercise 1

Choose the correct option to complete the short texts.

1 He's to blame. He *should have / would have* dealt with the problem sooner rather than leaving it so long. Things *wouldn't have / couldn't have* got so bad if he had.
2 The fire was my fault. I *shouldn't have / wouldn't have* left the cooker on while I was out.
3 It's my own fault. I *should have / would have* warmed up more before I started playing. I *wouldn't have / couldn't have* strained my back if I had.
4 It's the team's own fault they got knocked out. They *wouldn't have / shouldn't have* underestimated the opposition. They *should've / would've* taken the game more seriously. They *could've / should've* won if they had.
5 The game was pretty awful, but I suppose it *should have / could have* been worse – we *could have / would have* lost. A draw wasn't so bad.
6 Thanks for your help. I *shouldn't have / couldn't have* done it without you. I certainly *wouldn't have / shouldn't have* finished it on time anyway. That's for sure.

Exercise 2

Complete the sentences with the correct form of the words.

1

would / get	should / set off	should / warn

A: Sorry we're late. We _____ earlier and avoided the traffic. We _____ here much earlier.

B: Yeah, sorry, I _____ you about the traffic round here. It can be a nightmare at rush hour.

2

could / be	could / be	should / have

A: Poor Erika, getting knocked off her bike last night. Sounds like she had a lucky escape.

B: Yeah, but to be honest, she _____ lights on her bike. She's only got herself to blame. It _____ a lot worse. She _____ seriously injured.

3

could / give	should / not / leave	should / tell	would / not / enjoy

A: Hey, you _____ the concert so early last night. They came back on stage and played a couple more songs after you left.

B: Ah, that's a shame. But I was feeling really hot and it was a bit too crowded in there. I really needed some fresh air. I _____ it. And also, I had to get the bus.

A: I _____ you a lift. You _____ me!

5C THE PRESENT PERFECT SIMPLE AND CONTINUOUS

Use

We use the present perfect simple and present perfect continuous in a number of ways to connect the past with now.

- We use the **present perfect simple** to talk about something completed at some point before now, but which has a connection to the present.

  *Finally, we***'ve finished**!

  ***Have** you **fixed** the running machine yet?*

- We also use the **present perfect simple** to talk about how many times an action happened from the past up to now.

  *He***'s** already **managed** *eight or nine different clubs.*

  *She***'s been** *to the gym three times so far this week.*

- We use the **present perfect continuous** to talk about something that started in the past and continues now. There is usually a focus on continuous or repeated activity and on how long.

  *She***'s been training** *hard for six months now.*

  *He***'s not been feeling** *well for a while.*

  *I***'ve been trying** *to fix my computer since this morning.*

DID YOU KNOW?

When we talk about how long an activity continued up to now, there are certain verbs that we usually use with the present perfect simple instead of the continuous. We usually see these things as more permanent situations or states.

*We***'ve been** *here for over twenty years.*

*They***'ve known** *each other for a long time.*

Form

The **present perfect simple** is *have / has* + (*not*) + past participle.

*He***'s seen** *the film a few times.*

I **haven't been** *there yet.*

***Have** you **finished**?*

The **present perfect continuous** is *have has* + (*not*) *been* + *-ing*.

*I***'ve been going** *to the gym a lot.*

It **hasn't been working** *for a while.*

***Have** you **been training** much?*

Since, for and other time phrases

We use *since* and *for* when we talk about something that started in the past and continues now. We use *since* + a point in time and *for* + a period of time.

I've been doing yoga **since I was a student**.

I've been doing yoga **for over ten years**.

She's worked there **since about 2020**.

She's worked there **for a good few years now**.

We can also use phrases such as *always, never, all my life, all day, recently,* etc. when we talk about something that started in the past and continues now.

I've **always** *loved sports.*

I've been training a lot **recently**.

Exercise 1

Complete the sentences with the present perfect simple or present perfect continuous form of the verbs. Then, think about why the form is used in each case.

1 She _____ (try) to call him all morning, but she _____ (not / be able) to get hold of him.

2 I _____ (email) them several times already, but they still _____ (not / reply).

3 I _____ (go) skiing since I was a kid and I _____ (always / love) it, but I _____ (never / fancy) snowboarding.

4 She _____ (think) about dropping out of the course for a few weeks now. I think she _____ (struggle) to keep up with all the work they give her.

5 I _____ (mean) to ask Luis if he could help me for ages, but I _____ (not / find) the right moment to ask.

6 Apparently, we _____ (go) to the same gym for years, but we _____ (never / run into) each other there.

Exercise 2

Choose the correct option to complete the sentences.

1 *I haven't seen / I haven't been seeing* him all day. He must be off work.

2 *I've never had / I've never been having* any interest in golf. I don't know why, really, because *I've always loved / I've always been loving* most other sports.

3 *I've trained / I've been training* for the 10K a lot recently. *I've already got / I've already been getting* my time down to under 50 minutes.

4 What *have you done / have you been doing? We've waited / We've been waiting* for you *for / since* over an hour.

5 He *hasn't played / hasn't been playing* a single game *for / since* the first week of the season. He's still injured.

6 *I've played / I've been playing* a lot of chess recently. In fact, *I've played / I've been playing* just about every day *for / since* the last couple of weeks.

Exercise 3

Complete the sentences so they are true for you. Try to use both the present perfect simple and the present perfect continuous in your answers.

1 I haven't ... since ...
   I haven't played rugby I left school.

2 I've ... a lot recently.

3 I've always ...

4 I've never ...

5 I've ... for ...

6 ACCOMMODATION

6A MODIFIERS

We use modifiers to make adjectives, adverbs, nouns or verbs stronger or weaker.

Modifying adjectives

We can use *very / really / completely / totally / absolutely* to make an adjective or adverb stronger.
The hotel was **really nice**. The view from the balcony was **absolutely amazing**.
I'm **very tired**. In fact, I'm **completely exhausted**.

Note that we use *absolutely* with extreme adjectives (e.g. *amazing, boiling, awful, enormous, packed*) and we use *very* with more neutral adjectives (e.g. *nice, hot, bad, big, busy*).
It was **absolutely** enormous.
NOT It was very enormous.
It was **very** big.
NOT It was absolutely big.

We can generally use *really* with both kinds of adjectives.
It was **really bad**.
It was **really awful**.

We can use *a bit / quite / fairly / pretty* to make an adjective or adverb weaker.
The internet is **a bit slow**. I think the router is **quite far away**.
The beach was **pretty busy** today. It's normally **fairly quiet**.

Note that we generally use *a bit* to express a negative idea.
They look **a bit** cheap.
It's **a bit** expensive.
NOT It's a bit nice.

DID YOU KNOW?

We can use *(a bit) too* + adjective to say that something is more than we want or need.
The train is **a bit too expensive**. Let's go by bus.

A useful pattern is *a bit too … for my liking*.
This curry is **a bit too spicy for my liking**.

Modifying nouns

We can use *a complete / a total / a real / an absolute / a bit of a / hardly any / almost no* to make a noun stronger or weaker.
There were **hardly any** activities going on there. It was **a complete** waste of time.
It was **a bit of a** nightmare. **Hardly anything** went right. **An absolute** disaster, in fact.
We had **almost no** time. It was **a real** rush.

Modifying verbs

We can use *really / absolutely / totally / almost / hardly* to make a verb or verb phrase stronger or weaker.
I **absolutely loved** the place. I **really liked** the food.
We were **really enjoying** ourselves. I **hardly noticed** the rain.
I **totally forgot** to pack my bag. We **almost missed** the bus.

Exercise 1

Choose the correct option to complete the sentences. In some cases both options are possible.

1 The town we stayed in was *a bit / quite* dull, but the surrounding area was *very / absolutely* stunning. I *hardly / really* loved the place.
2 We had *hardly / almost* any rain while we were there, but there was *a bit / a bit of* a chill in the air most days.
3 The place gets *absolutely / very* packed with tourists in August and there are *hardly / almost* no vacancies in the hotels in the summer.
4 The place was a *real / really* tourist trap and everything was *absolutely / very* expensive.
5 The food was *a bit / quite* good. And it was *quite / fairly* cheap. But a lot of it was *a bit too / fairly* spicy for my liking.
6 The beach was *fairly / a bit* near, but it was *quite / a bit* too far to walk to. Luckily, the hotel pool was *absolutely / pretty* good.

Exercise 2

Read the first sentence in each pair. Complete the second sentence so that it has a similar meaning. Use between three and five words, including the word in bold.

1 We completely wasted our time.   **COMPLETE**
   It was _____ time.
2 It was unbearably hot in the tent.   **ABSOLUTELY**
   It _____ the tent.
3 There were almost no people in the town centre last night.   **HARDLY**
   There _____ the town centre last night.
4 Personally, I'd prefer it if the music wasn't so loud!   **BIT**
   The music _____ for my liking.
5 There was hardly anything to do during the day.   **ALMOST**
   There _____ during the day.
6 I liked the food a lot.   **REALLY**
   I _____ food.

6C HAVE / GET SOMETHING DONE

Use

We use *have / get something done* in two main ways:
- to say that someone does something for us, usually when we have arranged it and / or it is part of a service.
  We order our shopping online and **have** it **delivered**.
  We're **having** the house **decorated** at the moment.
  I generally **get** my hair **cut** once a month.
- to say that something unwelcome or bad happens to us. We do not normally use *get* in this way.
  I **had** my bike **stolen**.
  They've **had** their apartment **broken into** again.

Note that *have / get something done* is a kind of passive construction. In a normal passive structure, the focus is mainly on the object (e.g. **My bike** was stolen) but with *have / get something done*, the focus is on both the object and the person that the object belongs to (e.g. I had **my bike** stolen).

Form

The form is *have / get* + object + past participle. We can use *have / get* in a range of tenses.
We **have** our car **serviced** every year.
I'm **getting** my hair **cut** tomorrow.
I **had** my wallet **stolen**.
I **should get** my eyes **tested**.
I **had to have** my picture **taken** for the college website.
I'm **going to get** my hair **dyed** blond.
I'd never **have** my hair **cut** that short! It wouldn't suit me.

Exercise 1

Complete the conversations by reordering the words in italics.

1 A: *straightened / of / getting / thinking / my hair / I'm*. I'm fed up with this hairstyle.

   B: Really? I'd love to have curly hair like you.

2 A: *that photo / get / should / framed / you*. It's really nice.

   B: Do you think so? Maybe I will, then.

3 A: Someone broke into my friend's car and *stolen / had / she / her laptop and bag*.

   B: Oh no! That's awful.

4 A: I'm going to have to stop the car. The engine's overheating.

   B: I told you *should / we / it / had / have / checked* before we left.

5 A: I'm working at home this week. *redecorated / we / the office / 're having*.

   B: Ah, *had / we / ours / done* last month.

Exercise 2

Read the first sentence and complete the second sentence so that it has a similar meaning, using a *have / get something done* structure. Use between three and five words.

1 Our luggage was stolen from our hotel room.
   We _____ from our hotel room.

2 Don't touch the gate. It's only just been painted.
   We've just _____ so be careful you don't touch it.

3 My car is at the garage at the moment, being repaired.
   I _____ at the moment.

4 They should send someone to repair the air conditioning in here.
   They really ought to _____ in here.

5 I usually do my weekly shop online and they deliver it to my house.
   I usually do my weekly shop online and _____ to my house.

Exercise 3

Write comments for the situations. Use *have / get something done* and these words.

hair / cut	eyes / test	it / look at	it / deliver	windows / clean

1 Your computer keeps crashing.
   'I need to get it looked at.'

2 Your friend's windows are very dirty.
   'You need _____ .'

3 Your hair is too long and covering your eyes.
   'I really should _____ .'

4 Your friend's vision is not as good as it used to be.
   'You need _____ .'

5 Your friend can't collect something from the shop.
   'Why don't you _____ ?'

7 NATURE

7A NARRATIVE FORMS

When we tell a story about the past or describe a past event, we often use a combination of the three narrative tenses.

The past simple

We generally use the past simple to tell the main events of the story that follow each other. These events are often linked together using words such as *and*, *and then*, *after that*, *after*, *before*.

*We **pulled over** and **waited** for the rain to stop and then we **continued** our journey.*

*So, I **sat down**, **started** to read my book and then **fell** asleep. I **didn't wake up** and I **missed** my stop.*

The past continuous

We use the past continuous to describe an activity or situation that was already in progress and was interrupted by one of the main events of the story. We often link the two with *when* or *while*. Note that we only use *while* before the activity in the past continuous.

*I **met** my wife **when** we **were** both **living** in Slovakia.*

*I **was walking** by the river **when** a dog **ran** up to me and I nearly **fell** in.*

*I **had** an accident **while** I **was driving** to work.*

The past perfect simple

We use the past perfect simple to show that an action happened before one of the main events or before the story began. We often link the events with *when* and *by the time*.

*They**'d** already **left** by the time I **got** there.*

*When I **got** to work, I realized I**'d left** my keys at home.*

DID YOU KNOW?

Continuous tenses are sometimes used to emphasize the duration of an activity. Notice the time phrases.

*It **was raining the whole time** we were there.*

*We **were waiting for hours** for the fog to lift.*

Exercise 1

Choose the correct option to complete the sentences.

1 It was getting dark, so we *decided / were deciding* to go home while we could still see the path.

2 The roads were really dangerous because the snow *was melting / had melted* a bit the day before and had then frozen again overnight.

3 The sun was burning hot and I got really sunburned because I *was forgetting / had forgotten* to put any cream on.

4 The other day, I *sat / was sitting* in a café when someone said, 'Hello you!' It was an old friend from school, who I *didn't see / hadn't seen* for years.

5 I *got / was getting* caught in a storm while I was walking home, so I *stopped / was stopping* in a café until it had blown over.

6 I went away on holiday and when I *had got back / got back* I found that some kind of bug *ate / had eaten* all the flowers in my garden!

7 The fog *was coming down / came down* suddenly and took us by surprise. We then got completely lost and *had / were having* to phone for help.

8 It absolutely poured down all morning and by the time we *arrived / were arriving*, the campsite still *didn't dry out / hadn't dried out*, so the whole place was really muddy.

Exercise 2

Complete the text with the correct forms of the verbs.

A few months ago, I ¹_____ (fly) back from Bulgaria after a week visiting friends. It ²_____ (rain) quite hard and it was quite windy, but the plane ³_____ (take off) on time. So, we ⁴_____ (be) in the air for about five minutes when suddenly there ⁵_____ (be) a huge flash of light and a really loud bang. The plane had been struck by lightning. Everything was calm but we ⁶_____ (have to) return to the airport. They needed to get an engineer to check for damage to the plane, but can you believe it, the nearest available engineer ⁷_____ (have) dinner in Milan in Italy! About six hours later, he finally ⁸_____ (arrive). He ⁹_____ (spend) 60 seconds checking the plane and we finally ¹⁰_____ (leave) two hours after that. It was a very long day!

7B PARTICIPLE CLAUSES

A participle clause usually follows a noun. The participle clause gives more information about the noun in the same way that a relative clause does. A clause that uses a present participle (the -ing form) has an active meaning and a clause that uses a past participle has a passive meaning.

… a range of dishes **featuring** the insects (= a range of dishes **that feature** the insects)

… experiments **aimed at** combating illnesses (= experiments **that are aimed at** combating illnesses)

Exercise 1

Look at the sentences. Change the words in bold to a present participle (-ing form) or a past participle.

1 All the passengers **who were injured** in the accident have been released from hospital.
2 She works in an office **which overlooks** the main square.
3 Anyone **who finishes** in the top three gets a medal.
4 The owner of a lottery ticket **which was bought** in Chester almost six months ago has just one week left to claim the million-pound prize.
5 The people **who live** next door are really friendly.
6 Tickets **which were purchased** online will be automatically refunded.

Exercise 2

Complete the sentences using the correct form of the verbs.

1 The suffering _____ (cause) by vivisection is just awful.
2 Supplies are slowly starting to reach the areas _____ (affect) by the flooding.
3 She's part of a team _____ (investigate) the effects of a vegetarian diet on long-term health.
4 The police have said that some of the animals _____ (free) from the laboratories could be carrying diseases.
5 The government has promised to help rebuild all the properties _____ (damage) in the recent forest fires.
6 City Farms is a new project _____ (fund) by the local council and aimed at putting kids in contact with animals.
7 The low numbers of young people _____ (take) part in sport or _____ (do) regular exercise continues to be a cause for concern.
8 The group _____ (lead) the protests has issued a statement _____ (oppose) all forms of hunting.

8 CRIME AND PUNISHMENT

8A SHOWING DEGREES OF CERTAINTY WITH MODAL VERBS

Certainty

We use *must* or *can't* to show we are certain about something. This is often when we give our opinion or speculate about something and have no direct evidence.
*My keys **must be** here somewhere. I had them a moment ago.*
*He **must earn** a lot of money – he's always going on holidays.*
*You **can't be** serious. That's a crazy idea!*
*It **can't be** easy, doing three jobs at a time.*

The past form is *must / can't have* + past participle.
*It **must have been** awful. Poor you!*
*It's a no parking zone. She **can't have seen** the sign.*
*It **can't have been** easy being so poor.*

Uncertainty

We use *might (not)* or *could* when we are not certain about something. This is often when we give our opinion or speculate about something that is possible.
*It **could be** him who stole the money, but I'm not sure.*
*This **might be** Yuka's bag. It looks like it, but I'm not sure.*
*Dina **might not know** what happened. I'll call her and tell her.*

The past form is *might (not) / could have* + past participle.
*I suppose I **could've left** my passport in the hotel room. I **might not have lost** it, after all.*
*She hasn't replied to my email. I guess she **might not have seen** it yet.*

Note that we do not use *could not have* to express uncertainty.
Dina ~~could not have~~ known what happened. I'll call her and tell her.
She hasn't replied to my email. I guess she ~~could not have~~ seen it yet.

We can also use *may* instead of *might*. This is particularly common in more formal contexts, such as writing.
*We **may be** a few minutes late.*
*Police believe that high speed **may have played** a part in the crash.*

Exercise 1

Complete the sentences with *must (have), can't (have), might (have), could (have).*

1 They _____ be so fed up. That's the third time their house has been broken into this year.
2 It _____ be easy for them, bringing up six kids on one salary. But they never complain.
3 That _____ be the guy who stole your bike, but I'm not sure. It was dark and I didn't get a good look.
4 He's been working thirteen-hour days for weeks. He _____ be exhausted.
5 This doesn't look right. I think we _____ taken the wrong turning earlier.
6 It _____ been easy, only seeing your kids once a month. But it's great you see them more often now.
7 It _____ be great having a job where you travel all over the world. Lucky you!
8 There's no sign of them breaking in, so I suppose I _____ left the door unlocked. I'm pretty sure I did lock it, but I _____ be wrong.
9 It _____ been Harry that you saw – he was out of the country at the time. It _____ been someone else.
10 Your glasses _____ be somewhere here. You _____ looked very hard! They _____ be in the garden shed – you went in there a few minutes ago.

DID YOU KNOW?

We can use the continuous form of the verb (be + -ing) after *must*, *can't*, *could* and *might*.

He **can't be earning** much if he's only doing cleaning work.
We should get off the phone. She **might be trying** to call now.
I didn't time it, but I **must've been waiting** for over an hour.

Exercise 2

Read the first sentence in each pair. Complete the second sentence so that it has a similar meaning. Use between three and five words, including the word in bold.

1 The police believe it's possible the thieves got in through an open window. **MIGHT**

   The thieves _____ through an open window, according to the police.

2 I can't see how they did it other than knowing someone in the bank. **MUST**

   They _____ in the bank in order to do it.

3 I'll check she's not waiting for us outside. It's possible she is. **MIGHT**

   She _____ outside, so let me go and check.

4 He doesn't know what to do because I'm pretty sure he wasn't paying attention. **CAN'T**

   He _____ attention, or he'd know what to do.

5 I'm sure it took ages to write the report as it's so detailed. **MUST**

   That report _____ to write, given it's so detailed.

6 He's possibly the person I saw, but I'm not sure. **COULD**

   I think _____ who I saw, but I'm not certain.

8C NOUNS WITH PREPOSITIONS

To define or to add information to a noun, we can follow the noun with a preposition + the defining information. In the first example below, 'on research' tells us more about and defines 'focus'. The defining information is usually a noun, noun phrase, pronoun, gerund or *wh-* phrase.

- noun + preposition + noun / noun phrase / pronoun
  There needs to be more **focus on research**.
  We have **access to world-class facilities**.
  There seems to be no **reason for it**.

- noun + preposition + gerund (-*ing* form of the verb)
  I have no **interest in watching crime shows**.
  He had **no excuse for driving so fast**.

- noun + preposition + *wh-* phrase
  I have great **respect for what she has achieved**.
  There will be an **investigation into why it happened**.

Prepositions

There are no rules about which prepositions go after which nouns and you need to learn them individually (e.g. *a focus on*, *a responsibility towards*, *the difference between*). Sometimes, we use a different preposition depending on what we are expressing.

It had a big **impact on unemployment**.
Let's see what the **impact of the policy** is.
We gave a lot of **attention to the problem**.
They deflected **attention from the real problem**.
There was a **demonstration against the war**.
He gave a **demonstration of how it works**.

Exercise 1

Complete the sentences with the preposition + noun phrases in the boxes.

to rehabilitation	on punishing prisoners	with prisons

1 The main problem _____ is that we place too much emphasis _____ and don't pay enough attention _____ .

of academic study	of philosophy	of right and wrong behaviour

2 Ethics is a branch _____ that involves analyzing concepts _____ . The term comes from the Greek word ethos, which means 'character'. Ethics is also a field _____ .

Exercise 2

Complete the sentences with the noun + preposition combinations.

access to	addiction to	awareness of	ban on
criticism of	damage to	decrease in	involvement in

1 Police have arrested a leading politician for his _____ a corruption scandal.

2 The footballer admitted himself into a rehabilitation centre for treatment for his _____ gambling.

3 The government is considering a complete _____ the ownership of guns.

4 Better _____ the internet could help solve many of the problems that currently affect less developed countries.

5 The demonstration against rising prices of water turned into a riot, resulting in widespread _____ cars and buildings.

6 There has been some _____ the police handling of the incident last week in which a man was shot.

7 There's actually been a big _____ the incidence of street crime over the last few years.

8 Nowadays, there's much greater _____ the need for recycling and energy conservation.

Exercise 3

Choose the correct option to complete the sentences.

1 A I'm afraid there's no room *in / for* the class for another desk and chair.
  B We've got room *in / for* one more person in our car.

2 A Police have discovered a terrorist threat *of / to* the president.
  B The airport has increased security because of the threat *of / to* terrorism.

3 A What's the name of that film *with / about* Jet Li that came out last year?
  B It's a really interesting film *with / about* gun crime.

4 A The police have set up a meeting *about / with* the local residents *about / with* burglaries in the area.
  B The survey looked at attitudes *towards / among* young people *towards / among* politics.

5 A There's a demonstration *against / of* racism being held next week.
  B The students are going to put on a demonstration *of / for* what they've learned at the end of the course.

9 CAREERS AND STUDYING

9A CONDITIONALS WITH PRESENT FORMS

We can use a conditional sentence to talk about things that are possible or likely in the present or in the future. We use a present form in the *if*-clause and we can use a range of different forms and modal verbs in the result clause.

Look at the examples of the different functions. Note the form / modal verb that is used in the result clause.

Function	Form
to talk about general truths	*If I **ask** about doing other stuff, he **tells** me to be patient.*
to talk about definite future results	*If they **invest** more in education, it**'ll help** the economy.*
to make offers / promises	*I**'ll give** you a hand if you **need** help filling in the forms.*
to express possibility	*If I **get** this promotion, I **can / could / might buy** a place of my own.*
to give advice	*If it**'s** that bad, you **should think about** leaving!*
to talk about plans	*What **are** you **going to do if** you **don't get** the promotion?*
to express obligation	*If you **want** to get in, **you have to get** really good grades.*

Exercise 1

Write *if* sentences using the ideas below. Use the words in brackets to decide which structures to use in the result clauses.

1 you / fail three subjects / repeat the whole year   (obligation)
2 you / not feel well / take a day off sick   (advice)
3 you / ask my uncle for a job / you lose yours   (possibility)
4 I / be in big trouble / report not finished by Friday   (definite result)
5 things not get better at work / I / hand in my notice   (plan)
6 you're struggling / I / do my best to help   (offer)

Different present forms in *if*-clauses

We can use the present simple, present continuous, present perfect simple or present perfect continuous in an *if*-clause.

*I get paid extra **if I work** overtime.* (= always / whenever)
*If you**'re having** problems, you can always talk to me.* (= now / at the moment),
*If you**'ve finished**, could you make me a coffee?* (= already / before now)
*You can't concentrate properly if you**'ve been working** too hard.* (= from the past to now)

Exercise 2

Choose the correct option in each *if* clause.

1 If you *haven't heard / haven't been hearing* from them soon, maybe you should call them.
2 You should take some time off if you *aren't feeling / haven't felt* well.
3 We might all lose our jobs if the company *loses / has lost* any more money.
4 If you *work / have been working* here for more than two years, they have to give you a month's notice if they want to sack you.
5 If everything *goes / is going* according to plan, I'm going to go and work abroad for a year.
6 If *you're thinking / you think* of leaving your current job, I think we are looking for some new staff at my company.

DID YOU KNOW?

There are several fixed expressions which use *if*-clauses. Here are some useful ones:

If everything goes according to plan, the new office will open in August.
If the worst comes to the worst, I'll look for a new job.
If all else fails, I'll just have to work part time while I study.

Exercise 3

Correct the mistakes in the sentences.

1 If everything comes according to plan, we'll be with you by 6.30.
2 If the worst goes to the worst, I'll look for a new job.
3 If all other fails, I can always retrain and look for something new.
4 If nothing gets wrong, they'll be here next Monday.

9B CONDITIONALS WITH PAST FORMS

We can use a conditional sentence to talk about things that are unreal, imagined or hypothetical in the present, future or past.

Imagined / hypothetical present or future

We use a past form in the *if*-clause and we use *would* + verb in the result clause.

*Even if they **doubled** my money, I **wouldn't want** to work for them again.*
*If I **didn't have** so much work, I**'d go** away for the weekend.*
*I**'d walk** to work if it **wasn't raining**.*

Imagined / hypothetical past

We use the past perfect in the *if*-clause and we use *would have* + past participle in the result clause.

*It **would** probably **have been** a different story if I**'d been doing** it on my own!*
*He**'d have got** a much better grade if he**'d worked** a bit harder.*

We can use *might* instead of *would*. *Might* shows less definite results. We can use *might* in conditionals that refer to the present, the future or the past.

*If they **offered** me a big pay rise, I **might consider** staying in the job.*
*If it **hadn't been** for her, I **might never have heard** about the job.*

DID YOU KNOW

We can mix the present and the past in imagined / hypothetical situations.

This could be a past consequence of a present situation:
*If I **wasn't** in the army, I **would never have gone** somewhere like Haiti.*

Or it could be a present consequence of a past situation:
*If we**'d set off** a bit earlier, we **wouldn't be** stuck in this awful traffic.*

Exercise 1

Complete the text with one word in each gap (*didn't*, *hadn't*, etc. count as one word here).

If it hadn't [1]_____ raining that day I might [2]_____ have seen the advert. I usually cycled to work, but that day it was pouring down and I was late, so I took the metro. I was working for a TV company at the time and it was good, but I saw this ad and it said 'Imagine if you [3]_____ in your job for the rest of your life, how [4]_____ you feel? What do you think you [5]_____ have contributed to the world? Would you [6]_____ made your mark?' The advert really made me think and it led me in a completely different direction. I became a nurse. I liked the TV work, but I don't think it [7]_____ have been as rewarding, even if I [8]_____ been promoted and moved up the company. I doubt I'd [9]_____ so happy now if it [10]_____ been for that ad.

178

Exercise 2

Read sentence a and complete sentence b so that it has the same meaning.

1 A I'm amazed you didn't get angry when your boss said that to you.
  B If my boss _____ that to me, I _____ furious.

2 A Our present success is a direct result of all your hard work.
  B If it _____ for all your hard work, we _____ as successful as we currently are.

3 A I was very nervous in the interview. Maybe that's why I didn't get the job.
  B If I _____ more confident in the interview, I _____ the job.

4 A I know him better than you and I can tell you now: that was a stupid thing to say to him.
  B If you _____ him as well as I do, you _____ that to him!

5 A The money's terrible. I only stay because I find the work really rewarding.
  B To be honest, if I _____ the work so rewarding, I _____ my notice tomorrow.

6 A I only ended up doing this course because I didn't get the grades for the course I wanted to do.
  B If I _____ the grades I needed for the course I wanted to do, I certainly _____ this course.

10 SOCIALIZING

10A THE FUTURE PERFECT

Form

The future perfect is formed using *will / won't* + *have* + past participle.
They **will have done** all the painting by the weekend, so we can move in then.
Can I give it to you on Friday? I **won't have finished** it before then.

Use

We use the future perfect to talk about something that will be completed, or not completed, before a time in the future.
I **will have written** my essay by Thursday. (= My essay will be finished before Thursday.)
We **won't have finished eating** by nine. Can you call round a bit later? (= We will still be eating at nine.)

We can also use the future perfect for a situation which continues, but which has reached a significant point in time, such as an anniversary.
They**'ll have been** married for 50 years in November.
I**'ll have worked** here for five years next month.

We can also use *should* or *might* instead of *will* to show less certainty.
I **should have finished** by about six or so, but I'll call you if I haven't.
I **might have got** a new job the next time you see me!

Time references

We usually have a time reference with the future perfect. The phrases often begin with *by* (*by midnight, by this afternoon, by the time we get there, by the end of the year, by then,* etc.) and, less commonly, with *before* (*before midnight; before the end of the month,* etc.)

Exercise 1

Complete the sentences with the future perfect form of the verbs.

1 I'm helping a friend move house tomorrow, but we _____ (finish) by five, so call me then.

2 Next month, we _____ (live) in this apartment for two years.

3 It's absolutely pouring down now, but they said it _____ (ease off) by late afternoon.

4 Hurry up! The film _____ probably _____ (start) by the time we get to the cinema.

5 OK, see you at 7. Oh, _____ you _____ (eat) or shall we get something to eat here?

6 I read the other day that by the time you're 60, you _____ (spend) nine whole years watching TV! How depressing is that?

Common mistakes

• If they ~~will have fixed~~ **have fixed** the car, I can drive you to the airport this evening. I'll call you when I ~~will have finished~~ **have finished**.

  Don't use *will* in phrases with time adverbs (*when, until,* etc.) or *if-*clauses that refer to the future.

Exercise 2

Find five mistakes in the sentences. Then correct the mistakes.

1 Don't call before noon – I'll be in a meeting. But we should've finished by 1-ish.

2 We have lived here for ten years next July. Maybe we'll have a party to celebrate!

3 When do you think you'll have finished with the book? I promised I'd lend it to Jack when you will have read it.

4 I should've finished the report by the end of tomorrow. But I'll have let you know if it's going to be later than that.

5 You're arriving on Friday? I might already leave, I'm afraid! But if so, see you next time.

6 We'll have done all the necessary checks by the end of the week. When we will have done that, we'll issue you with the pass.

10C QUESTION TAGS

Use

We use a question tag to invite people to agree with or confirm what we are saying.
That was a great lecture, **wasn't it**?
She speaks French, **doesn't she**?

Form

Question tags are formed using an auxiliary verb (*be, do, have* or a modal verb) + a pronoun.

If there is an auxiliary verb (*be, have* or a modal verb) in the main part of the sentence, the question tag is made with the same auxiliary verb.
She**'s** left, **has**n't she?
He **can** speak French, **can**'t he?

If the main part of the sentence uses the verb *be*, the question tag uses an appropriate form of *be*.
He**'s** going to be late, **is**n't he?

If the main part of the sentence does not have an auxiliary verb (i.e. the present or past simple), the question tag uses an appropriate form of *do*.
He **plays** the guitar, **does**n't he?

With affirmative sentences, we use negative tags.
It **was** a great game, **wasn't it**?
They**'ve** already left, **haven't they**?
Teresa **lives** near there, **doesn't she**?

With negative statements, we use an affirmative tag.
*The meeting **shouldn't** take too long, **should it**?*
*She **hasn't** seen it, **has she**?*
*They **didn't** get there in time, **did they**?*

Note that with *I'm ...* , we use *aren't I?* in the tag. And with *I'm not...* , we use *am I?* in the tag.
*I'**m** invited to the party, **aren't I**?*
*I'**m** not invited, **am I**?*

Here are some other question tags and their uses.
*You **couldn't** save my place in the queue, **could you**?* (to make polite requests)
*Let'**s** start, **shall we**?* (to make polite suggestions)
*Pass me the salt, **would you**?* (to make polite commands – informal only)

DID YOU KNOW?
We don't add question tags to questions.
Are you doing anything this weekend, aren't you?
Do you want to go and get something to eat, don't you?

Exercise 1
Decide which two short conversations are correct. Correct the other four.

1 A: Would you like a coffee, wouldn't you?
   B: No, I'm fine, thanks. I've just had one.
2 A: You knew him quite well, isn't it?
   B: Yeah, we went to college together.
3 A: You couldn't lend me a pound, could you?
   B: Sorry, I haven't got any change on me.
4 A: You weren't at the last class, you were?
   B: No. I was ill. Did I miss much?
5 A: Lovely weather, isn't it?
   B: Fantastic.
6 A: Haven't you heard of One Direction, have you?
   B: No. Why? Should I have?

Exercise 2
Add the correct question tags.

1 She's Spanish, _____ ?
2 I'm on the list too, _____ ?
3 We need to be there by six, _____ ?
4 Let's go, _____ ?
5 You couldn't give me a lift, _____ ?
6 She's been there a few times, _____ ?
7 Give me a hand, _____ ?
8 He's going to be there too, _____ ?

DID YOU KNOW?
Other question tags are common in informal conversational English.
*You know where the cathedral is, **yeah** / **right**?*
*It's really good, **no**?*

Exercise 3
Replace *yeah?*, *right?* and *no?* with more formal tags.

1 You've been to university, no? *haven't you?*
2 It's a fantastic place to visit, no?
3 You know where to go, right?
4 We're going to meet them later, yeah?
5 She shouldn't be here, right?
6 They can't come tomorrow, right?

11B COMPOUND ADJECTIVES

Form
A compound adjective is two words that function as an adjective. This could be a combination of different parts of speech, such as number + noun (e.g. *24-hour*), noun + adjective (e.g. *world-famous*), noun + noun (e.g. *ground-floor*), adjective + participle (e.g. *broad-minded*, *easy-going*), adverb + participle (e.g. *highly regarded*).

As with many single-word adjectives, we can use compound adjectives + noun.
*She's an **award-winning writer**.*
*We stayed in a **five-star hotel**.*

Compound adjectives are usually hyphenated. However, you sometimes seem them without a hyphen. And you may see the same compound adjective written both with and without a hyphen.

| a five-star hotel | a family-run restaurant | a brightly lit room |

Note that many compound adjectives use the *-ing* form or the past participle of a verb.

| award-winning | south-facing |
| badly maintained | well-positioned |

We use the singular form of a noun in a compound adjective.
a six-hour flight NOT *a six hours flight*
a three-year-old car NOT *a three-years-old car*

Use
We often use compound adjectives in place of longer phrases. They make what we say shorter and more concise.
*She's an **award-winning** writer. = She's a writer who has won an award.*
*It's a **six-hour flight**. = The flight takes six hours.*
*It's a **well-positioned apartment**. = The apartment is well positioned.*
*It's a **2,000-year-old temple**. = The temple is 2,000 years old.*

Exercise 1
Read the first sentence in each pair. Complete the second sentence so that it has the same meaning, using a compound adjective.

1 The garden faces south.
   It's a _____ garden.
2 The building is very well maintained.
   It's a _____ building.
3 The hotel has five stars and it has won some awards.
   It's a _____ _____ hotel.
4 We stayed in an apartment which was equipped well and had three bedrooms.
   We stayed in a _____ _____ apartment.
5 We need to write an essay that has 3,000 words.
   We need to write a _____ essay.
6 We had some delicious tomatoes that had been dried in the sun.
   We had some delicious _____ tomatoes.
7 I know a lovely little restaurant by the sea run by a family.
   I know a lovely little _____ restaurant by the sea.
8 She's a scientist who is famous all over the world.
   She's a _____ scientist.

Exercise 2

Complete the sentences with compound adjectives using a word from each box.

densely	50	highly	Italian
meat	vegetable	300	

free	mile	populated	respected
rich	speaking	storey	

1 She's lives in the _____ part of the country. She also speaks German and French.
2 They're going to build a _____ skyscraper on the site.
3 Apparently, Monaco is the most _____ country in the world.
4 Professor Boyle is one of the most _____ academics in his field.
5 It's a _____ round trip. It'll take about five hours by car.
6 _____ and _____ diets are becoming more and more popular.

11C EMPHATIC STRUCTURES

There are two common patterns we use to emphasize how we feel. In these patterns, *what* … and *the thing that* … mean the same thing and work in the same way.

What The thing that	annoys me irritates me worries me amazes me 's great 's really scary I find strange I love I can't stand etc.	is	that … when … the fact that … the way … the amount of … the number of … verb + -ing … etc.

We can use the same pattern to talk about things that happened in the past.
*The thing that amazed me **was** the fact that people stopped for pedestrians at crossings.*
*What I found strange **was** that there were so few people there.*

Exercise 1

Complete the second sentence in each pair using the word in brackets, and any other words necessary, so that it emphasizes the feeling in the first sentence.

1 A The amount of pollution they have there is really worrying.
   B The thing _____ (worries) of pollution they have there.
2 A I find it strange that people prefer to drive rather than walk or cycle.
   B What _____ (find) that people prefer to drive rather than walk or cycle.
3 A When people get on the train while you're trying to get off, it really annoys me.
   B What _____ (annoying) getting on the train while you're trying to get off.
4 A The government increased the prices on the buses and it made people angry.
   B What _____ (angered) that the government put up the price of bus tickets.
5 A Being able to travel around the world with my job is great.
   B What _____ (love) able to travel round the world.

Exercise 2

Complete the sentences with your own ideas

1 One thing that drives me mad _____ .
   One thing that drives me mad is the increasing cost of living.
2 What always amazes me _____ .
3 What really worries me these days _____ .
4 One thing I loved doing as a child _____ .
5 The thing I find the most frustrating about learning English _____ .
6 What's great about learning English _____ .

12 HEALTH AND MEDICINE

12A POSITIVE EXPECTATIONS AND CHANGED PLANS

Be meant to / Be supposed to

We use *be meant to / be supposed to* + verb to talk about what we expect to happen, usually because it is planned or required or is the correct thing to do.
*Hurry up! We**'re meant to be** there in 20 minutes!*
*The meeting **is supposed to finish** at 10.30.*
*I**'m supposed to be seeing** a friend later, but I might cancel.*

Note that we often use *be meant to / be supposed to* + verb when we think something might not happen as planned, required or expected.
*We**'re meant to be going** to the beach this afternoon, but rain is forecast.*
*The taxi **is supposed to be** here at 9. Maybe I'll give them a call to see if it's on its way.*

We also use *be meant to / be supposed to* + verb to report what we've heard or we understand about something.
*Cold showers **are meant to be** really good for you.*
*I haven't seen the film, but it**'s supposed to be** really good.*

Should(n't) / Ought to

We can use *should / ought to* + verb in a similar way to *be meant to / be supposed to* + verb. However, we also use *should / ought to* to say what we think is probable or likely.
*If the traffic is OK, we **should be** there in about an hour.*
*The report **ought to be** finished by Friday.*

Exercise 1

Complete the sentences with the correct form of the words.

1 The meeting _____ (should / be) finished by three, so I should be able to call you then.
2 Look at the weather! It's awful and the kids _____ (supposed / be playing) tennis at 2 o'clock.
3 We _____ (supposed / be having) a meeting tomorrow, but there are so many people off with flu that we might have to cancel it.
4 I posted it this morning, so you _____ (ought / get) it in a day or two.
5 Have you been to that new Vietnamese restaurant? It _____ (meant / be) really good.
6 _____ we _____ (supposed / wait) at reception, or shall we go to her office?
7 I _____ (meant / be working) at home today, but they needed me in the office.
8 There _____ (supposed / be) a bus strike today. But they all seem to be running as normal.

Exercise 2

Complete the sentences with your own ideas.

1 We were meant to *go camping* , but rain was forecast for the whole weekend.
2 I was supposed to _____ , but it was cancelled at the last minute.
3 I'm supposed to _____ , but I really can't be bothered.
4 If all goes according to plan, I should _____ .
5 I've never been, but _____ is supposed to be a really nice place.
6 _____ is meant to be really good for you.

12C *NOT ONLY / NOT JUST …*

We can use *not only … but / it's also …* and *not just … but / it's also …* to show that two facts about a situation are important.
Many people go abroad for medical treatments. **Not only** *because it's cheaper,* **but also** *to have a holiday as well.*
I have private medical care. This **isn't just** *because the waiting time is much shorter,* **it's also** *that the service is much better.*
I go to the gym **not just** *to exercise,* **but also** *to catch up with friends.*

Exercise 1

Complete the sentences with a phrase from each box.

isn't just about	isn't just about	not just to
not only to	not only for	

but also to	but also because	but they do
it's also about	it's also about	

1 Medical tourism *isn't just about* cosmetic treatments, *it's also about* treating serious health issues, too.
2 I go to work _____ earn money, _____ I really enjoy it.
3 We want to move house, _____ get somewhere smaller, _____ move to a quieter area.
4 Exercising _____ feeling physically fit, _____ mental well-being.
5 I highly recommend this café – _____ the coffee, _____ some great pastries too.

DID YOU KNOW?

We sometimes start the sentence or clause with *not only*. When we do this, the subject goes after the auxiliary verb or the main verb *be*. Note that we add the auxiliary verb *do* in present and past simple sentences. This is the same word order as in questions.
Not only is it *an excellent restaurant, the food is very healthy,* **too**.
NOT *Not only it is an excellent restaurant, the food is very healthy, too.*
Not only did we wait *a long time,* **but** *the service was absolutely terrible.*
NOT *Not only we waited a long time, but the service was absolutely terrible.*

Exercise 2

Correct the mistake in the sentence beginnings. Then match the beginnings (1–4) with the endings (a–d).

1 Not only the hospital is close by,
2 Not only the hotel was pretty rundown,
3 Not only arrived they late for the meeting,
4 Not only have been several doctors dismissed,

a the hospital has been heavily fined too.
b but they were totally unprepared.
c it's also got an excellent reputation.
d the food was awful too.

Exercise 3

Complete the sentences with your own ideas.

1 I'm learning English not only … , but …
2 Studying isn't just to … , but it's also …
3 Not only do I … , but I also …

13 LIFE-CHANGING EVENTS

13A THE PAST PERFECT SIMPLE AND CONTINUOUS

Form

The past perfect simple is *had* + past participle.
They **had left** *by the time we arrived.*
I **hadn't been** *there before.*

The past perfect continuous is *had been* + -*ing*.
We **'d been thinking** *about moving for a while.*
She **hadn't been working** *there for long before she was promoted.*

Use

We use the past perfect to show that something happened before another past action or before a specific time in the past. The more recent action is usually in the past simple.
He **'d had** *a couple of big rows with his boss* **before he decided to leave.**
They **'d** *already* **finished** *the meeting by lunchtime.*
I **'d been looking** *for something else for ages* **before I found** *this job.*

Past perfect simple or continuous?

We generally use the past perfect simple for single events and to talk about how many times something happened.
We set off as soon as we **'d had** *breakfast.*
We **'d** *already* **met** *two or three times.*

We use the past perfect continuous to show something happened over a period of time.
I **'d been thinking** *about a change of career for a while.*
The company **had been losing** *money for years.*

DID YOU KNOW?

There are a few verbs that we generally do not use in the continuous form. These include verbs that describe states such as thoughts and mental states (e.g. *agree, be, believe, disagree, forget, hate, know, like, love, owe, prefer*) and possession (e.g. *have, belong, own*). For these verbs, we usually use the past perfect simple.
We **'d known** *each other for years.* NOT *We'd been knowing each other for years.*
I **'d always preferred** *working from home.* NOT *I'd always been preferring working from home.*

Time phrases

With the past perfect, we often use time phrases that show sequence (e.g. *by the time, before, after, already, as soon as*) and time phrases that show duration (e.g. *for a while, for ages, for three hours, for days / weeks / months / years, always* and *never*). Note that we usually use the past perfect simple with *always* and *never*.
The meeting had finished **by the time** *I got there. I* **'d been stuck in traffic** *for over an hour*.
I bought a car **as soon as** *I* **'d passed** *my driving test.*
I **'d always wanted** *my own car.*

Exercise 1

Choose the correct option to complete the conversations.

1 A: So what made you decide to become a zoologist?
   B: *I'd always been / I'd always been being* interested in science and *I'd always wanted / I'd always been wanting* to work with animals, so it just seemed like a sensible choice.

2 A: How did you end up in this job?
  B: *I'd looked / I'd been looking* for something for ages, and *I'd had / I'd been having* a few interviews, but nothing came of any of them, so in the end I took the first thing I got offered. To be honest *I'd never really considered / I'd never really been considering* this type of work, but I'm quite enjoying it.
3 A: Why did you move out?
  B: Well, my brother and I *hadn't got / hadn't been getting* on for quite a few months, so in the end I decided it was time to move out and get a place of my own.
4 A: How did you two get together?
  B: Well, we were at uni together. *I'd asked / I'd been asking* her out three or four times before, but *she'd always said / she'd always been saying* no, so you can imagine my surprise when she finally said yes!

Exercise 2

Complete the sentences with the past perfect or past simple form of the verbs. Where both the past perfect continuous and past perfect simple are possible, use the continuous form.

1 We _____ (plan) for it for ages, but it still _____ (come) as a bit of a shock. Once the kids _____ finally _____ (leave) home, the house _____ (seem) so quiet and empty. It'll take some getting used to!
2 He _____ (do) the lottery for years and _____ never _____ (win) anything at all, so you can imagine how much of a shock it _____ (be) when he _____ (find out) he _____ (win) £100,000.
3 We _____ (drive) from Batumi to Tbilisi and we _____ (be) on the road for a few hours when my husband suddenly _____ (remember) he _____ (leave) the door unlocked! We had to turn round and go all the way back again!
4 It was quite odd, really, because she _____ (tell) everyone for ages how much she was looking forward to retiring, but then after she finally _____ (retire) it was like she just _____ (not know) how to fill her days and she _____ (be) really bored.

13B *BE ALWAYS / CONSTANTLY -ING, WISH* AND *WOULD*

Be always / constantly + -ing

We generally use the present simple to talk about habits.
He **borrows** my clothes all the time.

However, to express annoyance or irritation about a habit or repeated activity, we can use the present continuous with *always / constantly*.
He**'s always borrowing** my clothes. It's so annoying.
They're so aggressive. They**'re constantly getting** into fights.

Wish + would

We use *I wish + would(n't)* + verb to show we want people to stop or start doing something or to behave differently.
I **wish** the kids **would help** out more.
I **wish** he **wouldn't shout** so much.

Exercise 1

Write full sentences using the ideas below.

1 He / constantly / interrupt her / when / she / talk
2 I wish / she / play her music so loud / while / I / try / study
3 My brother / always / borrow / my bike without asking
4 My boss / constantly / give / me extra work to do
5 I wish / he / speak to me in that way / all the time
6 They / always / joke / and / mess around
7 I wish / my kids / help / around the house a bit more
8 My neighbours / always / shout / at each other

Common mistakes

- *She's such a slob. She ~~is never doing~~* never **does** *any exercise.*
- *He ~~is never listening~~* never **listens**. *It's so annoying.*
  Don't use the present continuous to emphasize things that do not happen. Use the present simple.

- *I wish she ~~would live~~* **lived** *nearer.*
- *I wish he ~~would be~~* **was** *happy.*
  Don't use *wish + would* to talk about states, character or appearance. Use the past simple.

- *I wish I ~~would work~~* **worked** *less.*
- *I wish I ~~would have~~* **had** *more money.*
  Don't use *would* after *wish* if the subject is the same. Use the past simple.

Exercise 2

Find six sentences which have mistakes. Then rewrite them correctly.

1 I wish he would tidy up sometimes. Constantly he's leaving his stuff all over the place.
2 She's so stubborn. She's never admitting she's wrong! It's so annoying.
3 He's so manipulative. He's trying always to make me feel guilty.
4 I wish he would be more assertive and that he'd defend himself a bit more.
5 She's so cheerful. She's always smiling and laughing. I wish I would be a bit more like her.
6 They're constantly talking and disrupting the class. I wish they just shut up for once.
7 I wish they wouldn't argue so much. They're constantly shouting at each other.
8 My sister always borrowing my clothes. I wish she'd just ask for once.

14 BANKS AND MONEY

14A PASSIVES

Form

We form passives using different forms of the verb *be* + past participle.
My wages **are** *usually* **paid** *into my account on the 22nd.* (present simple)
A new security system **is being installed** *at the moment.* (present continuous)
Your new card **was sent out** *to you last Monday.* (past simple)
They said cash withdrawals **were being made** *in Morocco.* (past continuous)
The cheque **has been cleared**, *but you* **will be charged** *for this.* (present perfect simple / will)
I suddenly realized I'd been tricked. (past perfect simple)
They said the decision **might be delayed** *but that it* **should be finalized** *by the end of the month.* (modal verbs)

Use

We use passives to say what happens to someone or something (rather than what someone or something does). The most common reason for using a passive is when we do not say who or what does the action. This is usually because the person or thing is obvious (e.g. *millions of emails are sent every day*), unknown (e.g. *my bank account has been hacked*) or unimportant (e.g. *the first online banking service was launched in 1997*).

Sometimes, however, we use the passive and we also want to say who or what performed the action. We add this information using *by*.

*I **was offered** yet another credit card **by my bank** last week!*
*The dollar **has been strengthened by the news**.*
*Online banking **was launched by my bank** in the late 1990s.*

Exercise 1

Complete the sentences with the correct passive form of the verbs.

1 The computer's very slow this morning, I'm afraid. The system _____ (update) at the moment.
2 I pay all my bills by standing order, so the money _____ (send) automatically at the end of every month.
3 I spoke to someone yesterday and they told me the money _____ already (transfer) _____ .
4 My credit card _____ (reject) three times yesterday and I'd like to know why.
5 We can't accept this cheque, I'm afraid. Look, it _____ (not / sign) yet.
6 It's not my fault! Up until last week, all my correspondence from the bank _____ (forward) to the wrong address.
7 According to our records, the letter _____ (send) to you on the 28th of last month.
8 We have all your details and you _____ (contact) as soon as a decision _____ (make).

Exercise 2

Rewrite the sentences using the passive so the meaning is the same.

1 They opened the bank in 1865.
The bank _____ .
2 Someone has stolen my wallet and passport.
My wallet _____ .
3 People send millions of spam emails every day.
Millions _____ .
4 The bank told me that they would refund the money.
I _____ that the money _____ .
5 A group of billionaires started the charity in 2020. They predict that next year, it will have taken over a million children out of poverty.
The charity _____ .They predict that next year, over a million _____ .

14B WISH

We use *wish* to talk about something imaginary or hypothetical – something we want to be different, but which is impossible. To express this hypothetical aspect, *wish* is followed by past forms.

wish + past simple

We use *wish* + past simple to talk about a present situation.
*I **wish** I **was** better with money. I'm always in debt.*
*I sometimes **wish** I **had** a car, but I can't afford one.*

wish + past perfect

We use *wish* + past perfect to talk about the past. We often use it for past regrets.
*I **wish** I**'d invested** the money instead of spending it.*
*I imagine he **wishes** he**'d never sold** that painting. He sold it for £6,000 and it's worth ten times that figure now.*
*I **wish** I**'d been paying** attention. I'd know what to do if I had.*

wish + could / could have

We use *wish* + could + verb to talk about ability and possibility in the present.
*I **wish** I **could help**, but I've got people over for dinner.*
*I sometimes **wish** we **could stop** working, but we can't.*

We use *wish* + could have + past participle to talk about ability and possibility in the past.
*I **wish** I **could have done** something, but it was impossible.*
*I really **wish** I **could have gone**, but I was just so busy.*

DID YOU KNOW?

We use *wish* + would to say that we want something to change or be different in the future.
*I **wish** the government **would invest** in schools more.*
*I **wish** he **wouldn't waste** his money the way he does.*

Exercise 1

Complete the dialogues with the correct form of the verbs.

1 A: I wish we _____ (think) about it earlier.
   B: Oh well. We didn't. But we'll know for next time.
2 A: I wish I _____ (not have to) fill in my tax return!
   B: I have an accountant to do mine. Do you want me to give you her number?
3 A: I wish the government _____ (cut) taxes the other month.
   B: Yeah? I think we need to be paying more!
4 A: I wish I _____ (book) my holiday abroad months ago.
   B: Me too. It's all so expensive now, especially flights.
5 A: I wish I _____ (can play) the piano. I've wanted to be able to play it since I was a kid.
   B: Well, it's never too late to learn.
6 A: I wish I _____ (can go) with you last night. It sounds like you had a great time.
   B: Yeah, we did. And we missed you. Sill, next time, yeah?
7 A: I wish it _____ (not rain) so much around here.
   B: Yeah, it can rain a lot, especially at this time of year.
8 A: I wish my neighbours _____ (stop) playing that awful music all the time. It's driving me mad.
   B: You should complain to the landlord – it's their responsibility.

Exercise 2

Complete the sentences with your own wishes.

1 I wish I could …
2 I really wish I hadn't …
3 I wish I could've …
4 I wish I had …
5 I wish I was …
6 I wish I'd …

15 FOOD

15A LINKING WORDS

We use linking words for a number of reasons.

To express order / sequence

- We usually use *when, before, after* and *once* + clause to link two events within a sentence. *Once* has a similar meaning to *when* and *after*.
  ***When** the water is boiling, add the rice.*
  ***After** the rice has cooked, add the spices.*
  ***Once** the onions have turned brown, take them off the heat.*
  *Fry the vegetables **when** the oil is hot enough.*
  *We went for a meal **before** (we went to) the show.*
- We usually use *when, afterwards* or *after that* to connect two ideas across separate sentences. However, they can join two halves of a sentence when they are used with *and*.
  *Wash the chickpeas. **Then** / **After that** / **Afterwards,** put them in water to soak.*
  *Mix the ingredients and **then** / **after that** / **afterwards** boil them for a few minutes.*
  *Peel the carrots and **then** / **after that** / **afterwards** cut them into thin slices.*

- *Until* shows that something continues up to a particular point in time.

  *Fry the onions slowly **until** they are brown.*
- We use *while* + clause to show that things happen at the same time.

  *He had a phone call **while** he was having dinner and had to leave.*

  ***While** you're finishing the cooking, I'll get the table ready.*
- We use *during* + noun to show that something happens 'inside' another time or event.

  *He had a phone call **during** dinner and had to leave.*

  *I don't usually have dinner before nine **during** the week.*

To express reason and purpose

- We use *to* + verb phrase. This is sometimes known as 'the infinitive of purpose'.

  *Wash the mushrooms **to** remove any dirt.*

  *I'm going to the shop **to** get some milk.*
- We use *so (that)* + clause. We can use either *so* or *so that* with the same meaning.

  *Marinade the meat for an hour **so that** it doesn't dry out.*

  *Drink plenty of water **so** you don't dehydrate.*
- We use *as* + clause. *As* has a similar meaning to *because*.

  *Cook it on quite a low heat, **as** you want to make sure the meat is soft and tender.*

  ***As** Jenny doesn't eat meat, we went to a vegetarian restaurant.*

To express contrast

- We use *although / even though* + clause to link contrasting ideas within a sentence.

  *I like to make it quite spicy, **although** I know many people prefer it milder.*

  *We eat there quite a lot, **even though** it's quite expensive.*
- We use *however* in a second sentence. Note the different positions *however* can go in.

  *She's mainly vegan. **However**, she occasionally eats eggs.*

  NOT *She's mainly vegan, however she occasionally eats eggs.*

  *It was pretty cold. We still went for a picnic, **however**.*

  *I think it tastes disgusting. A lot of people, **however**, love it.*

To express condition

- We use *if* + clause. See Unit 9 for more about *if* sentences

  *It'll burn **if** you heat it too quickly.*

  ***If** the sauce is too thick, add a little more milk.*
- *Provided* has a similar meaning to 'if you make sure'.

  *It's fairly easy to do, **provided** you give yourself enough time to prepare everything.*

  ***Provided** you can get all the ingredients, it's quick and easy to make.*
- We usually use *in case* to express that we are prepared for something that might happen.

  *I'll email you the recipe later **in case** you forget how we did it.*

  *Shall we make some veggie food **in case** anyone doesn't eat meat?*

Exercise 1

Complete the sentences with appropriate linking words. In some cases, there is more than one possibility.

1 I'll pack some snacks _____ we get hungry.
2 He let the milk boil over, _____ I asked him to keep an eye on it.
3 They'll cook whatever you want, _____ you order in advance.
4 Do you fancy going for a coffee _____ the meeting has finished?
5 Cook the pasta for about ten minutes. _____ , drain it and mix it with the sauce. And _____ the pasta is cooking, you can maybe prepare the salad.
6 I'll get some more snacks, _____ we don't run out. And I'll get some more non-meat ones _____ some people are vegetarian.
7 He drank three coffees _____ the meeting! Perhaps he needed it _____ stay awake!
8 Fry the carrots _____ they are soft. _____ , add the peppers and mushrooms and fry for another two or three minutes.
9 I don't buy these biscuits very often _____ I find them so addictive. _____ I've had one, I have to finish the whole packet!

15C PATTERNS AFTER REPORTING VERBS

Different reporting verbs are followed by different patterns.

Reporting verb + *to* + verb

agree	arrange	claim	decide	intend
offer	pretend	promise	refuse	threaten

*He **agreed to come** with me.*
*She **offered to help** us.*

Reporting verb + *-ing*

admit	consider	deny	imagine
miss	recommend	suggest	

*The company **denied being** involved.*
*She **recommends trying** that new restaurant.*

Reporting verb + person + *to* + verb

advise	ask	encourage	invite	persuade
remind	tell	urge	warn	

*My parents **encouraged me to go** to university.*
*She **asked me to give** her a hand.*

Reporting verb + preposition + *-ing*

admit to	apologize for	confess to	insist on	worry about

*We **apologized for being** late.*
*She **insisted on paying** for the meal.*

Reporting verb + person + preposition + *-ing*:

accuse somebody of	blame somebody for	criticize somebody for
forgive somebody for		

*They **accused me of breaking** the window.*
*She **forgave him for forgetting** her birthday.*

Reporting verb + *(that)* clause

admit	arrange	claim	confess	decide	deny
imagine	insist	pretend	promise	recommend	suggest
threaten	warn	worry			

*He **insisted that** it wasn't his mistake.*
*They**'re suggesting** that we meet a bit earlier.*

DID YOU KNOW?

Some reporting verbs have more than one pattern.
*He **decided to leave** early.*
*He **decided that he would leave** early.*
*He **admitted causing** the problem.*
*He **admitted to causing** the problem.*
*He **admitted that he had caused** the problem.*

Exercise 1

Choose the correct option to complete the sentences.

1. In the end, the waiter offered *giving / to give* us the starters for free as we'd been waiting so long!
2. I was going to have the chicken soup, but the waiter persuaded me *trying / to try* the pumpkin ravioli instead.
3. A new campaign is being launched today, urging people *not to waste / not wasting* food.
4. The company confessed to *use / using* out-of-date ingredients in their products.
5. The company promised *offering / that they would offer* a full refund.
6. They insisted *knowing / to know / that they knew* nothing about it.
7. My boss suggested *to apply / me to apply / that I apply* for his job when he leaves.
8. He's considering *to make / making / that he's making* a complaint about the service.
9. The doctor recommended *to cut down / cutting down / me to cut down* on red meat as far as possible.
10. The government has been criticized for *not to do / don't do / not doing* enough to combat food fraud.

Exercise 2

Four of the sentences contain a mistake. Correct the incorrect sentences.

1. They've agreed changing the packaging to make it clearer about the ingredients.
2. David recommended trying the new pizza place by the main square.
3. Harry insisted to pay for everything, which was very kind of him.
4. They encouraged that I apply for the job.
5. Sam's offered to take us all for dinner this evening. Are you free?
6. He threatened taking the restaurant to court over the food poisoning he got.

16 BUSINESS

16A THE FUTURE CONTINUOUS

Form

The future continuous is *will be + -ing*.
I**'ll be waiting** for you in reception.
We**'ll be starting** the meeting in a few minutes.
How long **will** you **be staying**?

Use

We use the future continuous to talk about something in progress at a time in the future. We often use it for plans and arrangements or what we expect to be happening.
We**'ll be moving** to the new offices in July.
I can't make Friday. I**'ll be attending** a conference in Bolton.
That's a good question. I**'ll be talking** about that later on.

One common use of the future continuous is to talk about a plan or arrangement that is connected with or fits with another action or event.
I**'ll be talking** to the area manager later, so I'll raise your concerns with her.
I**'ll be popping out** to the café in a while. Can I get you anything?
Will you **be seeing** Max later? I promised I'd get this report to him today.

Exercise 1

Complete the sentences with the future continuous form of these verbs.

advertise	drive	stay	stop	work

1. I _____ to the airport at six. Let's speak before I leave.
2. My boss has just given me a load of extra work. Looks like I _____ late tonight!
3. How long _____ you _____ in Milan? I'll be there on the Friday if you're still there.
4. I _____ for lunch in about half an hour. We can talk then if you like.
5. We _____ the new post in a couple of weeks or so. I think you'd be an excellent candidate.

Exercise 2

Match the existing plans (1–8) with the follow-up comments (a–h).

1. Will you be translating the website content into any other languages?
2. Your order will be going out today by special delivery,
3. They'll be launching the product in the US first,
4. When will she be starting her new job?
5. Will they be taking any new staff on during the summer?
6. I'll be going past the canteen,
7. Will you be using the computer later?
8. He'll be retiring in the summer,

a. so it should be with you first thing tomorrow.
b. Because I must remember to ring and wish her luck.
c. Because that could be one way of breaking into some overseas markets.
d. so we won't have to put up with his moaning for much longer.
e. Because I'll watch that film I missed last night if you're not.
f. so I might buy one when I'm in New York next month.
g. Because I'll apply if they are.
h. so I'll get you a coffee, if you like.

Exercise 3

Complete the sentences with your own ideas. Use three of these time phrases.

in ten minutes	at 7.30 this evening	at midnight
at 8 tomorrow morning	this time tomorrow	next Saturday afternoon
this time next week		

I'll be having dinner at 7.30 this evening.

1. I'll be _____ .
2. I'll _____ .
3. I _____ .

16C EXPRESSING OBLIGATION AND ABILITY

Replacing *must* with forms of *have to*

Must and *have to* have a similar meaning and they are often interchangeable. We use them to express present obligation or strong necessity.
You **must / have to show** some ID to get in the building.
We absolutely **must / have to secure** this contract.

However, when we express obligation / necessity using a past, future, present / past continuous or present / past perfect form or using an *-ing* form or infinitive, we use *have to*.
Everyone **had to attend** the meeting.
The office is being decorated, so we**'re having to work** from home this week.

*This is the third time this month I**'ve had to talk** to you about this.*

*If we'd done more market research, we **wouldn't have had to redesign** it so soon.*

*It's a risk investors **are going to have to take**.*

*I sold my car last month, so I**'ve been having to take** public transport to work since then.*

*This device allows you to share files without you **having to rely on** a computer.*

*Is it usual **to have to work** at weekends in your company?*

Force and make

When something creates an obligation for someone to do something, we use *force* or *make*. Note we use *force* + *to* + verb and we use *make* + verb (without *to*).

*The negative feedback that we got **forced us to look** at the design again.*

*If we'd done more market research, it would've **made us think about** our product a bit more.*

Replacing can with forms of be able to

Can and *be able to* have a similar meaning and they are sometimes interchangeable. We use them to show a present ability or possibility. Note that *can* is more common.

*I **can't** / **'m not able to attend** the meeting I'm afraid.*

***Can** you / **Are** you **able to work** this weekend?*

However, when we express ability / possibility using a future or present / past perfect form or using an *-ing* form or infinitive, we use *be able to*.

*We**'ll** soon **be able to generate** our own electricity.*

*Over the last few years, we**'ve been able to keep** ahead by developing new products.*

***Being able to speak** another language has made a huge difference to my life.*

*I'd love **to be able to code** computer programs.*

DID YOU KNOW?

We can sometimes use both *could* or *be able to* to talk about the past.

*The first mobile phones **could / were able to store** only about ten phone numbers.*

However, we only use *be able to* (not *could*) when the meaning is 'managed' or 'succeeded'.

*In the end, we **were able to fulfil** all our orders before Christmas.*

Enable, allow, let

When something gives you the ability or possibility to do something, we use *enable*, *allow* or *let*. Note that we use *enable* / *allow* + somebody + *to* + verb and we use *let* somebody + verb (without *to*).

*The loan **enabled us to buy** more stock.*

*Working from home **allows me to choose** my own hours.*

*The development will **let the department cut** costs massively.*

Exercise 1

Complete the sentences with the phrases in the boxes.

having to	am going to have to	had to
've had to	makes them	forced us to

1 Sorry I didn't make it at the weekend. We had a bit of an emergency at work and I _____ go into the office.
2 This is the third time this week I _____ reinstall the software.
3 We've got a problem at work. I'm afraid I _____ cancel our meeting this afternoon.
4 The disappointing sales _____ rethink our advertising strategy.
5 Their boss often _____ work late, sometimes until eight or nine.
6 _____ get up at five every morning is the biggest downside of the new job.

'll be able to	being able to	to be able to
's been able to	enabled us to	allows me to

7 She _____ speak several languages since she was quite young, I think.
8 I don't know the answer right now, but I _____ let you know in a day or two.
9 I like _____ work from home. I love the flexibility it gives me.
10 I'd love _____ work just three days a week.
11 Having flexible hours _____ spend more time with my family.
12 Restructuring the department _____ increase productivity quite considerably.

Exercise 2

Read the first sentence in each pair. Complete the second sentence so that it has a similar meaning. Use between three and five words, including the word in bold.

1 We've been able to step up production thanks to the new investment.   **ENABLED**
   The new investment _____ up production.
2 With this device, you can monitor how much electricity you're using.   **LETS**
   The device _____ how much electricity you're using.
3 It's great working from home. I don't need to get up so early!   **GET UP**
   The best thing about working from home is not _____ so early.
4 We've reached the factory's capacity, so we can't expand at the moment.   **WON'T**
   Without a new factory, _____ expand.
5 They only found out because he forced me to tell them.   **MADE**
   They wouldn't have found out if he _____ them.
6 We had to abandon the project in the end.   **FORCED**
   We _____ abandon the project in the end.

Irregular verbs

Infinitive	Past simple	Past participle
be	was / were	been
beat	beat	beaten
become	became	become
begin	began	begun
bend	bent	bent
bite	bit	bitten
bleed	bled	bled
blow	blew	blown
break	broke	broken
bring	brought	brought
build	built	built
burn	burned / burnt	burned / burnt
buy	bought	bought
catch	caught	caught
choose	chose	chosen
come	came	come
cost	cost	cost
cut	cut	cut
deal	dealt	dealt
dig	dug	dug
do	did	done
draw	drew	drawn
dream	dreamed / dreamt	dreamed / dreamt
drink	drank	drunk
drive	drove	driven
eat	ate	eaten
fall	fell	fallen
feed	fed	fed
feel	felt	felt
fight	fought	fought
find	found	found
fit	fit / fitted	fit / fitted
freeze	froze	frozen
fly	flew	flown
forget	forgot	forgotten
get	got	got
give	gave	given
go	went	gone
grow	grew	grown
hang	hung	hung
have	had	had
hear	heard	heard
hide	hid	hidden
hit	hit	hit
hold	held	held
hurt	hurt	hurt
keep	kept	kept
know	knew	known
lead	led	led
lean	leaned / leant	leaned / leant
learn	learned / learnt	learned / learnt

Infinitive	Past simple	Past participle
leave	left	left
lend	lent	lent
let	let	let
lie	lay	lain
light	lit	lit
lose	lost	lost
make	made	made
mean	meant	meant
meet	met	met
pay	paid	paid
prove	proved	proven
put	put	put
read (/ri:d/)	read (/red/)	read (/red/)
ride	rode	ridden
ring	rang	rung
rise	rose	risen
run	ran	run
say	said	said
see	saw	seen
sell	sold	sold
send	sent	sent
set	set	set
shake	shook	shaken
shine	shone	shone
shoot	shot	shot
show	showed	shown
shut	shut	shut
sing	sang	sung
sink	sank	sunk
sit	sat	sat
sleep	slept	slept
smell	smelled / smelt	smelled / smelt
speak	spoke	spoken
spell	spelled / spelt	spelled / spelt
spend	spent	spent
spill	spilled / spilt	spilled / spilt
spread	spread	spread
stand	stood	stood
steal	stole	stolen
stick	stuck	stuck
swim	swam	swum
take	took	taken
teach	taught	taught
tell	told	told
think	thought	thought
throw	threw	thrown
understand	understood	understood
wake	woke	woken
wear	wore	worn
win	won	won
write	wrote	written

Vocabulary reference

1 ENTERTAINMENT

1A USING PAIRS OF ADJECTIVES FOR EMPHASIS

When we describe things, we often use pairs of adjectives that have similar meanings to emphasize what we mean. We sometimes repeat the same adverb with each adjective.
*It's **very moving** – just very, **very sad**.*
*It's **great**, absolutely **amazing**.*

3 THINGS YOU NEED

3B WORD FAMILIES

Suffixes – word endings – often indicate a particular word form. For example, the suffix *-er* or *-or* often indicates a noun that describes what people do: *a collector, a hoarder, a writer, a teacher*. All these nouns have connected verbs: *collect, hoard, write, teach*. When you learn connected word forms, try to also learn the collocations that go with these words.

6 ACCOMMODATION

6C IDIOMS

In Exercise 2, you heard these two idioms: *You're taking the mickey* and *I'm completely out of pocket*.

An idiom is a group of words that means something different to the meaning of the individual words. You can sometimes work out the meaning of an idiom from the words and the context. If you look up the idiom in a dictionary, it's usually listed under the entry for the noun.

7 NATURE

7C METAPHORS

You will know the word *water* as in *drink some water*, but in one of the conversations in Exercise 4 you heard this: *I've been watering [the plants] every day*.

Most words have more than one meaning. Sometimes you can tell a word is being used in a different sense because the form of the word is different (here, *water* is a verb in the present perfect continuous). Sometimes the word has a connected meaning as here (give water to plants), but sometimes it is less clear, and you need to look at the words around it to work out the meaning in this context, as in these examples in this unit.
*The snow's beginning to **settle**.* (= it's something snow does)
*It'll really **settle** your stomach.* (= it's something you do to your stomach)

If you think of words as often being part of collocations and phrases, you will also start to notice other vocabulary connected to them. This will boost your understanding of how words work.

13 LIFE-CHANGING EVENTS

13C VALUES AND CONCEPTS

When we talk about values (e.g. *honour, courage*) and when we talk about a concept in general or an abstract concept, we don't usually use articles (*a / the*).
*People here find **death** an awkward subject.*
***Family** is core to the Hindu faith.*

14 BANKS AND MONEY

14C METAPHORS CONNECTED TO MONEY

Many words and expressions, such as those connected to money, are used metaphorically. Often this metaphorical usage is more common than the literal usage.
*The **odds** of winning the UK lottery are 45 million to one.* (literal)
A: *What are the **odds** he'll be late?* (metaphorical)
B: *Oh, he's bound to be!*

15 FOOD

15B PREFIXES

In the article, the author mentioned a dish that was *overcooked* and *under-seasoned*. We make lots of words by using prefixes like *over-* and *under-* before a root word. They modify the meanings of the words they are added to. For instance, an *overcooked* dish is one that has been cooked for too long, while an *under-seasoned* dish does not have enough seasoning, e.g. salt, and is tasteless.

Information files

1B Exercise 3, READING

Student A

EGYPT

One of the most successful Egyptian movies ever – at least within the country itself – is 2018's *El Badla* (The Suit). The film is usually described as an 'action comedy', and the plot revolves around the adventures of two friends who are both struggling with their careers. They get invited to a get-together of old school friends, which they both wrongly assume is a fancy-dress party. They decide to dress up as police officers and, before long, they realize that everyone thinks they're the real thing. Aware of the opportunities this now offers them, they carry on wearing the costumes in their daily lives, not realizing the danger this will lead them into. A series of crazy adventures follow until they are finally forced to deal with some dangerous gangsters and corrupt cops. The film was so successful that in 2018 it became the first Arabic-language film to be screened in Saudi Arabia for 35 years.

DENMARK

The most successful Danish film ever is *The Purity of Vengeance*, the fourth crime thriller in a series that is based on Jussi Adler-Olsen's hugely popular *Department Q* murder mystery books. As with many Scandi dramas, the story starts with the discovery of some dead bodies and the investigation that follows uncovers some dark parts of the country's history. In particular, detectives focus their investigations on a small island called Sprogø, where women who didn't act according to strict social expectations were sent to live and work – against their will – right up until the 1960s. The film has a great cast, the main characters are beautifully developed and it's very gripping, with enough twists and turns to keep you on the edge of your seat the whole way through. The film is fast-paced and whilst it is obviously very commercial, it also manages to tackle serious issues around sexism and power in society, and the need to face the past.

1C Exercise 11, SPEAKING

Student A

Some of the following language might also help:

> The painting shows …
> In the background / At the back of the picture, you can (just)
>   see …
> In the foreground / At the front of the picture, there is …
> To the right / left of the (man) …
> In the (bottom / top right hand) corner of the painting, you can
>   (just) see …

3A Exercise 1, VOCABULARY

a hammer

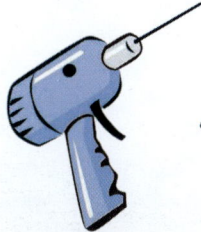
a drill

a saw

a torch

a stepladder

a nail

a screw

toothpaste

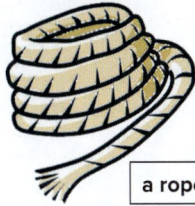
a rope

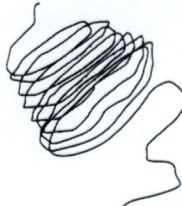
wire

a pan

a cloth

a dustpan and brush

a mop and bucket

glue

a corkscrew

a tin opener

a lighter

a rubber

correction fluid

a stapler

scissors

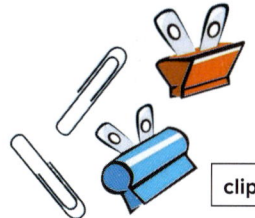
clips

sticky tape

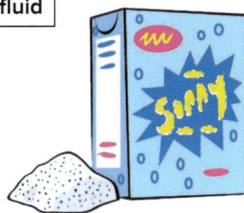
washing powder

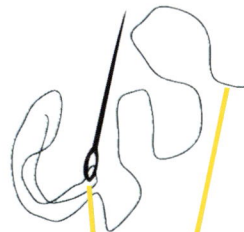
a needle and thread

an iron

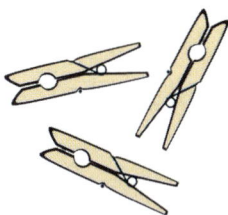
clothes pegs

a charger

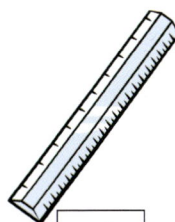
a ruler

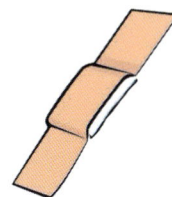
a plaster

a bandage

3A Exercise 12, CONVERSATION PRACTICE

Student A

Look at the four situations below. Think about what you need to ask your partner for in each of these situations.

1   The strap on your bag has broken.

2   You've dropped your ring and it's rolled under a cupboard and you want to try and get it out.

3   You've dropped a bottle of oil on the floor and it's smashed.

4   You knocked over a flower vase in the house you're staying in and a bit of it has broken off.

4A Exercise 12, CONVERSATION PRACTICE

Student A

Look at the role card and choose one opinion from each row. It can be true or not.

Think of a question you might ask to get this opinion and one or two examples / reasons for the opinion you chose.

When you are ready, ask one of your questions to start the conversation.

Listen to Student B's response. Continue the conversation on that topic by agreeing, giving an example / reason or presenting an alternative view. Keep going until one of you asks another question.

Either …	Or
The government's economic policies are good.	The economy is good in the capital but elsewhere there are problems.
You don't like the targets / policies to tackle the climate crisis.	You think the government has some good green policies but could do more.
Public services have generally been improving.	Public services have generally stayed the same or got worse.
The prime minister / president has a good image in the world.	The government's foreign policy isn't good or is not important for you.
The government will probably stay in power after the next election.	The opposition will probably win power in the next election.
There is one particular thing you'd like to see the government do more on.	You think there are lots of areas where the government should be doing things differently.

6B Exercise 9, READING

To: Jacksonjane@shotmail.ml

Re: Surprise, surprise!

Hi Jane,

Hope this address still works for you. I bet this is a bit of a surprise! It's my fault, of course. I realize I've isolated myself a bit. If you're annoyed with me and don't want to know or respond, then fair enough.

Anyway, this is just to let you know that I'm going to be over in England and it'd be really good to get back in touch – and introduce you to my wife and new son, Huang Fu. See picture attached.

Email me!

Matt

7B Exercise 3, READING

Pair B

Victory in bullfighting fight

The Spanish Parliament has voted to lift a ban on broadcasting live bullfighting on the state-run channel RTVE. Alongside giving space in the early evening schedule for live bullfights, the proposal calls for space to be given to documentaries and reports on the sport.

The lifting of the ban will be seen as a victory by bullfighting fans in an ongoing debate about the sport, which they see as under threat. While there were over 1,400 bullfighting festivals in Spain last year, with more than three million spectators, the numbers attending are in decline and a recent survey by the BBVA foundation found 76% of the population were opposed to the use of bulls for fighting.

The bullfighting industry is also threatened with rising costs, and it depends on festivals being subsidized by local government and on the European Union providing upwards of twenty million euros a year to bull farmers. However, many of these subsidies are being reviewed and may end altogether.

While opponents highlight the cruelty of the sport and argue it is unsuitable TV viewing for children, supporters insist it is a popular art form and a celebration of risk and bravery which has a special place in Spanish culture.

It's an argument which, in parliament at least, supporters of bullfighting have won.

Controversial research lab finally opens

A controversial animal research laboratory funded by Oxford University has finally opened after the project was delayed by sixteen months because of threats and intimidation by members of extremist animal rights groups. The first company involved in the construction of the lab decided to pull out of the project amidst fears for the safety of both site workers and the firm's board members.

The eighteen-million-pound centre will bring together researchers from various parts of the university to carry out experiments investigating conditions such as cancer, heart disease and diabetes. The university says the centre will provide better care for the animals used in the experiments, 98% of which are rats and mice and 0.5% primates such as monkeys.

There's been ongoing controversy since the project was first announced. Campaigners against animal experiments (also known as *vivisection*) held regular demonstrations claiming that vivisection is cruel, unreliable and unnecessary. However, more radical activists in the anti-vivisection movement also tried to intimidate people involved in the project by publishing their addresses online and sending threatening letters. Other groups then responded with demonstrations in support of the centre.

While the university says they are looking to reduce the need for animals in research, scientists insist the centre will play a vital part in finding cures for diseases that affect millions of people.

FILE 8 Unit 11

11A Exercise 12, CONVERSATION PRACTICE

Student A

You are going to collect a car you have booked online. It's a small family car with a little bit of space in the boot. You are travelling with your partner (who might do some of the driving) and your five-year-old daughter (who hates being in cars).

- The car rental assistant may try to sell you some extras.
- Ask about them and decide if you want them or not.
- Think of three other questions you will need to ask.

FILE 9 Unit 11

11B Exercise 2, READING

Student B

The World on Wheels

Since the age of 15, Albert Casals has travelled all over the world, often on his own, and on **a shoestring budget** of around three euros a day. This includes hitchhiking from his homeland Catalunya to New Zealand. All that is pretty remarkable in itself, but even more so when you consider Albert is a wheelchair user. Now translated into English, his journals and reflections on his adventures are a funny and inspiring read. We see him **negotiating the difficulties** that travel throws up with his optimistic, can-do attitude and understand that, for Albert, travel is less about geography and seeing sights and more about meeting people and **encountering new ways of living**.

The Motorcycle Diaries

The first time I saw this film, it inspired me to quit my job and buy a motorbike to travel throughout South America. Watching it again with my partner, who I met on that journey, **brought back all those memories** and reminded me of what makes travel great. For those who don't know it, the film depicts a road trip of the young Ernesto 'Che' Guevara and his friend Alberto through South America. On their journey from his home in Buenos Aires to Guajira in Venezuela they negotiate the typical difficulties of travel – breakdowns, lack of money and food, misunderstandings and arguments. But they also **experience great hospitality** and see things that **open their eyes** and broaden their minds.

Un Gran Viaje (A Grand Tour)

Pablo Strubell's Spanish podcast aims to show how a grand tour is a possibility for anyone. He interviews a huge range of people, some with **a clear itinerary**, others wandering where they fancy. For example, there's the so-called backpacker granny *(abuelita mochilera)*, who's toured round 74 different countries by public transport in her 25-odd years of retirement. Or the couple who went on a seven-year, round-the-world bicycle trip – and had two children while they were still on the road. Strubell himself is a 'grand tourist'. At 30, he **dropped everything**, including a well-paid job as a salesman, in order to spend seven months backpacking along the so-called Silk Road from Turkey, through Iran and 'the Stans' to China. He**'s never looked back since**.

FILE 10 Unit 12

12B Exercise 10, SPEAKING

Student A

1 A man who's in hospital after a heart operation has just inherited $10 million. His family are afraid the shock might kill him so they asked his surgeon if there's any way she could tell him. So the surgeon goes to the patient and says, 'Joe, what would you do if you were left $10 million in a will?'

   'Well, I'd give it all to the doctor who saved my life.'

   At which point, the surgeon drops down dead!

2 A man goes to his doctor and says his wife is worried about him because he can't do all the things around the house that he used to do. When the examination is complete, the man says, 'I can take it. Tell me in plain English what is wrong with me.' 'Well, in plain English,' the doctor replied, 'you're just lazy.' 'OK,' said the man. 'Now give me the medical term so I can tell my wife.'

3 'Doctor, Doctor. I think I need glasses.'

   'You certainly do, Sir. This is a hairdresser's!'

FILE 11 Unit 14

14A Exercise 12, CONVERSATION PRACTICE

Student A

For three conversations, you are the customer.

1 You want to open a new account.

3 You want to take out a loan – decide how much.

5 You want to transfer some money overseas.

For three conversations, you are the bank clerk.

2 Student B wants to apply for an overdraft. You can do this, but there will be a charge.

4 Student B wants a new cash card. You can't produce one now. One can be sent out within two weeks.

6 Student B thinks they have been the victim of fraud. They do not have insurance and the bank can't refund any losses.

15A Exercise 1, VOCABULARY

almond	mint	tomato	grape	broccoli	plum
raisin	turnip	hazelnut	octopus	parsnip	coconut
trout	courgette	parsley	eel	rosemary	fig
ginger	orange	kidney bean	chick pea	sweet potato	sweetcorn
scallop	peach	cabbage	pumpkin	radish	celery
pepper	fennel	spring onion	chilli	salmon	beetroot

16A Exercise 10, CONVERSATION PRACTICE

Student A

Scenario 1

There are some problems with teamwork in your company. You think it would be good to do some kind of team-building exercises. Phone a colleague to get their input. Arrange a meeting to discuss the issue further with one or more other people.

Scenario 2

Someone from a company you supply is going to call about the latest of several problems they have had. Sort out the current problem. Give an excuse for the ongoing problems but arrange a meeting to come up with some solutions.

FILE 14   Unit 16

16C Exercise 11, SPEAKING

Pair A

Choose one of these products and follow the instructions.

1 a machine to allow your dog to get exercise without having to take it for a walk

2 a program that can edit your online profile and delete any embarrassing or potentially career damaging information

3 a chain of stores that sells specialist high-quality chocolate and personalized chocolate products

- Come up with a name for the product.
- Think of the retail price and how much profit you'll make on each item.
- Explain how the product works and why it's better than the competitors' – if there are any.
- Think of some questions to ask the other pair when they present their products (and which they might ask you!). For example: *What's the estimated size of the market?; What's the company's projected turnover / profit? What are the projected sales?*
- Think about how much money you want Pair B to invest and why. What stake of the company will you give them in exchange?
- Be prepared to negotiate if they offer you something.
- Discuss how you'll present your product and who will say what in the pitch.

FILE 15   Unit 12

12B Exercise 10, SPEAKING

Student C

1 A hypochondriac went to the doctor. 'Doctor. You've got to refer me to a consultant. I've got liver disease.' 'How could you possibly know that?' replied the doctor. 'There's no discomfort and no outward signs of illness with liver disease.' And the patient said, 'You see! Those are my precise symptoms.'

2 A man goes to a doctor after hitting his head in an accident. After examining the man, the doctor said, 'Well, I've got some bad news and some good news. The bad news is you've got a terminal disease and will be dead within six months.' 'Oh my gosh! Well what's the good news?' 'Well, you've also got amnesia, so you'll forget all about it!'

3 'Doctor, Doctor. Have you got something for a bad headache?' 'Of course. Just take this hammer and hit yourself on the head. Then you'll have a bad headache.'

FILE 16   Unit 1

1B Exercise 3, READING

Student B

THAILAND

While many films fit fairly neatly into a particular genre, the highest-grossing Thai film of all-time, *Pee Mak*, really doesn't. Perhaps best described as a romantic comedy-horror with a difference, the film was an astonishing success not only at home, but all across Asia. *Pee Mak* is set in the 19th century and draws on Thai legends and folklore. The plot isn't easy to summarize, but in short, the hero Mak returns from a war with four friends he has saved from certain death. He invites them to meet his wife and his young son, who was born while he was away fighting. However, before long, the friends come to realize that little is what it seems to be in Mak's village – and even with his family. Don't be fooled, though: the film isn't as dark as this might suggest. There are plenty of laugh-out-loud funny moments and at the heart of the film is a strangely moving love story.

BRAZIL

While the Brazilian film industry has gone from strength to strength over recent years, nothing has been able to compete with the smash hit series of comedy films, *Minha Mãe é uma Peça* ('My mom is a character'). The first film was released in 2013 with the sequel coming three years later; the plot in both revolves around a mother who feels that her kids don't appreciate her and so decides to take action and reclaim her life. However, it is the third film in the series that has been by far and away the most successful, as the now-divorced supermum of the title prepares for life without her many kids, who are now all leaving home and starting new lives. A word of warning, though: despite being about family life, it may not be ideal family viewing and it contains a fair bit of swearing and some very adult themes.

1C Exercise 11, SPEAKING

Student B

Some of the following language might also help:

The painting shows …
In the background / At the back of the picture, you can (just)
    see …
In the foreground / At the front of the picture, there is …
To the right / left of the (man) …
In the (bottom / top right hand) corner of the painting, you can
    (just) see …

FILE 18   Unit 3

3A Exercise 12, CONVERSATION PRACTICE

Student B

Look at the four situations below. Think about what you need to ask your partner for in each of these situations.

1   You've got some new shoes which are rubbing on the back of your heels and you don't want your heels to get sore and bleed.

2   On a picnic, the tab on the top of a tin or can has broken off so you can't open it easily.

3   A screw on your glasses has come loose and the arm of the glasses has fallen off.

4   You need to change a light bulb, but you can't reach the light even if you stand on a chair.

FILE 19   Unit 4

4A Exercise 12, CONVERSATION PRACTICE

Student B

Look at the role card and choose one opinion from each row. It can be true or not.

Think of a question you might ask to get this opinion and one or two examples / reasons for each opinion.

When you are ready, listen to Student A's question and give your response.

Listen to Student A's response. Continue the conversation on that topic by agreeing, giving an example / reason or presenting an alternative view. Keep going until one of you asks another question.

Either ...	Or
The government's economic policies are good.	The economy is good in the capital but elsewhere there are problems.
You don't like the targets / policies to tackle the climate crisis.	You think the government has some good green policies but could do more.
Public services have generally been improving.	Public services have generally stayed the same or got worse.
The prime minister / president has a good image in the world.	The government's foreign policy isn't good or is not important for you.
The government will probably stay in power after the next election.	The opposition will probably win power in the next election.
There is one particular thing you'd like to see the government do more on.	You think there are lots of areas where the government should be doing things differently.

FILE 20   Unit 11

11A Exercise 12, CONVERSATION PRACTICE

Student B

You work for Right Car Rentals. Student A is going to collect a car they have booked online from you.

- Decide if you have any special offers this week.
- Point out that the car runs on diesel not petrol.
- Try to sell some extras – you get 15% commission if you do!
- Decide how much to charge for the following extras:
  - GPS
  - Additional insurance to cover damage to tyres and windscreen
  - Comprehensive insurance to cover damage to the vehicle, injury or loss of life, theft of property, etc.
  - A baby seat (for children under two) or a booster seat (for children from two to eight)
  - Cover for any additional drivers

FILE 21   Unit 12

12B Exercise 10, SPEAKING

Student B

1   A man walks into a doctor's office. He has a cucumber up his nose, a carrot in his left ear, and a banana in his right ear. He says, 'Doctor, Doctor – what's the matter with me. Is it serious?' The doctor replies, 'Not at all. You're not eating properly.'

2   A doctor is consulting a colleague. 'I have this patient who is suffering from Jimbomba – it's a rare tropical disease. It's very contagious.'

'Ah yes. Interesting, I had a patient who suffered from that some years ago.'

'Really? What should I do?'

'I recommend a diet of pizzas and pancakes.'

'Pizzas and pancakes. That's a pretty radical solution. Will it really cure them?'

'Probably not, but it's the only food that'll fit under the door.'

3   'Doctor, Doctor, I'm on a diet and it's making me really irritable. Yesterday I actually bit someone's ear off.'

'Oh dear! That's a lot of calories!'

14A Exercise 12, CONVERSATION PRACTICE

Student B

For three conversations, you are the bank clerk.

1   Student A wants to open an account. You need to see relevant ID.

3   Student A wants to take out a loan. You can't lend this much to someone with such a bad credit history.

5   Student A wants to transfer money overseas. This is fine, but there will be a 5% commission charge.

For three conversations, you are the customer.

2   You want to apply for an overdraft. Decide how large.

4   You have lost your card and need a new one.

6   According to your bank statement, 1,500 euros were withdrawn from your account last week in Belgium. You've never even been to Belgium!

FILE 23   Unit 16

16A Exercise 10, CONVERSATION PRACTICE

Student B

Scenario 1

Your colleague is going to call you to talk about some problems with teamwork in your company. Listen to their concerns and offer one or two suggestions when asked, including having a meeting to discuss the issue further.

Scenario 2

You are phoning a supplier to your company to chase up an order. You've been having ongoing problems and feel it would be good to have a meeting with one or more other people to discuss these further and see if you can come up with some solutions.

FILE 24   Unit 16C

16C Exercise 11, SPEAKING

Pair B

Choose one of these products and follow the instructions.

1   a key ring that is fitted with a balloon that automatically inflates on contact with water

2   a special sauce from a particular country for cooking a dish or to have on the side

3   a special box for shoes that enables you to remove smells instantly

•   Come up with a name for the product.

•   Think of the retail price and how much profit you'll make on each item.

•   Explain how the product works and why it's better than the competitors' – if there are any.

•   Think of some questions to ask the other pair when they present their products (and which they might ask you!). For example: *What's the estimated size of the market?; What's the company's projected turnover / profit? What are the projected sales?*

•   Think about how much money you want Pair A to invest and why. What stake of the company will you give them in exchange?

•   Be prepared to negotiate if they offer you something.

•   Discuss how you'll present your product and who will say what in the pitch.

Audio scripts

Lesson 1A, Listening, Exercise 1

1 Yeah, all the time. My headphones are glued to my ears! I like all kinds of stuff as well – reggaeton, hip-hop, even some pop.

2 Not as much as I'd like to, because I really love it – especially musicals. I mean, I do go now and then, but the seats are so expensive I can't afford to go more than a couple of times a year.

3 Very rarely, to be honest. I guess I might in the summer – if it's very hot. I find it a bit boring, just going up and down the pool. It's not really my kind of thing – and I'm not very good at it either.

4 Probably less than I think I do, if you know what I mean. It's often on in the background, you know, but I don't pay much attention to it most of the time. I do sometimes watch the big matches if they're on – and the occasional film – but apart from that, most of it's rubbish.

5 Yeah, I guess so. I usually play football on a Wednesday and I go running now and then. I generally cycle to college as well – unless it's raining.

6 No, not as a rule. I tend to watch films on demand through my TV at home. Oh, and I download quite a lot of stuff too.

7 Yeah, at the weekends, of course. I go shopping, go to the cinema, go clubbing sometimes. I don't tend to during the week, though, because I have to get up early for school and I've got homework, and basically my parents prefer me to stay at home.

8 Not as much as I used to. I was addicted to this online game for a while until I started to realize it was a problem. I'd sometimes play for five hours a day! I sometimes play other games now, but I've learned to control it all a bit more!

Lesson 1A, Listening, Exercises 9 & 10

A: So, what kind of things do you do in your free time?

B: I guess films are my main thing.

A: Really? Do you go to the cinema much then?

B: Oh, all the time. I mean, I go at least once a week, but I'll often go two or three times!

A: Wow! That is a lot!

B: Yeah. I mean, it depends what's on, of course.

A: Right.

B: What about you? Do you go much?

A: Now and then, if there's something I really want to see, but I'm happy just to watch at home.

B: Really? But if you're watching an action movie with all the special effects, don't you want to see it on the big screen?

A: Yeah, I guess, but to be honest, I'm not that keen on action movies anyway, so …

B: Really? I mean, what about the Avengers films? Or *Batman*? Stuff like that?

A: Yeah, *The Suicide Squad* was OK, I suppose, but I'd rather see other things.

B: Actually, there was this great Korean film on TV last night – *Oldboy*.

A: Oh yeah, I started watching it, but I turned over.

B: You didn't like it?

A: Not really. It was so over-the-top. That scene where he eats the live octopus! I don't know. It was all a bit too weird for my liking. Didn't you find it strange?

B: I guess it is a bit, but that's what I like about it. They actually did an American remake of it, but I prefer the original – I've seen it loads of times.

A: Really? OK. As I say, it's not really my kind of thing. I prefer a good drama. So what other films are you into?

B: Oh, all sorts. I mean, I'm really into action films and stuff like that, but I'll watch most things really. As I say, I go most weeks, so, you know …

A: Have you seen *Green Book*?

B: Yeah. Have you?

A: No, but I've heard it's good. I should probably try and catch it sometime.

B: Yeah, you should. It's astonishing. I was in tears by the end.

A: Yeah?

B: Yeah. It's quite upsetting in places, quite disturbing – but the two main characters are just incredible … and it's based on a true story as well, I think.

A: I'll check it out then.

B: Yeah, you should. Honestly, it's brilliant.

Lesson 1C, Listening, Exercises 7 & 8

Now, if you follow me through into the next room, we come to two paintings by a 17th century Dutch artist who was both widely admired and reasonably successful during his lifetime. Born in Leiden in 1629, Gabriel Metsu moved to Amsterdam around 1655 and produced over 40 major works. Sadly, though, he died at the age of 37, at a time when his career was going particularly well, and since then he has been rather forgotten, which seems a bit of a shame, to be honest.

These two pieces were meant to be hung together as companion pieces. In the painting on the left, a young man is writing a letter and on the right, we see a young woman reading a letter. The viewers are supposed to understand that he is composing a love letter to her, and that here she is digesting it. On the surface, these may look like fairly conventional, fairly realistic pieces, but look more carefully and you soon realize that they are actually very open to interpretation.

The man appears to be a member of the upper-middle classes, and his surroundings create the impression that he's well travelled: through the open window, we can see a globe in the room behind him and there's an expensive Turkish rug on his table. To his right, there's an Italian-style landscape hanging on the wall, which suggests he's a man of the world. Meanwhile, the woman, who is also expensively dressed, seems to belong more to the domestic world. Painted in bolder colours, she looks calm and content as she reads.

However, not everything is as it first appears. Beneath the surface of the calm domestic world lies trouble. In the foreground of the painting, we see a shoe. Perhaps the suggestion is that the woman was so excited to receive her letter that she jumped up and didn't even notice it'd come off. To the right of the picture, we see the woman's maid pulling back a curtain, behind which we see two ships on a stormy sea. This could well be a symbol of the difficult, stormy nature of love, especially when partners are separated. Look carefully and you'll notice too that the servant has another letter to deliver – presumably to the man shown here.

Although he is depicted in darker, more subtle shades, there are visual clues that the man is also experiencing strong emotions. The rich red of the cloth and the bright light pouring in through the window suggest he has a heated mind. The underlying message now seems clear: passion can disturb and disrupt.

UNIT 2

Lesson 2A, Listening, Exercises 6 & 8

M = Mai, I = Ivana

M: What a lovely day!

I: Yeah. It's nice, isn't it? It's been a really warm autumn.

M: So, where are we?

I: Well, the bit we've just been through, with all the high-rise buildings, is what we call New Belgrade. It's quite a popular area these days and lots of businesses have moved here over recent years. Now I don't know if you can see it or not, but just behind us, over to the right, is the Arena, where all the big concerts and sports events are held. It's one of the biggest entertainment venues in Europe.

M: Wow! OK. Right.

I: You might've seen it on TV – it's the place they held the European basketball finals a few years ago.

M: Oh, right. To be honest, I'm not really that keen on basketball. It's not really my kind of thing.

I: No? Oh well. Fair enough. Anyway, now we're crossing over the River Sava into Old Belgrade.

M: Wow! The river looks wonderful.

I: Yeah, it's great. In the summer, we often go out on little boats or have dinner down by the waterside.

M: Oh, that sounds lovely. And what's that big bridge over there?

I: That's the Ada Bridge. It's not that old, actually. It only opened about ten years ago.

M: It looks great.

I: Looks even better when they light it up at night.

M: Mmmm.

I: And just down there, there's a little street called Gavrila Principa Street, which is where Manakova Kuca – Manak's House – is located. It's a kind of cultural museum and it has an amazing collection of old national costumes and jewellery and stuff.

M: OK. I'll check that out if I have time. What's that building over there?

I: Oh, that's St Mark's Church.

M: Wow! It's a stunning building. How old is it?

I: Not that old, actually. It was built in the late 1930s or something, but it's on the site of a much older church. It contains the tomb of Stefan Dusan, who was perhaps the greatest Serbian emperor ever.

M: Oh, OK.

I: And if you want to walk around here later, you're quite close to the Kalemegdan Fortress, one of the most historic buildings in Belgrade. There's the Victor Monument up there as well, which was put up after the First World War. It's one of the city's most famous landmarks.

M: Right. Well, I'll have to remember to take my camera with me up there, then.

I: And now we're coming up to Dedinje, which is one of the wealthier parts of the city. It's where all the celebrities and the old aristocratic families live – and a lot of the embassies are based here as well.

M: The houses are lovely round here.

I: Yeah, they're amazing.

Lesson 2C, Listening, Exercises 2 & 3

1: Honestly, if I had my way, we'd be just sitting in a café and watching the world go by, but Paul likes to take something back for the family. It's such a waste of money. Just look what's on display here! It may all be handmade crafts, but it all looks just incredibly ugly to me. I bet local people never have this stuff in their homes. I mean, … oh good grief here he comes! What is that? I've no idea why he's looking so pleased with himself. And there's no way that'll fit in our hand luggage. I think I'm going to have to 'accidentally' drop that on our way to the airport.

2: I hadn't particularly wanted to go on it. They kept insisting and in the end, I gave in. I was actually fine on the first bit, but it seemed to just keep speeding up and all those spins and twists … The kids were screaming with laughter, but I was just screaming in fear and couldn't wait to get off. Honestly, I thought I was going to throw up.

3: We had found a place and although the money's very tight, we thought we could afford it. But then next day we heard someone from out of town had put in a bigger offer. We're seeing another place tomorrow, but the same thing is bound to happen because it's such a competitive market with people wanting a holiday home or to escape the city completely. I grew up here and it is a bit upsetting to think that my choices are to either move away or to be stuck with my parents forever.

4: I'm glad to announce that our plans for this new hotel resort and spa are due to be approved next week, despite the opposition. Our arguments were accepted, but I apologize if you faced any protesters as you arrived today. Apart from the jobs we'll create in the resort itself, the development is likely to attract tourists to the whole region, so everyone will benefit. And just from a selfish point of view, I think a lot of us will be happy to finally have a decent golf course round here.

5: Hi, Maria, its Andrew. I'm here at the ticket office and have got the tickets. You know there are restricted numbers, and I was afraid they'd sell out. I mean, the main collection of vintage vehicles is always interesting, but this exhibition on Formula One is supposed to be amazing. Anyway, I'll wait here, but let me know how long you'll be. It opens in an hour and I want to go in before it gets too busy.

Review 1, Grammar, Exercise 4

1 It's going to boost the club's income.

2 I'd listen to his stuff all the time when I was younger.

3 I'm sure it'll be worth it in the end.

4 It's likely to present a huge challenge in the coming years.

5 It's due to be completed in 2030.

6 It might take years to repair the damage.

UNIT 3

Lesson 3A, Developing conversations, Exercise 7

1

A: What's the name of that stuff you use to put posters up?

B: Can you be a bit more specific?

A: Yeah, sorry, I mean that stuff – it's a bit like chewing gum or something, but it doesn't actually feel that sticky.

B: What? You mean Blu Tack®?

A: Yeah! Is that what they call it?

2

C: It's, um … what do you call those things climbers use? They're made of metal. They're like a hook.

D: What? You mean the thing you use to connect yourself to the rope?

C: Yeah, they have a sort of clip thing that opens and shuts. You see people using the small ones as key rings sometimes.

D: Yeah, yeah. I know exactly what you mean. I don't know! Do they have a special name? Aren't they just clips?

Lesson 3A, Listening, Exercises 9 & 10

A: I brought you a present.

B: Wine?

A: No! I know you don't drink. No, it's Californian grape juice. I had some at a friend's the other day and it was really delicious.

B: Really?

A: Apparently, they have all sorts of varieties.

B: Yeah? Well, thanks! Shall we have some now?

A: Sure! Have you got a corkscrew?

B: Ah, that's a point, actually. I'm not sure I have. Let me have a look. There's so much stuff in these drawers. Most of it's rubbish. I really should clear it out. Mmm. I don't think there's one here. Can't you use a knife?

A: I don't think so.

B: You need a stick or something to push it down. Would a pencil do?

A: It wouldn't be strong enough.

B: What about a wooden spoon? You could use the handle.

A: Yeah, that should do. Let's see … Oh no!

B: Oh, it's gone everywhere!

A: Sorry! Have you got a cloth?

B: Yeah. I think we need a mop and bucket as well.

A: Sorry.

B: Don't worry about it. These things happen. You might want to rub some salt into that shirt or it'll leave a stain.

A: Really?

B: Well, it works for other things.

Lesson 3C, Listening, Exercise 3

Hello. Welcome to *Rights and Reason*. On today's show, we'll be discussing the importance of dealing with customer complaints; the government's proposed new laws on data protection; and we'll be talking about the hazards of buying a second-hand car.

Our first item came out of a post on the *Rights and Reason* web page from a listener, Fei Han. Last month, Fei bought a pair of shoes in a well-known store. When he opened the box at home, he discovered one of the shoes had an insole missing. Fei says he put off going back to the store because he didn't want the stress. In fact, he says he even thought about keeping and using them, but unsurprisingly, found them too uncomfortable to walk in. So eventually he took them back. And this is where the problems really started.

The assistant told him it wasn't company policy to sell individual parts separately and that he should have checked the shoes at the point of sale. He was even accused of losing the insole himself! The assistant said he could only prove this wasn't the case by checking the CCTV cameras after the store closed that day. Fei left a contact number, but heard nothing and went back three days later. After explaining the situation again, this time to the store manager, Fei was finally offered a new insole. Unfortunately, when he got home he discovered it was the wrong size, at which point he gave up! Now, to discuss this case and the wider implications for customer services …

Lesson 3C, Listening, Exercises 5 & 7

P = Presenter, JS = John Squire

P: Now, to discuss this case and the wider implications for customer services, we have John Squire from the Institute of Customer Care. Welcome, John. So what do you think of this case?

JS: Yes. Thank you. I mean, clearly Fei shouldn't have been treated like that and given the final outcome, what exactly have they achieved? It's almost a perfect example of what NOT to do.

P: But was he just unlucky? Was it just one bad shop assistant?

JS: Well, possibly, but it can be a sign of a deeper problem in the company. In some shops and companies, a culture can develop where staff see complaints as the customers causing problems. They think the customer is being deliberately awkward or even trying to cheat the company. That means the assistants don't really listen to the customer or take the issue seriously.

P: OK. So are you saying the customer is always right?

JS: No, no. Not at all. There are instances of people complaining repeatedly in order to get compensation and extra benefits – and, of course, sometimes the customer is at fault. However, you should always start from the view that they do have a valid claim and allow them to speak. Listen. Consider what the customer wants. Also consider what's the cost of resolving the situation – even if you do have doubts. I mean, in Fei's case even if he was lying – and who on earth loses part of their shoe – how much would replacing that part cost?

P: Indeed. And there's a bigger cost to poor care, isn't there? Your institute's produced some interesting statistics on this recently – I mean it's cheaper to keep customers.

JS: Absolutely. Estimates suggest the cost of retaining a customer is a fifth of the cost of finding new ones, and customers are actually four times more likely to use or recommend a service again if a problem is sorted out efficiently.

P: And the recommending is important to remember, too?

JS: Absolutely. Even if your business doesn't deal with lots of regular customers or repeat visitors – I don't know, like in a tourist attraction for example – the best advertising is word-of-mouth. And that also means treating all customers equally; kids, tourists, whoever – because they can all give recommendations.

P: Are poor attitudes to customers only an issue here?

JS: Well, probably not, but I know that some cultures do have a different approach. In Japan, for example, if people complain, it's in the spirit of improving a service rather than seeking compensation. We say complaints should be seen in this way here too – as a gift. For every person who complains, there'll be 25 who are also dissatisfied, but who said nothing. A person who complains has made an effort. They are providing valuable feedback and show how you can improve products and services. Companies often pay to get feedback and here they're getting it for free! In short, the message is: take customer care seriously whoever the person is and train staff to do it well.

P: John Squire, thank you very much.

Lesson 4A, Listening, Exercises 4 & 5

A: So what do you think of your president?

B: Oh, I don't really like him, to be honest.

A: Really? Whenever I see him on TV, he looks good – he seems like someone who wants to make a difference.

B: Ah, it's all image. I mean when he gained power he talked a lot about tackling the climate crisis and boosting opportunities for young people, but they've almost done the opposite!

A: Really?

B: OK, they banned plastic bags and made a big thing about setting tough targets on climate change, but since then they've increased investment in roads and cut tax on gas … it makes no sense.

A: I know what you mean. Something similar happened here too.

B: And as for opportunities for young people? They've just put up the fees for university. It costs, like, about $10,000 now!

A: Wow! How do you manage? Isn't the cost of living really high too?

B: Tell me about it! Especially rent! It's so expensive, I just have to hope I can find a decent job.

A: And what is the job situation like?

B: Well, if you listen to the government, everything is brilliant. Since they've been in power, we've avoided a recession and we've created millions of jobs, but from what I see, so many of those jobs are insecure and badly paid. People are just getting into debt in order to make ends meet – and with so many people in debt, who knows what might happen?

A: I see. So, when's the next election? Can't you vote against them?

B: It's next year, but I'm not sure it's going to be worth voting.

A: No? The opposition don't have other policies?

B: Yeah they do, but I don't know – can I trust them?

A: I know what you mean, but it's always worth voting. I mean, like, our government has done a few controversial things – stuff I didn't agree with – but, you know, they've done good things as well. I mean, the economy's really booming.

B: Maybe you're right – or maybe I should think about going to your country after college.

A: You should. Honestly, there's such a skills shortage that companies are paying really good money now. They're desperate for people.

B: You don't think the language would be a barrier?

A: Not necessarily. Quite a few multinational companies have set up here recently and they all use English. And anyway, you'd pick up the language after a while. They've actually done a lot to cut bureaucracy too, so it's much easier for people from other countries to get work here now.

B: Yeah? I would like to work abroad someday, so … thanks for the tip.

Lesson 4A, Developing conversations, Exercise 10

1 A: I don't know how people can make ends meet.
  B: Tell me about it! I only earn enough to cover the basics and I've got a good job.

2 A: The job market is so competitive at the moment.
  B: I know what you mean, but if you're prepared to be flexible there's plenty of work.

3 A: The pace of life is so fast here.
  B: I know! It's exhausting. I feel like I spend my life just rushing around.

4 A: There's so much crime, you can't go out at night!
  B: Yeah, maybe. Mind you, it's not like that everywhere. If you avoid certain areas, it's perfectly safe.

5 A: They haven't done anything to boost tourism.
  B: Yeah, I know what you mean. Mind you, look what they've done to improve poor areas. That's great.

6 A: This country is so bureaucratic!
  B: Tell me about it! I had to fill in four forms in three different places to be able to work here!

Lesson 4C, Listening, Exercises 3 & 5

1: A new law that could see social media companies defined as publishers is being debated in parliament today. Publishing companies are responsible for checking facts, whereas social media companies currently aren't. Similar moves have been taken in the EU in an attempt to reduce fake news and hate speech online. If the bill's passed, social media companies could be sued for lies and abuse posted on their platforms.

2: Police today are investigating an assault on a young man which has left him seriously injured in hospital. Police believe the incident was racially motivated, based on evidence from security cameras which caught a group of youths running from the scene of the attack. Anti-racist campaigners are planning a march at the weekend in support of the victim.

3: The government will today launch an initiative called Housing First. The plan aims to reduce the number of people living on the streets by simply giving them a flat without conditions – it doesn't matter why the people ended up on the street. The idea has already had success in Finland, where it's national policy. It has massively reduced homelessness and led to savings in other areas such as health and policing.

4: A woman at a leading law firm has won an unfair dismissal case. Judith Fenton took the company to court when she was sacked after revealing she was pregnant. The company had claimed it was struggling and cut other jobs at the same time, but the court rejected the argument and awarded £20,000 in compensation. According to one campaign group, there are over 50,000 similar cases every year, but only around one per cent take legal action.

5: Ten people were arrested today in demonstrations demanding the introduction of a new law giving rights to nature. Countries such as Mexico, Panama and New Zealand have similar laws, which allow legal action on behalf of habitats damaged by human activity. Demonstrators stopped traffic into the capital as some glued themselves to roads. It took police five hours to remove them all. The government said they oppose the idea and called the protests foolish and dangerous.

Review 2, Grammar, Exercise 4

1 You use a sort of brush thing to clean it.
2 When I switched it on, I found it was faulty.
3 You should've been offered a replacement.
4 Prices have risen so much we can't make ends meet.
5 The lower the tax, the greater the incentive to earn more.
6 When it comes to coffee, the stronger, the better.

UNIT 5

Lesson 5A, Listening, Exercises 5 & 8

1

A: What are you up to later?

B: Oh, I'm going to a belly dancing class.

A: You're doing what?

B: Belly dancing. You know, like …

A: Yeah, I know what it is. I just had no idea that you did that.

B: Well, I don't really. It's actually the first class.

A: Oh, OK. So why belly dancing?

B: I've been thinking about doing something to get a bit fitter and I've never liked sport particularly. I find jogging and swimming and stuff like that a bit boring, you know – and then I saw this class advertised and I thought it'd be fun.

A: Right. Got you. I should probably do something as well. I've done hardly any exercise since January.

B: Really? You'd never know. You look fine.

A: Well, I don't feel it! I'm really unfit as well. I had to run for the bus this morning and it took me about ten minutes to get my breath back!

B: Well, why don't you come with me?

A: I don't know. I think I'd feel a bit self-conscious.

B: Come on! You can't be worse than me. I'm totally uncoordinated! It'll be a laugh.

A: Well, maybe.

2

C: Are you around this weekend at all?

D: Not really, no, I'm going to a judo workshop all day Saturday.

C: You're going where?

D: To a judo workshop. It's like a master class with this top Japanese teacher.

C: Wow! I didn't even know you did judo. How did you get into that?

D: Oh, we actually used to do it at school. In PE, we had the option to try out all kinds of sports and I just really got into it, and then I joined a club, and then I started competing a bit more seriously, you know.

C: I had no idea. Well, what about Sunday? I'm going to have a wander round the big street market in the morning.

D: To be honest, I think I'm just going to have a lie-in and chill out at home. I'll be exhausted after Saturday.

C: Fair enough. Just the thought of doing that kind of exercise makes me sweat!

3

E: What're you doing this evening? Do you fancy meeting later?

F: No, I can't. I've got my … um … my, um, knitting group tonight.

E: You've got what?

F: My knitting group.

E: Since when?

F: I've been doing it for about six months now. I took it up because I was going through a very stressful period at work and a friend suggested doing it. She said it'd help to calm me down, so I joined this group and it's been really good. I feel much less stressed now and I actually really like the knitting. I just find it very, very relaxing.

E: OK, but isn't it all just women in this group?

F: Well, I guess I am the only man, but given that I work in such a male-dominated area, it's actually nice to just mix more and meet new people … you should try it yourself! Get out and meet some different kinds of people!

E: Hmm. Yeah. Maybe.

Lesson 5C, Listening, Exercises 2 & 3

C = Chloe, P = Paola, K = Kyle

P: I must go and send my cousin an email in a minute.

C: Oh, OK.

P: I've been meaning to go round and see him, because he's not been well, but Kyle's a bit reluctant to drive me round there because it'd mean spending time with my uncle.

C: Really? What's wrong with him?

K: He's just a bit odd, that's all.

P: He's not, he's just …

K: Annoying?

P: No!

K: Eccentric in the extreme? Exhausting?

P: Chloe – just ignore him. Kyle – you can be so horrible sometimes.

K: Listen, Chloe, the last time we went to see him he had a thing about handstands. We were sitting outside a café, just having a coffee and chatting, and he suddenly just got up and did a handstand – right next to all the tables! He kept it up for about half an hour!

C: That does sound a bit unusual. How old is he?

P: About fifty.

C: Fifty!

K: I told you! He's not normal.

P: Oh come on! He's just one of these people who can't sit still. I mean, he's always loved sport and when he does something new, he really gets into it. Like he took us ice-skating once. Do you remember?

K: How could I forget?

P: I mean, we were exhausted after about an hour, but he just kept on skating – and we watched him going round and round for another hour.

K: It was like he'd just completely forgotten we were there! And what about the hang-gliding?

C: Hang-gliding?

P: Yeah, he used to go hang-gliding. Obsessed with it, he was. He went practically every weekend for about three years.

K: Until he had an accident. He fell something like a thousand metres without a parachute.

C: You're joking!

P: No, it's true.

C: So what happened?

P: Well, he'd borrowed someone else's glider for some reason, and they didn't have a parachute, but he went up anyway.

And he was caught in really bad weather and the hang-glider broke and he fell.

C: And he wasn't badly injured?

P: Well, he went through some trees, which broke his fall. He had hairline fractures in his shoulder and his neck and some minor cuts and bruises, but basically he was OK. He was incredibly lucky he didn't die.

C: Absolutely!

K: Anyway, then we saw him about three weeks later roller-skating in the park, even though he still had his neck in a brace!

C: But he did give up the hang-gliding after that?

P: Not exactly, no. He tried it once more – to overcome any fear. I mean, he just wanted to prove to himself he could do it, but since then … no. The last few years he's been really into windsurfing. He's actually always liked it – he did it when he was younger – but the last few years, that's been his main obsession. He lives on the coast, so he goes nearly every day.

C: Right. I'm starting to think Kyle might be right!

K: And you haven't heard all of it. For the last few months he's been rubbing lemon juice into his skin and his hair every day! He says it gets rid of dandruff and he was going on and on about how amazingly healthy it is.

P: OK, OK! It's true. He is a little bit odd but he's a nice guy and he's fun to be with.

K: In small doses!

UNIT 6

Lesson 6A, Listening, Exercises 4 & 6

1

A: Have you ever been to Hungary?

B: Yeah, I went to the Sziget Festival a couple of years ago.

A: You went where?

B: The Sziget. I don't know if I'm pronouncing it right, but it's an enormous music festival in Budapest. It's held on this island in the middle of the Danube.

A: Oh right. So where did you stay?

B: We camped on the festival site. It was a bit of a nightmare, actually, because it absolutely poured down while we were there. The whole place was flooded and we got absolutely soaked – tent, sleeping bags, everything. And it was so muddy, everything got filthy. It was crazy.

A: Couldn't you stay somewhere else?

B: Well, we actually did in the end. We met these really nice Hungarians who lived in the city and they put us up for a couple of nights.

A: Wow, that was generous! So would you go again?

B: Absolutely. We had a great time, in spite of the weather. I hardly slept the whole time we were there. There was so much going on.

2

C: Did you go away in the holiday at all?

D: Yeah, I went to Turkey.

C: In August? Wasn't it a bit hot?

D: It was absolutely boiling, but then I love the heat – and you get quite dry heat there.

C: I guess. So did you enjoy it?

D: Yeah, it was brilliant. We stayed in this absolutely amazing place on the south coast – right on top of the cliffs, overlooking the sea.

C: Sounds nice.

D: It was. Wait, I've got a picture of it somewhere on my mobile.

C: Let's have a look. Wow! Look at that sunset. That's stunning!

D: I know. It was like that nearly every night.

C: That's great. Were there any other places nearby? It looks as if it's in the middle of nowhere.

D: It was a bit isolated, yeah. It was a few kilometres along this narrow track to the nearest village – well, town – but they had a minibus to take people there in the morning and to bring them back in the evening.

C: Wasn't that a pain, having to rely on the bus? Didn't they run more often than that?

D: No. It was a bit annoying, but considering how cheap the place was, you couldn't complain. And there was a little beach near the hotel. There was a path down between the cliffs – and the beach was almost deserted, which was lovely.

C: I'm not surprised. Sounds like hard work.

D: It was a bit of a struggle climbing back up, but it was worth doing once.

C: I guess. It doesn't sound like my kind of thing though.

Lesson 6B, Listening, Exercises 2 & 3

One often hears that something was a culture shock – most often when people arrive in a new country, but also when they enter other kinds of new environments. However, it is usually described as being similar to jet lag – something that you experience for a couple of days and then get over – with the suggestion being that all you need is a good night's sleep and then you'll be fine!

The reality is, however, that undergoing any big change – whether it's moving house, changing jobs or going to university – will bring about a 'culture shock'. Far from being a single event which is quickly forgotten, it is rather a process which may take several months – even years – to fully recover from.

The psychologist Dr Cathy Tsang-Feign calls this process 'acculturation' and highlights four distinct phases that nearly everyone goes through. These are: elation – the joy and wonder you first have, where everything is so new and different; resistance – when things settle into a routine and you start to see everything which is bad in your new situation. You start looking back through rose-tinted glasses on your life before the change. This resistance is then followed by the transformation phase, where you swing more to the other extreme and start looking down on your previous existence and its culture. You may refuse to mix with people you used to know or who speak the same language. You might start to see them in a more negative light when you do. Finally, people reach a state of integration, where cultural differences are acknowledged and accepted and people appreciate both their own heritage and their new life.

In an ideal situation, everyone goes through these four stages, but not everyone finishes the complete cycle. This can cause problems because they often don't recognize the phases of acculturation. For example, some people drop out of university in their first year, saying they don't relate to the middle-class values or that it has nothing to do with reality and so on. In reality, these opinions are actually a symptom of the resistance stage. In other cases, people get stuck in a transformation phase, which may stop them moving on to new experiences or lead to them cutting themselves off from their roots, from people they've known for years and years. That can lead to a deep sense of unhappiness and to feelings of frustration.

Lesson 6C, Listening, Exercises 2 & 3

1

A: I have a booking under the name of Bergen.

B: Hmm. I'm sorry, sir. We have no record of any reservation.

A: That can't be right. I spoke to someone just over a week ago.

B: Well, did you receive a confirmation by email or text?

A: Should I have?

B: That's our normal procedure, yes.

A: No. I haven't had anything.

B: Well, I'm afraid there's nothing I can do.

A: Haven't you got any rooms available?

B: I'm afraid not.

A: Oh, that's great, that is.

2

C: Hello. I was wondering if you could help. My room's not very warm. Is there any way I can turn down the aircon?

D: I'm afraid it's all controlled centrally.

C: Can you seriously not do anything about it? I mean, you seem to have it on full blast. It's absolutely freezing!

D: I'm sorry, but we haven't had any other complaints about it.

3

E: What do you mean you're not going to give us our deposit back?

F: Well, as I'm sure you'll appreciate, the damage is going to have to be paid for somehow.

E: Damage? What damage? The place is in the same state it was in when we moved here.

F: Ah well, you see … I can see you've used Blu Tack® on the wall – I'm guessing you had posters up in here probably.

E: Yes, but …

F: Well, look at all the marks. That'll all need cleaning and repainting.

E: Well, I hardly think that's worth a whole month's rent.

F: It's not just that, though, it it? It's a combination of things. There have been knocks to the paintwork, there's general wear and tear … when you take everything into account, it soon adds up.

E: What? To over a thousand pounds? You're taking the mickey! I can't believe you think we're going to pay that! It's ridiculous!

4

G: I told the landlord the roof was leaking time and time again.

H: I know. I remember you telling me about it ages ago.

G: And he promised it'd get fixed, but they just kept putting it off. Look, this wall is dripping wet! Honestly, I'm furious about it!

H: I'm not surprised. Still, I think you were right to have it looked at and get it repaired. I mean, it's not good to live in such a cold, damp place.

G: No. I know. And the damp's not good for the property either, is it?

H: You'd think they'd understand that, really, eh.

G: The thing is, though, it's left me completely out of pocket now.

Review 3, Grammar, Exercise 3

1 I've been meaning to go there for a while.

2 She's had her hair done.

3 I shouldn't have put it off for so long.

4 It was a bit of a nightmare to be honest.

5 You should've told me. I could've dealt with it.

6 I've been struggling to keep up.

UNIT 7

Lesson 7A, Listening, Exercise 4

A: We got caught in this incredible storm on our way to visit friends in Rome.

B: Yeah?

A: Yeah, it was amazing! One moment we were in sunshine, the next we saw like a line on the road ahead and we drove through it and it was hail! Incredible – these enormous hailstones just started bouncing off the car! They were as big as golf balls. Honestly, they were hitting the car so hard, they nearly broke the windscreen.

B: Really?

A: Well, maybe I'm exaggerating a bit, but they were pretty big and it was pretty scary.

B: I bet.

A: And then the lightning started. It was lighting up the whole sky. In the end, we pulled over to the side of the road till it all blew over.

B: Right.

A: And then it cleared up again – almost as quickly as it'd started.

B: It's amazing, isn't it? It actually reminds me of a time I was in Sardinia. We were visiting this little village somewhere, the name of which escapes me. Actually, I guess we should've realized because it'd been boiling all day – very humid and sticky – and then in the evening we were just taking a walk along the beach – you get this great view across the bay to Alghero.

A: Uh huh.

B: And anyway, suddenly we saw this incredible forked lightning across the bay followed by a faint rumble of thunder, and it just continued. It was so spectacular, we were just, like, transfixed watching it because, you know, it was still dry where we were. It was amazing – I could've watched it for hours, but then suddenly it started spitting and then just two seconds later the heavens opened and it started pouring down.

A: Oh no.

B: And of course we hadn't brought an umbrella or anything, so we just ran to the nearest café we could find, and honestly, it can't have been more than a minute but we got absolutely soaked. I must've poured something like a litre of water out of my shoes.

A: Incredible.

B: I swear – sitting there in the café I think it was the wettest I've ever been!

Lesson 7C, Listening, Exercises 4 & 6

1

A: Oh dear! Those don't look very healthy.

B: I know. I bought them to cheer up the flat a bit. You know, a bit of colour and greenery, but they just look depressing now! It's strange. I've been watering them every day.

A: Maybe that's it. The soil's probably too wet. I think it rots the roots.

B: You're joking! You mean I'm drowning them?

A: I guess so!

2

C: What are these flowers? They're lovely.

D: They're terrible!

C: Why? What do you mean?

D: They're just so invasive! They take over the whole place. None of the other plants can survive – and they're really difficult to get rid of as well.

C: But they look so nice.

D: Yeah, but they're not native to this country and they're destroying the local varieties.

C: That's too bad. I still like them, though.

3

E: I wanted to take my hosts something to say thank you for having me to stay and so I bought some flowers.

F: Fair enough.

E: Anyway, I handed them over – and you know that feeling when you suddenly realize you've accidentally upset someone, yeah? The woman kind of gave me this tight smile and nodded, but, you know, they were quite a big bouquet.

F: You kind of expect something different, yeah?

E: Exactly. Anyway, she said something to her husband and he took them away and there was a bit of an awkward silence and then we just carried on with the evening.

F: How weird!

E: Yeah. I thought so, but then I was telling someone about it and they told me people there only give those flowers when someone's died!

F: Oh no!

E: It was like I was cursing her or something – hoping she'd have a funeral!

4

G: You're going to do what?

H: Gather mushrooms. Isn't 'gather' right?

G: Yeah, yeah – gather, pick, whatever. It's just, I don't know, I've never met anyone who does it.

H: No? Everyone does it here in Poland. Why don't people do it in Britain?

G: Well, it's dangerous, isn't it? Don't you worry about picking the wrong one and poisoning yourself? Some of them are lethal, aren't they?

H: We're brought up doing this. We know from when we're children what's OK and what's not. And it's good – you feel more connected with nature. Last time we went we saw a deer – really close.

G: Yeah? Wow! It sounds great.

5

I: Here, take this. It should help.

J: What's in it?

I: It's just a herbal tea my gran makes. It's basically fennel seeds and leaves with a touch of lemon and honey. She swears by it.

J: I've never had fennel.

I: It's nice. It's got an aniseedy kind of taste. It's great. It'll really settle your stomach.

Lesson 7C, Vocabulary, Exercise 9

1 a There's an insect that attacks the roots of the tree, causing it to die.

　b There are many problems affecting the country, but the root cause is the poor education system.

2 a I have several tomato plants on my balcony, but they're not doing very well.

　b The film is basically about the police trying to find out where the bad guy has planted a bomb.

3 a She worked as an actress for years without much success, but since winning the Oscar her career is blossoming.

　b The best time to go is in spring because of all the blossom on the trees.

4 a Most people agree that the economic crisis stemmed from mistakes made by the banks and the high level of private debt.

　b If you cut the stems of the flowers under water, apparently the flowers last a lot longer.

5 a You need to take a leaf out of your sister's book and do a bit more to help people.

　b I love this time of year, when the leaves have turned red and yellow, but haven't fallen yet.

6 a We don't think there is much room for growth in this market so we're thinking about areas we might branch out into.

　b A big branch was blown off in the storm and landed on our car.

7 a I bought some seeds to grow some herbs in my kitchen, but I haven't planted them yet.

　b It's just the seed of an idea at the moment. I haven't really got very far developing it.

UNIT 8

Lesson 8A, Listening, Exercises 4 & 5

1

A: How was your holiday?

B: Fine – apart from getting robbed.

A: Oh, you're joking! What happened?

B: Well, it was stupid, really. I should've been more careful. I was sitting in a café and these lads came up to me with a map asking for directions. I said I didn't understand and they walked off. Then I suddenly realized my bag was gone.

A: Oh no!

B: I'd left it under my chair and one of them must've grabbed it while they were talking to me.

A: That's terrible! Did it have much in it?

B: Fortunately not. My purse was in my pocket.

A: Still, it can't have been very nice.

B: Yeah, it was a bit upsetting, but I didn't let it spoil the holiday.

A: Well, that's good.

2

C: Who was that on the phone?

D: It was the bank. They wanted to know if I'd spent $800 in Manila.

C: Manila? That's like 5,000 kilometres away!

D: I know. I guess someone must've got hold of my card details somehow.

C: Sure, but how did they manage to get it halfway round the world?

D: Apparently, they have machines which can swipe the card and grab all your details, then they just sell the details to whoever over the web.

C: Right. So have you got any idea when it happened?

D: No. I mean, it could've have been when I bought those new trainers on the internet, but then again it might equally have been in the local supermarket.

C: You reckon? Maybe you should just pay for everything in cash.

D: Yeah, right! That's not very practical!

C: I'm just saying. Anyway, what about the money? Will you get it back?

D: Yeah, they said it's fine.

C: That must be a relief.

D: It is.

3

E: Er, what are you reading?

F: Oh, it's just about all these animals and stuff they've seized this year.

E: Oh right.

F: No it's incredible. Look at this picture.

E: Oh my word – that's awful. There's a whole elephant! Why would you want a whole stuffed elephant?

F: I don't know, but it says it's worth two hundred thousand, so someone with more money than sense.

E: ... and a large living room.

F: Exactly. Get this, though. Apparently, they raided a motel room and they found this guy with two live crocodiles in the bathroom and a lion in the back of a van outside.

E: No!

F: Yeah!

E: Imagine if someone had gone in to clean the room.

F: It'd be a bit of a shock. Do you think he was transporting them together?

E: It sounds like it. I suppose he must've drugged them. They'd fight otherwise.

F: I guess. Who do you think would win?

E: I'd say the crocodile. Didn't you say there were two of them?

Lesson 8A, Developing conversations, Exercise 7

1 That's dreadful! Was anyone killed?

2 That must've been awful! Were you OK?

3 Oh no! Did they take anything very valuable?

4 That's dreadful! What were the parents thinking?

5 What a shame! Were you insured?

6 That's terrible! Did you report it to the police?

7 You're joking! Do they know who did it?

Lesson 8C, Listening, Exercises 5 & 7

There's nothing unusual in a film actor first learning their trade in the theatre. What is remarkable, though, is when that theatre is based in a jail – and the film star is still a prisoner serving a life sentence for murder.

Aniello Arena first hit the big screen when he starred in *Reality*, an award-winning film in which he played a simple man whose life is destroyed when he becomes obsessed with achieving fame in a reality TV show. Since then, Arena's had numerous roles in film and theatre – all done on day release from Volterra prison, where he's jailed.

Arena grew up in a poor area of Naples, where he became involved with criminal gangs. He committed his first offence at a very young age and then, at 23, he was convicted of killing three members of a rival gang – though he insists he was innocent of the murders.

In Volterra prison, he was introduced to drama through the Fortezza theatre company, which provides acting lessons to prisoners. The company performs classic and contemporary plays within the prison, but also outside, taking them on tour round Italy. The company's founder, Armando Punzo, believes drama allows prisoners to look inside themselves and deal with difficult personal issues, which means they can achieve potential they didn't know they had. That was certainly the case for Aniello Arena, and the Fortezza theatre company may well point a way forward to reduce crime in the long term.

In many countries, public opinion and political pressure often demand harsher punishment for criminals. But evidence suggests this tough approach doesn't do much to reduce reoffending. For example, in the UK, where prisoners get long sentences and are often locked in small cells most of the day, almost 40% will commit a repeat offence within a year of release and over 70% reoffend within nine years. Norway used to have a similar rate, but it's now down to just 20% after a year and 25% after five years.

The Norwegian prison system has some similarities with what the Fortezza theatre company does. Rather than placing an emphasis on punishing inmates, both give more attention to rehabilitation. Norway has no death penalty and a maximum sentence of just 21 years, so prisons are more about preparing prisoners for their eventual release than simple punishment.

Bastøy, the nation's only island jail, is a good example of this approach. Prisoners are provided with meaningful work and the resources and responsibility to develop themselves. For example, literacy classes are a priority, as a lack of reading skills is seen as a prime reason why young people drop out of education and fall into crime. In Bastøy, prisoners also have access to classes on everything from IT skills to trades such as carpentry or plumbing. All this helps ensure prisoners are employable on their release and therefore less likely to reoffend. On top of this, Bastøy prisoners are encouraged to meet and interact with people from outside prison, which is believed to also aid rehabilitation.

The Fortezza theatre company is also providing prisoners like Aniello Arena with new skills and interaction with the outside world.

Review 4, Grammar, Exercise 4

1 Someone might have got hold of your details.
2 They must've broken in through the back door.
3 There's no point in trying to look for them.
4 It was pouring down and then it turned to hail.
5 I got soaked because I'd forgotten to bring a coat.
6 I was standing there and this guy came up to me and grabbed my bag.

UNIT 9

Lesson 9A, Listening, Exercise 4

M = Melissa, R = Richard

M: So how're you finding your job? Is it going OK?

R: Oh, it's all right, I suppose. It's not what I want to do long term, though.

M: No? How come?

R: Oh, it's just so menial! I'm not using any of the skills I learned at university – and my boss is just dreadful! He never delegates any real responsibility. Instead, I just seem to spend most of my time running round making him cups of tea and photocopying things and if I ask about doing other stuff, he just tells me to be patient and then starts going on about how he did the same when he started at the company.

M: Well, maybe it's true.

R: Oh, I don't know. I was talking to this woman who joined at the same time as me and she said she was learning loads in her department – being really stretched, apparently. It makes me think it's maybe more about me!

M: Oh, I am sorry! If it's that bad, maybe you should think about handing in your notice?

R: I don't know. I guess it might get better if I just give it a bit more time.

M: Well, you'd think so. I mean, it is a big company, isn't it?

R: Mmm, but maybe that's it, you see. Maybe it's a bit too big. Anyway, I can't see myself staying there long term.

M: No? Well, if you decide to make a move, I'm sure you'll be fine. You're bound to get lots of offers.

R: I don't know about that, but it's nice of you to say so!

M: It's true!

Lesson 9A, Listening, Exercise 5

M = Melissa, R = Richard

R: Well, anyway. What about you? How's your job going?

M: Oh, you probably won't want to hear this, but it's great, yeah. It's going really well.

R: Well, I'm glad at least one of us is happy, anyway!

M: Yeah, it's actually been pretty amazing. I've been getting loads of on-the-job training – and they've been letting me go into college one day a week as well, to improve my skills. It's been really stimulating. I've also been meeting clients quite a bit. Oh, and I gave my first big presentation last week.

R: Wow! Sounds great. Did it go OK?

M: Yeah, it went really well. I've got my first business trip coming up next month – to New York. And I'm applying for promotion at the moment too.

R: Really? Already? Do you think you'll get it?

M: Hopefully, yeah, but you never know, do you?

R: Oh, you're bound to. You'll probably get a pay rise too. From the sound of it, you're their star employee. I can just see you in five years' time, running the entire firm.

M: Ha!

R: And if the worst comes to the worst, I'll end up knocking on the door of your office, begging you for a job!

Lesson 9B, Listening, Exercise 2

The charity Education and Employers recently carried out some research into the jobs young people aged between eight and eighteen wanted to do when they were older. They then compared their findings with projected labour market demands – and what they found shocked them!

The top choices for young people of all ages involved occupations in the fields of culture, media and sport. The problem is, such career aspirations have little in common with the kinds of jobs in hospitality, finance, healthcare and education that we will need people to fill in the years to come.

One of the reasons why young people may not have mentioned jobs in these fields is that they simply aren't aware of their existence. Many children's ambitions are limited by what they're exposed to and it's much harder to be something if you can't see that something in your everyday life. Young people clearly need to learn about a wider range of possible professions . . . and it might also help to realize that the successful people they see on TV often started out in far more menial jobs.

For example, using the hashtag firstsevenjobs, astronaut Buzz Aldrin revealed that he started out washing dishes. From there, it took him just three moves to become one of the first people to walk on the moon. Not bad, eh?

Similarly, before he became famous for creating the hit musical *Hamilton*, Lin-Manuel Miranda could be found asking, 'Would you like fries with that?' And the playwright didn't only work at McDonald's – he also operated a drinks machine at his aunt's store.

While more traditional first jobs such as delivering newspapers have largely been replaced by roles in the retail and hospitality sectors, the basic principle of dreaming big but sometimes having to start small still applies – and rather than measuring ourselves against the successes of others, we might all benefit from seeing the many small steps and side tracks that led to them.

Lesson 9C, Listening, Exercise 4

Hello. Welcome, everyone. For those of you that don't know me already, I'm Pihla from Finland, and I'm here studying Economics as part of the student exchange programme. Today I'm going to talk about PISA. So, hands up everyone who has heard of PISA. OK. Quite a lot of you. Now, hands up everyone who thought I was talking about the Italian city with a leaning tower? OK – well, I'm afraid you're wrong. No – this PISA is the Programme for International Student Assessment, which is used to compare education systems round the world.

So, what I'm going to do today is take a closer look at this project. I'll begin by explaining how PISA works, before moving on to look at and comment on some of the results. Then I'll go on to conclude that, from a Finnish perspective, the results from PISA are not necessarily the most helpful way of measuring success.

Lesson 9C, Listening, Exercises 6 & 7

OK. Well, basically PISA consists of three tests in Maths, Science and Reading, organized by the Organisation of Economic Cooperation and Development – OECD for short. The tests were first run in 2000 and are usually set every three years. Currently, around 600,000 fifteen- and sixteen-year-olds from 79 different countries take part. The average marks for each country's students give the country's rank. The idea is that to compete economically, you need to improve education.

So, moving on to the results, the table here shows the average scores from the last set of PISA tests for maths, science and reading for a selection of countries. As you can see, China

is over 60 points ahead of my country, Finland. Such a big difference may be down to better education, but it may also be because of the kinds of kids who were tested. Unlike in all the other countries, students tested in China came from just four out of the country's 32 administrative districts.

More importantly, focusing on rank is a problem. Finland, for example, has fallen from being best in 2000. I have seen some headlines here saying 'the miracle is over' and 'plunging' standards. But there were only 40 countries taking part in 2000, whereas now it's nearly double that, and our score has actually dropped by just over four per cent – not exactly 'plunging'. When you look at percentages instead of points, you may also note that although we are 21 places and 35 points ahead of Iceland, that's actually only just over seven per cent.

So should we care about PISA? Well, I guess it's good to have an independent test, but I don't think we should change our education system to get better marks in it. These marks don't really tell you what education is like. In South Korea, kids typically study twelve or more hours a day, and we sometimes do half that! We believe in giving kids time to develop social skills and to exercise. And does it really matter in terms of the economy? Qatar is one of the richest countries in the world, and yet it doesn't even make the top fifty. In short, I think each country should decide what it wants from its education system – and avoid comparisons.

UNIT 10

Lesson 10A, Listening, Exercises 3 & 4

N = Nina, L = Linda, V = Viti

N: So how much longer have you got?

L: Three more days. By four o'clock on Friday, we'll have finished every single one. I can't wait!

V: Me neither. The Physics one yesterday was a nightmare.

L: I know! I'm sure I failed it.

N: You must be sick of it all.

V: I am. If I revise much more my head's going to explode!

L: Just keep telling yourself: three more days, three more days.

N: So shall we go out and celebrate on Friday, then?

V: That sounds like an excellent idea.

L: Yeah, I'd be up for that as well. Do you have anywhere in mind?

N: I thought that Equinox might be fun.

L: Where's that?

N: Oh, don't you know it? It's the big club on the main square in town. It's great.

V: If you like that kind of place! I have to say, it's not my kind of thing. I can't stand the music they play and besides, it's really not my kind of crowd there.

N: Oh! I thought it was OK when I went there, but if you'd rather go somewhere else, that's fine by me.

L: Well, personally, I'd quite like to get something to eat at some point, if that's all right with you.

V: Yeah, that sounds good. Any thoughts on where?

L: Well, Rico's is always a good bet.

V: Oh, it's such a rip-off, that place. Last time I went there, I spent something like €60. Can't we go somewhere cheaper?

N: How about that Brazilian place near the station?

V: Guanabara? Yeah, that'd be fine with me. Linda?

L: Yeah, whatever. I'm easy. They have music down there later on, don't they?

N: Yeah, they do samba after ten.

V: It sounds ideal. So what time do you want to meet? Seven? Seven thirty?

N: I'm working till six and it'd be nice if I could go home first, so could we make it eight? I'll have had time to get changed and freshen up a bit by then.

V: Yeah, fine.

N: And I'll phone and book a table – just to be on the safe side.

L: OK. I'll ring a few other people and see if anyone else is up for it – and see you down there.

N: OK. Brilliant. Bye.

V: Bye.

Lesson 10C, Listening, Exercises 5 & 7

1

A: Sorry, but you couldn't pass me the salt, could you? Thank you. They look nice.

B: They are. They're lovely. Have you tried that aubergine dip? It's delicious.

A: Hmm. I have to say, I'm not that keen on aubergines. There's something wrong with them as a vegetable.

B: You're joking! Aubergines – they're the king of vegetables! Although strictly speaking, of course, they're technically a fruit.

A: OK.

B: They're so versatile. You can fry them, grill them, have them mashed, stuffed, barbecued …

A: Right.

B: Did you know that they used to use the skin as a dye? The Chinese apparently used to polish their teeth with it!

A: Who knew? I've clearly not given aubergines a proper chance. Anyway, listen. Sorry, but I've just seen my friend Mercedes. I must just go and grab her. I've been meaning to talk to her all evening. Bye!

2

C: So how do you know Niall?

D: Who?

C: Er … the person whose party this is.

D: Oh right. Well, he's like the friend of a friend of my flatmate. I don't know why I'm here, really. I feel a bit left out. My flatmate dragged me here because she thought she wouldn't know anyone – and now she's met someone. Oh – that's her over there, with that blond guy. I think I might just go. How do you know Niall anyway?

C: I'm his fiancée! You did know this is a party to celebrate our engagement, didn't you?

D: No, actually. I didn't. Congratulations, though! It's a great party.

3

E: I'm glad I'm not the only one who couldn't stand it in there any more.

F: Tell me about it! It was so stuffy in there, wasn't it? You could hardly breathe.

E: I know. They need some air conditioning or something, that's for sure.

F: I thought I was going to fall asleep at one point there it was so hot.

E: The speaker wasn't exactly helping either, though, was he?

F: He didn't really grab my attention much, no. Hey, um … look, I think I might just go and grab a coffee instead of going back in, so …

E: Oh, sounds like a good idea. Do you mind if I join you?

4

G: Is this the queue for the toilet?

H: I'm afraid so.

G: I love your top.

H: Oh, thanks.

G: It's quite unusual. Where did you get it?

H: I actually picked it up in a second-hand clothes stall. It was only five pounds.

G: Really? That's fantastic! I never bother looking in places like that. I mean, there's a second-hand place near me, but the stuff in there always looks in pretty poor condition. That looks brand new, though.

H: I think it's quite old actually, but the stall I got it from is just fantastic – just really nice stuff.

G: Mind you, it's so difficult getting stuff in my size.

H: I can imagine. It must be hard. I've got a friend who's maybe your height and she's always moaning about it as well. That dress is lovely, though.

G: It's great, isn't it? I actually just found this place online. Oh look – it's your turn.

5

I: Sorry, but I couldn't help overhearing. Did you say you've just come back from Accra?

J: Yeah. Why? Do you know it?

I: Yes, quite well, actually. I spent two years there back in the 90s.

J: Wow! What were you doing there?

I: My husband was based at the embassy there, so …

J: Really? It must've been quite different back then. It's a real boom town at the moment.

I: So I've read, yes. It was relatively quiet when we were there and the infrastructure was still very much a work in progress, but we loved it. We met some wonderful people there and were able to see a bit of the countryside as well. I'm sure it's changed a lot, though.

J: For sure. It's attracting a huge amount of inward investment. In fact, my firm is planning to open an office there, so I was over there sorting that out.

I: Oh, that's great. I'm really pleased to hear it. Anyway, sorry. I didn't want to stop you chatting.

Lesson 10C, Grammar, Exercise 10

1 A: Miserable weather, isn't it?
  B: Yeah, awful. It's been like this for weeks now, hasn't it?
  A: I know. I can't remember when I last saw the sun.
2 A: You don't remember me, do you?
  B: It's Li, isn't it?
  A: No. It's Lian.
3 A: Excuse me. You haven't got a light, have you?
  B: Yeah. Here you go.
  A: Thanks.
  B: You couldn't lend me a pound, could you?
  A: No, sorry.
4 A: You missed the class on Monday, didn't you?
  B: There wasn't one, was there? The school was closed for the holiday, wasn't it?
  A: No. Mind you, you didn't miss much. It wasn't very interesting.
  B: Well, to be honest the whole course is a bit disappointing, isn't it?
5 A: I love that jacket. It's from Zara, isn't it?
  B: No, I got it from a vintage shop in town.
  A: Really? You wouldn't happen to have the address, would you?
  B: No. Sorry. I honestly can't remember.

REVIEW 5, Exercise 4

1 If you're struggling to cope, maybe you should delegate more.
2 I guess things will improve once I get the hang of the new system.
3 If the worst comes to the worst, you'll just have to hand in your notice.
4 It was a shame all that food went to waste, wasn't it?
5 If it hadn't been for her, I wouldn't be where I am today.
6 With anyone else, I would've felt awkward if they'd said that.

UNIT 11

Lesson 11A, Listening, Exercises 6 & 7

A = Assistant, C = Customer

A: Hi. How can I help you today?

C: Hi. I reserved a car online. Here's my booking confirmation and driving licence.

A: Yep. OK. Let's have a look. Right. We have your car ready, but we're running a special offer this week. You can upgrade to the next range for just two euros a day, so you could have an estate car if you like.

C: It's OK. We don't have much luggage.

A: Are you sure? It's a bit more powerful as well.

C: No, I actually prefer something smaller – it's more environmentally friendly.

A: Fine. You requested an automatic, yes?

C: That's right.

A: OK. Would you like our additional insurance cover for all damage, including tyres and windscreen?

C: Isn't that already included in what I paid online?

A: No. I think it's in the small print – and this is only three euros extra a day.

C: How often does that happen?

A: Well, it's up to you, but better safe than sorry, isn't it?

C: I suppose so. OK, then. It is quite cheap.

A: Fine. Can I just have your credit card? That's for the full cover, the cost of the fuel and also your deposit on the car – which you'll get back on return.

C: Sure, so should I return it with the tank full?

A: No, just return it empty. It's diesel, by the way.

C: OK.

A: And just to remind you there is a mileage limit of 150 per day. Unless you want to pay for unlimited …

C: No that's OK.

A: OK. So could you just sign where I've marked with a cross? You may want to check the car as well before you leave. There are some scratches here and here, and a small dent in the rear door. But as you're covered there's no real need to worry.

C: OK. I'll look.

A: Have a good trip.

Lesson 11A, Listening, Exercise 8

A = Assistant, C = Customer

A: Hello. Right Car Rentals.

C: Oh, hello. Could you help. My name's Diego Sanchez. I was in this morning and picked up a car from you.

A: Oh, hello, Mr Sanchez. How's it going?

C: Not that well, to be honest. I'm actually calling because we have a problem with the car. I was driving along the motorway and something flew up at the windscreen and cracked it.

A: Oh, I am sorry to hear that. How bad is it?

C: Quite bad. It's a very big crack. I'm uncomfortable driving with it like this.

A: OK. I totally understand. You'll need to ring our breakdown service. The number's written in the book that came with the car.

C: Oh, OK. I'll do that now. How long do you think they will be?

A: We guarantee they'll be with you within four hours.

C: Four hours? Is that really the quickest someone can get here?

A: I mean that's the guarantee, but it's usually less, so fingers crossed. At least you got insurance!

Lesson 11A, Developing conversations, Exercise 10

1 A: The taxi fare to your hotel will be €100.

  B: €100? That's expensive!

2 A: The cheapest ticket we have left is $875.

  B: $875? If that's the cheapest, I dread to think how much the most expensive is!

3 A: Our flight leaves at five in the morning.

  B: Five in the morning! That's going to be a killer!

4 A: It's a bit old, but it's a nice car! I could let you have it for £3,500.

  B: £3,500? I was thinking more like £150, personally!

5 A: If you just wait at the station, I should be able to get there within an hour or two.

  B: An hour or two? It'd be quicker for me to walk!

6 A: I'm afraid the contract does state that there's a €50 penalty if you return the car more than an hour late.

  B: €50? Where on earth does it say that?

Lesson 11C, Listening, Exercises 4 and 5

1

We left the car outside the flat we were staying in, but when we came out in the morning, we found a market stall where our car had been! It had been towed away. What annoyed me was that the only sign warning that there was a market was 60 metres away at the end of the street. It cost us 150 euros to get the car released and there was an 80 euro fine on top of that. They said I could appeal against the fine, but as I don't live there, I thought it'd be too difficult.

2

I've failed six times now. The thing that I find most difficult is parking. I can do it OK when I'm with my instructor, but during the test my nerves get the better of me and I always mess it up. Actually, last time I failed for going through a red light, but to be fair I think that even that was down to the parking. I was getting so worked up in anticipation about doing it, I got distracted and missed the lights changing.

3

My first big trip on my own after getting my licence was to see a friend in another city. On the motorway I stuck to the inside lane and didn't overtake anyone, but then entering the city was a nightmare. I was already struggling to follow my sat nav in a new place, but then people were driving right up close behind me, flashing their lights and swearing at me. What annoys me is the fact that I have a sign on my car boot saying I'm newly qualified, but they didn't make any allowances. It's like they'd never been in my shoes.

4

If you ask me, you should have to pass a test to ride those electric scooters. They may be environmentally friendly and all that, but they're lethal. Riders seem to think that rules don't apply to them. They swerve in and out of the traffic and make you brake suddenly. Then at other times they race along the pavement as if it's a road. The other day I almost got run over myself when I stepped out of a shop and one suddenly shot past.

5

The other day I was driving along and I suddenly came across a huge hole in the road. I couldn't swerve to avoid it because of traffic coming in the opposite direction so I just went through it and the tyre burst. I managed to brake and control the car a bit, but I still ended up going into a barrier at the side of the road. It could've been worse. I was shaken, but otherwise uninjured. What concerns me now is the failure to maintain our roads. I can't be the only one to experience something like that, but would others have been so lucky?

UNIT 12

Lesson 12A, Listening, Exercises 4 & 5

1

M = Michelle, Y = Yusuf

M: Hello.

Y: Oh, hi Michelle. It's me, Yusuf. Listen. I'm just ringing to say we're not going to make it to the restaurant later. Katie isn't feeling very well.

M: Oh dear. What's up?

Y: Well, actually, she had a bit of a panic attack earlier while we were out.

M: You're joking!

Y: No. We were in this shop and she was saying her chest felt tight and she felt a bit dizzy.

M: Oh no! Is she all right now?

Y: Yeah, she's OK. She had a little sit down and it passed, but she'd rather stay in tonight. She told me to say how sorry she is.

M: Don't be silly! Tell her there's no need to apologize and I understand.

Y: Thanks. I will.

M: What brought it on? Do you know?

Y: Well, she won't admit it, but I think she's just a bit burned out with the stress of work. She finds it difficult to switch off and I hear her tossing and turning at night …

M: That's quite worrying. Has she been to see anyone about it?

Y: No, not yet. Actually, we're meant to be going away for a few days next week, but now I don't know whether we should stay here and get an appointment or leave it till we come back.

M: Well, maybe all she needs is a break.

Y: Mmm. Maybe.

M: I know you're worried, but if it's only a few days … . Why don't you see how she is when you get back?

Y: I guess.

M: Anyway, send her my love and tell her I'm thinking of her.

2

C = Caitlin, N = Nina

C: Hello. Nina? Hi. It's me, Caitlin.

N: Hi! Where are you? I was expecting you at six.

C: Yeah, sorry, but Lachlan's had some kind of reaction to something he ate. We're in Rome hospital.

N: You're joking! Is he all right?

C: Yes, yes. He's fine now. He's with the nurse and they're running some tests to try and find out exactly what he's reacting to.

N: No! So what actually happened, then?

C: Well, we were in the middle of lunch and he suddenly said he was feeling a bit weird. And then all of a sudden his lips just started swelling up and he was really struggling to breathe.

N: That sounds terrifying. Is he all right now, though?

C: Yes, yes, honestly. We rushed him to the hospital – someone from the restaurant actually took us – and they dealt with him very quickly. He had an injection to reduce the swelling and they gave him oxygen to help him breathe.

N: Oh, Caitlin. You sound so calm. It must've been awful.

C: Well, I was panicking at the time, but everyone here has been so good to us. Anyway, listen, they're going to keep him in overnight – to be on the safe side.

N: Oh, right.

C: Sorry. I know we're supposed to be coming to the concert tonight.

N: Don't be silly! Lachlan's health is much more important than a concert. When do you think you'll get here tomorrow?

C: It shouldn't be too late. The doctor's going to come at nine, so if he says Lachlan's OK to leave, we should get to yours by lunchtime.

N: OK. Well, listen. Give him a hug from me and don't worry about rushing to get here tomorrow.

Lesson 12B, Exercise 9

A man goes to a doctor // and says, // 'Doc, // I think there's something wrong with me. // Every time I poke myself // it hurts. // Look!' // And he starts poking himself. // He pokes himself in the leg. // 'Ouch!' // He pokes himself in the ribs. // 'Aagh!' // He pokes himself in the head // and he literally screams in agony. // 'Aaaaagh! // You see what I mean, Doc? // You see how bad it is? // What's happening to me?' // And the doctor replies, // 'Yes. // You seem to have broken your finger!'

Lesson 12C, Listening, Exercise 5

Like other aspects of travel, so-called 'medical tourism' was hit badly by the pandemic in 2020–21. Since then, though, the industry has bounced back to previous levels and is set to boom over the coming years. Part of that boom is also actually down to the pandemic because hospital waiting lists, especially for non-urgent procedures, have risen significantly.

Dental work, plastic surgery or a hip replacement may not be urgent, as the underlying conditions are not likely to be life-threatening. However, waiting, possibly for years, to be treated through public health can be hugely upsetting for patients, who may be living with pain or need daily help. It's therefore unsurprising that many decide to go private – not only within their home countries but also abroad. Countries such as Spain, Turkey, India and Thailand have very high-quality hospitals offering treatment at a lower cost compared to other places. On top of that, they offer patients great tourist facilities after their treatment.

Having said that, medical tourism isn't only about minor operations, it's also about treating serious illnesses. Some clients are seeking cutting-edge cures for cancer or the best surgeons for an organ transplant.

While many countries are rightly proud of their ability to attract medical tourists, the industry is not without its critics and here to discuss some of the issues I have Karl Meyer, a medical lawyer, Ila Pandey, a manager at a leading Indian hospital promoting medical tourism, and Pepa Morales a health and patients' rights campaigner.

Lesson 12C, Listening, Exercises 7 & 8

P = Presenter, KM = Karl Meyer, IP = Ila Pandey, PM = Pepa Morales

P: So the first question might be, is it safe? Ila, I've certainly heard horror stories.

IP: Well, I'm sure there are some bad providers, but if you go somewhere reputable like our hospital, it's perfectly safe and patients often get better treatment than at home. The outcomes for heart surgery at our hospital are among the best in the world – that's why people come here.

P: Karl?

KM: I basically agree. Many hospitals are accredited by independent bodies, which ensure quality, so you're very safe with those. However, all medical procedures have risks and the recovery process can be unpredictable. People can catch secondary infections, especially when they're recovering in a very different climate. This can lead to extended stays or a return to hospital, which might not be covered by insurance.

IP: I personally think the issue of being exposed to different kinds of diseases from a new environment is exaggerated. Most clients travel from neighbouring countries or from other regions within the country – and where there is a concern, we put extra measures in place.

P: I see – but even the best hospitals make mistakes, Karl?

KM: Absolutely. And if you're not a citizen of the country, suing a hospital can be a nightmare. Apart from language barriers, unfamiliar legal systems can be incredibly difficult to negotiate.

IP: Again, I can only say our hospital has a strong complaints procedure.

P: Understood. So far, we've focused on patients' experience. What about wider implications on society though? Pepa, I think you have concerns about this.

PM: Absolutely. Basically, as I see it, when we expand medical tourism, we do it at the expense of public services.

P: You mean, if you treat patients from abroad, you don't treat as many local patients?

PM: Essentially – yeah.

P: Ila, what would you say to that?

IP: I don't agree. I'd say any investment in high-quality healthcare is good for a country. In India we've seen a brain drain over many years …

P: A brain drain?

IP: Basically, the country trains doctors and nurses to a high level, but then countries like the US and Canada attract them away with better pay and conditions. As I see it, medical tourism could help reverse that trend by allowing us to pay doctors more.

PM: I totally agree that richer places exploit developing countries by essentially buying medical staff from abroad rather than doing the training themselves. But I don't see medical tourism as the answer. Not only does it take doctors from the public sector, but it also attracts staff and patients to big cities, so local services actually get worse.

P: Ila?

IP: Obviously, I don't agree. Some of our doctors work in the public sector too and we provide some grants for those in need … but ultimately, I guess this is a political issue and I'm not a politician.

P: I think we can all sympathize with that. Let's leave it there. Thanks to all my guests.

Review 6, Exercise 3

1 We did a six-month tour of South America by public transport.

2 Not only did he lose all his money, they took his passport too.

3 What I found strange was that there were so few people there.

4 It shouldn't be that hard to find accommodation.

5 I'm supposed to be going out later, but I don't really feel like it.

6 We not only completed it, but we did it in record time.

UNIT 13

Lesson 13A, Listening, Exercises 4 & 5

1

A: Hey, did you hear about Kerry?

B: No. What's happened?

A: Well, you remember she was doing a Chemistry degree, yeah?

B: Yeah.

A: Well, apparently, she's dropped out.

B: Seriously? How come? Wasn't she in her final year?

A: Yeah. I think she only had about six more months to go.

B: Wow! What a shame. So what brought that on, then? Do you know?

A: Well, from what I've heard, it was basically stress related.

B: What? Because of the workload?

A: Partly that, I think, yeah, but as I understand it, she'd also recently split up with her partner, who she'd been with for years.

A: Oh, I had no idea. That's a lot to have to deal with, eh?

B: Yeah. I mean, it's not completely unexpected because the last time I saw her, she did tell me that things hadn't been good between them for a while, and then she found out they'd been cheating on her. Apparently with several different people. And that was the final straw.

B: Well, in that case, she's better off without them, then.

A: I guess.

B: So what's she going to do now? Any idea?

A: Not a clue. I'll try and give her a call later on.

B: Well, send her my love.

2

C: Have you seen Ollie recently?

D: No, not for ages. Have you?

C: Yeah, I saw him last week. We went for a drink.

D: Right. How is he?

C: Oh, he's good. Really good, actually. You know he left his job at Byflix?

D: No! Really? I was told he was doing well there.

C: He was, he was, but he'd actually been thinking about leaving for a while – basically ever since he started going out with Leila.

D: Who's Leila?

C: When was the last time you saw him?

D: It must've been about a year ago. As far as I know, he wasn't seeing anyone then.

C: Oh, maybe. Well, anyway, she's Finnish. They met on holiday. She lives in Helsinki. They were commuting between here and there more or less every two weeks, but in the end, he decided to quit his job and move there.

D: You're joking!

C: No. Apparently, she's got a really good job so they can afford to both live off just her salary.

D: So what's he going to be doing with his time, then?

C: Well, he said he'd sent round CVs to a couple of companies, but if that came to nothing, he was going to retrain as an English teacher.

D: Really? Well, that's a change for the better!

Lesson 13C, Listening, Exercises 3 and 5

1: I went to a wedding in Sweden last year. It wasn't so different to other weddings I've been to, but there were a few things that did really strike me: firstly, there was a lot of singing during the reception, which I joined in with – even though I'm tone deaf! Then there were lots of speeches. Anyone could make a toast and speak. And when the groom left the room for whatever reason, male guests would leap up and kiss the bride … which was a bit odd!

Another thing I discovered is that when the couple exchange vows, the person who says 'I do' loudest is supposed to be the one who'll wear the trousers in the marriage.

2: Here in Japan, the second Monday in January is called Seijin No Hi – Coming-of-Age Day. Everyone who turns twenty that year is invited to a big reception organized by the local authority to mark the fact they're now legally adults. The girls wear traditional Japanese outfits, worth thousands of pounds, which is why most girls just hire them for the day. The guys usually wear suits, but some do dress more traditionally too. At the reception there's a lengthy speech by the local mayor to congratulate them and remind them of their new responsibilities and small gifts are handed out to everyone. Family and friends usually gather outside the town hall to take photos. Then we go out and party the night away.

3: People here in the US find death an awkward subject. In Puerto Rico, I think we have a healthier, more open attitude. When someone dies, the funeral company usually preserves the body so it can be displayed in a coffin. However, recently there's been a trend to dress the bodies and place them in a themed setting, such as sitting on their motorbike. The body's on display at least two days so everybody – friends, family, neighbours, children and adults – can pay their respects and take photos with the body before it's buried. This is all part of celebrating their life and the photo is an important record of the event. It's part of a person's history and honouring the dead is very important, which is why we also visit the graves of loved ones every year.

4: I have just had my first baby, Aadit. Family is core to the Hindu faith so there are several rites connected to birth and children. Right after the birth, the baby is washed and then the father brushes a mixture of honey and butter on the baby's lips. He then whispers special holy words in the baby's right ear as a blessing for his future life. I had quite a difficult labour but seeing my husband do that was so beautiful, I immediately forgot all the pain and exhaustion. We didn't actually name the baby till ten days after the birth, because a priest consults an astrological chart to find the position of the stars and choose the initials of the name. Later in the year we'll mark other events like the baby's first trip outside and the first time he has solid food.

UNIT 14

Lesson 14A, Listening, Exercises 4 & 6

1

A: Hi. I'd like to open a bank account, please.

B: Certainly. Do you have some form of identification with you?

A: Yes, I've got my passport here. Is that OK?

B: Yes, that's fine, but we also need proof of your current address. Do you have a utility bill – a gas bill or electricity bill or anything – with you?

A: No, I don't, I'm afraid. You see, I'm not directly paying bills at the moment. I'm living in a shared house, a student house, and I just pay a fixed amount every month.

B: OK. Well, do you have any proof of income or a National Insurance number at all?

A: No. No, I don't. I told you. I'm a student. I'm not working. I have my passport, my driving licence from back home, three cheques I want to deposit and this letter from my uni.

B: Oh, can I just have a quick look at that? Ah. OK, I see. Right, well this should be fine. What kind of account were you after?

A: Just a normal current account.

B: OK. Well, what we can do is give you a three-month trial period on a current account, which will cost you £10 a month, and if you do decide to stay with us after that, the £30 will be refunded.

A: OK. Well, I guess that's fair enough.

B: Great, so if you could just fill out these forms …

2

C: Hi. I'm flying to Caracas and I need to get hold of some Venezuelan currency. I'm not sure what it's called, I'm afraid.

D: No problem. I'll just check for you. Yes, there we are. It's the bolivar. How much are you looking for?

C: I'm after about £500 worth, please.

D: I'm not sure if we actually keep that currency in stock. Let's see. I'm awfully sorry, madam, but I'm afraid you're out of luck.

C: Oh, OK, that's a bit annoying.

D: We do have reserves of the less popular currencies from time to time, but more often we tend to order them in.

C: Right – yeah, I won't have time.

D: I'm terribly sorry. Would US dollars do? As I understand it, they're often accepted instead of the local currency. Otherwise, I'm sure you can just change money once you arrive or make a withdrawal from a cashpoint there.

C: In theory, yes, but I've been caught out before thinking that. Maybe I'll get some dollars just to be on the safe side.

D: Of course. How much would you like?

C: I'll take 300, please.

D: OK. That'll be £206.75.

C: Really? What's the exchange rate?

D: We're currently selling at 1.48 to the pound and then there's 2% commission on all transactions.

C: Right. Well, that's slightly more than I was expecting, I must say. Can I pay by Visa?

D: Yeah, of course. Just pop the card in there. And just enter your PIN number. Thanks.

Lesson 14B, Reading, Exercise 5

The husband bought bricks and hired builders. Before too long, the pile of silver was almost gone, but their mansion remained unfinished. The husband decided to see if the moneybag would produce more silver, so without his wife's knowledge, he opened the bag for a second time that day. Instantly, another lump of silver rolled out. He opened it a third time and received a third lump.

He thought to himself, 'If I go on like this, I can get the house finished in no time!' He completely forgot the old man's warning. However, when he opened the bag a fourth time, it was empty. This time not one bit of silver fell out. It was just an old cloth bag. When he turned to look at his unfinished house, that was gone as well. There before him was his old hut with its leaking roof.

The poor man fell to his knees in despair, crying, 'How I wish I'd never opened that bag! Now everything is lost.' His wife came over to comfort him, saying, 'Not all is lost. We still have each other. Let's go back to the mountain and cut firewood like we did before. That's a more reliable way of earning a living.'

And from that day on, that's exactly what they did.

Lesson 14C, Listening, Exercises 5 and 7

Zak: Here's an offer. If you give me one dollar each week, I promise to give you $2.6 million at some point in the future. There's just one catch, when I say 'at some point in the future', I mean at any point within the next quarter of a million years! Tempted? I bet you aren't. So why is it that so many people gamble on lotteries when the odds are nearly one in fourteen million? Probably because the whole marketing of lotteries downplays the odds against winning and emphasizes the dream, the ease of getting money, and the 'good causes' that are funded by the profits lotteries make. But I don't see subsidizing things like opera and Olympic sportsmen as a good cause. And it's not good when profits simply go to the government or the company that runs the lottery.

Not only does the advertising of lotteries tend to obscure this tiny chance, it also sends this subtle message – people don't need to work hard or get a good education to become wealthy; all you have to do is choose six numbers and your dreams will come true. And then also consider what those dreams are. Are they for a better society and health care? Peace and understanding? No! It's a mansion and a Ferrari for me! These are values – anti-educational, money-driven and selfish – that go against society. No doubt Stacy will argue that, in fact, it's all innocent fun and that the stakes are small, but not only do lotteries damage society in this way, they also bring pain to individuals. Take these words from John, a gambling addict from Sydney, for example: 'I sometimes gambled away my whole paycheck and had nothing left with which to pay the mortgage or feed the family. In the end, I'd bet on anything – horse races, rugby, roulette, even what the weather would be like – but it all started with lottery tickets. I wish I'd never seen one.'

There's more at stake than we imagine. Gambling destroys people's lives and nine times out of ten it starts with lotteries. They're a tax on the poor and benefit the rich and they undermine social values. They really should be banned.

Lesson 14C, Listening, Exercise 8

Stacy: I'm sure I can't be the only one here who found Zak's comments about problem gambling very moving. I'm afraid, though, that I also found them rather misleading. Of course, compulsive gambling is not something that any of us would approve of, right? It not only causes pain to the gambler, but it also hurts their family and friends. However, addictive behaviour comes in many shapes and forms: for many people, if it wasn't gambling, it might well be drugs or shopping or work. Banning lotteries won't reduce addictive behaviour – even if it were true that nine out of ten gambling addictions started with the lottery. By the way, I'd be interested to hear the source of that figure as I'm not quite sure I believe it.

But just for a moment, let's say it was true, and that nine out of ten gambling addicts really do start with lotteries, should we also consider banning cigarettes on the basis that heroin addicts started by smoking? Or prohibit credit cards because some people go on to be shopaholics and run up huge debts? No.

In the end, I actually agree with Zak – we should take responsibility for our future wealth. It's just that where he suggests we do that by banning the lottery and investing in education, I believe that people should do it by learning self-control.

Which brings me to his point that the lottery somehow goes against hard work and education. With the greatest respect, I just don't buy it! People don't spend money on the lottery instead of studying and working hard – it's on top of it. Similarly, lottery dreams don't replace friendship, they add to it. The real equivalent of spending money on a lottery ticket is buying, say, an ice cream. Neither are necessary for living – they provide pleasure. Let's face it, gambling in one form or another has featured in human society since time began, because it's fun! The only difference is that, unlike ice cream, the lottery ticket, however remote the chance is, might just possibly bring you the additional benefit of riches.

From that standpoint, it's a sound investment. Now Zak may not find lotteries exciting or wish that he had a Ferrari, but I do – and I can't see that there is anything anti-social in that or anything worth banning.

Review 7, Grammar, Exercise 4

1 She found out he'd been lying to her for ages.
2 I wish he wouldn't shout at me so often.
3 It was just announced that he's been fired.
4 They said it'd already been delivered, but I haven't received it yet.
5 I wish I could've been there to see it.
6 I wish I'd never said anything about it now!

UNIT 15

Lesson 15A, Listening, Exercises 5 & 6

A: Mmmm, this is delicious!

B: Thanks.

A: What's in it? It's got a bit of a lemony taste.

B: Yeah, that's the lemongrass.

A: Lemongrass?

B: Yeah, it's this … actually I don't know what you call it – a herb or spice. It looks sort of like a spring onion, you know. It's like a greyish-white stick. Anyway, you drop it in the sauce while it's cooking and it gives it a kind of citrusy flavour.

A: You don't eat it then?

B: No. It's got kind of a woody texture – it's pretty tough – so you just pick it out at the end.

A: Right – and the orangey colour … is that from carrots?

B: No. It's pumpkin and red lentils.

A: Pumpkin?

B: You know, like a big orange squash – like a melon or something – but rounder and the flesh is harder.

A: Oh yes, of course. Pumpkin – I know this word.

B: Yeah, so you use that or sometimes I use sweet potato instead.

A: Right. So how do you make it?

B: Oh, it's dead easy. You get a large onion and a couple of cloves of garlic and ginger and you chop them all really finely. I actually sometimes use a food processor. Then you put some oil in a pan and heat it up and you just throw everything into the oil, with a couple of bits of lemongrass, and I sometimes put in a whole chilli as well – just to spice things up a bit – you know, like to flavour the oil.

A: Right.

B: And then you cook it quite quickly, but you have to keep stirring 'cos you don't want it to burn. Otherwise, it can be a bit bitter.

A: OK.

B: Then you throw in the pumpkin. Oh, I should've said you have to cut it up into cubes.

A: How big?

B: I don't know – about an inch – a couple of centimetres? It doesn't matter that much – you blend it all in the end.

A: I meant how big should the pumpkin be?

B: Oh sorry! Yeah, I don't know – they vary so much in size. Biggish, I guess, but not like the huge ones.

A: OK, and then what? You just add water and boil it?

B: Yeah, more or less. You add lentils – roughly a cupful – and a tin of coconut milk.

A: Oh right. Coconut milk.

B: Yeah, actually I often use less, because I find it a bit much otherwise. And then I add about a litre or so of chicken stock and, as you say, bring it to the boil and then once it's boiling, you reduce the heat and leave it for fifteen minutes or so – till the pumpkin's soft, anyway – and then just blend it till it's smooth.

A: So when do you take out the lemongrass?

B: Oh right, yeah. Sorry. Basically, after it's simmered – at the end. It sort of floats to the surface. You just get it out with a spoon.

A: And the green herbs?

B: Well, you can use different things. I usually sprinkle a bit of chopped parsley, but basil's nice as well. And obviously a pinch or two of salt, although personally I got out of the habit of using too much because my dad's got a heart condition and he can't have too much.

A: Right. Well, it's great.

B: Yeah, I like it. Actually, I sometimes do it as a sauce – just everything in reduced quantities – and I cook pieces of cod or chicken in it.

A: Mmm. Sounds great.

Lesson 15C, Listening, Exercises 2 & 4

1: A UN report found that an estimated 923 million tonnes of food produced each year goes uneaten. The report also urges governments and businesses to do more to reduce waste at a time when 690 million people are still suffering from severe hunger and there are increasing concerns about the effect of farming on the climate and biodiversity. Campaigners accused the government here of failing to take the issue seriously and demanded that the government introduce anti-waste laws like those found elsewhere. South Korea has banned all food going to dumps and the capital Seoul has reduced waste by 10% through special bins that weigh the food and charge citizens for what they throw away. The food is then recycled as compost and animal feed. France also has a law which requires grocery stores to donate all their unsold fresh food to food banks and charities. A government spokesman defended its record and said the best way forward was to promote good habits through education rather than legislation.

2: The Swedish fast-food chain, Max Burgers, has won an award for introducing the first climate-positive menu. The company, which operates across Europe, has also reduced food waste to just 1%. While we may be used to dishes being labelled for allergies and calories, Max Burgers rates all its dishes for their carbon footprint from farm to plate. It pioneered plant-based burgers over a decade ago and promises to make 50% of all sales plant-based. It offsets the carbon from its meat dishes by planting trees. Meat production is a major source of greenhouse gases and climate experts recommend moving to a vegetarian diet as a key way to reduce emissions. Another of the award winners was Forest Green Rovers in the UK, known as the greenest professional sports team in the world. All players eat a vegan diet and the team's kit is made from recycled coffee grounds.

3: Scientists have discovered quite by accident a new way of catching scallops that could prevent major damage to the seabed. The researchers had been investigating whether lobsters and crabs could be caught using small lights, rather than with small fish as bait. At the end of the experiment, they found that the lobster baskets had failed to attract any crabs, but they did contain large numbers of scallops. Scallops have around two hundred tiny reflective eyes, which may explain why they were attracted to the disco lights. The discovery could be a huge breakthrough in sustainable fishing. While some scallops are collected by divers, the most common method is to use heavy machines that scrape the seabed, killing much of the other sea life and leaving long-lasting damage.

4: A major fast-food chain has caused something of a Twitter storm in China with the latest limited edition of its popular dessert. The company has added a sprinkling of dried coriander crumbs and a coriander and lemon sauce to its famous soft vanilla ice cream. Some claimed the dessert was a fantastic blend of sweet and spicy, while others suggested it was a crime against humanity and said just the idea of it made them want to throw up. The unusual combination is not the only cause of the debate. Scientists have shown that some people possess a particular gene which means they experience coriander as having a soapy taste. Fortunately, for those people the new flavour is only on sale for a few days.

UNIT 16

Lesson 16A, Listening, Exercise 4

I = Ivan, C = Claudine

C: Hello. Claudine Hellmann speaking.

I: Oh, hi, Claudine. This is Ivan calling, from Madrid.

C: Oh hi, Ivan. How're things?

I: Pretty good, thanks. A bit hectic – as usual for this time of year – but, you know, hectic is good. Anyway, listen, I'm just calling, really, to try to arrange a good time to talk through the sales strategy ahead of the coming season.

C: Yeah, that sounds good. When were you thinking of?

I: Well, to be honest, the sooner, the better. Would next week be good for you at all?

C: Well, if you wouldn't mind, I'd rather wait till the week after. I'll be visiting Spain for a trade fair so I could fit in a day with you then.

I: Oh, is that the one in Valencia?

C: Yeah, that's right. Are you going?

I: No, I'm afraid not.

C: That's OK, I can easily come to head office. What day would work best for you?

I: The Tuesday would suit me best. That's the 24th, preferably.

C: OK, great. I can make any time after ten.

I: OK. I'll pencil it in. Perhaps I could actually get Piotr from Warsaw to come over too. Face to face is always better and it'd be good to have input from another market.

Lesson 16A, Listening, Exercise 5

C = Customer Services Operator, V = Vicente Serrano

C: Hello, Customer Services.

V: Hi. I wonder if you can help me. I'm phoning to chase up an order I placed with your company some time ago – and that I still haven't received.

C: I'm sorry to hear that. Let's see what we can do. Would you happen to have the order number there?

V: Yeah, I do. It's EIA-290-3969.

C: Right. I'm just checking that now and I can't actually see any record of the transaction. When was the order placed?

V: The 29th of August, so that's over a month ago now. It should be under my name – Vicente Serrano.

C: Ah, OK. I've got it now. I'm afraid there must've been some kind of mix-up in the system because it doesn't appear to have been sent out yet. I do apologize. I'll get that off to you ASAP.

V: OK. Well, at least that explains that, then!

C: Again, I'm really sorry about that, Mr Serrano.

V: It's OK. These things happen.

C: Thanks for being so understanding. I've just put that through and it'll be going out today by special delivery, so it should be with you first thing tomorrow. That's at no extra charge, of course.

V: Great. Thanks. Would you mind just emailing me confirmation of that?

C: No, of course not. Can I just take your email address?

V: Sure. It's Serrano– that's S-E-double R A-N-O underscore f at meccanica dot com. That's meccanica with a double c.

C: Got it. OK. I'll send that through in a minute.

Lesson 16C, Listening, Exercise 3

P = Presenter

P: *Shark Tank* returns for a new series this week. The programme started out in Japan as *Money Tigers* and has now spread to over 40 countries under various titles including *Dragon's Den* and *Lion's Cave*.

For those unfamiliar with the format, each week four or five budding entrepreneurs try to raise money to expand their business in return for a stake in their company. The businesspeople pitch their ideas to a group of potential investors – the sharks of the title – who are already very successful company owners and are investing their own money.

After each presentation, the sharks interrogate the entrepreneurs to find out more about their business. During this questioning, the sharks either declare they are out or make an offer. The rules of the show demand that the sharks must offer all the money requested, but they may negotiate the percentage share in the company.

The various versions of the show have seen a huge variety of proposals that have attracted investment, such as Buggybeds, a device that detects bed bugs before they become a problem; Piñata2Go, a foldable version of the Mexican party game; and Wonderland, a style magazine for the super-rich. And of course, there are many more proposals that have been rejected.

Here to discuss the show's popularity and if it's actually good business, I have two guests: Luis Pereira, CEO and business mentor, and the social media entrepreneur, Ebony Smith.

Lesson 16C, Listening, Exercise 5

P = Presenter, L = Luis Pereira, E = Ebony Smith

P: Ebony, if I can start with you, why do you think the show is so popular?

E: Well, obviously the main reason is that it's promoting good ideas and it allows hard-working people to succeed, which is essentially a very positive message. In countries where it's run for several seasons, viewers may have literally seen the products on their supermarket shelves, so they know how the investment might enable people to become millionaires. It's making dreams come true, right?

P: Luis?

L: Yeah, absolutely, that's great. I think of the paint manufacturer in Brazil who won the biggest ever investment there, and you can't but be happy for the guy. But I wouldn't say the show is overwhelmingly positive. Just think of the title, *Shark Tank*. Sharks are aggressive and I think sometimes the investors are a bit too vicious in their criticism. Unfortunately, that attitude attracts viewers too, but I'm not sure it's something we should be encouraging in business.

E: Yeah, I mean, obviously that is a key part of the programme. Clearly, the producers of the show pick people to pitch and some are probably chosen because they are weak, to create drama and even laughter. But you know, even then, I think the sharks do those entrepreneurs a service by being cruel to be kind. People can become so obsessed with their idea that they don't see the flaws and can just pour more and more money into the venture. So maybe they need some vicious criticism to make them stop before they lose everything.

L: Maybe. But I think they're also rude and over the top, for less serious reasons. Sometimes people mix up their figures or mess up their pitch, but that doesn't make it a bad business. I always think of the guy on the UK show who created the Tangle Teezer, which is a brush for long hair that lets you get rid of knots painlessly. It wasn't a great presentation, and he revealed he hadn't sold many units, but they just tore him apart. It was unnecessary – and it turned out they were wrong, too, because the product has gone on to sell millions.

P: So he had the last laugh, then.

L: Yeah, but it represents the wrong approach. This is why I prefer the term 'business angel' or 'coach'. When you have small businesses looking to expand, they don't just need money, they need advice and mentoring. Maybe I'm wrong, but the sharks only seem interested in people who are already successful and need no help – like Buggybeds that was mentioned earlier. They were profitable when they came on the show.

P: So you don't think they'll have benefited from being on the show?

L: No, I wouldn't go that far, no. They will have obviously got great publicity and had a big boost in sales – I'm sure they're happy with how things have gone. And no one's forcing anyone to accept an offer.

E: Exactly. And the sharks don't always make money either. There's been some research on the UK programme and quite a few of the businesses only just broke even, or ceased trading altogether.

L: Yeah, so I suppose I'd like to see more of that reality and less aggression. I'd like to see more about how they help these businesses day to day and why they succeed or fail.

E: Yeah, me too. But I think that's a different programme and it doesn't stop me loving *Shark Tank* as it is.

P: Me neither. And for all those fans like us, the new series starts at 9 p.m. this Wednesday on Channel 3.

Review 8, Grammar, Exercise 4

1 Once you've finished that, come and tell me.

2 It'll allow us to check stock levels more efficiently.

3 I'll be seeing him later, so I can ask him if you want.

4 Would you consider branching out into other areas?

5 After the riots, they're threatening to ban public protests.

6 We'll be launching it next week, provided there are no last-minute issues.

NATIONAL GEOGRAPHIC
LEARNING

National Geographic Learning,
a Cengage Company

**Outcomes Upper Intermediate Student's Book,
3rd Edition**
Hugh Dellar and Andrew Walkley

Publisher: Rachael Gibbon

Senior Development Editor: Laura Brant

Content Editors: Alison Sharpe and Clare Shaw

Director of Global Marketing: Ian Martin

Senior Product Marketing Manager: Caitlin Thomas

Heads of Regional Marketing:

  Charlotte Ellis (Europe, Middle East and Africa

  Justin Kaley (Asia and Greater China)

  Irina Pereyra (Latin America)

  Joy MacFarland (US and Canada)

Senior Production Manager: Daisy Sosa

Content Project Manager: Ruth Moore

Media Researcher: Jeff Millies

Operations Support: Hayley Chwazik-Gee

Senior Designer: Heather Marshall

Senior Media Producer: Monica Writz

Art Director (Video): Macy Lawrence

Inventory Manager: Julie Chambers

Manufacturing Planner: Eyvett Davis

Composition: MPS North America LLC

Audio Producer: Tom, Dick & Debbie Productions Ltd.

Contributing Writer: Jon Hird (Endmatter)

For permission to use material from this text or product,
submit all requests online at **cengage.com/permissions**
Further permissions questions can be emailed to
permissionrequest@cengage.com

Outcomes Upper Intermediate Student's Book, 3e
ISBN: 978-0-357-91772-5

Outcomes Upper Intermediate Student's Book with
the Spark platform, 3e
ISBN: 978-0-357-91771-8

National Geographic Learning
Cheriton House, North Way,
Andover, Hampshire, SP10 5BE
United Kingdom

Locate your local office at **international.cengage.com/region**

Visit National Geographic Learning online at **ELTNGL.com**
Visit our corporate website at **www.cengage.com**

Printed in Greece by Bakis SA
Print Number: 01 Print Year: 2023

FSC
MIX
Paper from
responsible sources
FSC® C169932
www.fsc.org

Credits

Illustration: All illustrations are owned by © Cengage.

Photography:

Cover © Jennifer Hayes/National Geographic Image Collection

2 (tl1) AP Images/Emilio Morenatti, (tl2) Rudolf Wichert/laif/Redux, (tl3) © James L. Stanfiled/National Geographic Image Collection, (cl1) © XPacifica/National Geographic Image Collection, (cl2) © Jimmy Chin/National Geographic Image Collection, (bl1) © Alison Wright/National Geographic Image Collection, (bl2) Robin Utrech/AFP/Getty Images, (bl3) Matt Cardy/Getty Images News/Getty Images; **4** (tl1) Desiree Stover/NASA, (tl2) Xavierarnau/E+/Getty Images, (tl3) Majonit/Shutterstock.com, (cl1) Lionel Bonaventure/AFP/Getty Images, (cl2) Dpa picture alliance archive/Alamy Stock Photo, (bl1) NurPhoto/Getty Images, (bl2) Barna Tanko/Alamy Stock Photo, (bl3) © Lynn Johnson/National Geographic Image Collection; **6–7** (Spread) AP Images/Emilio Morenatti; **8** Emmanuel Dunand/AFP/Getty Images; **11** BFA/Alamy Stock Photo; **12** The Wanderer above the Sea of Fog, 1818 (oil on canvas)/Friedrich, Caspar David (1774-1840)/Hamburger Kunsthalle, Hamburg, Germany/Bridgeman Images; **13** (tl) Young man writing a letter, circa 1664-1666 (oil on panel)/Leemage/Bridgeman Images, (tr) Young woman reading a letter - Painter by Gabriel Metsu (1629-1667), circa 1664-1666 (oil on panel)/LEEMAGE/National Gallery of Ireland, Dublin, Ireland/Bridgeman Images; **14–15** (Spread) Rudolf Wichert/laif/Redux; **16** (c) FreshSplash/E+/Getty Images, (br) Pablo Camacho/Age Fotostock; **18** Federico neri/Shutterstock.com; **19** (tl) Sean Drakes/LatinContent Editorial/Getty Images, (cl) Lloyd Vas/Shutterstock.com, (bl) Wirestock, Inc./Alamy Stock Photo; **20** Maremagnum/Corbis Documentary/Getty Images; **23** Andrew Merry/Moment/Getty Images; **24** (tl1-tr2) © Cengage; **26–27** (Spread) © James L. Stanfiled/National Geographic Image Collection; **28–29** (Spread) PhotoAlto/Alamy Stock Photo; **31** ED/CS/IKEA/Camera Press/Redux; **33** Randy Duchaine/Alamy Stock Photo; **34–35** (Spread) © XPacifica/National Geographic Image Collection; **36** © Lynn Johnson/National Geographic Image Collection; **39** Didier Marti/Moment/Getty Images; **40–41** (Spread) Toshi Saski/Alamy Stock Photo; **43** Zoonar/N.Sorokin/Getty Images; **44** (tl1-tr2) © Cengage; **46–47** (Spread) © Jimmy Chin/National Geographic Image Collection; **48–49** (Spread) Igor Alecsander/E+/Getty Images; **51** Loic Venanace/AFP/Getty Images; **52** Bhairav/Dreamstime.com; **54–55** (Spread) © Alison Wright/National Geographic Image Collection; **56** Tatiana Popova/Shutterstock.com; **57** Olmarmar/iStock/Getty Images; **59** (tl) F8 studio/Shutterstock.com, (tr) Andriy Kravchenko/Alamy Stock Photo, (b) Chrislofotos/Shutterstock.com; **60** Kit Leong/Shutterstock.com; **62** Alan Walker/Alamy Stock Photo; **64** (tl1-tr2) © Cengage; **66–67** (Spread) Robin Utrech/AFP/Getty Images; **68–69** (Spread) Vicki Mar Photography/Moment/Getty Images; **71** (t) AP Images/The Yomiuri Shimbun, (bl) Mark Moffett/Minden Pictures; **72** Denys Barbier/Alamy Stock Photo; **73** Panther Media GmbH/Alamy Stock Photo; **74–75** (Spread) Matt Cardy/Getty Images News/Getty Images; **76** Andrew Michael/Alamy Stock Photo; **78–79** (Spread) Maremagnum/DivisionVision/Getty Images; **81** (cr-tl) (b) Album/Alamy Stock Photo; **83** Sean Prior/Alamy Stock Photo; **84** (tl1-tr2) © Cengage; **86–87** (Spread) Desiree Stover/NASA; **89** 10'000 Hours/DigitalVision/Getty Images; **91** BearFotos/Shutterstock.com; **93** Hero Images Inc./Alamy Stock Photo; **94–95** (Spread) Xavierarnau/E+/Getty Images; **97** Jack Hollingsworth/Photodisc/Getty Images; **98** South China Morning Post/Getty Images; **99** Joe Brown/CartoonStock; **101** © Tino Soriano/National Geographic Image Collection; **102** Martin Berry/Alamy Stock Photo; **104** (tl1-tr2) © Cengage; **106–107** (Spread) Majonit/Shutterstock.com; **109** Marilyn Nieves/E+/Getty Images; **111** (tl) Source: Netflix, (cr) Source: Penguin Random House Australia, (bl) © Ran Peng; **113** Jeffrey Isaac Greenberg 8+/Alamy Stock Photo; **114–115** (Spread) Lionel Bonaventure/AFP/Getty Images; **117** Brinkstock/Alamy Stock Photo; **119** ZUMA Press Inc/Alamy Stock Photo; **120** (c1) Twenty1studio/Shutterstock.com, (c2) Cinderella Design/Shutterstock.com, (c3) Anton Shaparenko/Shutterstock.com, (c4) Nadya_Art/Shutterstock.com, (c5) CharacterFamily70/Shutterstock.com; **122** Justin Kase zsixz/Alamy Stock Photo; **124** (tl1-tr2) © Cengage; **126–127** (Spread) Dpa picture alliance archive/Alamy Stock Photo; **129** LWA/Dann Tardif/DigitalVision/Getty Images; **131** AscentXmedia/E+/Getty Images; **132** IndiaPix/IndiaPicture/Getty Images; **134–135** (Spread) NurPhoto/Getty Images; **137** AFP/Getty Images; **141** ManoAfrica/iStock/Getty Images; **143** Oliver Killig/DPA/Getty Images; **144** (tl1-tr2) © Cengage; **146–147** (Spread) Barna Tanko/Alamy Stock Photo; **149** Foxys_forest_manufacture/iStock/Getty Images; **151** (tr) Daria Bass/500px/Getty Images, (cr) Imagebroker/Alamy Stock Photo, (br) zi3000/Shutterstock.com; **152** Dan Pearson/Alamy Stock Photo; **154–155** (Spread) © Lynn Johnson/National Geographic Image Collection; **157** Jeffbergen/E+/Getty Images; **159** Pius Utomi Ekpei/AFP/Getty Images; **161** Adam Rose/Disney General Entertainment Content/Getty Images; **162** Riccardo Lennart Niels Mayer/Alamy Stock Photo; **164** (tl1-tr2) © Cengage; **191** Heritage Image Partnership Ltd/Alamy Stock Photo; **193** Best-photo/iStock/Getty Images; **194** (tr)Will Steeley/Alamy Stock Photo, (br) Uwe Deffner/Alamy Stock Photo; **198** Sunday Afternoon on the Island of La Grande Jatte, 1884-86 (oil on canvas), Seurat, Georges Pierre (1859-91) / The Art Institute of Chicago, IL, USA/Bridgeman Images.

Acknowledgements

The Outcomes publishing team and authors would like to thank EC English for their collaboration on the new videos in this edition, and all of the students and staff at EC Dublin and EC Brighton who took part in the filming.

The team would also like to thank the following teachers who provided detailed and invaluable feedback on this course.

João Rodrigo Lima Agildo, Colégio São Luis, São Luis; Verliscia Alexander, EC Malta, St Julian's; Patrick Allman, EC Bristol, Bristol; Francesc Martí Aluja, EOI Lleida, Lleida; Jose Luis Piñeira Alvarez, EOI Tolosa, Tolosa; Marcel lí Armengou, EOI Terrassa, Terrassa; Desmond Arnold, EC Cambridge, Cambridge; Holly Bailey, EC Brighton, Brighton; Elisabet Prím Bauzá, EOI Manacor, Manacor; Daniel Beus, Fukuoka Communications Center, Fukuoka; Mónica Salgado Blesa, EOI Palma, Palma de Mallorca; Frederik Bolz, University of Bochum, Bochum; Malachy Caldicott; EC Oxford, Oxford; Elisa Roca Burns, EOI Palma, Palma de Mallorca; Eva Cantuerk, University of Bochum, Bochum; Ana Belén Gracia Castejón, EOI Palma, Palma de Mallorca; Ana María Serra Comas, EOI Palma, Palma de Mallorca; Michael Crowe, EC Dublin, Dublin; Rebekah Currer-Burgess, EC Bristol, Bristol; Luca de Santis, EC Dublin, Dublin; Hilary Donraadt, EC Dublin, Dublin; Julia Drzechovskaja, EC Dublin, Dublin; Jordan Duggie, EC Brighton, Brighton; Rachel Fenech, EC Malta, St Julian's; Armando Fernández, EOI Palma, Palma de Mallorca; Fabiana Fonseca, Associação Brasil América, Recife; Bruno Franco, Luzianna Lanna, Belo Horizonte; Natalia Fritsler, University of Bochum, Bochum; Lukas Galea, EC Malta, St. Julian's; Antonio Berbel Garcia, EOI Almeria, Almeria; Maria dels Angels Grimalt, EOI Palma, Palma de Mallorca; Honorata Grodzinska, Future, Gorzów; Abigail Hackney, IH Manchester, Manchester; Alicky Hess, EC Dublin, Dublin; Silvia Milian Hita, EOI Prat, El Prat de Llobregat; Richard Hill; EC Cape Town, Cape Town; Roxana Irimieia, BBE Languages, Bogota; Bronia Jacobs, EC Cape Town, Cape Town; Natalia Jakubczyk-Gajewska, Warsaw University of Life Sciences (SGGW), Warsaw; Georgine Kalil, Berlin; Jameelah Keane, EC Manchester, Manchester; Shelly Keen, EC Bristol, Bristol; Dariusz Ketla, Warsaw University of Life Sciences (SGGW), Warsaw; Gabriela Krajewska, University of Wrocław, Wrocław; Peter Kunzler, Gymnasium Kirchenfild, Bern; Juana Larena-Avellaneda, EOI Telde, Telde; Isabelle Le Gal-Maier, VHS Rottweil, Rottweil; Angela Lloyd, Polytech Brandenburg/Havel, Brandenburg an der Havel; Kenya Lopes, Luzianna Lanna, Belo Horizonte; Sandra López, EOI Palma, Palma de Mallorca; Lucía Marotta, EC Dublin, Dublin; Francesca Mesquida, EOI Manacor, Manacor; Nico Moramarco, EOI Santander, Santander; Sian Morrey, University of Sheffield, Sheffield; Vinicius Nobre, Toronto; Sue Nurse, University of Sheffield, Sheffield; Giuseppe Picone, Milan City Council, Milan; Maria Eugenia Perez Primicia, EOI Palma, Palma de Mallorca; Piotr Przywara, Warsaw University of Life Sciences (SGGW), Warsaw; Manlio Reina, EC Dublin, Dublin; Laura Rota i Roca, EOI Sabadell, Sabadell; Salvador Faura Sabe, EOI Sabadell, Sabadell; Justin Sales, Edinburgh College, Edinburgh; Paloma Seoane Sanchez, EOI Laredo, Laredo; Aïda Santamaria, EOI Palma, Palma de Mallorca; Sean Scurfield, EOI Santander, Santander; Pilar Riera Serra, EOI Palma, Palma de Mallorca;Tetiana Shyian, University of Bochum, Bochum; Vinicius Silva, Colégio Bandeirantes, São Paulo; Anna Soltyska, University of Bochum, Bochum; Glenn Standish, IH Torun, Torun; Andreas Tano, Makarios Christian School, Jakarta; Tran Thi Thu Giang, TEG international Education Centre, Hanoi; Sam Verdoodt, EC Malta, St Julian's; Aline Vianna, Colégio Humboldt, São Paulo; Rachael Worrall, IH Manchester, Manchester; Mehmet Yildiz, Bezmialem Vakif University, Istanbul

Authors' acknowledgements

Thanks to Alison Sharpe, Clare Shaw, Nicole Elliott, Rachael Gibbon and Laura Brant for their meticulous reading of our work and to all at National Geographic Learning for the continued support and enthusiasm.

Thanks also to all the students we've taught over the years for providing more inspiration and insight than they ever realised. And to the colleagues we've taught alongside for their friendship, thoughts and assistance.